FIRECRACKERS

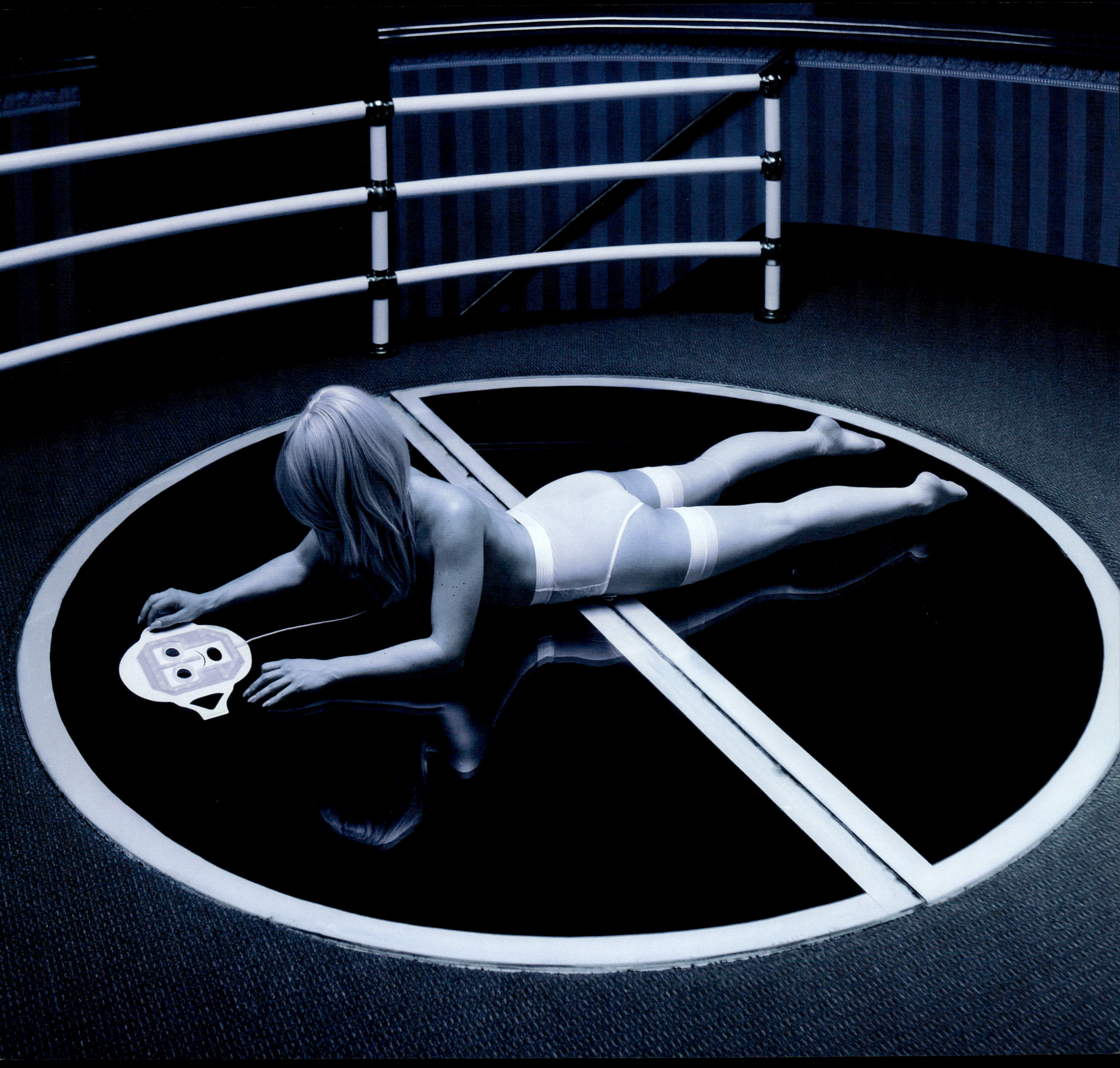

FIRECRACKERS

CONTEMPORARY FEMALE PHOTOGRAPHERS

FIONA ROGERS &
MAX HOUGHTON

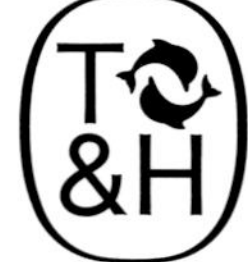

Page 2: Juno Calypso, *Solitary Love Affair*, 2016

Captions give, where applicable, the title, date
and series of each photograph. Where photographers
wanted to say more about a particular work, extended
captions can be found at the end of
the book.

First published in the United Kingdom in 2017 as
Firecrackers: Female Photographers Now by
Thames & Hudson Ltd, 6-24 Britannia Street,
London WC1X 9JD

This paperback edition published in 2025

Designed by Sarah Boris

EU Authorized Representative: Interart S.A.R.L.
19 rue Charles Auray, 93500 Pantin, Paris, France
productsafety@thameshudson.co.uk
interart.fr

A CIP catalogue record for this book is available from
the British Library

ISBN 978-0-500-29723-0
01

Manufactured in China by Imago

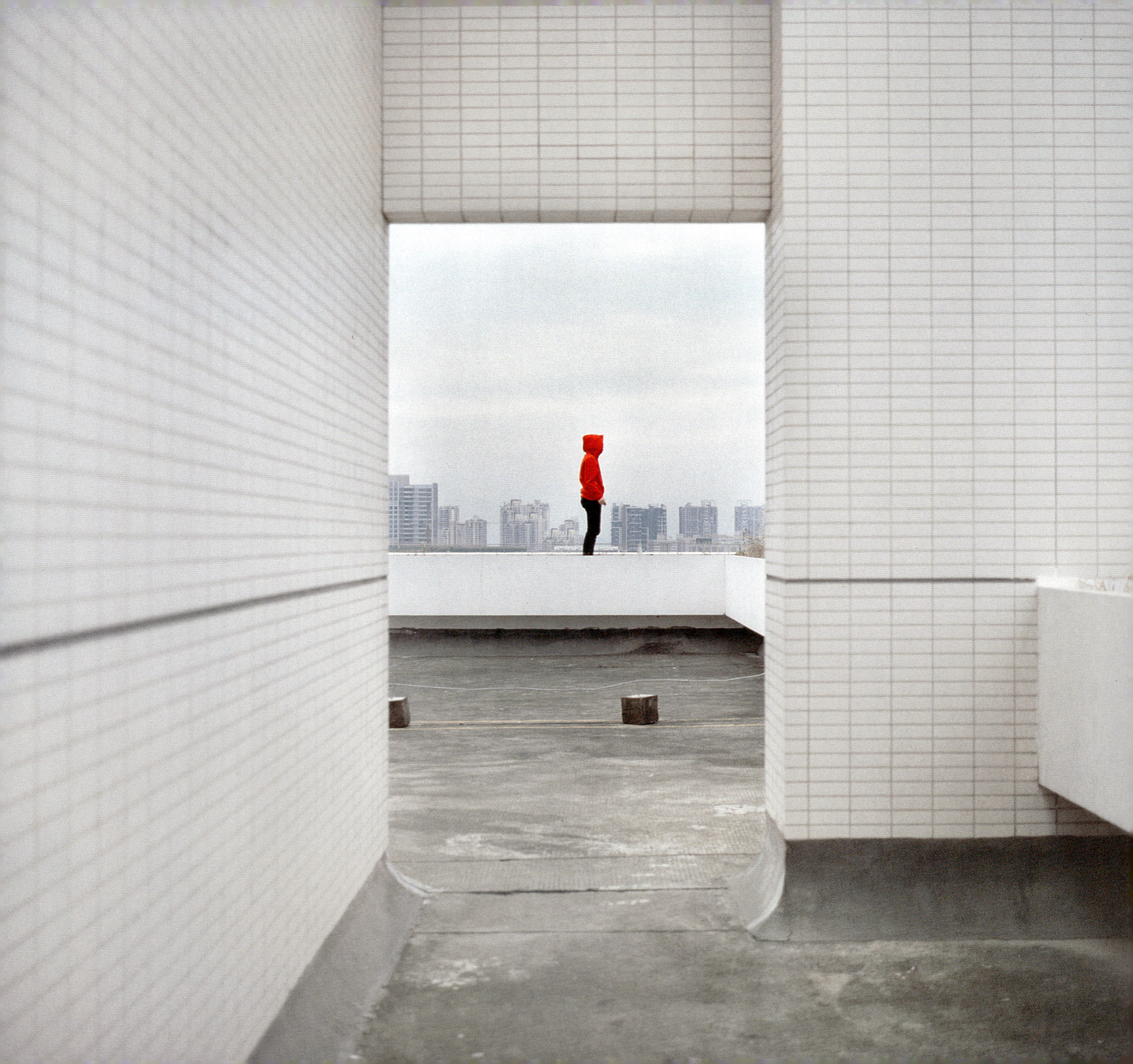

INTRODUCTION

Firecracker, like most 'awareness raising' initiatives, was borne out of
a sense of frustration. I had worked in photography for a long time and
was fortunate to have encountered many amazing female photographers,
but I was concerned about a lack of professional representation for them
and, at the same time, my own inability to offer support.

During a trip to Australia I met the remarkable photographer, curator
and editor Lee Grant. She introduced me to her platform, Light Journeys*,
a showcase for Australian female artists working with photo-media.
It was an inspiration – and thankfully Grant was flattered rather than offended
by my plagiarism. This chance encounter led to the birth of Firecracker.

Firecracker started life online in 2011. I named it after the affectionate
childhood nickname my father gave me for being a little disruptive and short-
tempered. I could think of no better name for a collection of artists who were
all 'firecrackers' in their own way, each one creating an individual explosion
and making her mark in this highly competitive industry.

In tandem with our increasingly social and visual world, Firecracker grew
organically and I now see it primarily as a network – a hub for the promotion
of work of the highest calibre; somewhere to engage with the best artistic
talent working today; a space to support growth and exchange, where dialogue
between artists and professionals can be encouraged. It operates somewhat
like a collective and some of the photographers have even begun to refer to
themselves as 'firecrackers'.

The development of the Firecracker Photographic Grant in 2012 allowed this
idea to expand into something more meaningful – talent could be recognized
and the grant could contribute to the sustainability of practice-based female
artists. Each year the grant provides a photographer with funding to support
a documentary project. It also emphasizes the importance of networking,
ensuring the projects get into the hands of professionals who can make a
longer-term impact on the photographers' careers. To date, and through the
continual and generous support of Genesis Imaging, the grant has championed
five international photographers, three of whom are featured in this book.
In 2014 the idea of this 'exchange network' was expanded to include the
Firecracker Contributors Award: an annual opportunity for photographers to
thank the hard-working women of the photo industry through an open-call
nomination process. Here, the mentors, commissioners and educators helping
to support all facets of photography and the visual arts can be celebrated.

FIONA ROGERS

I am grateful to Max Houghton for agreeing to be my co-editor and author.
We both felt it was largely an organic experience; the challenges were more
about who not to include, due to a finite number of pages, rather than who
to include. There are a number of omissions and wonderful photographers
we could not, did not, include – Laura Pannack, LaToya Ruby Frazier, Rena
Effendi, to name a few. We did not have specific 'criteria', but our emphasis
was on the contemporary, the best or the surprising. We wanted to show
photographers you had no doubt heard of, but whose work you maybe hadn't
seen in any major presentations. We also wanted to represent a breadth
of subjects, aesthetic styles and backgrounds.

The geographical scope of the book presented us with some challenges too.
Firecracker initially showcased the work of photographers who had been born
or resided in Europe, so we had to strike a balance between actively seeking
out more international photographers and not making arbitrary decisions based
on box-ticking. A welcome by-product of this, however, is that Firecracker has
become more inclusive and I'm now looking forward to working with a wider
selection of photographers from around the world.

Firecracker has provided me with a creative outlet for the extraordinary
women I've met throughout my career, but photography is an industry that is
undeniably crowded by (white) men. It's by no means the only industry in which
this happens, of course. Life imitates art and vice versa. With so few women
represented at the highest levels in contemporary art, politics and the media,
it's no wonder there is a lack of diversity in photography – and it's not just
a gender issue either (but that's another story, and indeed another book).
Of course, you cannot build an initiative about women without attracting
comments about its exclusivity, or sexism, or encountering its reductive nature,
and I'm often at odds with the contradictory nature of it all.

Essentially, I'd like Firecracker to be a means of celebration. A celebration
of photography, a celebration of game-changers, a celebration of women and,
above all, a celebration of great work now. This book has become the vehicle
for this celebration at this very moment, and maybe there will be others. I hope
that within the final selection you too will delight in the diverse range of
practices, from the abstract to the journalistic, from the deeply personal to
the clinically scientific, and everything inbetween. I also hope that it may
spark some debate in the continuous dialogue about gender imbalance and
female representation. That Firecracker pun was most definitely intended.

*Light Journeys has since ceased to curate regular features but stands as an archive
of fifty-eight incredible Australian photographers at www.lightjourneys.org.au

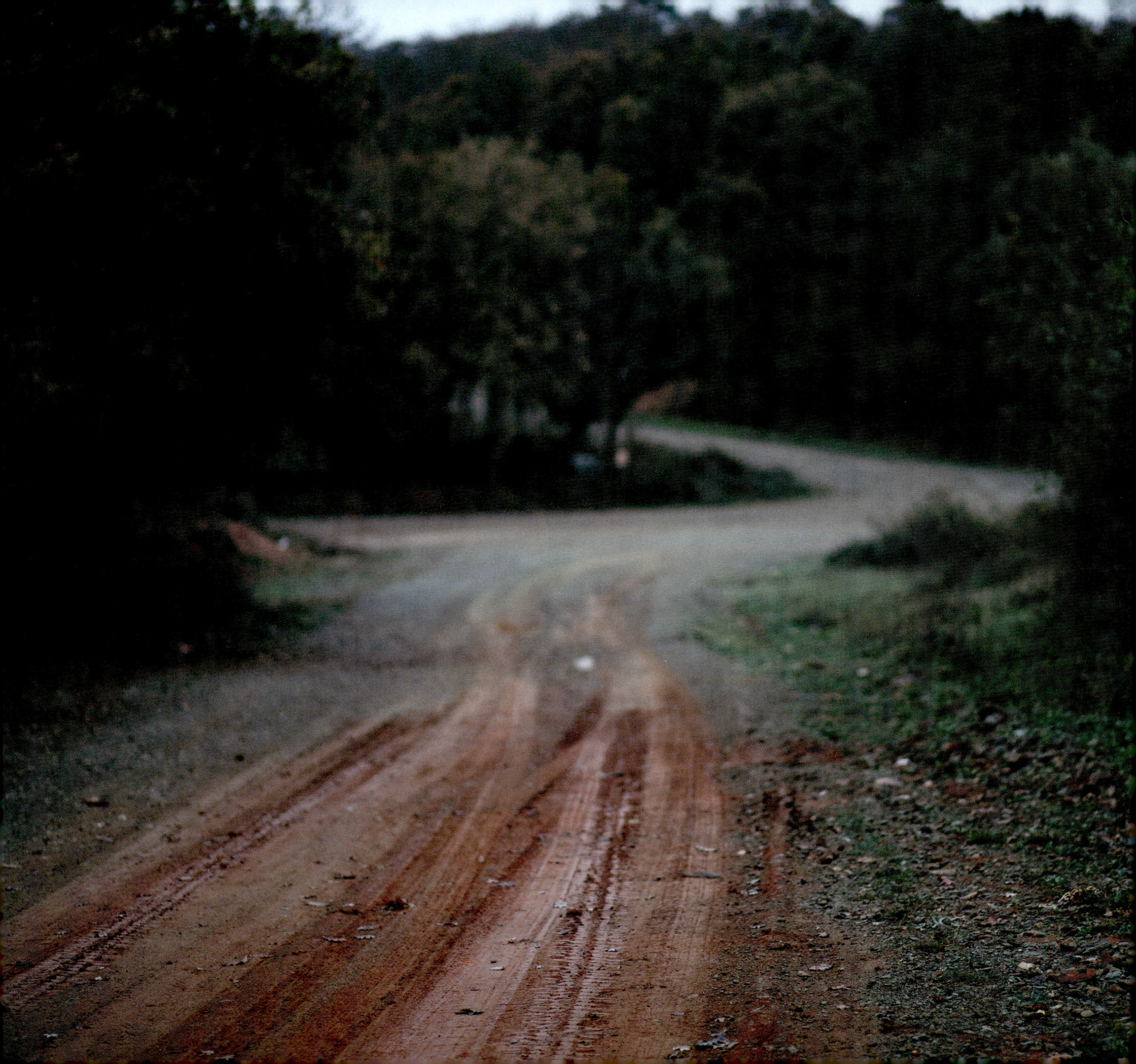

FOREWORD: TRAVELLING LIGHT   MAX HOUGHTON

'It's the job of photographers to see more, to travel light when it comes to preconception, to go into the dark with their eyes open.'*

The beauty of collecting series of photographs made by women is that our plane of seeing converges with theirs, and we can see the world as they do...a world that has more often than not been delineated, explained and ruled by men. That's not to say the brilliant photographic work in this book was made to a feminist agenda, but, when considered as a whole, the power of the female gaze, and its absence in certain areas, comes to the fore.

In our obsessively visual culture, how things are seen has a monumental effect on how they are then known or understood. Photography is exceptionally well placed to bring forth new kinds of knowledge; it's also the pre-eminent mode of communication in our Insta-world. It's a relatively young medium, and increasingly everyone feels they can take ownership of it because the technology is widely available via mobile phones (although, culturally, it's not a given that photography is a welcome or relevant practice). Technological determinism aside, the question of who is looking is vital.

If the photographs on the following pages share specific territory, it is located in their spirit of inquiry, and a desire to create new forms of imagery if the story can't be told traditionally. The obvious common ground here is that the photographer in each case is female, but although this is a selecting principle it is first among equals. I am interested in the eye that makes the photograph, and what it sees. How women see the world has not dominated discourse, and whenever the opportunity arises to redress this imbalance, it is necessary to seize it. Women are not a minority, nor are they a minority in photography, but their opportunities have historically been very different. It is essential that we make space for female visual artists, unless we are content to be locked inside repeated

male visions of the world; an infinite hall of mirrors. Cool girls prefer the waltzer to send you spinning on.

To make an art book with exclusively female work will always be seen as a kind of provocation. Importantly, this is not a book for women, by which I mean, of course, that it is a book for everyone. Drawing attention to a creative practice on the grounds of gender alone is, in a way, reductive. It might, however, be seen as an entirely normative practice if we recall the Guerrilla Girls poster from 2015. It was an update of their 1985 incursion, which pointed out that of all the museums in New York that year only one – MOMA – had bestowed a solo show upon a woman. Thirty years later MOMA had exhibited two that year, while the other 'big three' (the Solomon R. Guggenheim Museum, the Metropolitan Museum of Art and the Whitney Museum of American Art) had increased their numbers from zero to, er, one in each case. I don't think the curators were asked to account for their male selections.

We could continue with statistics, much more life-affecting than those of the art world, in relation to gender inequality worldwide. With job insecurity, the gender pay gap, unpaid work, the prevalence of violence against women, FGM, forced marriage, under-representation in politics...the 21st century does not look like a good place to be a woman. We are talking about entrenched practices of patriarchy and unfreedom and the reason we are still talking about such issues is because they persist. One of the ways in which feminist philosophy since Simone de Beauvoir has had an impact is in opening up a space for freedom to flourish. 'Only the freedom of others can keep each one of us from hardening in the absurdity of facticity', de Beauvoir writes.

I think what we see on these pages is a pursuit of freedom, both personal and artistic. These young women, from various continents, are documenting contemporary life, which will become part of future history. The photographers travel freely, for the most part, though not always without political or cultural constraint. They tell stories that move them and, in turn, move us. Within these scant pages are narratives of corruption, change, fantasy, inequality, love, conflict, prejudice, power, terror, fear and hope, told with empathy or wit, and always with an extraordinary aesthetic sensibility. In this way, the new history of the world unfolds without a template. Power is, slowly, changing hands, and some of these hands are holding a camera, using it to bring light to ideas or things or people or places that might otherwise remain in the dark.

Certain themes have arisen from the work we have chosen, which are ripe for rethinking from a female perspective. We see women escaping the sexual gaze of men. Threads can be drawn back to the wonderfully subversive work of Alice Austen, whose image of 'Trude and I, Masked, Short Skirts, 11pm, Thursday Aug. 6th 1891' broke free of Victorian patriarchy. Austen pictured herself and her lifelong lover Gertrude Tate doing exactly what they pleased at an hour that would certainly be deemed ungodly. This spirit of mischief can be seen in the work of Juno Calypso, who pulls the rug from under the beauty industry, upsetting its sadistic range of implements, and pokes further fun at the commodification of love – in honeymoon hotels. Love and betrayal are dishes best served cold, as seen in the photography of Natasha Caruana. Her photographs of men attempting to conduct extra-marital affairs are anything but sexy or glamorous, and instead depict the awkward and rather abject nature of the transaction taking place. How adroitly she turns the tables.

Women looking at men is a neat reversal of that most prevalent gaze. Germaine Greer wrote vividly of this phenomenon in her book *The Boy*, in which she acknowledged the right of women not only to look, but also to derive pleasure from looking. It is fascinating to observe French photographer Scarlett Coten inviting men she meets on the streets of Morocco and Egypt to come and be photographed. It is not necessarily a sexual gaze she casts, but one that is not at all customary in the societies she has chosen to document, on her own terms. Evgenia Arbugaeva fell into the role of Arctic explorer most naturally, hiring a helicopter to turn up unannounced at a meteorological station in the Russian Arctic at new year, to make an unforgettable visual portrait of a lone Russian weatherman. Through her eyes we see and sense the vastness of the polar night.

Cultural preconceptions of gender are also given a shake-up by visual artists. Afghan-American artist Behnaz Babazadeh creates edible burkas and photographs herself wearing them. Her evaluation of her birth country's mores would almost certainly never have happened without 9/11. Her identity is always on the move, and she is able to express that uncertainty through photography with sensuality and joy. Ethiopian-born Aïda Muluneh uses the traditional African art of body painting to express something new and very personal about her relationship to her country. Her sharp understanding of the power of the image has led her to set up a photo festival in Addis Ababa, her country's capital, which is gaining global attention.

The search for the lost mother is a trope in male writing from Proust to Barthes, so it is especially interesting to observe three young women trying to recover paternal memory through photography. Diana Matar created a melancholy visual language of loss and absence in relation to the political disappearance of her father-in-law in Libya. Mariela Sancari advertised for men of the age her father would have been if he was still alive to stand in his place, and be photographed by her. The results are haunting. Diana Markosian, whose work on Armenian history we present here, has also used her photography to reconstruct a father–daughter relationship that was abruptly severed. Such stories are unexpected and forge new paths in contemporary discourse in relation to what is considered significant, and who is permitted to put forth such ideas.

War and conflict are subjects with which it is vital to engage women, as Virginia Woolf made brilliantly manifest in her work *Three Guineas*. She includes photographs within her text, which she uses to provoke a dialogue with the hawkish man to whom she writes. She is aghast at the military regalia worn by parading men: 'Your clothes in the first place make us gape with astonishment. How many, how splendid, how extremely ornate they are – the clothes worn by the educated man in his public capacity!' She describes in detail the cult-like behaviour of the British military, which is habitually accepted without comment. She then embarks upon a comparison with acceptable dress for women, and the glaring double standards at play. It's witty and shocking at the same time. Woolf created a unique intellectual space to voice her opposition to war, and the male discourse that created it. It is fascinating that she did so using a) photographs and b) clothing to make the pacifist statement of the century. Lee Miller would later document what women wore in wartime – as well as, of course, photographing the dead of Dachau and herself in Hitler's bathtub – and, fortunately, we have female photographers today who are also focusing on conflict from unexpected angles. Here we can share the vision of Anastasia Taylor-Lind, who documented the makeshift armour of Ukrainian men, and their weapons crafted from table legs or metal rods, during the country's political upheavals in 2014. Her other observation, 'Men fight wars; women mourn them', brought us photographs of the flowers left by women in Maidan Square in Kiev to commemorate the fallen. In another important body of work that helps us better understand the nature of contemporary conflict, Poulomi Basu sought access to mothers of ISIS fighters and, in contrast to the expected discourse of terror, told poignant stories of lost sons. Laura El-Tantawy went in pursuit of her Egyptian identity at a moment when her country erupted into turmoil; her photographs and intensely personal narrative are an enduring take on the human cost of conflict.

As we can see on every page in this book, photography can be used to create a language that doesn't presently exist to convey the complexities or subtleties of contemporary life. We are very proud to show contemporary photography at its dazzling best here. The attraction of the image for me is that it's never just one thing; photography won't be pinned down, easily defined, or limited. This is what makes it such a potent medium for women whose work and ideas are equally unclassifiable: they are able to tell the stories they want to tell. Thus unburdened, they travel light.

*The epigraph is a doctored quotation from essayist Rebecca Solnit. Where I have inserted 'photographers', she refers to 'writers and explorers' in her essay 'Woolf's Darkness' from the collection *Men Explain Things to Me*, Granta, 2014.

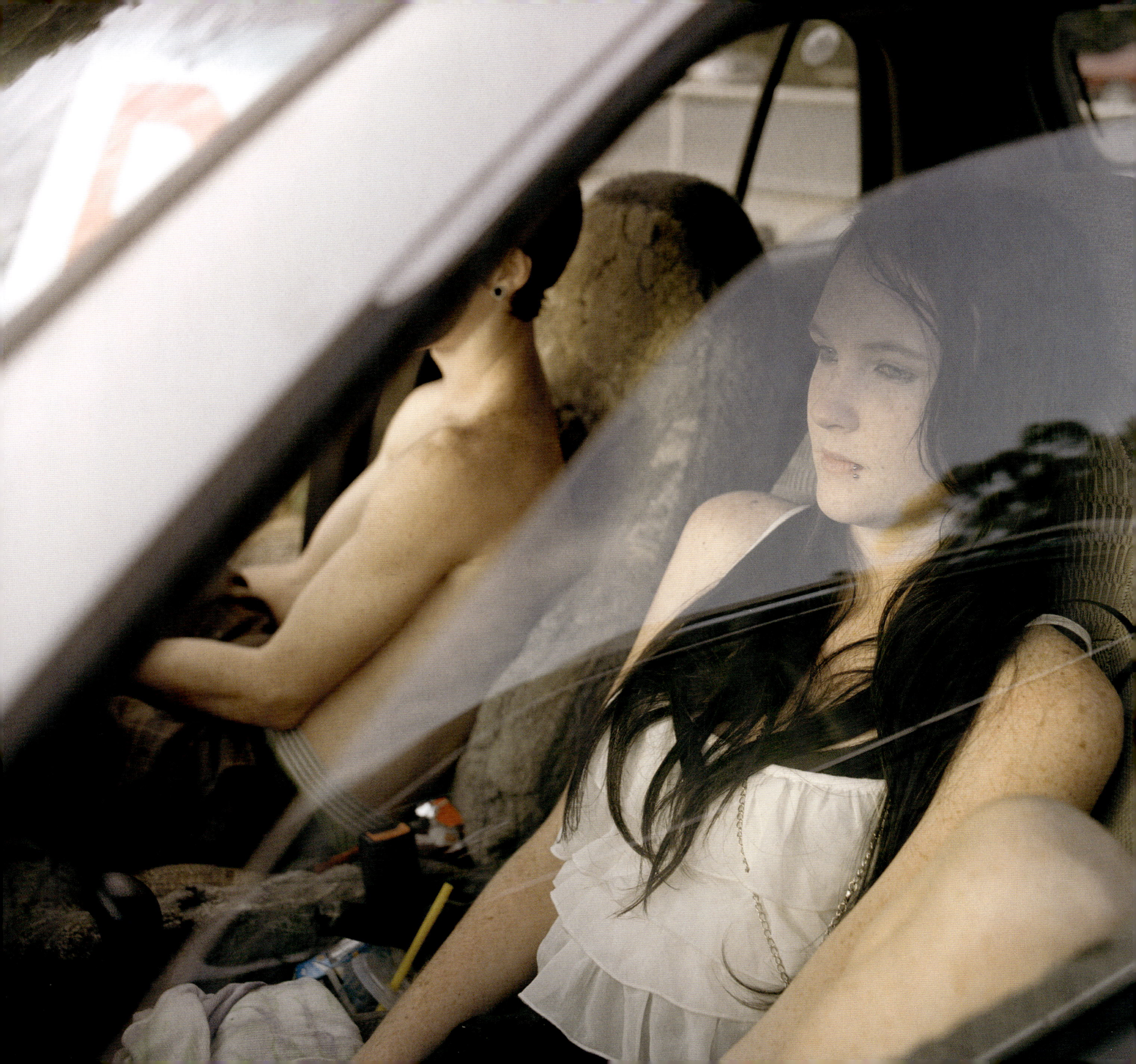

YING ANG

The narrative surrounding Australian–Singaporean photographer Ying Ang's *Gold Coast* plays out like a complicated detective novel. With a distinctly film-noir quality straight from the David Lynch school of anticipation, the photographs present a knife-edge tension and the feeling that under the sunny Australian disposition all is not as it seems.

And it is not. *Gold Coast* may be brimming with images of picket-fenced suburbia, but Ang exposes a seedy underbelly of corruption, murder, drugs and racism behind the luminous 'Pleasantville' façade of the place where she grew up.

Now pitched as the tourism centre of Australia, the Gold Coast was once an undesirable stretch of dangerous coastline: the waves were too big and the bull shark problem was too great for it to appeal as a family destination. However, government corruption, which was particularly prevalent in the 1960s and peaked with the real-estate boom of the 1980s, led to the false characterization of the area as a modern-day utopia. It quickly became a place where shysters could reinvent themselves, 'a sunny place for shady people', as the media coined it, while the more law-abiding community hid behind manicured lawns and overlooked the problems to keep an artificial paradise alive.

Ang moved from Singapore to Queensland when she was ten years old, and so is much more than a casual observer of a rotten core. She was a reluctant witness to several crimes; words such as 'rape', 'amphetamines', 'murder' and 'extortion' were part of her everyday vocabulary growing up. The daughter of a local socialite and philanthropist, as a teenager Ang was often of interest to the local papers. After witnessing a multiple murder, media attention grew and thus the two opposing narratives, one representing the 'false glamour' of her new home, the other epitomizing the sordid and dark reality, became significant in Ang's life and her work. Her experience quickly revealed that the affluent 'dream' her family had been sold, along with many others, was in reality an insidious nightmare.

In *Gold Coast* Ang's images are presented as icons of safety, visual metaphors that we recognize as familiar and safe: clean streets, tall and shiny buildings, children playing. But this scene is always disrupted by something subtle yet ominous: a girl looks over her shoulder, a storm begins to break, a spider envelops its next meal. Ang successfully deploys her photography to highlight the power of perception: how potent the superficial can be in influencing opinion, providing distraction and creating a mirage from the truth.

Gold Coast's narrative is perhaps best represented in the eponymous book (self-published in 2015). Photographs highlighting a prosperous lifestyle, such as Ang's own grandiose dining room, are juxtaposed by the inclusion of newspaper clippings – a naked couple slashed to death, a girl who starved after her mother died. The unease is further supported by the book's layout, with some pictures tilted at a confusing 45-degree angle and some sliced halfway across the next page, creating a disorientating, multi-layered effect.

Ang's diverse background in political science, biotechnology and communications provides her with a rounded and anthropological approach to her artistic practice. A prolific book and zine publisher, Ang delights in the tangible and the meditative. Her considerations of design and form are instructions to touch, to feel and to engage.

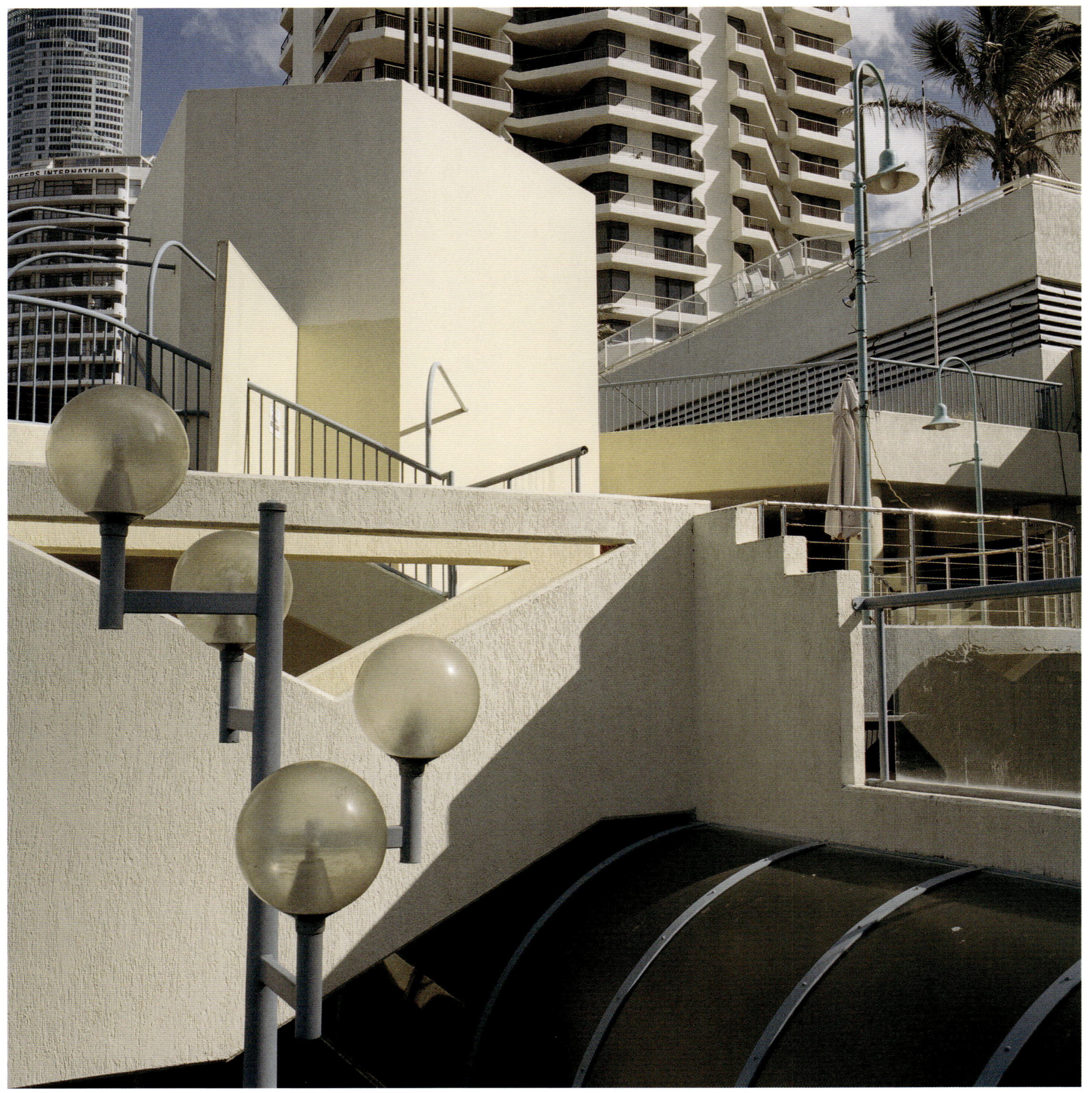

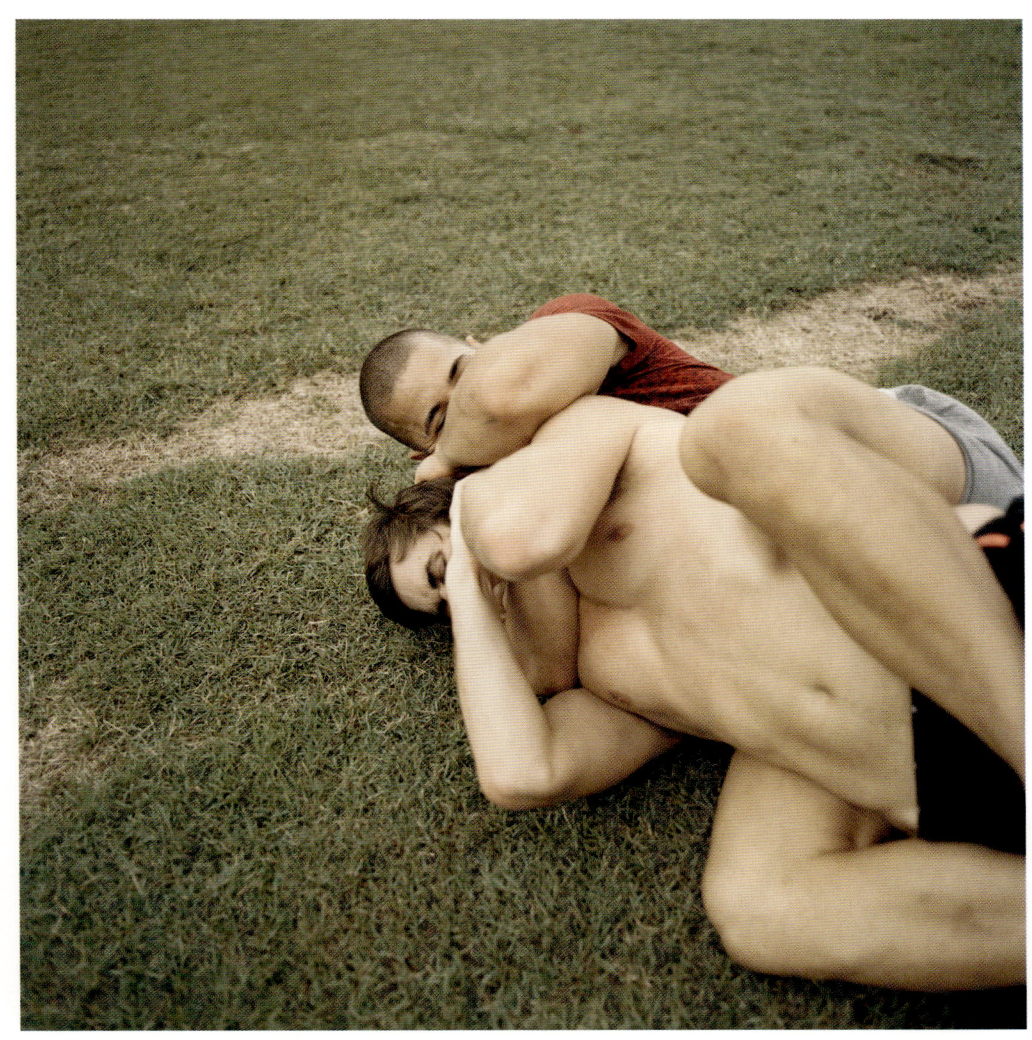

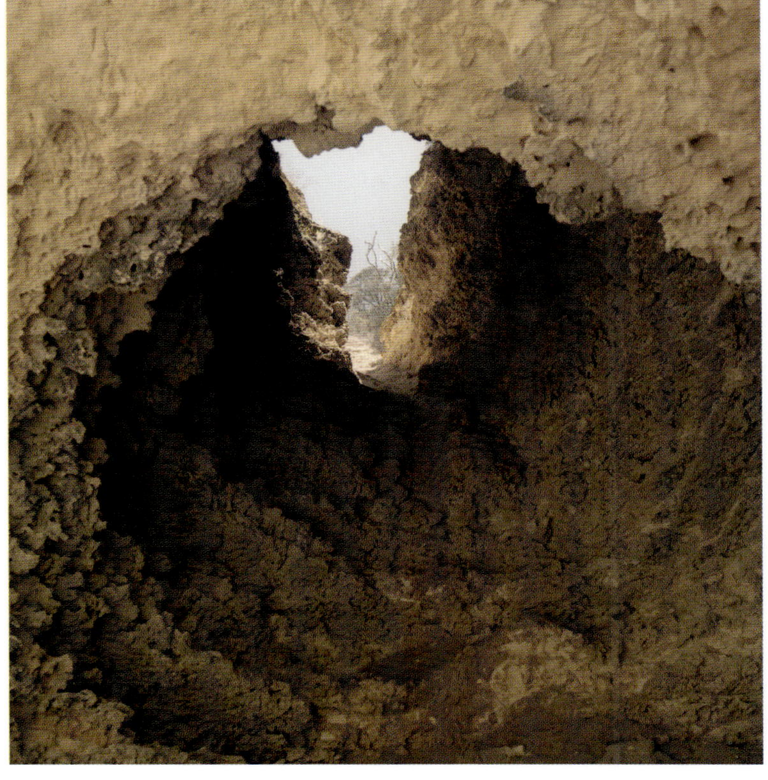

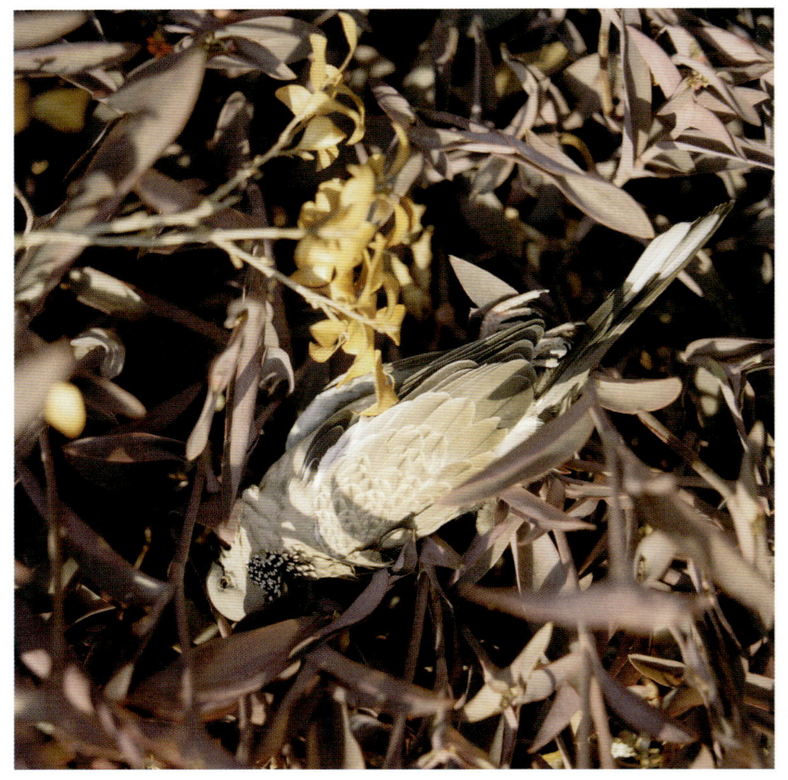
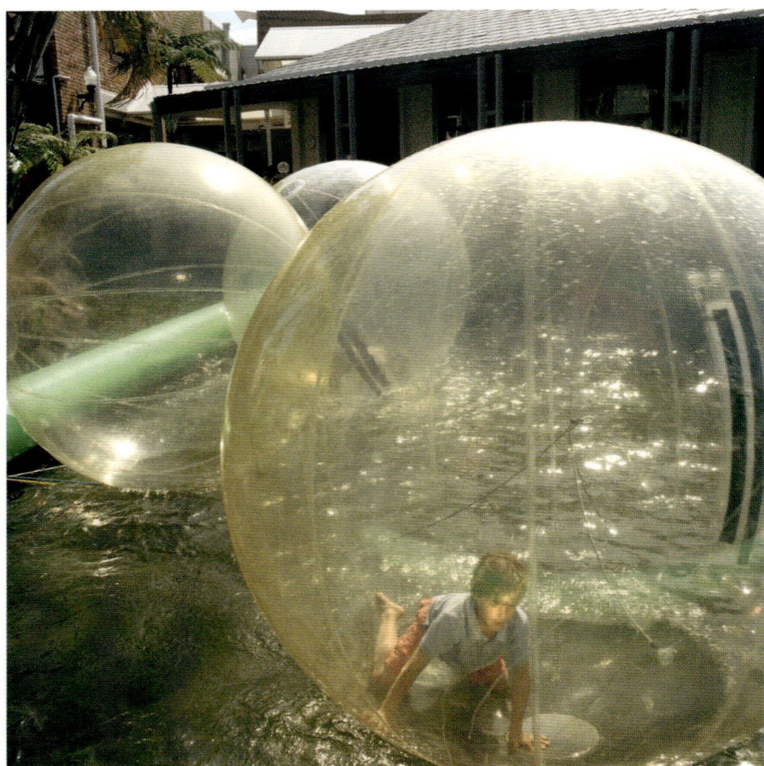
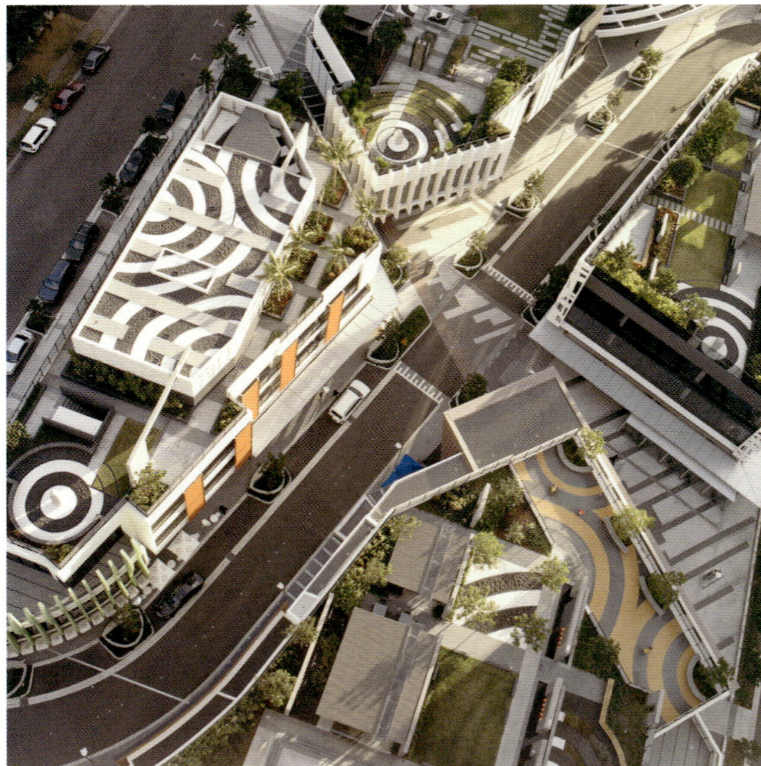
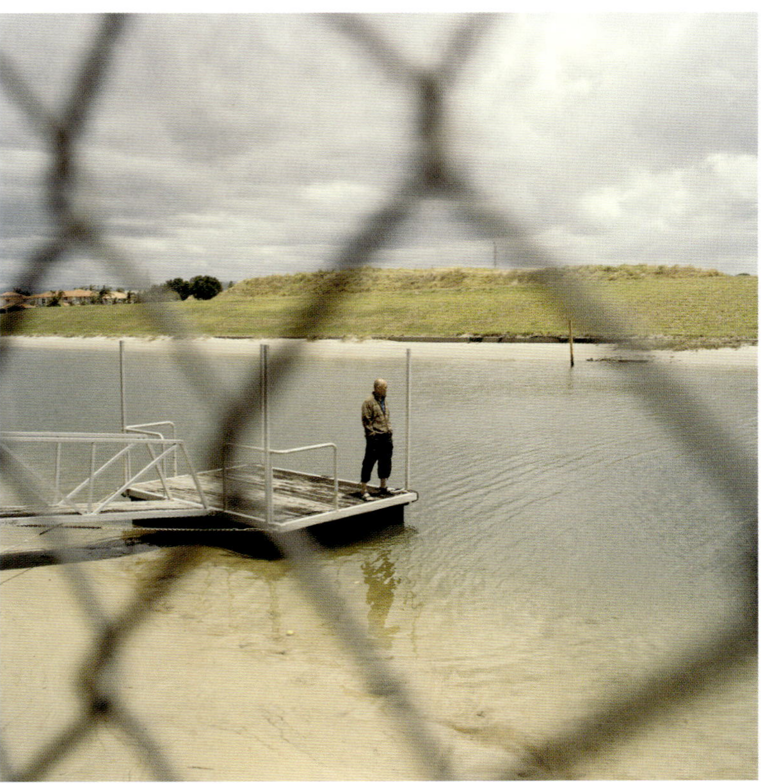

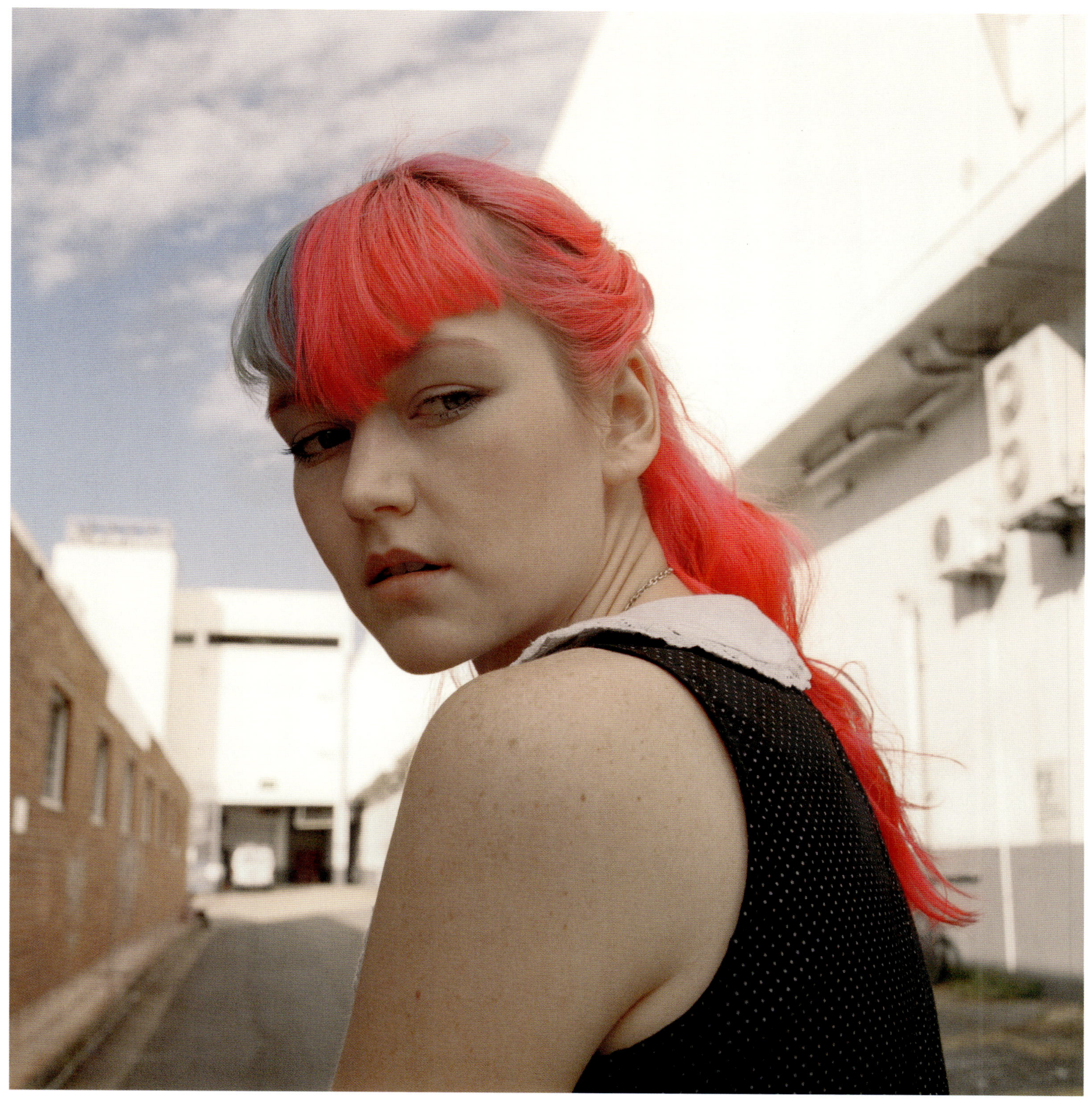

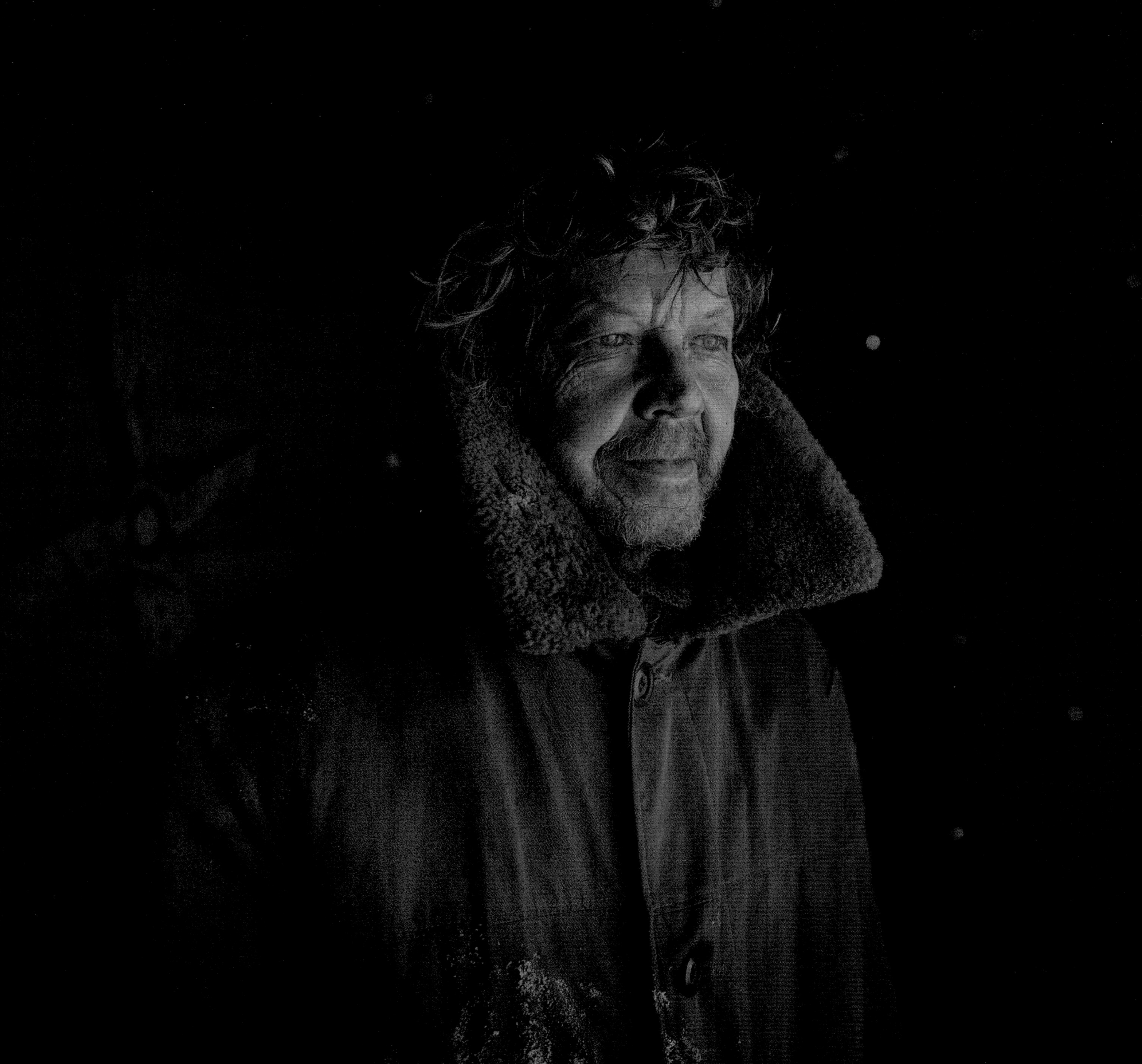

EVGENIA ARBUGAEVA

...

In her determination to tell this story,
Arbugaeva hired a helicopter, and landed,
at new year, bearing gifts of oranges
...

In an interview with a UK newspaper, Evgenia Arbugaeva said that after perestroika people saw no future in her home town of Tiksi, Russia. Her family left the town, once a Soviet military base on the Laptev Sea, in 1991 and moved south. They were part of a vast migration to Yakutsk, known as the world's coldest city, in Siberia. She was eight years old, and this move, or the changes it wrought, created maps and scenes in her young mind that she would later re-create as a photographer.

Arbugaeva has worked extensively in Tiksi since – in pursuit of the snowstorms and polar winds that spun the stories of her childhood. She has written evocatively of this experience, from a child's perspective, looking on in wonder at the green light cast by the aurora borealis, the golden tones of the tundra, the blueberry-blue created by the first sunlight after a polar winter. Her photographs conjure this same magic because she understood the capacity of the brilliant snow to act as a giant reflector, resulting in images bathed in light and colour. Her past has become the future that never was.

Arbugaeva has continued to be attracted to isolation, and to the very specific landscape of the Arctic region. After the fairytale quality of her Tiksi images, she wished to capture its darkness. Her commitment to this desire saw her spend two months on an icebreaker ship, visiting twenty-two weather stations, reminiscent of one she visited with her father as a child. She found her ideal location in Khodovarikha on the Pechora Sea, and in Vyacheslav Korotki (known as Slava), her ideal subject. In her determination to tell this story, after Slava did not respond to her request to visit, she hired a helicopter, and landed, at new year, bearing gifts of oranges, champagne and a bird. The parrot was, of course, not intended as a prop, but a photograph of man and bird, seemingly content in each other's company, poses poignant questions about freedom.

The portraits of Slava might be expected to reveal a lonely eccentric; rather, they express a distinction between solitude and loneliness. In Slava, we see a man in his natural habitat, whether out to sea in the boat he constructed, or recording air temperature, illuminated by the northern lights. Arbugaeva describes Slava as having no sense of self as such; that he dissolves into his environment. She has noticed that something of the Arctic seas remains in his eyes.

Even though it is her home territory, Arbugaeva still carries out research. For *Weatherman*, as the series came to be called, she immersed herself in cello music, and studied classical Russian and European oil paintings. She certainly invokes melancholy with her dark, fluid compositions. The photographs communicate something profound about a landscape that remains almost completely mysterious to the Western eye.

Arbugaeva is following a very great tradition of Russian exploration. Among her observations in Slava's wooden home was a newspaper cutting of Yuri Gagarin. Encouraged by her parents, and experiments in her father's darkroom, she left Siberia in 2009 to study at ICP in New York, eventually becoming the recipient of their prestigious Infinity award for a young photographer in 2015. Her voyages to the outermost parts of the earth are bound to continue.

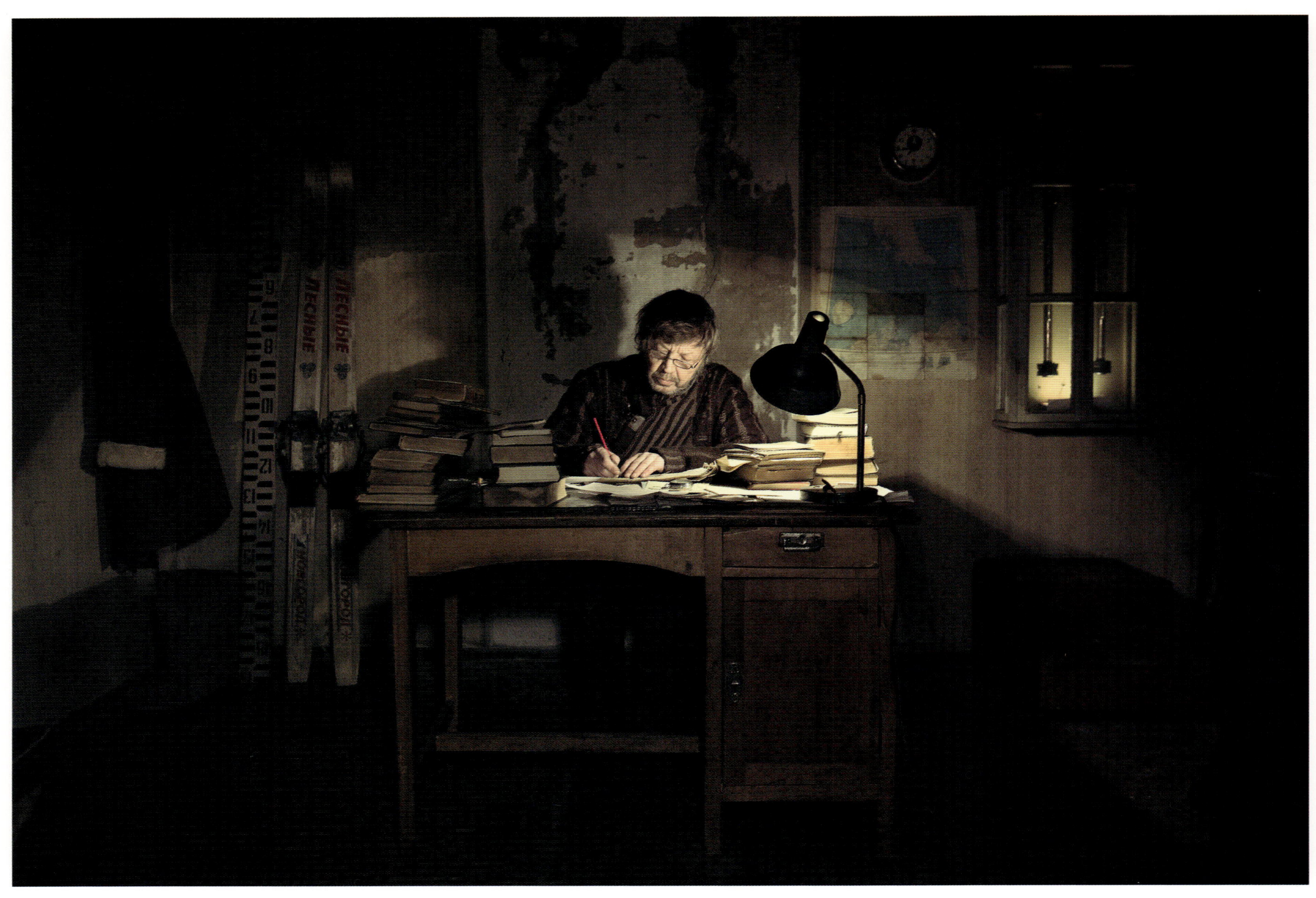

Weather Man series, 2014

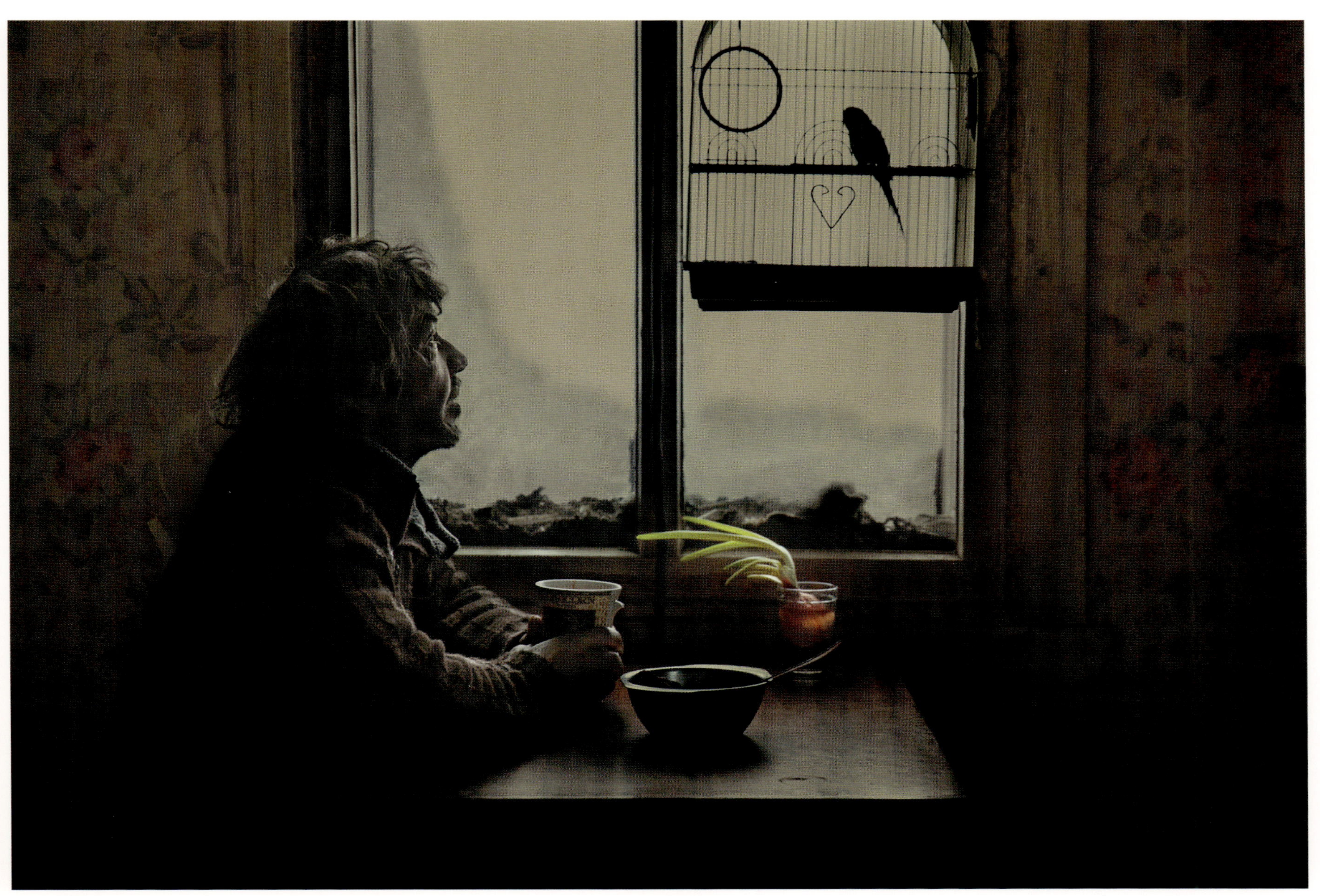

Evgenia Arbugaeva   21

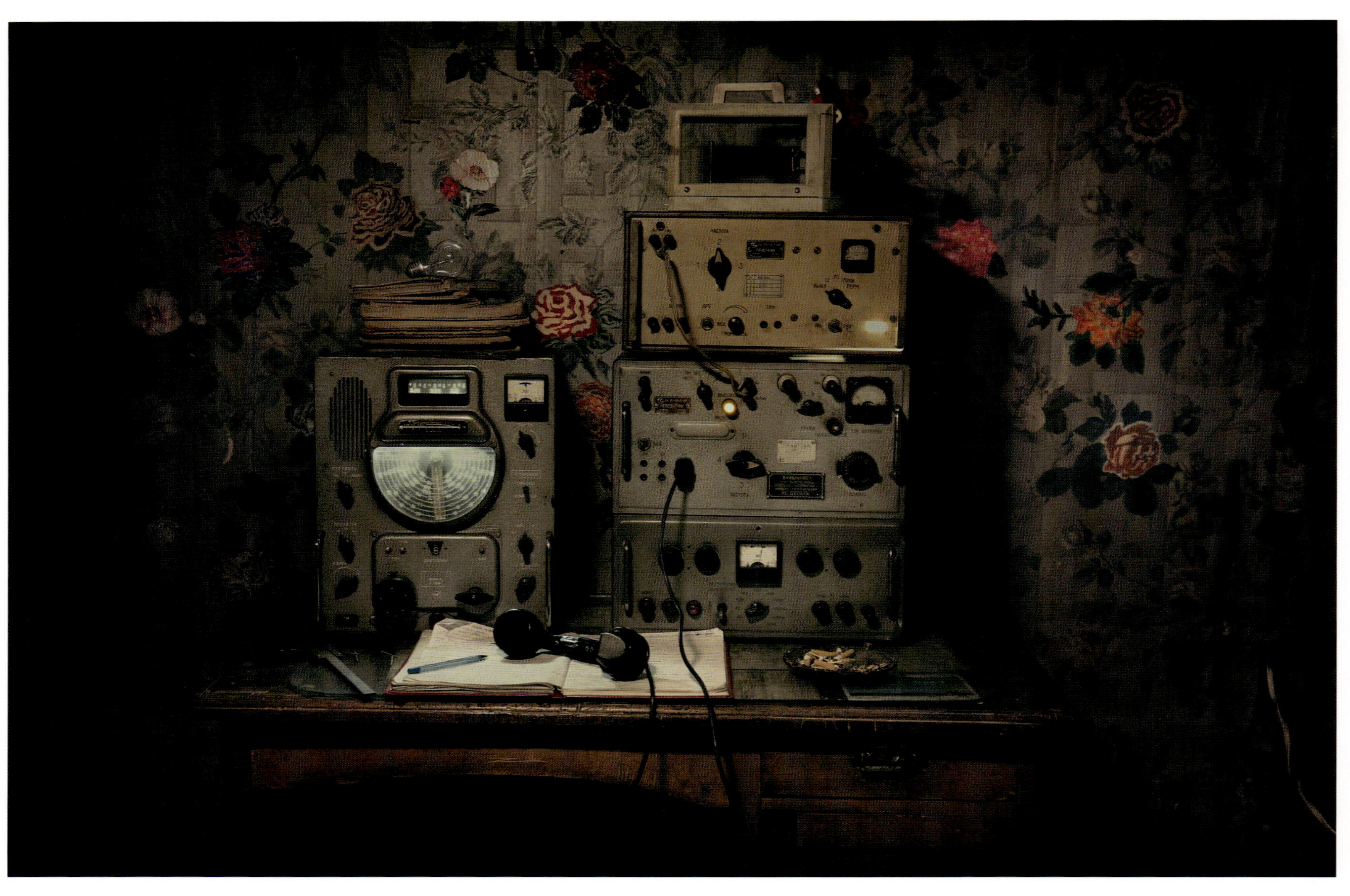

Weather Man series, 2014

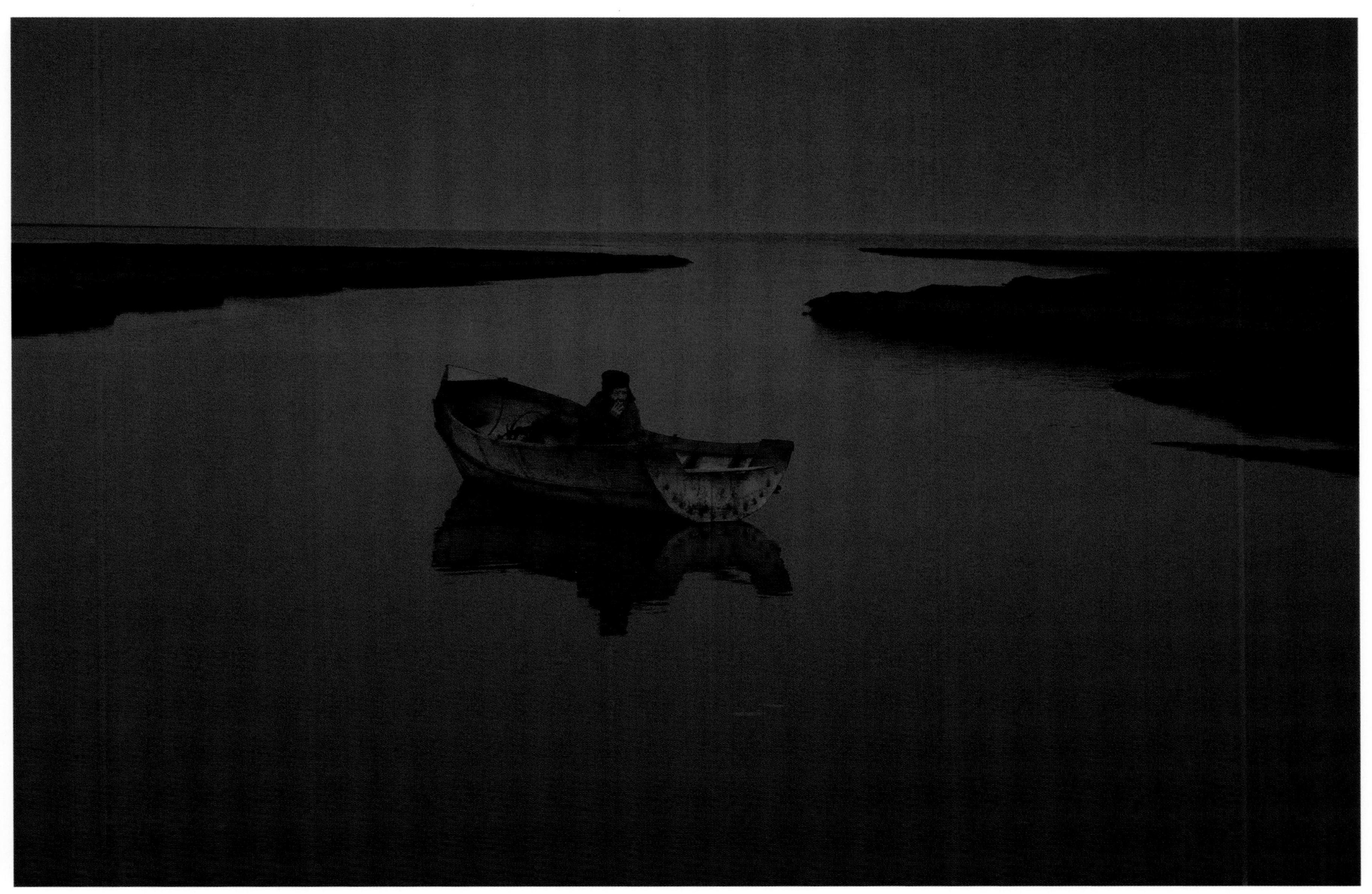

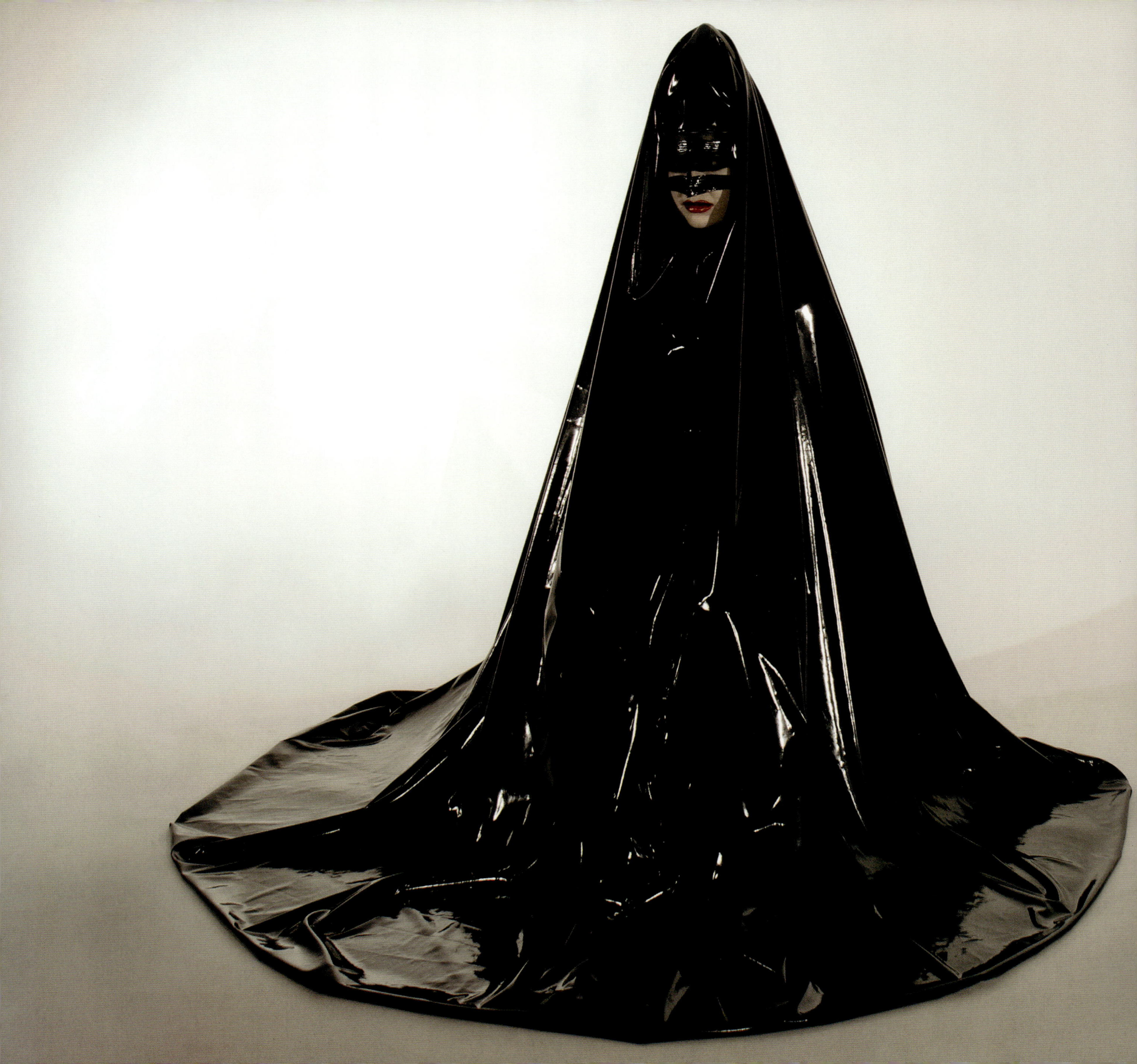

BEHNAZ BABAZADEH

The image of a veiled woman has become one of the most politically charged images of our time. The head-to-toe burka, with a slit only for the eyes, is the most controversial of all the modes of veiling from a non-Muslim point of view.

The *Edible Burka* by Afghan-American photographer Behnaz Babazadeh plays on people's fears – of otherness, of political correctness – to create an unforgettable work that led to a TED talk on her unique cross-cultural practice. Arriving in the US from Afghanistan (via Iran) as a very young child, Babazadeh remembers the reaction to her desire to wear pretty fabric around her face, as was her custom. It wasn't considered necessary in her new life. Then, as a teenager in the aftermath of 9/11, her desire to understand the mores of a country many Americans had scarcely heard of until then propelled her towards a creative practice.

An academically trained designer, Babazadeh turned to photography to document her elaborate experimentation. It has become the evidence of her inquiry. While she was still studying, she heard about a woman in the UK known as Latex Lady, a BDSM submissive who had burkas custom-made in latex as her preferred form of restrictive clothing. Her view of the burka was as a utilitarian garment that could help her live her daily life; a view diametrically opposed to the usual Western perception of the Taliban's sartorial preference. Babazadeh made a film inspired by this attitude – *Burkaphilia* – and also began a series of conversations with her grandmother, through which she came to understand how her culture's outlawing of intimacy of any kind before marriage left women and men with no idea how to behave on their wedding night. Babazadeh's creative response was to further explore the idea of the burka as a fetish object.

The desire to create an edible burka grew from a personal need to create an east-west dialogue, akin to the one taking place in her own mind. When she arrived in the US as a small child she was utterly seduced by American candies. Her favourite were fruit roll-ups, so it was natural to utilize that source of comfort – with its vivid redness that signified lust, love, war, danger – to open the lines of communication. Babazadeh embarked upon a time-consuming construction process, in which she built the essential form of the burka using around 500 strips of fruit roll-ups (save the ones otherwise consumed). She then climbed into the structure, awaiting her portrait. She repeated this experiment with candy corn, sour gummy worms and gummy bears.

Her body therefore became the research object. Babazadeh was excited by the reaction of the American public – benign, intrigued, even aroused ('Men will always find ways to find women attractive', she says). She was able to generate discussion about how women from the Middle East are perceived in the West, and was thrilled by encountering such an unexpected emotional reaction. Her latest additions to the series depict her in the traditional blue burka of her country, in ordinary American settings. With every day that passes, Babazadeh is leaning towards where the work is taking her, learning about her own history, and sharing her knowledge with those who want to look.

Black latex burka, film still from *Burkaphilia*, 2012

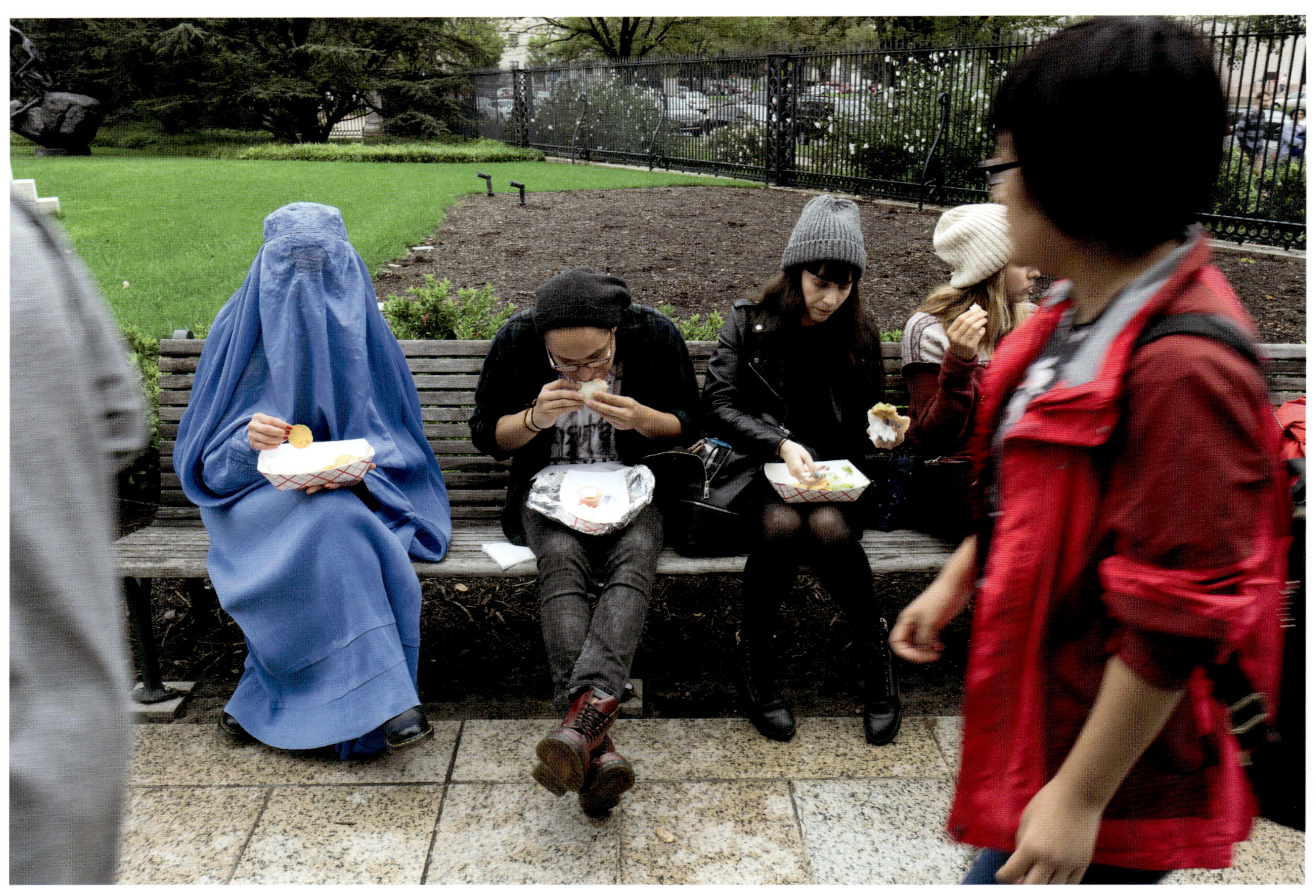

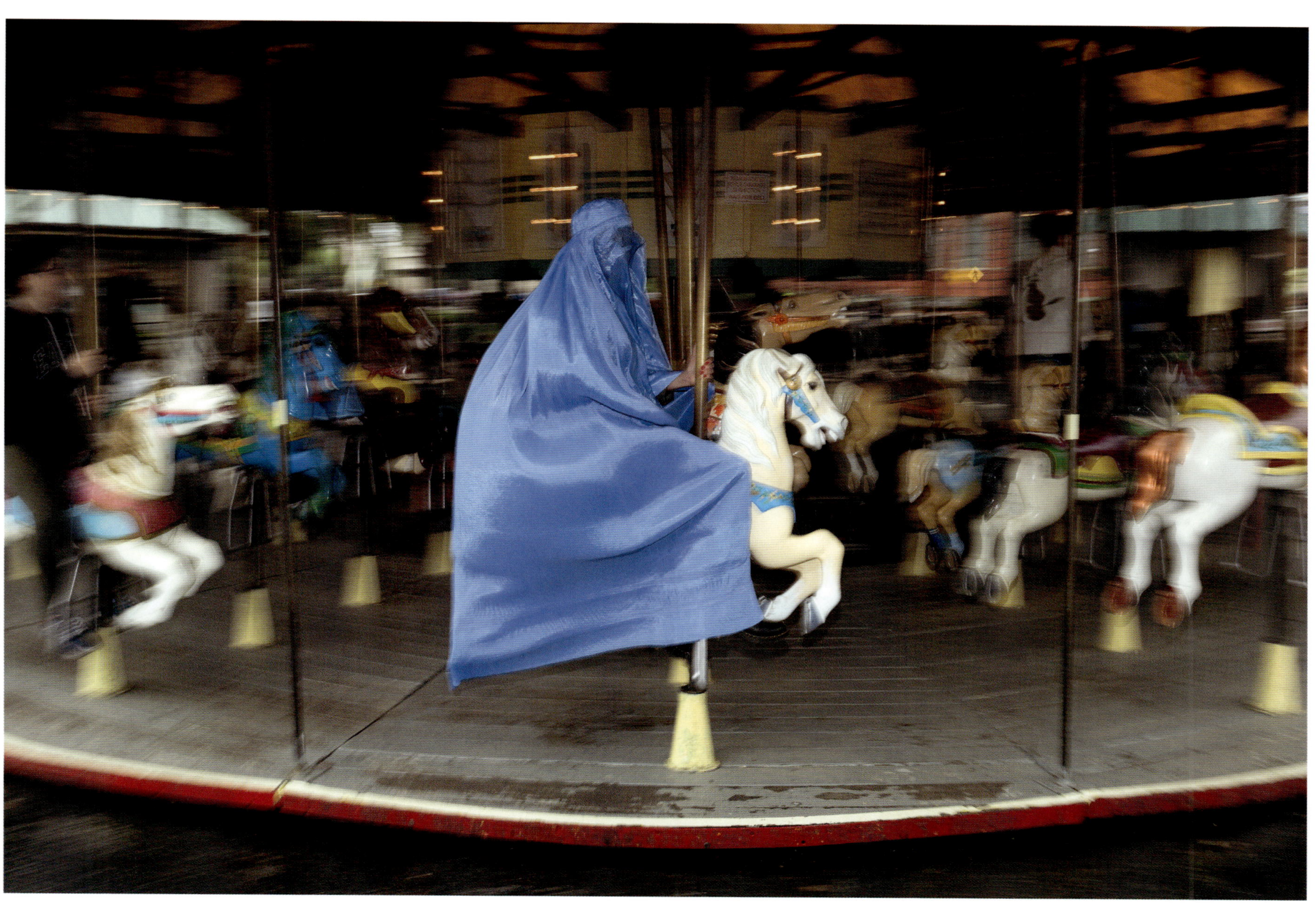

On the Carousel, 2016, Burka Diaries series

Behnaz Babazadeh   27

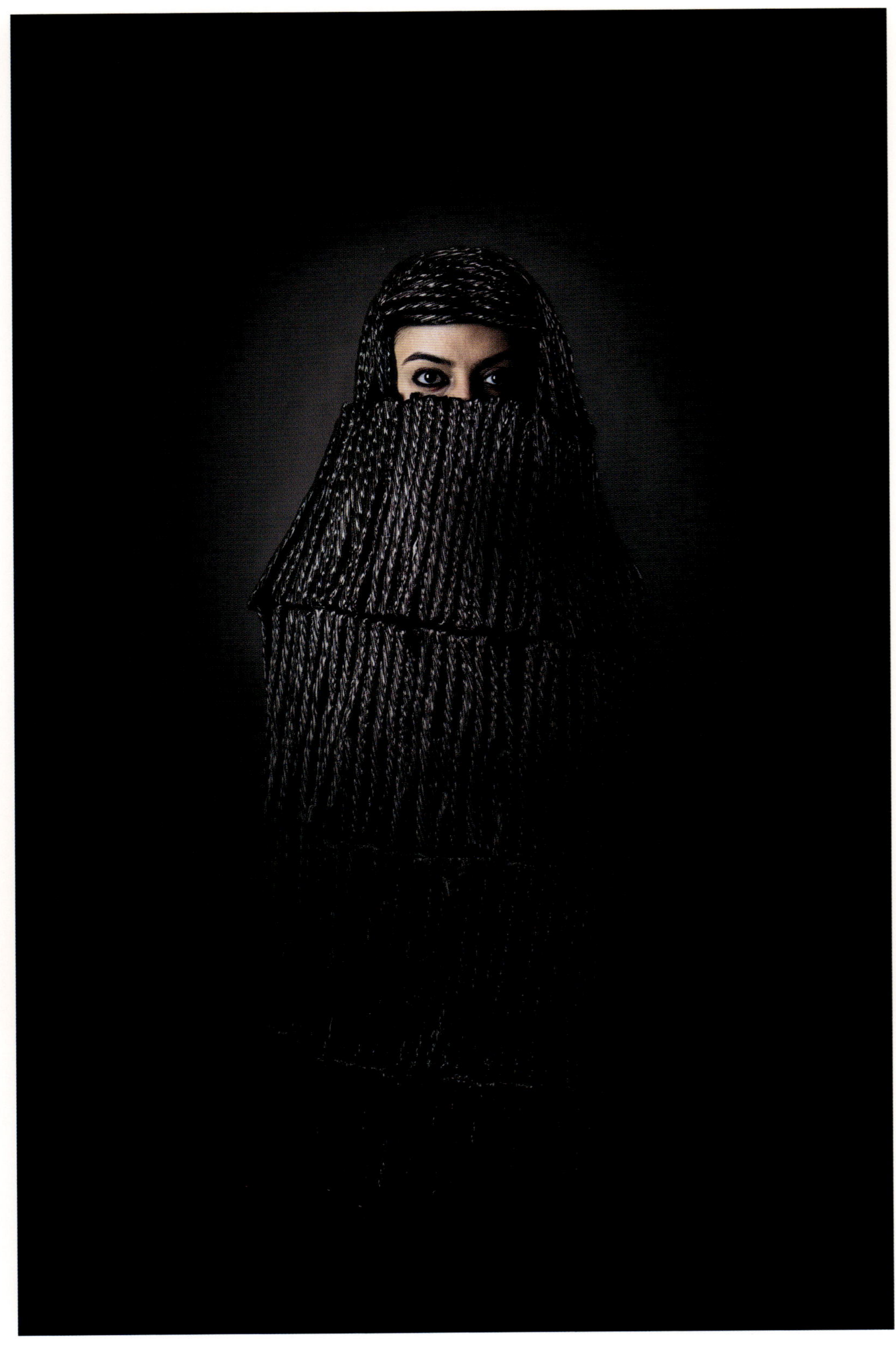

    Firecrackers

Black Burka, Twizzlers Licorice, 2015

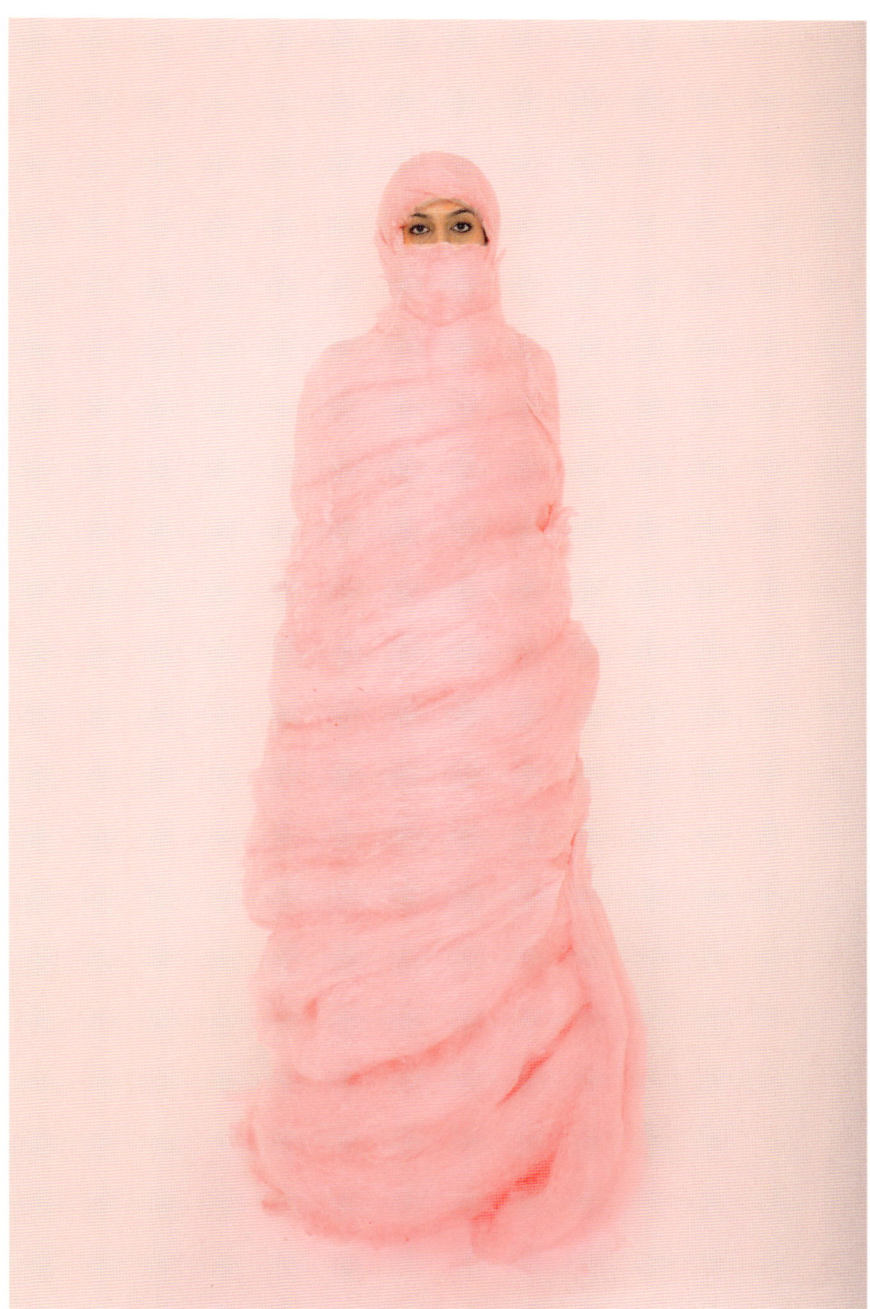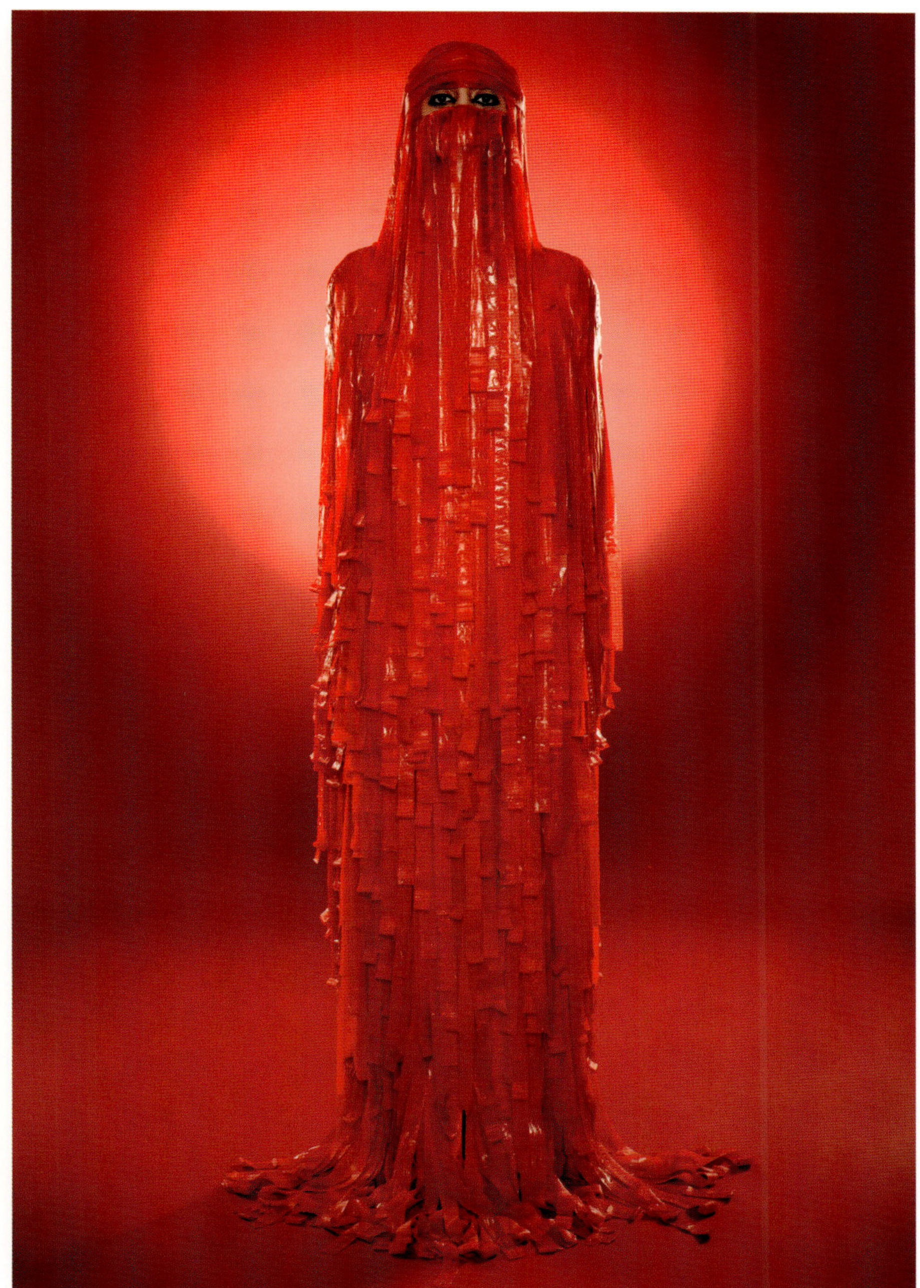

Above left: *Pink Burka, Cotton Candy, 2014;*
above right: *Red Burka, Fruit Roll-Up Licorice, 2012*

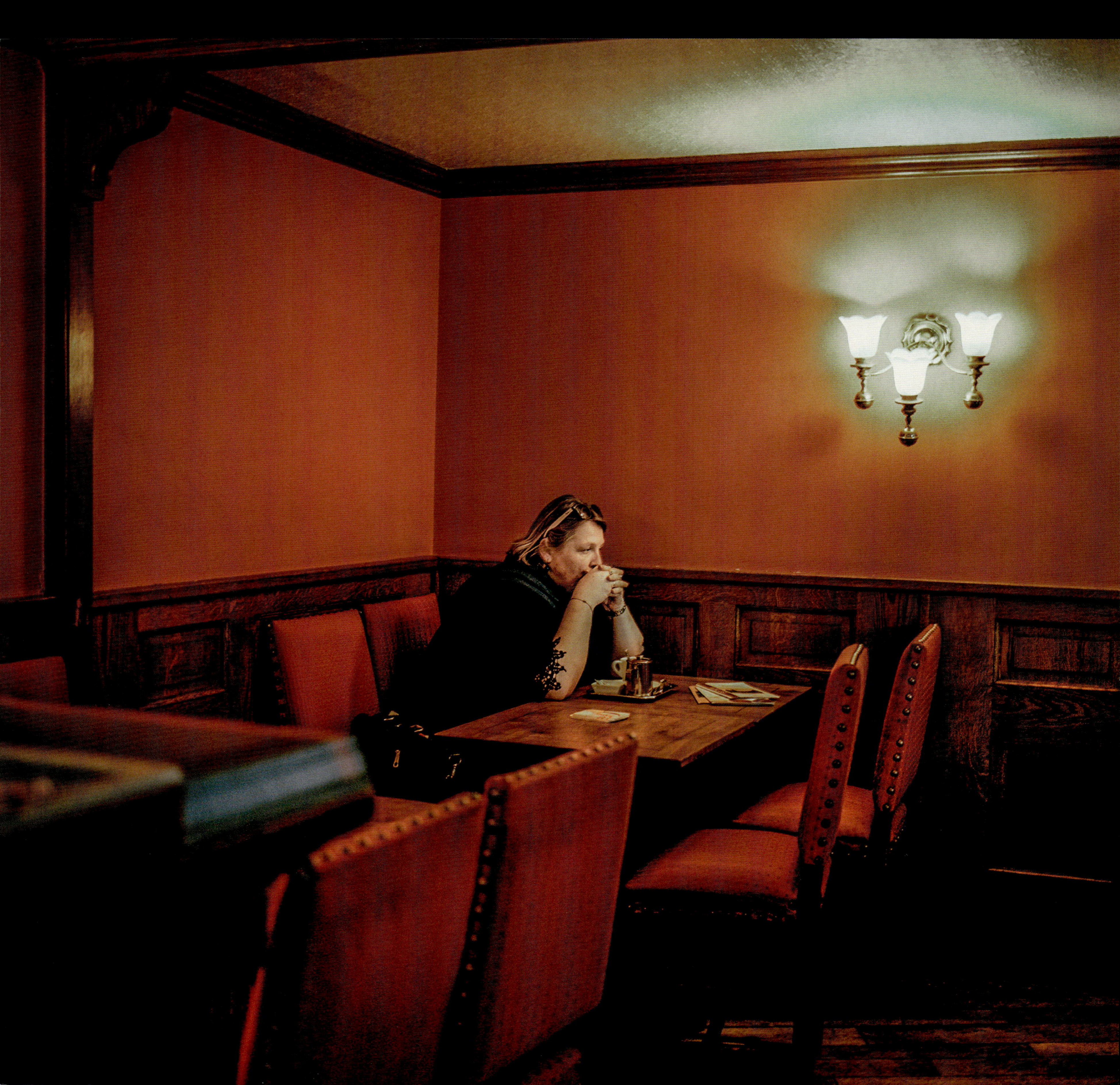

POULOMI BASU

...

Basu photographs inside the homes of the absent sons, which are filled with photographs, possessions and mementos of the young men

...

Since the ISIS attacks on Paris in November 2015 a spotlight has been shining on Belgium. According to a survey conducted in December 2015 by Soufan Group, Belgium is believed to be home to more foreign ISIS fighters per capita than any other European country. The group estimate that 470 young men have been radicalized and influenced by the opportunity to leave provincial Brussels and give their lives to the creation of a caliphate, secure in the knowledge that they will most likely die as martyrs.

Indian photographer Poulomi Basu has integrated herself in the community of Vilvoorde on the outskirts of Brussels, which is often referred to as a 'hotbed' of jihadism. She has photographed the mothers of ISIS fighters, uncovering the trauma of those left behind as they try to deal with their grief, confusion and, frequently, their guilt.

Basu describes Vilvoorde as a fragmented and alienated place. She photographed three women who all have their own tales to tell about their lost sons. Saliha's nineteen-year-old son, Sabri, fabricated a wedding so that he could travel to Turkey and then into Syria where he was killed just four months later. Chantal's son left in 2012 and is believed to still be in Syria. Martine's eighteen-year-old son was disillusioned by the lack of opportunity in his home town and by negative reactions to his Arabic surname. He left in 2014 and was killed during an attack on the Deir Ez-Zor airport in Syria a year later.

Basu has given a potent and moving account of the desperation and isolation experienced by these women, who are often ostracized by their communities, and the brave efforts they undertake to fight back against radicalization and support other suffering parents.

Basu draws on metaphors such as reflection to present ideas of duality. Images of her subjects staring into nothing create a tangible, desperate sense of waiting. She includes landscapes of mundane suburban towns and photographs her subjects alone in areas that should be bustling with life. She photographs inside the homes of the absent sons, which are filled with photographs, possessions and mementos of the young men. The message seems to be one of anonymity: this could happen to anyone, in any town, in any country.

A powerful addition to Basu's narrative is the inclusion of Facebook messages between Saliha and her son – their only means of contact once he left. Her sense of longing and his apathy read as many exchanges might between a mother and her son were it not for the repeated use of religious words and concepts – 'hamdoulah' (praise be to God) and 'Don't let go of Islamization'.

Basu sometimes refers to the project by the title *Paradise Lies at the Feet of Your Mother,* a concept borrowed from the Koran. The mothers have now galvanized into lobbying groups and the phrase was used in an open letter to their sons in an attempt to bring them back from Syria. Much work is now taking place with the mothers as key partners in the fight against extremism – it is understood a mother is often the first to recognize behavioural changes in her child and perhaps better placed to counteract it.

Basu tackles this emotionally layered construct with the elegance of a seasoned visual journalist: one who is used to talking about the hardships of women. It's a story that arguably only another woman could tell. Themes of identity and gender run through most of her work. In *To Conquer Her Land* she recounts India's first women soldiers deployed at the Pakistan border, while the award-winning project *A Ritual of Exile* explores practices that subjugate menstruating women in South Asia under the guise of religion.

Basu has had numerous commissions, notably from non-profit entities. A recent grantee of the Magnum Foundation Emergency Fund and co-founder of Just Another Photo Festival across India, she continues to democratize photography, making sensitive stories public and delivering them to new audiences.

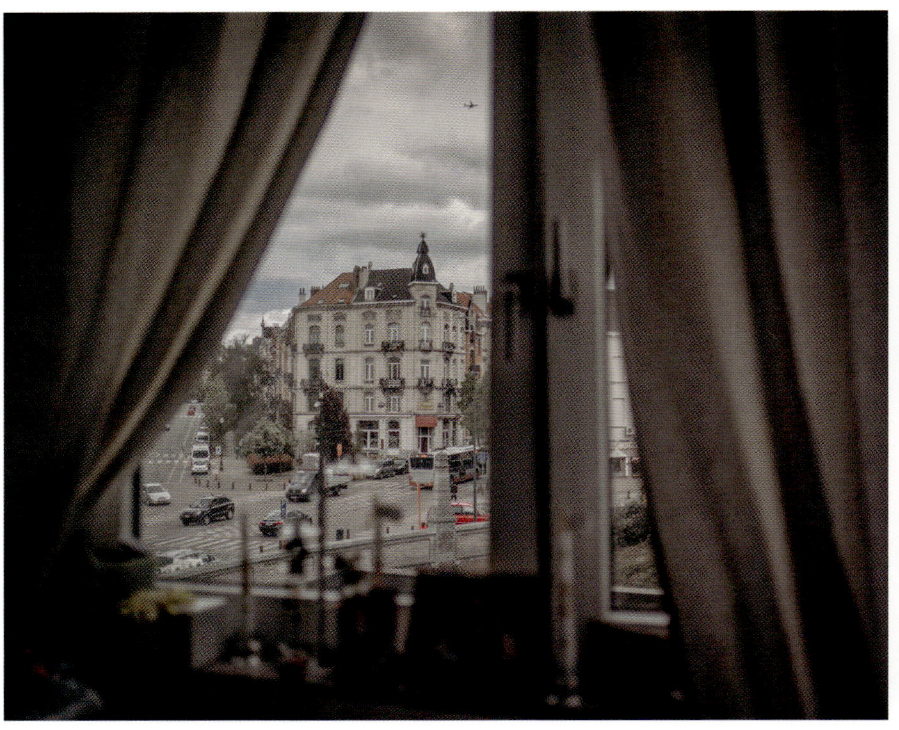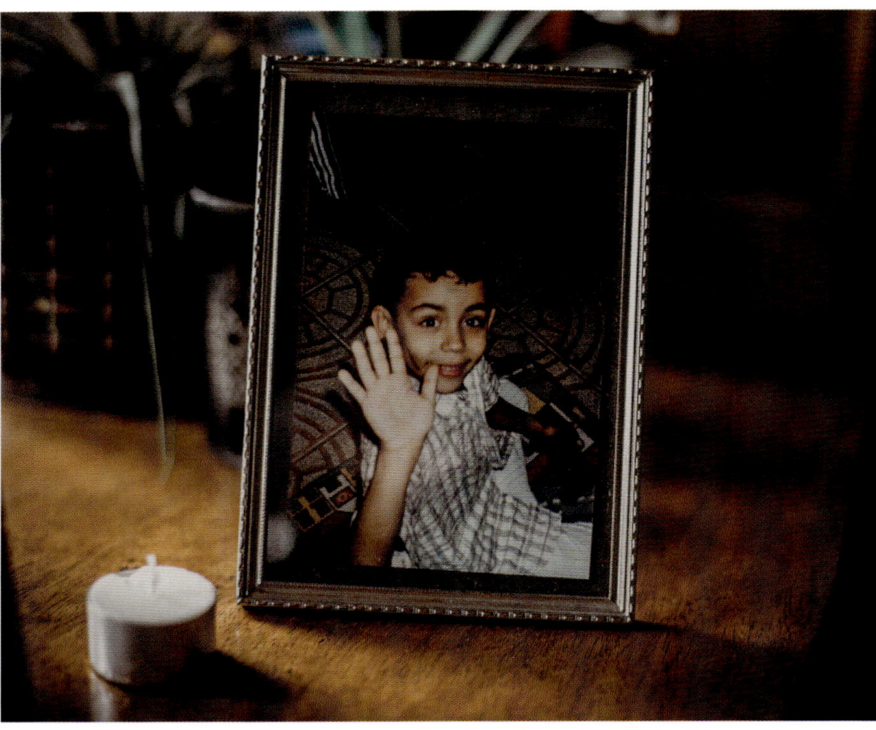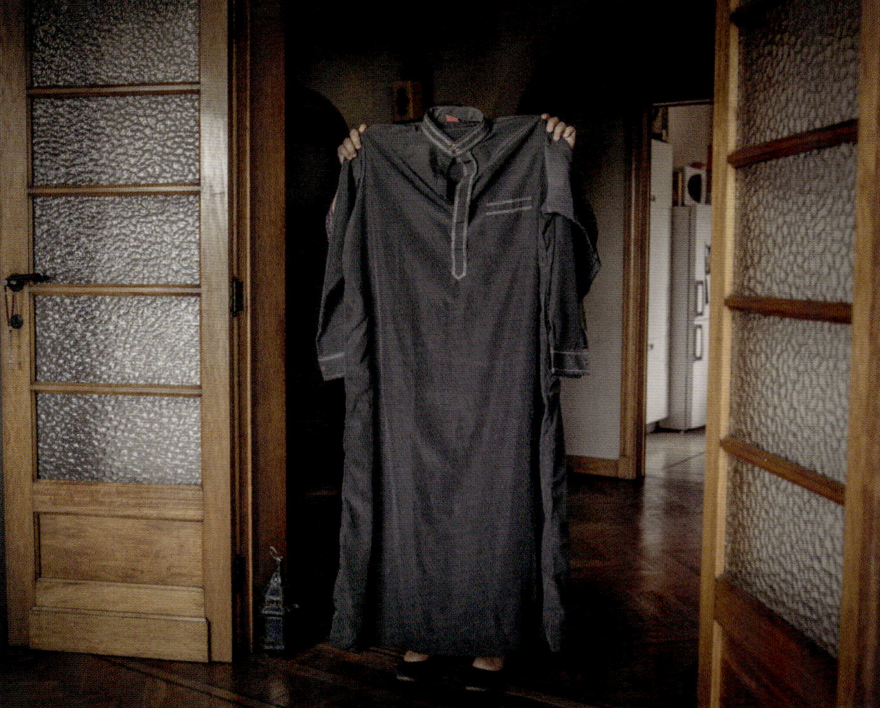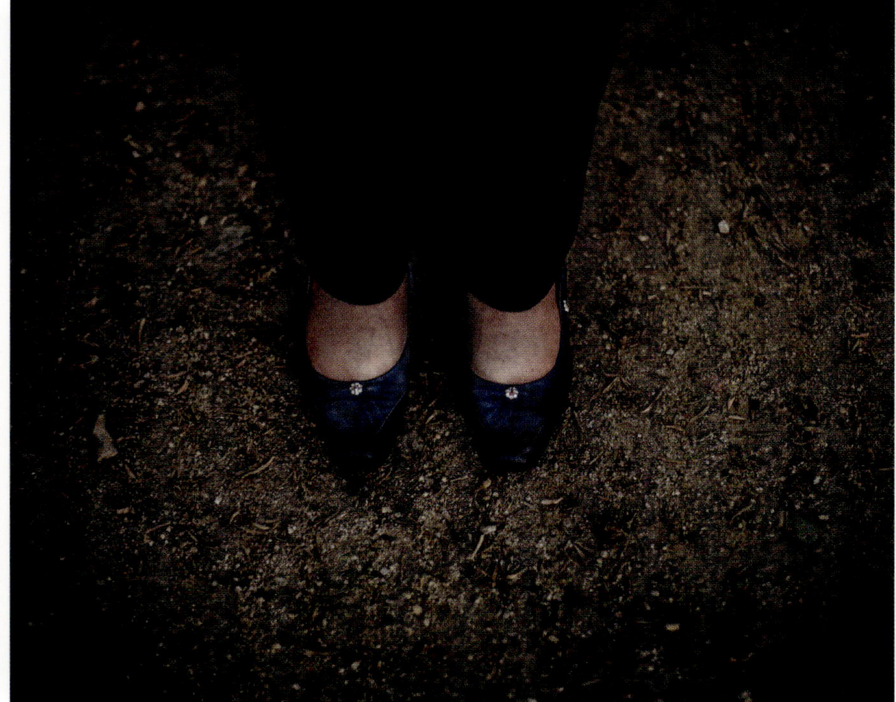

Untitled, 2015, Paradise Lies at the Feet of Your Mother: Mothers of Isis Foreign Fighters series

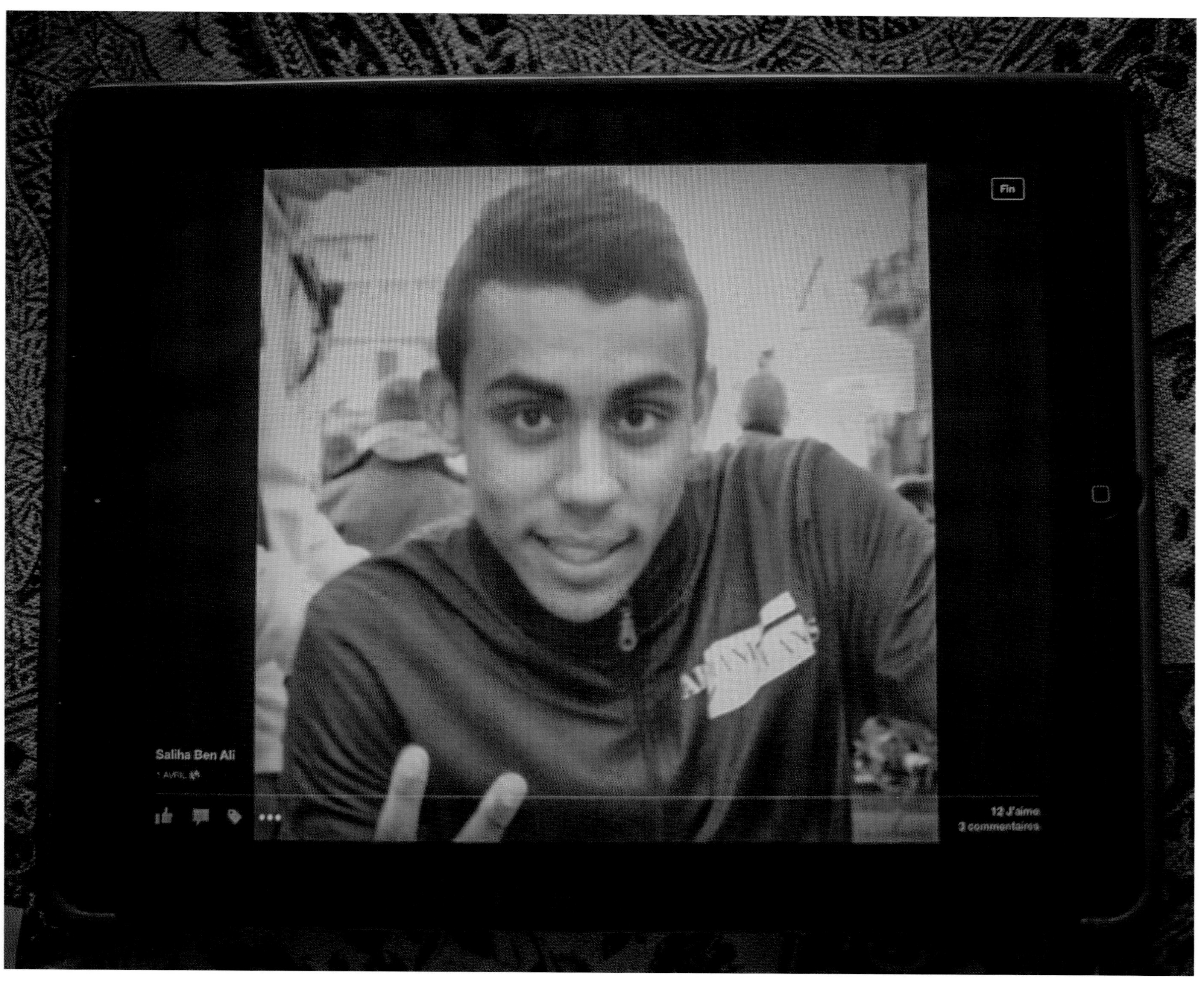

Untitled, 2015, Paradise Lies at the Feet of Your Mother: Mothers of Isis Foreign Fighters series

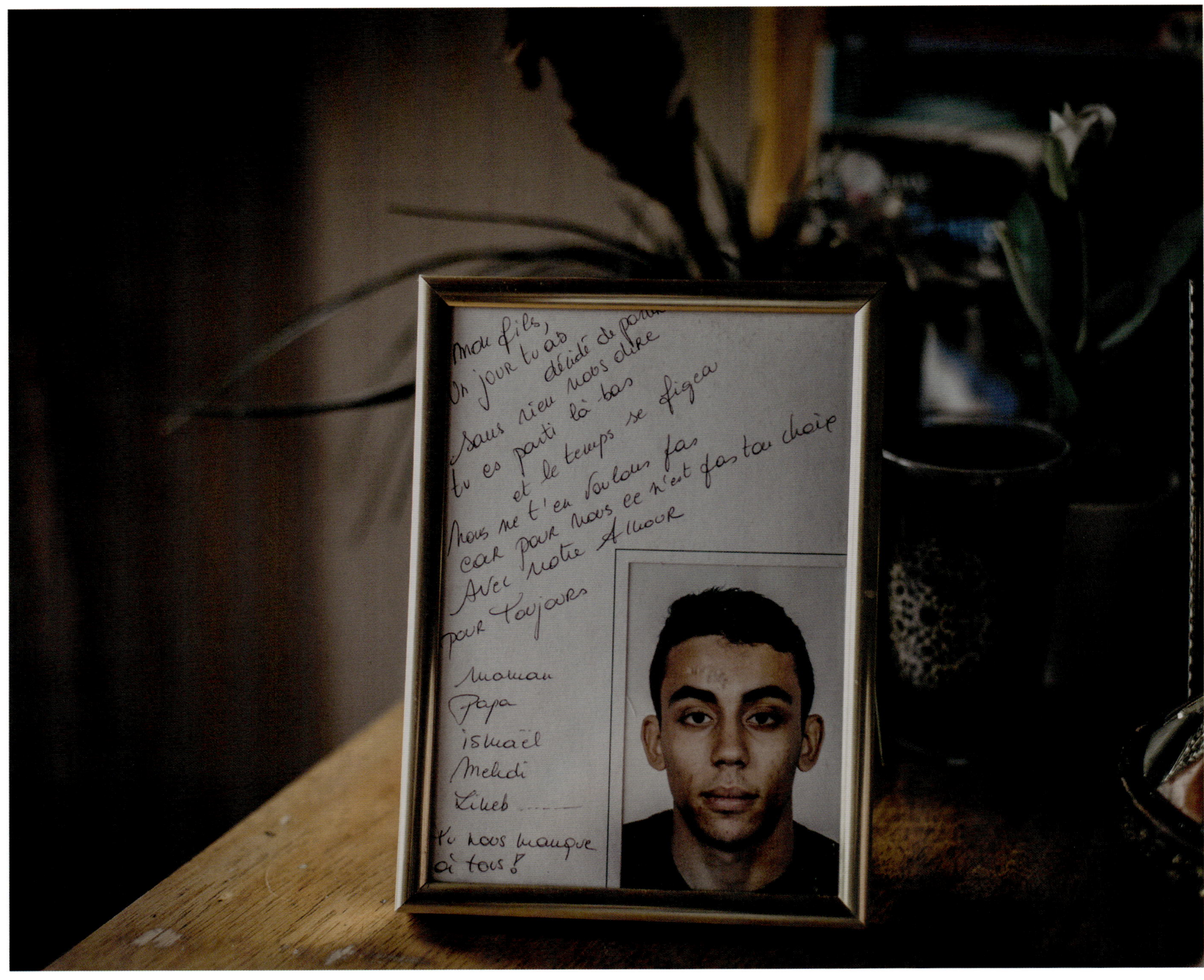

Untitled, 2015, Paradise Lies at the Feet of Your Mother: Mothers of Isis Foreign Fighters series

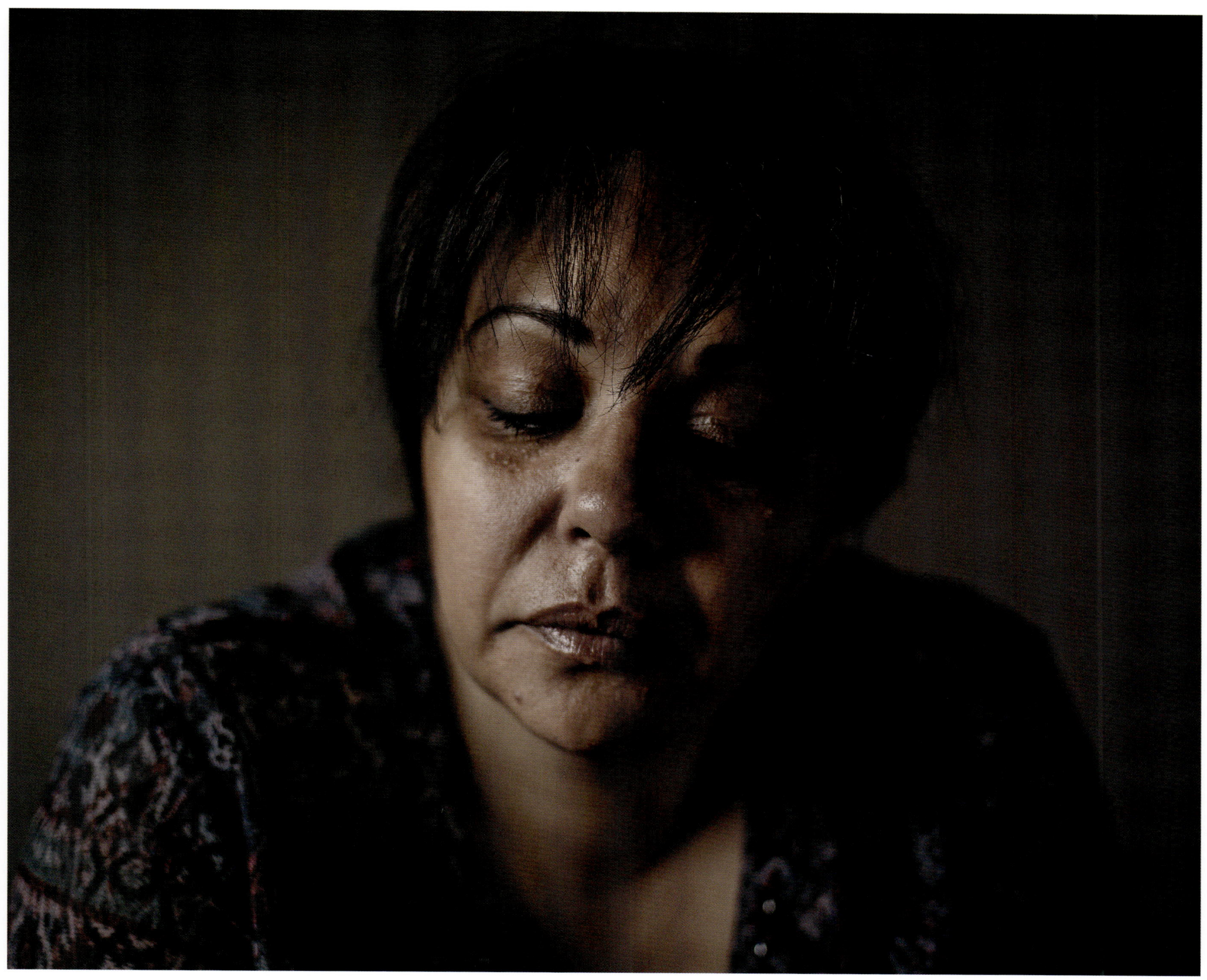

Untitled, 2015, Paradise Lies at the Feet of Your Mother: Mothers of Isis Foreign Fighters series

Poulomi Basu 35

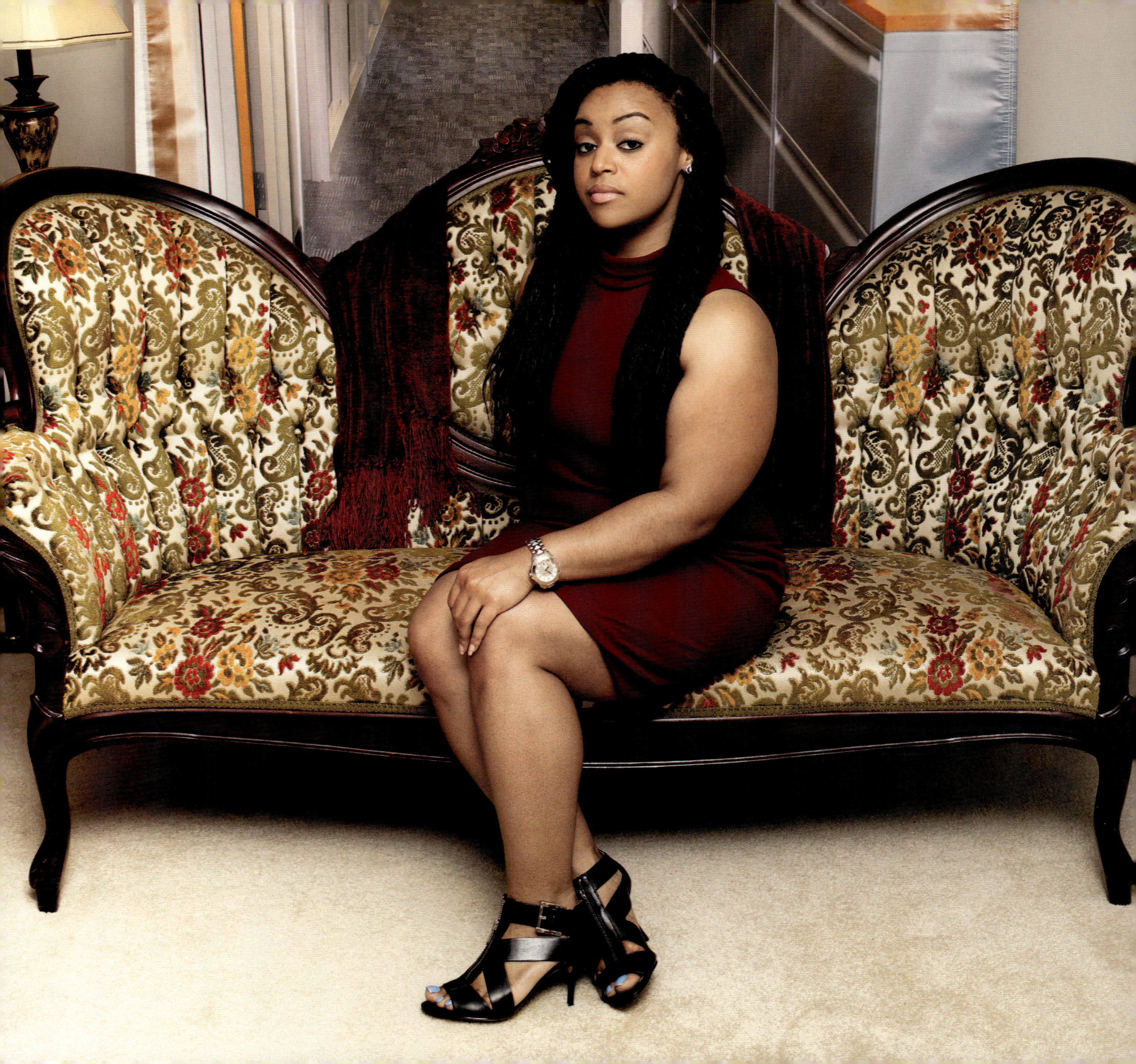

ENDIA BEAL

Endia Beal is an American artist, educator and activist for social, racial and gender equality. She graduated from the University of North Carolina and has an MFA from Yale University School of Art. She is currently the director of Diggs Gallery and an associate professor of art at Winston-Salem State University.

Beal has made a significant contribution to the history of photography for minority women of colour through her work – a history that is still being written. As well as looking at racial and gender stereotypes, Beal's work explores life in corporate America, workplace diversity, the often uncomfortable spaces women of colour occupy within this, and the concessions they make to 'fit in'.

Her 2013 work *Can I Touch It?* took a cross-section of white, middle-aged women and gave them a variety of black hairstyles. The women are featured in buttoned-up attire, with cornrows, braids, finger waves and afros, shot in the style of traditional corporate portraits. The idea was inspired by Beal's personal experience of the office environment: 'My colleagues were very fascinated by my Afro, like overly fascinated', she explains. 'I found myself in this situation of discomfort, and knowing that if I straightened my hair, I was kind of appealing to a norm, to fit in that space.

But if I wore my hair like how I normally like to wear it, it became a petting zoo.'

The work is also featured in a three-minute video, where a spoken-word artist provocatively describes how she's going to 'let them touch me', and where Beal's male co-workers are subjected to a degree of embarrassment as she asks them to describe what it was like to touch her hair.

Beal's continuing interest with objectification, 'the other' and functioning in the corporate space led to her project *Am I What You're Looking For?*, which won a Magnum Foundation Emergency Fund award. The series borrows inspiration from James Van Der Zee's *Harlem Renaissance*.

The project portrays young African-American women transitioning from academia to career paths. Photographed in their homes, against the (visible) backdrop of the IT department at Yale (where Beal interned), Beal encourages the girls to be authentic and as comfortable as possible – to wear what they deem to be a 'professional' outfit and to act as if they are preparing for a job interview. Considerations are given to outfits, shoes, hairstyles, tattoos, but also body language. Some of the women are strikingly confident in sky-scraper heels, while others are more moderate. Eyes are downcast, and

they appear not to know what to do with their hands.

Beal asks, 'What does that feel like, being in that space, knowing that you have to prepare for a performance? Knowing that what you look like may not necessarily fit the ideal choice?' Her work highlights the clash between individuality and conformity – something experienced by many young people of all races – but also seeks to question who defines 'appropriate' professional behaviour for young, ambitious women of colour. Beal's work serves as both a positive reinforcement and an important dialogue in expanding workplace diversity, while reassessing the cultural norms.

Jessica, 2015, *Am I What You're Looking For?* series

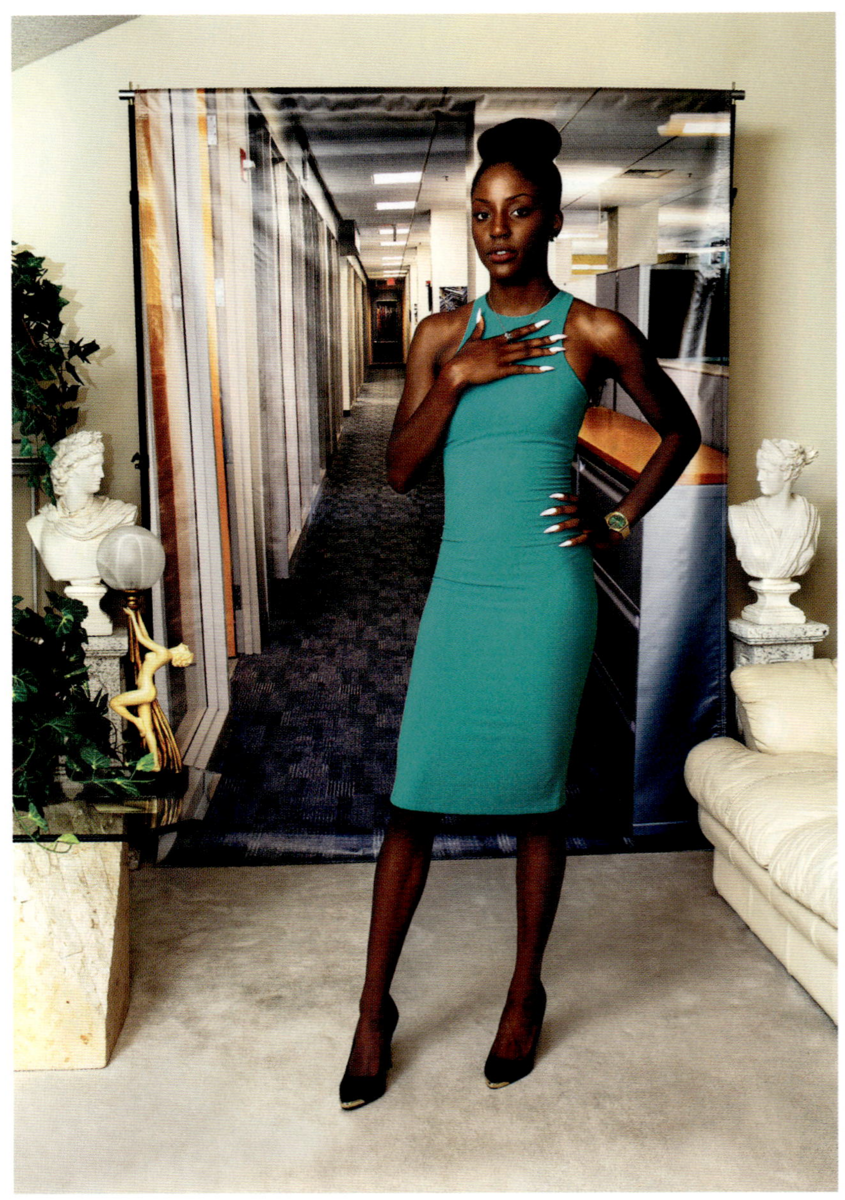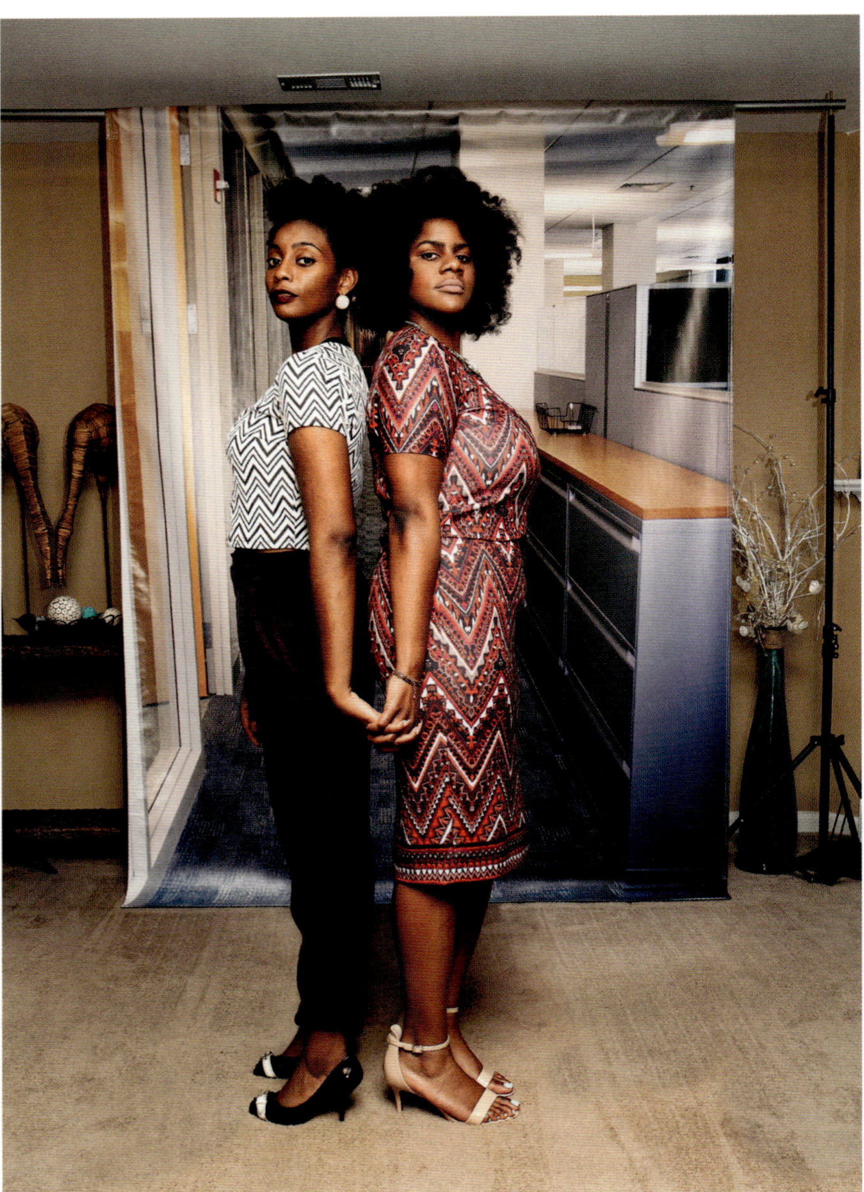

    Firecrackers

Left: Mel, 2016;
right: Kyandra and Shakiya, 2016; both *Am I What You're Looking For?* series

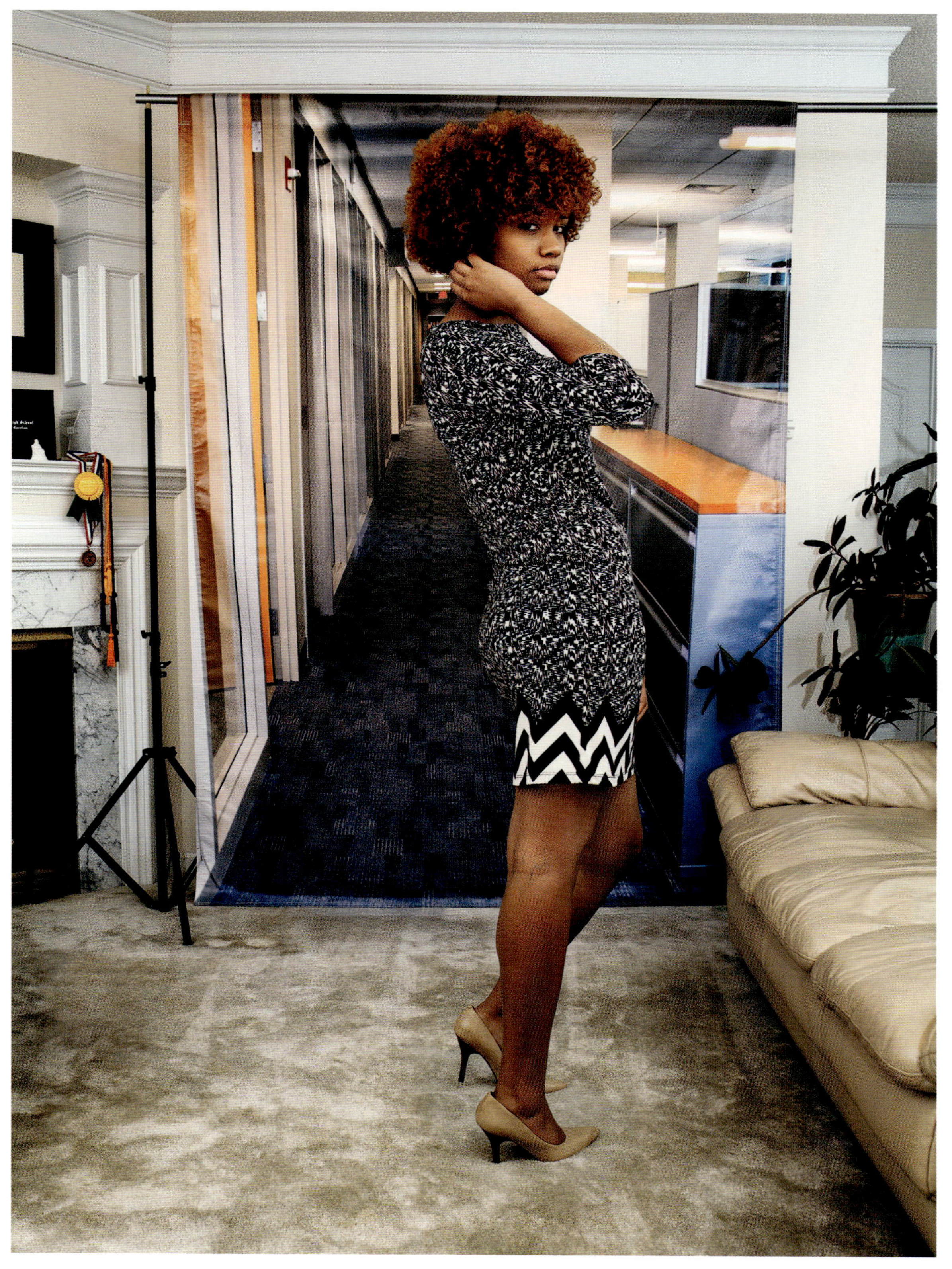

Taylor, 2016, *Am I What You're Looking For?* series

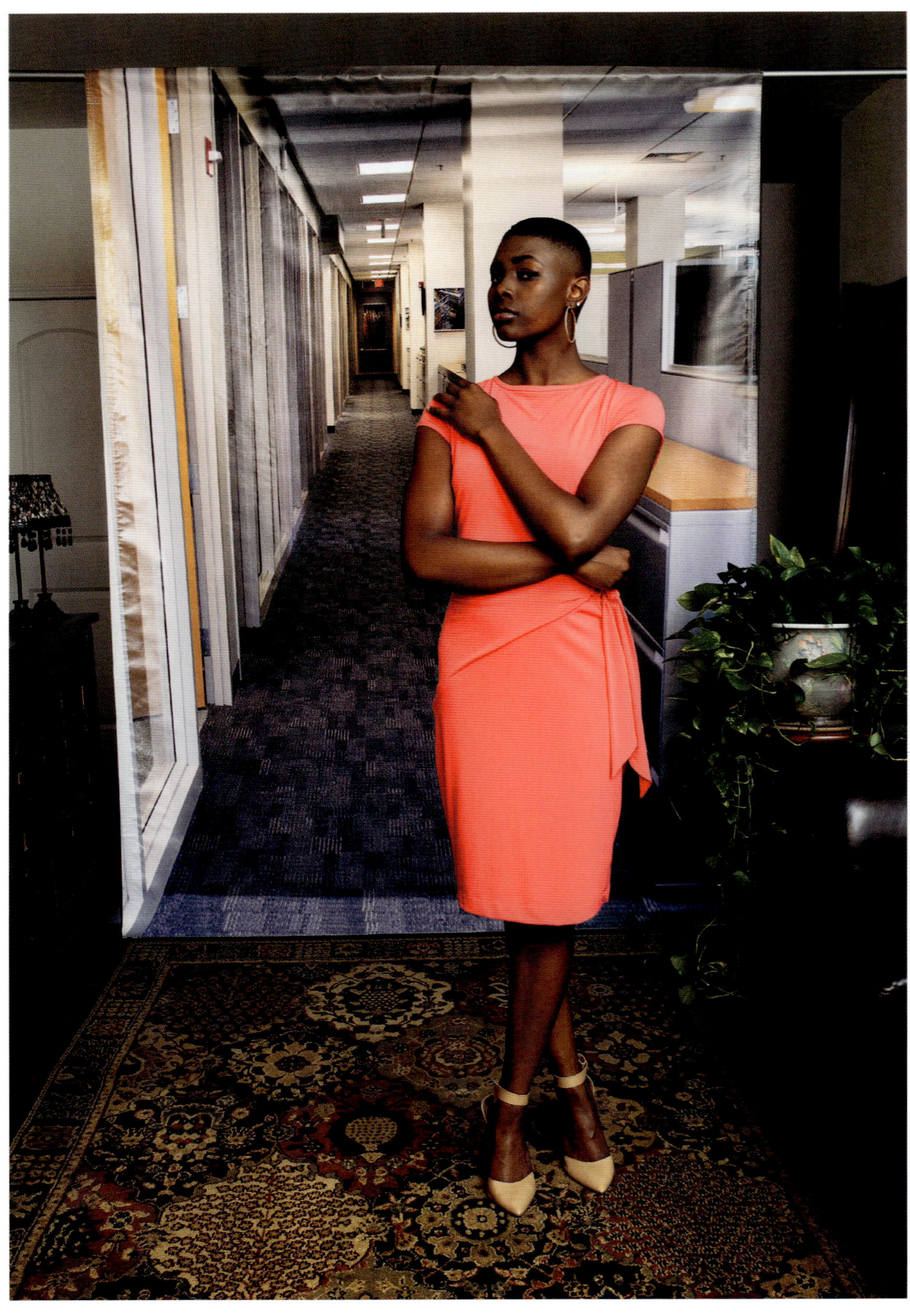

Tianna, 2016, *Am I What You're Looking For?* series

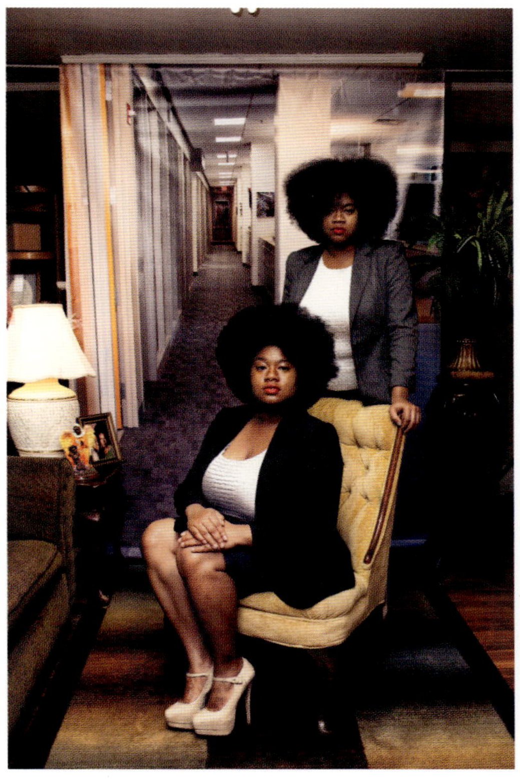

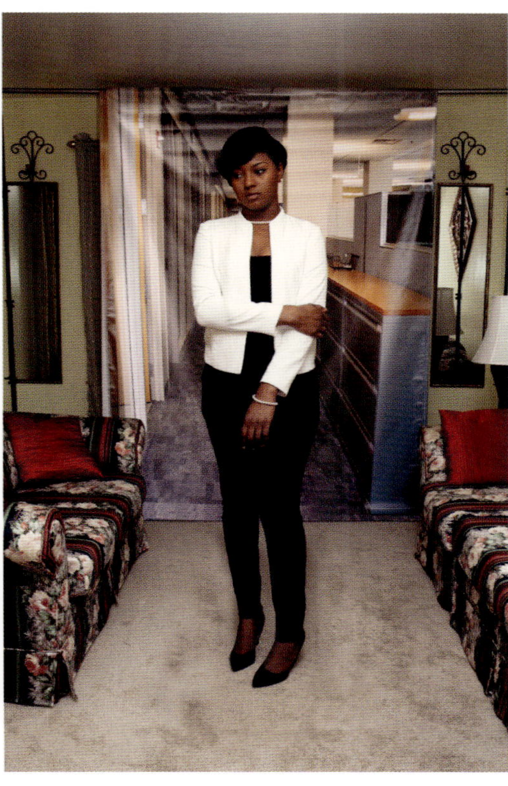

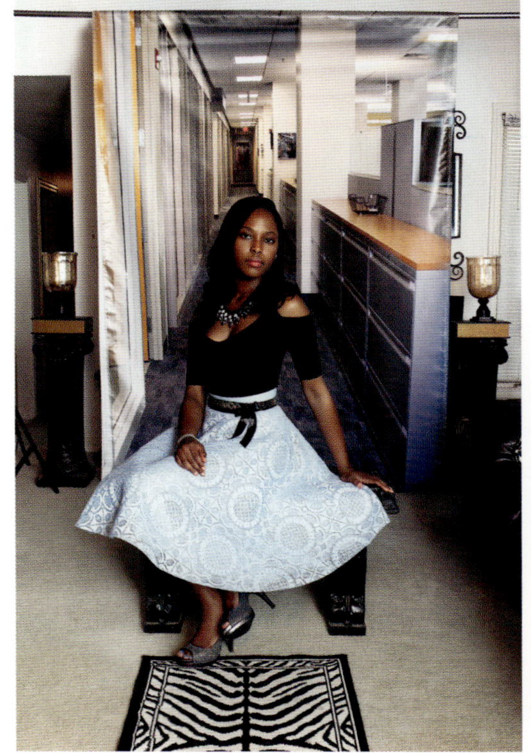

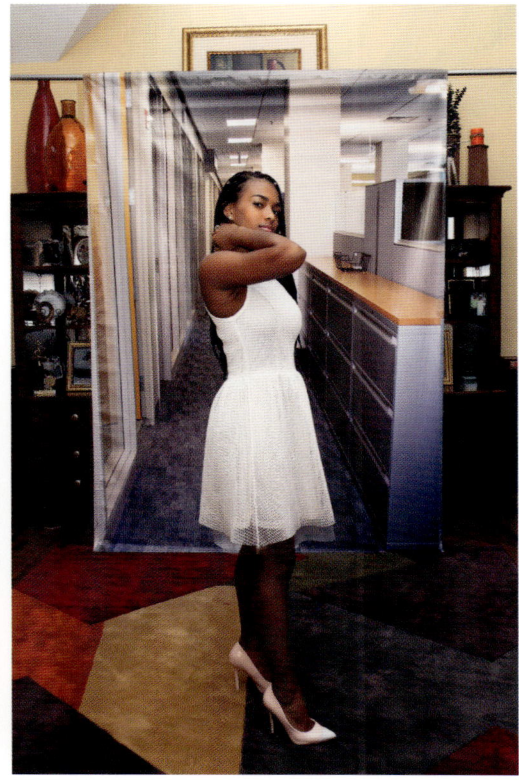

Top left: Sabrina and Katrina, 2016;
top right: Dontia, 2015;
above left: Annie, 2016;
above right: Aja, 2016;
all *Am I What You're Looking For?* series

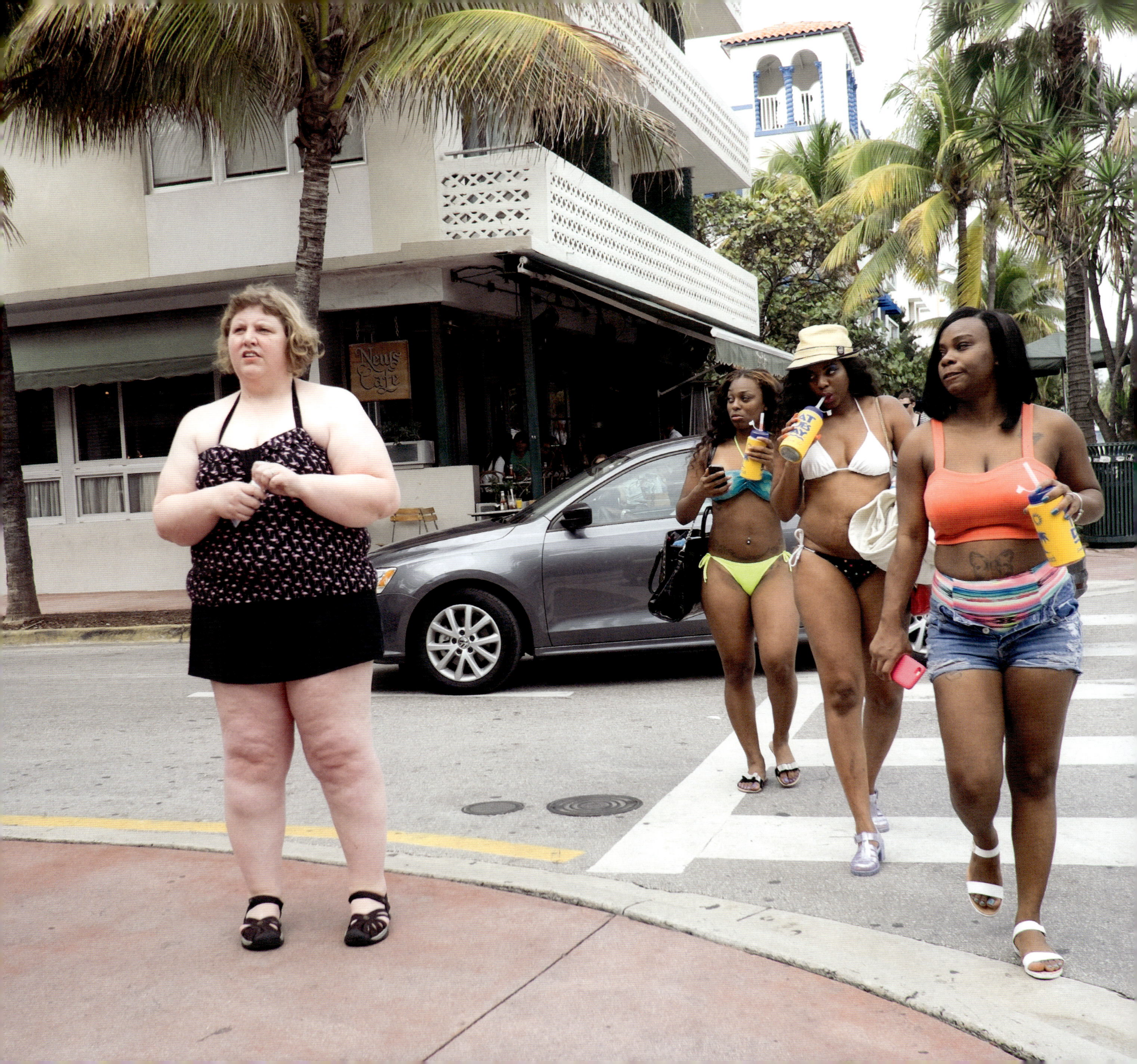

HALEY MORRIS-CAFIERO

…

Morris-Cafiero's work is an unflinching, brave and bold reassessment of 'the gaze'

…

In *Wait Watchers*, American photographer Haley Morris-Cafiero acts as part-performer, part-provocateur to raise questions about society's prejudices and preferences. Her work is an unflinching, brave and bold reassessment of 'the gaze' and a study of the audience as an implicated party.

Using a camera mounted onto a tripod and a remote fire or an assistant, Morris-Cafiero travels to high footfall areas such as the Champs-Elysées in Paris or Las Ramblas in Barcelona and records people's reactions to her and, unavoidably, to her physical size and shape. She began the project in 2010 when she noticed that a man being photographed in Times Square in New York was more focused on sneering at her rather than paying attention to the task in hand.

Since then, the success with which Morris-Cafiero manages to capture the palatable disdain for her body is at once shocking and depressing. But the photographer empowers herself, cleverly turning the negative gaze back onto the viewer and, in doing so, makes a spectacle of the audience itself.

There are three gazes within this complicated and layered story. The first is from the often contemptuous eyes set on Morris-Cafiero; the second is that of us – the viewer – and our interaction with those scornful eyes;

and the last gaze belongs to Morris-Cafiero herself, her eyes on us, her invisible audience. Her penetrative gaze seems to challenge us and is a provocation to take a stand. The story is reminiscent of a modern-day Narcissus, except rather than falling in love with our reflection, we are horrified at what Morris-Cafiero shows us about our own prejudices, stereotypes and societal norms.

Of course, we cannot read the exact thoughts of all Morris-Cafiero's subjects, and it is equally possible that those caught in the act of staring are stunned by their own reactions. Perhaps what is more telling about the work than the photographs themselves are the comments that followed when the series went viral and Morris-Cafiero found herself hailed simultaneously as hero and villain. Comments varied from predictable responses relating to her 'needing' to style her hair, do some exercise, stop eating doughnuts and put on make-up: 'Fat lump of lard. Stay off the donuts and go running. Makes me ill just looking at her'. This negativity is juxtaposed with powerful messages. 'You are brilliant and amazing and courageous and I wholeheartedly understand the intent of this project'.

The comments sit as polar opposites in *The Watchers* (published by the Magenta Foundation, 2015). In the book the negative

responses act as a catalyst for a current work-in-progress tentatively titled 'Self Improvement', where Morris-Cafiero takes the 'advice' of her fat-shamers and documents herself exercising, having a makeover and shopping for clothes. The concept again looks to raise issues about social norms and explores the counter-intuitive responses from those mocking rather than encouraging her attempts to engage with society's expectations and follow that advice. In sacrificing herself through her work, Morris-Cafiero becomes a representation of anyone who has been made to feel uncomfortable under the gaze of another; indeed for anyone who has ever felt like an outsider.

News Café, 2015, *Wait Watchers* series, Miami Beach, Florida

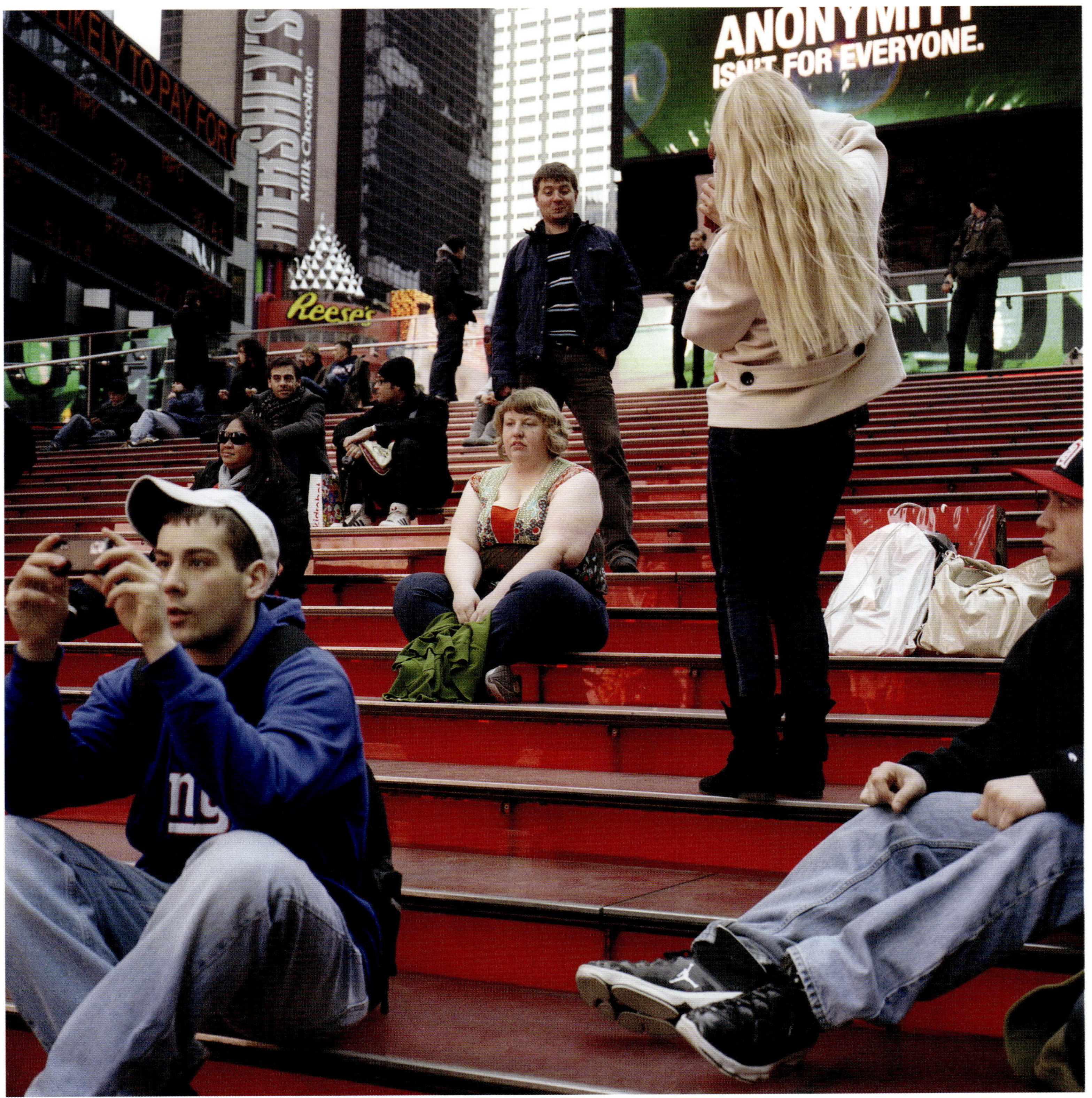

Anonymity Isn't for Everyone, 2010, Wait Watchers series, New York

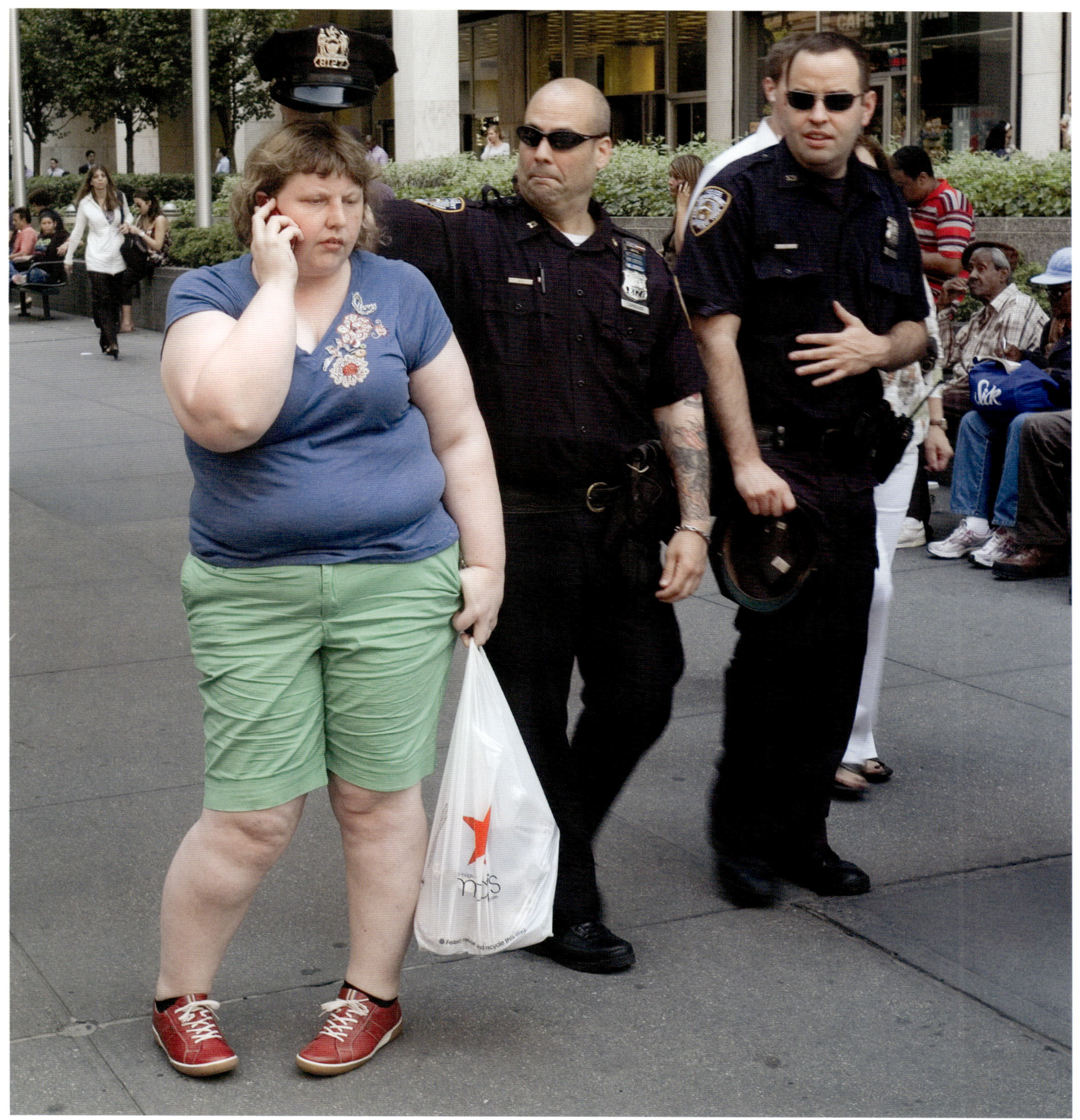

Haley Morris-Cafiero   45

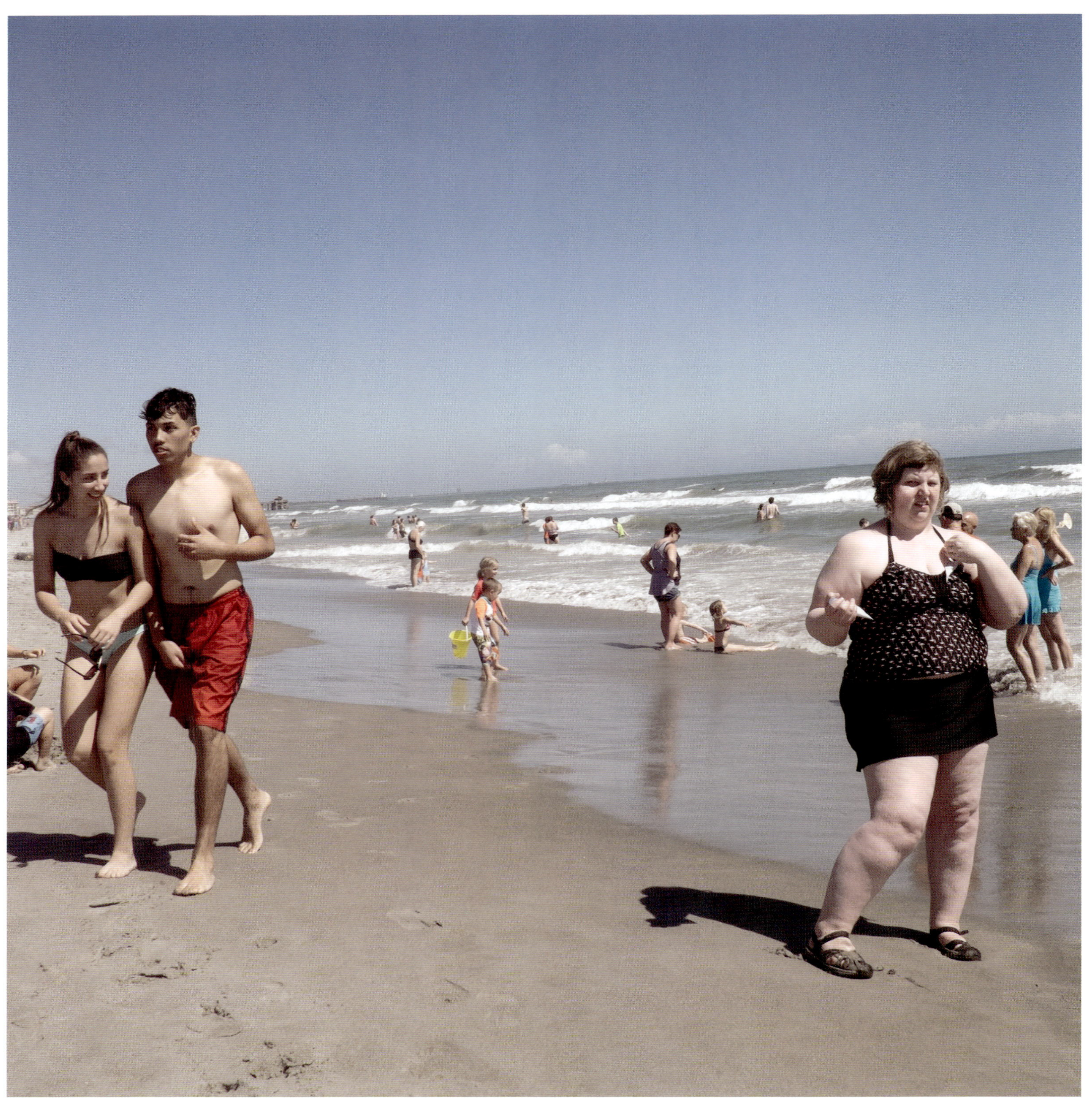

    Firecrackers

Sunscreen, 2015, Wait Watchers series, Cocoa Beach, Florida

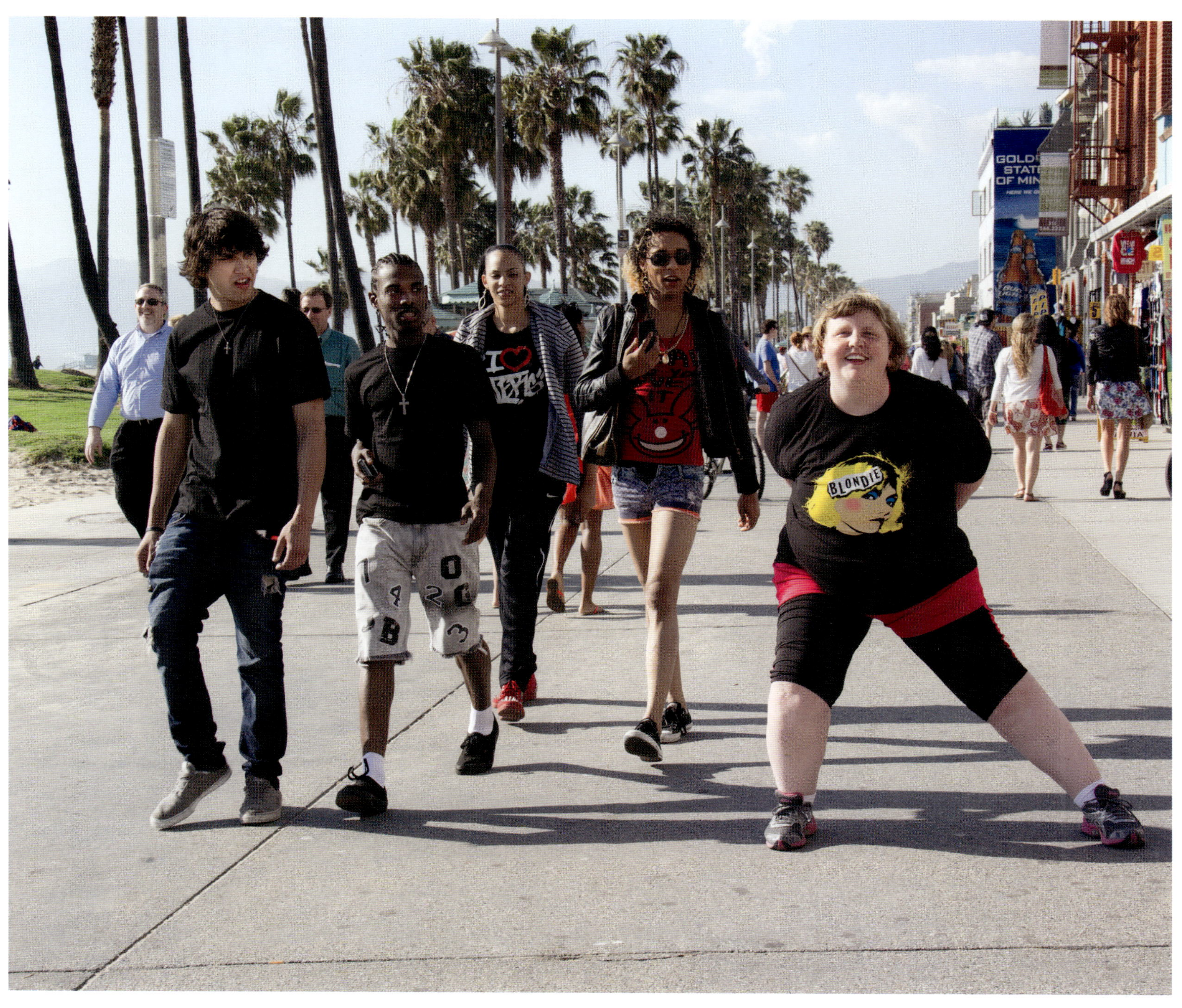

Blondie, 2014, Wait Watchers series, Venice Beach, California

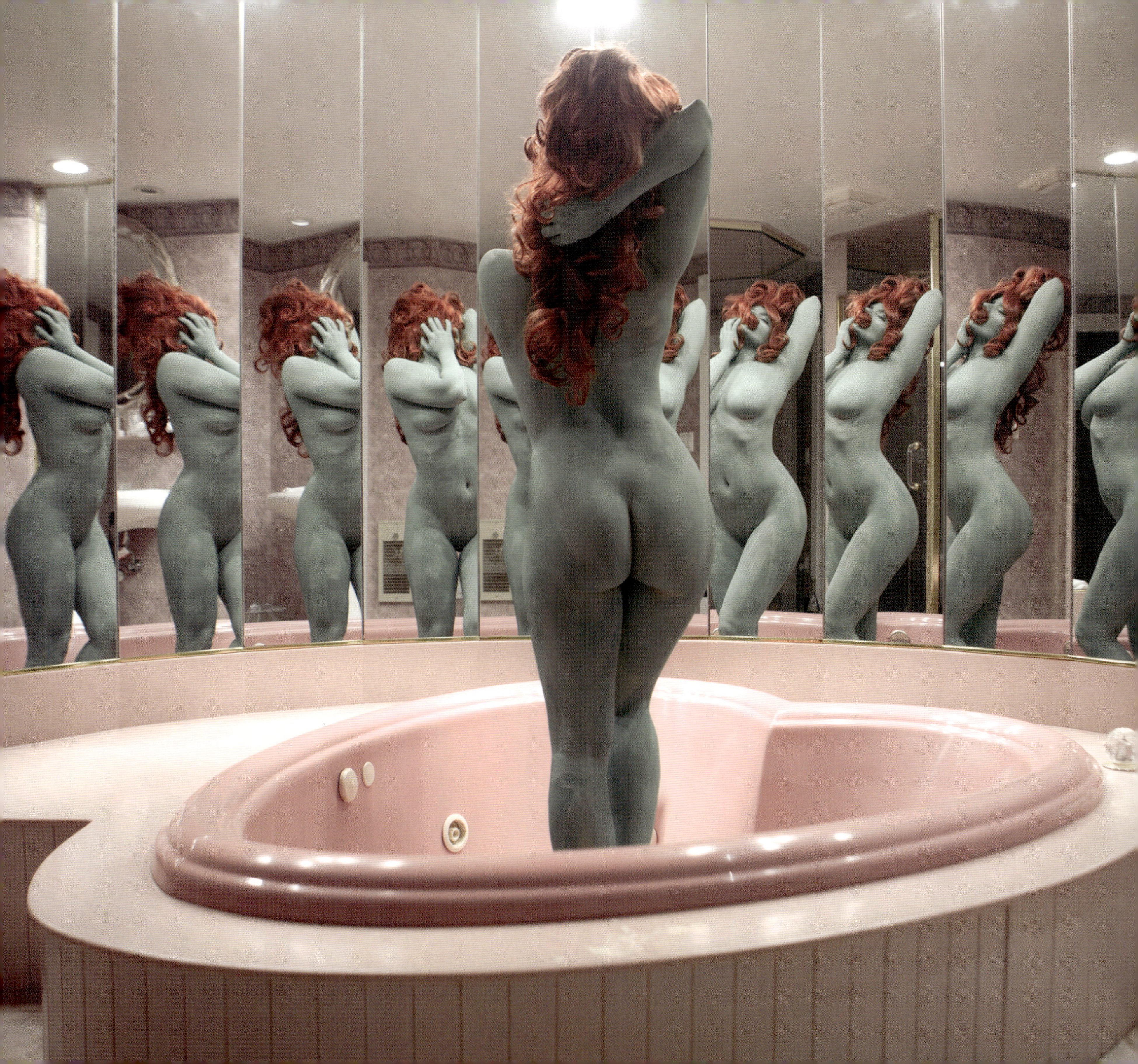

JUNO CALYPSO

With a name uniting a Roman goddess with a Greek sea nymph, perhaps Juno Calypso's destiny was foretold. Her contribution to contemporary feminist discourse is significant, witty and entirely natural. Calypso is both photographer and subject, continuing a relationship with the camera that began as a teenager, which she channels through her 'extended self', Joyce.

If one colour is associated with Calypso, it is confectioners' pink. She uses it with abandon, and plays with our own thoughts about this bizarrely gendered colour until we too find our cultural assumptions absurd. Another defining factor of her work to date is her use of props, which she sources on eBay (where else?). She has an eye for items designed for use by women in acts of ritualistic self-improvement: wrinkles will be banished! Fat will melt! Body hair will vanish! And then, obviously: love will appear! Calypso buys these objects – her own bedroom must be a cabinet of curiosities – and Joyce tries them out. As she does so, she becomes a kind of B-movie alien, undergoing procedures earthly creatures could never comprehend. Indeed, over several images, Joyce turns green; becomes multiple; becomes a disembodied hand. She is legion.

Calypso's use of location is as specific as her character and composition. She photographs in rented accommodation in her native London, or at her mother's home in the room where she was born in Dalston. Her most ambitious shoot took place at the Honeymoon Hotel in Pennsylvania. Drawn across the Atlantic by online images of a pink heart-shaped hot tub, she entered a world of tense expectation tinged with inevitable disappointment. Calypso had forewarned us of this mood in *Popcorn Venus* (2012), in which she, blonde-wigged, ascends from a giant wedding cake, presented on a table laden with sad salami, putrid prawns and pink fizz.

The politics of food are never far away in Calypso's oeuvre. We see her lying prone, an arm's length away from an open can of luncheon meat, or a tin of frankfurters, one protruding priapically. Her interest does not appear to be connected to consumption, however. Her eye seems to focus on the process that has reconfigured an animal/crustacean/crop into something so far removed from its original form it has become unrecognizable. It is certainly unpalatable.

It is rare for such a young photographer (Calypso was born in 1989) to have such a gift for observation; for understanding the constructs underpinning our society at this precise moment in time; for presenting them to us without preaching; for fully harnessing the power of the feminine aesthetic and using it as a kind of mirror. Since graduating from London College of Communication in 2012, she has won multiple awards including the British Journal of Photography International Photography Award, and has exhibited her work in London with TJ Boulting and with Flowers Gallery, New York. It is heartening to see the image used as such a vital tool in communicating a complex network of projected weirdness that women are expected to swallow whole and, ideally, without thinking. In this way, Calypso is a most dangerous photographer: she thinks. Beautifully.

A Dream in Green, 2016, The Honeymoon series

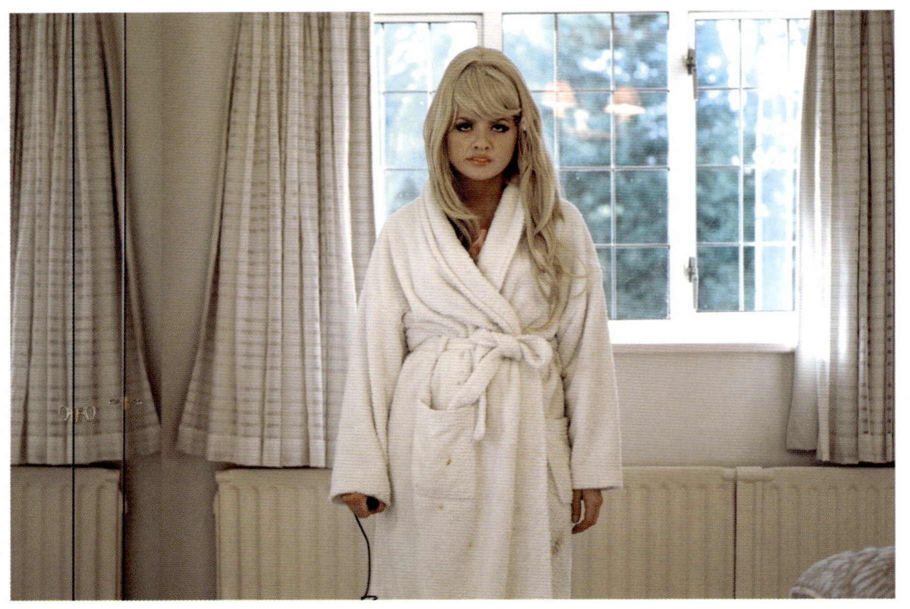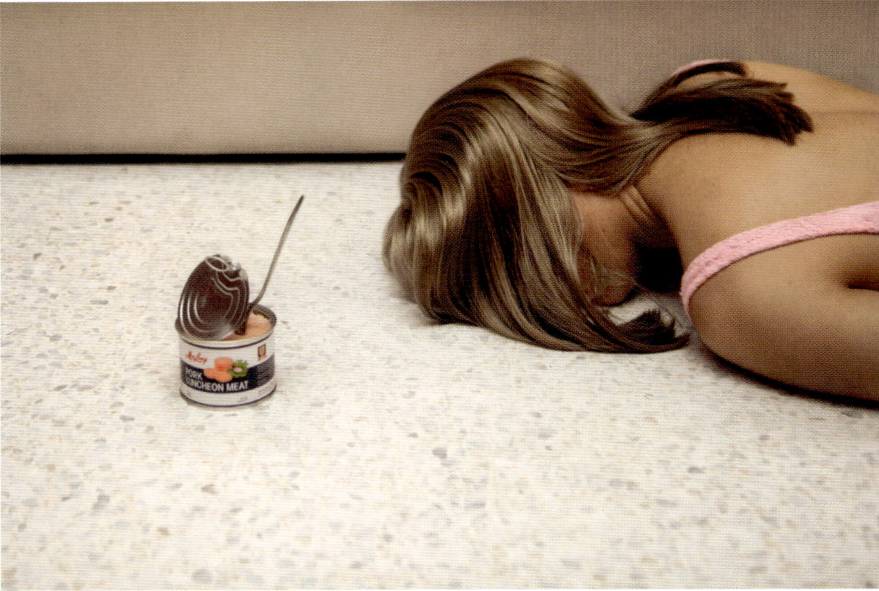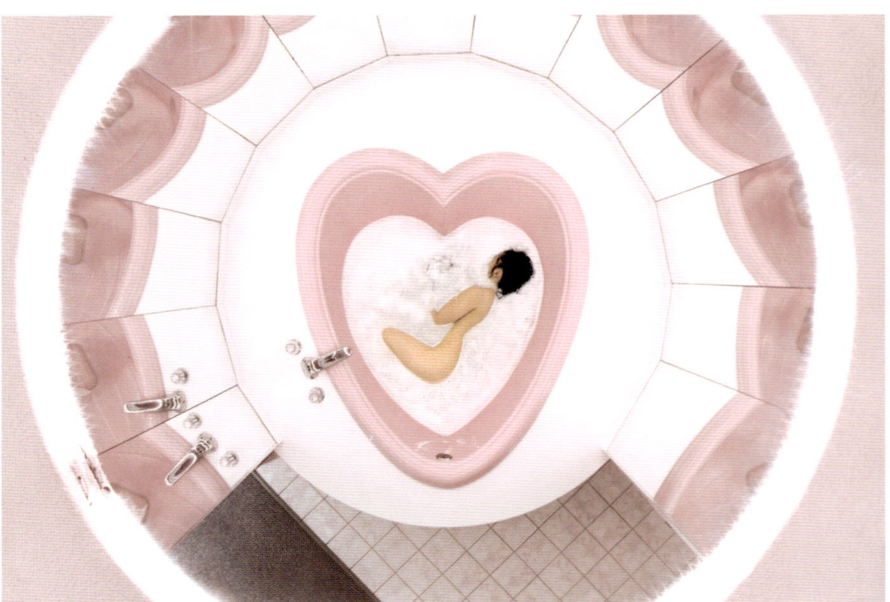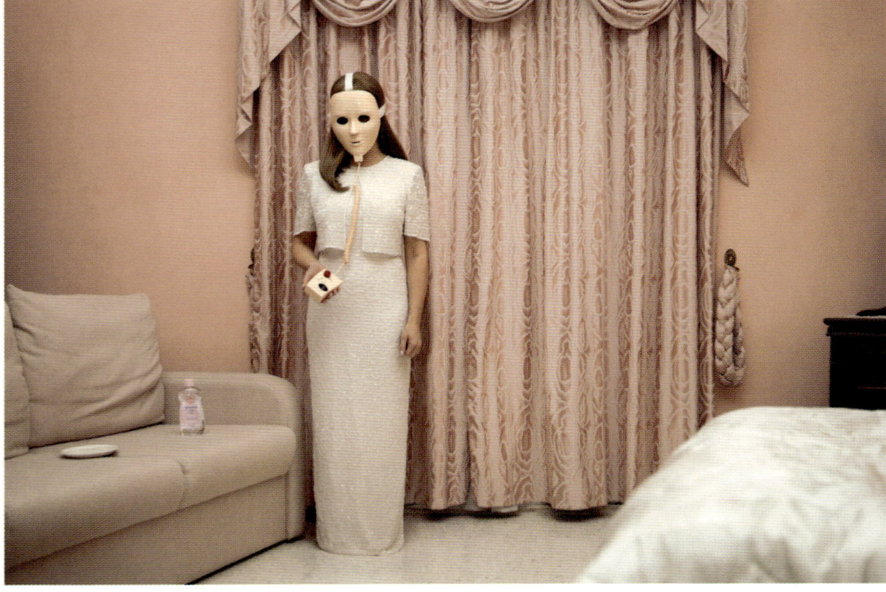

Top left: *Artificial Sweetener*, 2012, Joyce series;
top right: *Reconstituted Meat Slices*, 2013, Joyce series;
above left: *Sensory Deprivation*, 2016, The Honeymoon series;
above right: *12 Reasons You're Tired All The Time*, 2013, Joyce series

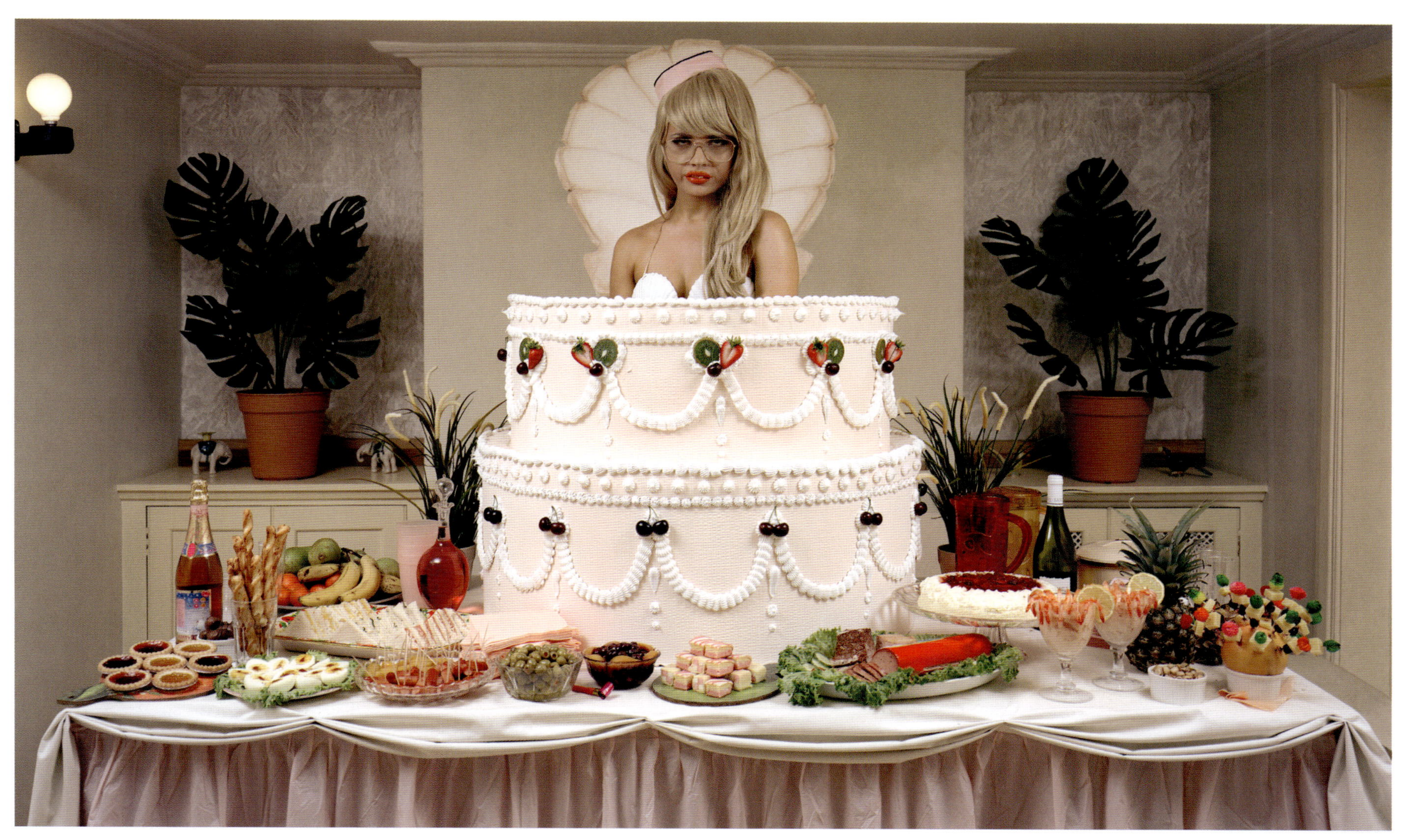

Popcorn Venus, 2012, Joyce series

Juno Calypso   51

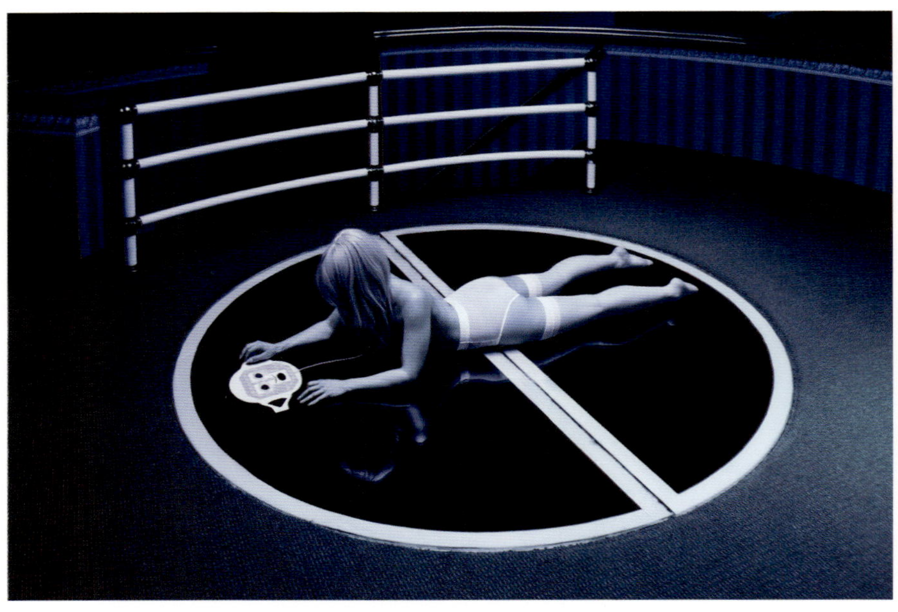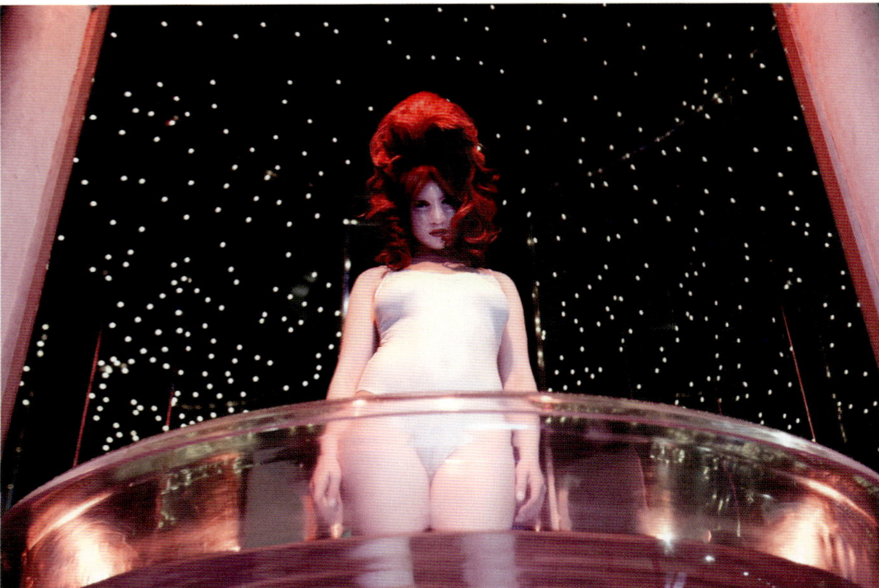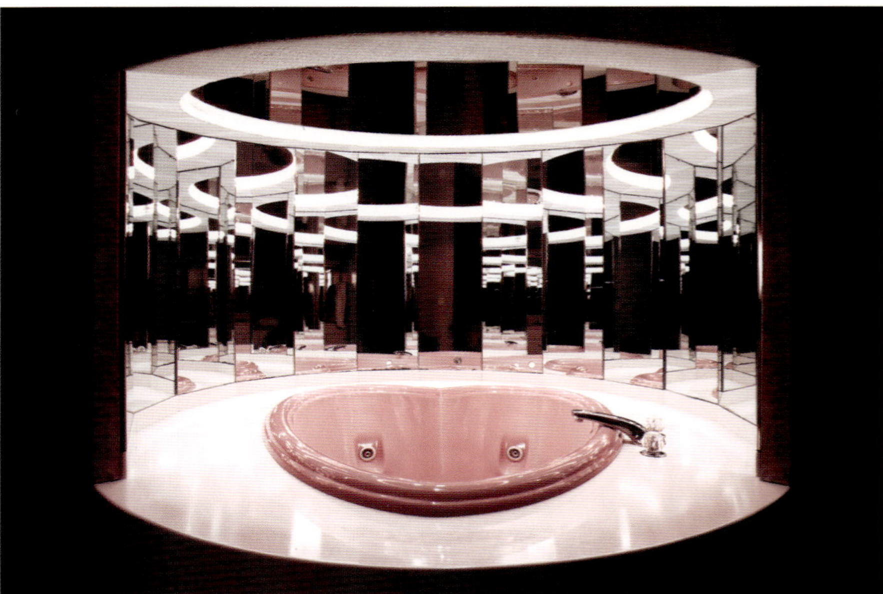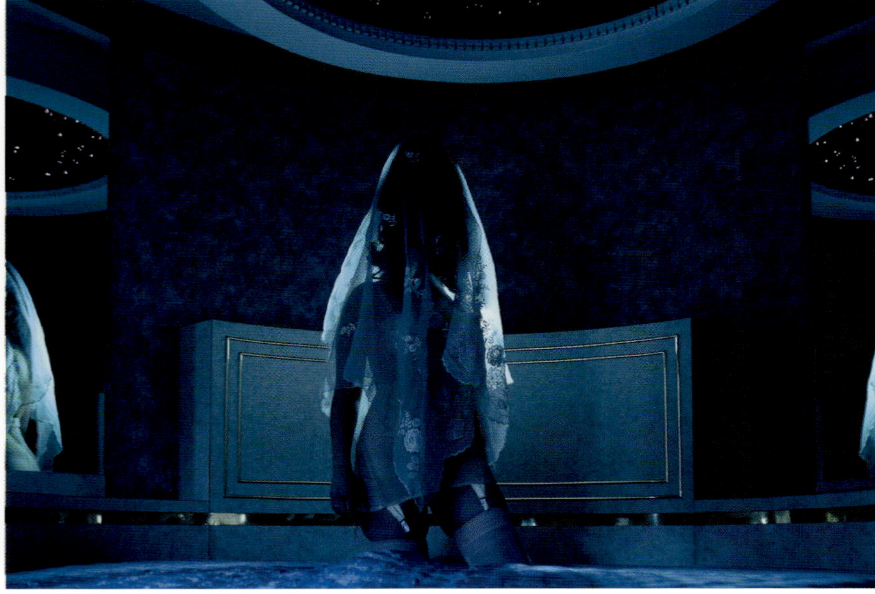

Top left: *A Solitary Love Affair*, 2016;
top right: *The Champagne Suite*, 2015;
above left: *The First Night*, 2015;
above right: *The Fantasy Suite*, 2016; all *The Honeymoon* series

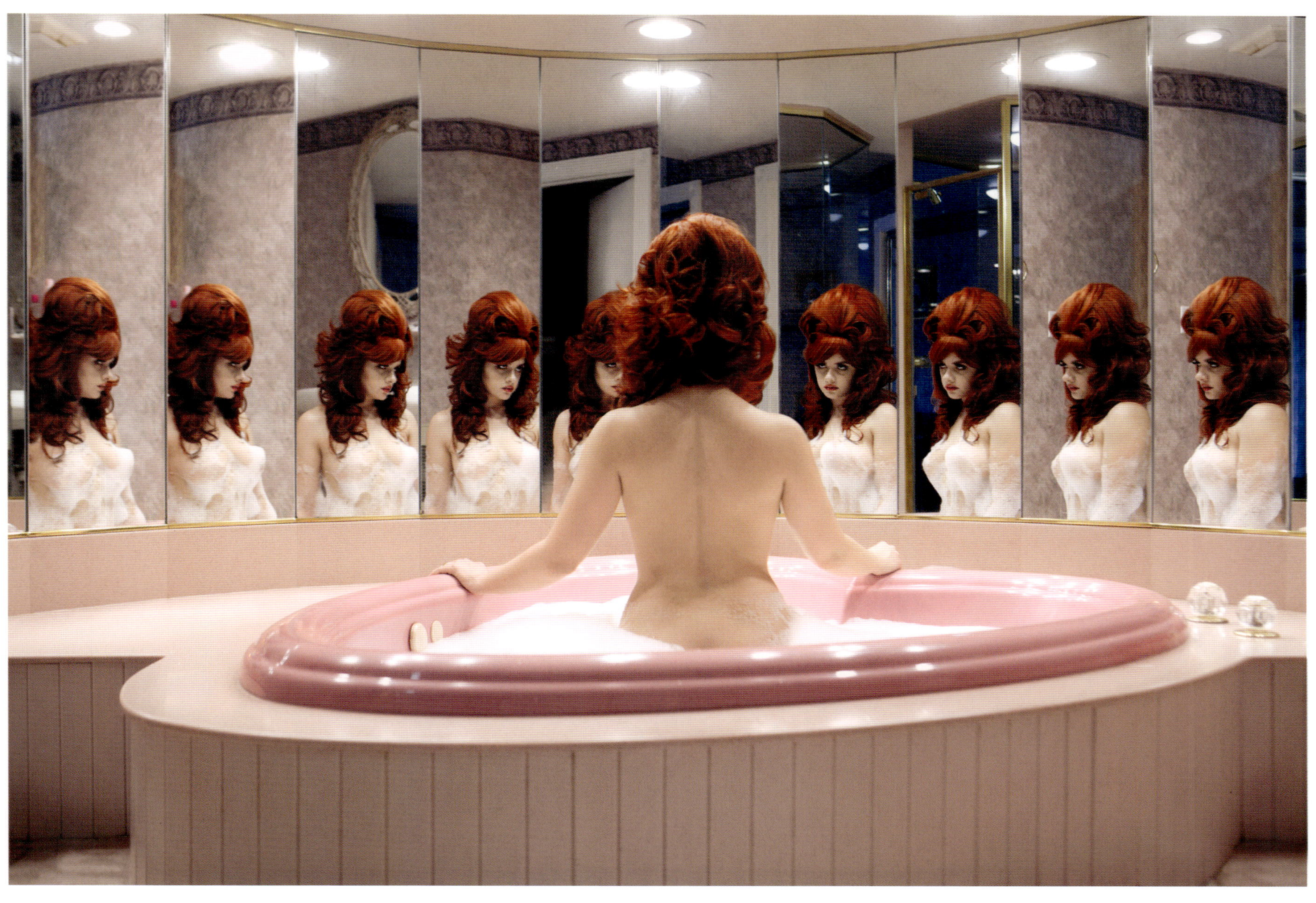

The Honeymoon Suite, 2015, *The Honeymoon* series

Juno Calypso   53

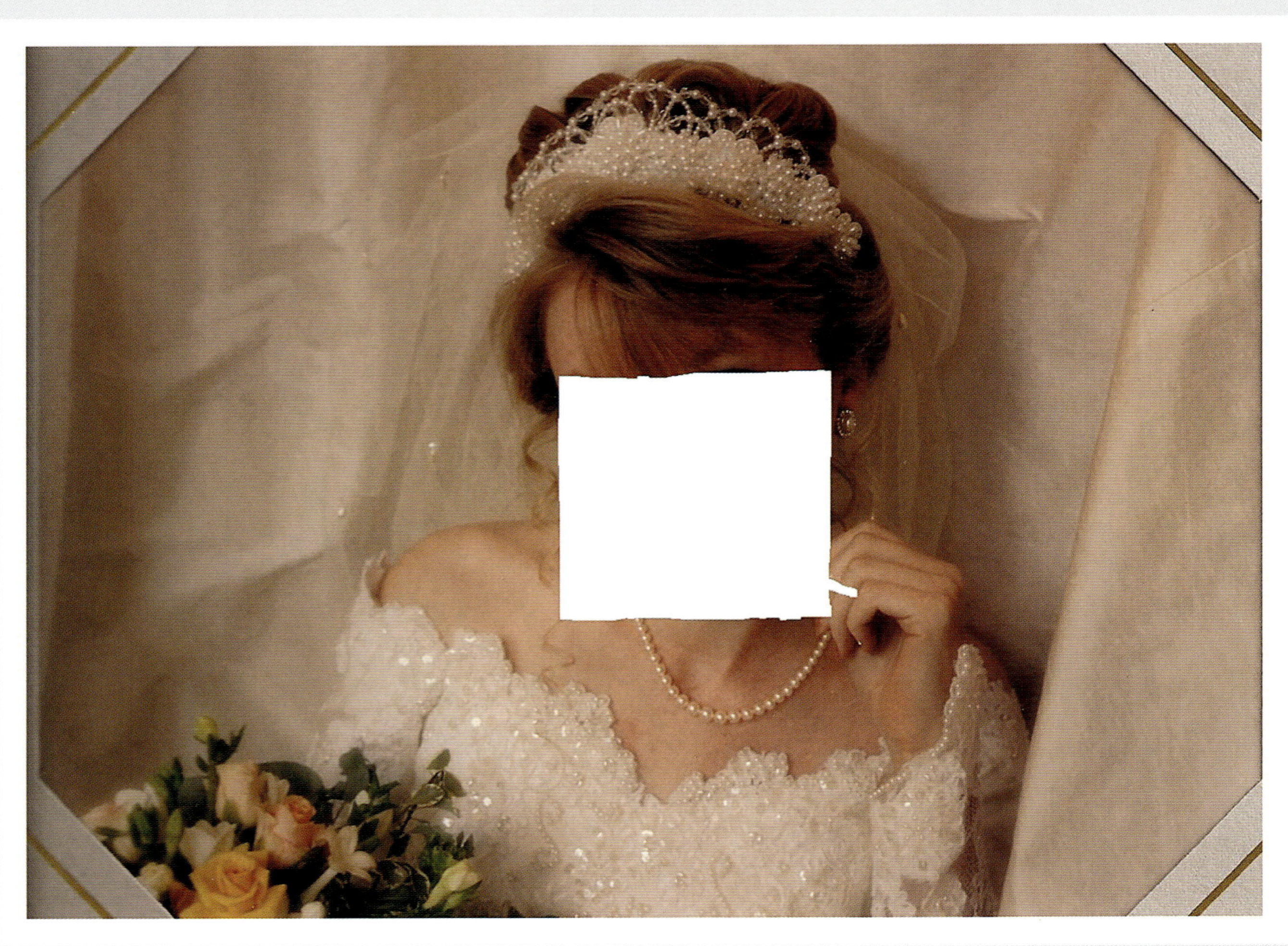

NATASHA CARUANA

...

Caruana is asking us not to judge,
but to observe the transactional nature
of all relationships
...

Growing up as the daughter of a circus clown gave Natasha Caruana a taste for performance within her photographic practice. Her work follows and creates narratives of love, betrayal and fantasy in all their hues, while at the same time questioning how technology influences relationships.

In her series *Fairytale for Sale*, Caruana trawled the internet for used wedding dresses available to buy. She communicated with the brides, who, in the interests of privacy, had removed their faces from their original pictures. Caruana's involvement is simply to gain access to the original image at a high enough resolution so she can re-publish it. The image, however, undergoes a transformation – from wedding photograph to sales image – and as this change takes place, the bride loses her identity. She loses face. Through this idiom we can understand the sense of shame that might attach itself to a failed marriage, or a change in financial circumstances that might lead to the selling of a wedding dress. Of course, it may just be a pragmatic desire to make space in a wardrobe, or to use the money to buy a cot. But in the discarding of this essential garment of the wedding ritual, without the happy face of the bride, the fairytale wedding production disintegrates into ghostly theatre.

With *Married Man*, Caruana mined her own private life – visiting dating websites for married men who wish to conduct affairs – in order to expose the accepted dynamic of male/female relationships. Here the technology is basic: a throw-away camera to frame non-identifying details of the evening spent with the duplicitous man. The complicity of the female in this type of betrayal, as well as the artist's intention, serve to complicate the ethical stance and the viewer's role in this voyeurism further. This becomes even more layered when we realize that, in her wider photographic practice, Caruana focused on a love affair in which the artist was *The Other Woman*. The abject air exuded by the resulting photographs – of women hiding behind furniture or trees – reveals that if glamour was ever on the menu in such assignations, it was not a dish that travelled well. Caruana is asking us not to judge, but to observe the transactional nature of all relationships. It is not comfortable viewing.

The role of woman as instigator comes naturally to Caruana, who is happy to portray herself as a sexual being with her own desires and moral code. She continues this trajectory with *Love Bomb*, in which she once again scours the internet, this time for recipes to galvanize or destroy love and lovers. She expands on this theme in *At First Sight* to

explain the inexplicable human phenomenon of falling in love instantaneously, at the moment of meeting. This work was made during the residency she was awarded in 2014, with BMW at Musée Nicéphore Niépce, Chalon-sur-Saône, France, and inspired a hugely varied aesthetic response from Caruana. She photographed scientific experiments that she happened upon by chance, used illustrations from school classroom French medical charts and exhibited books as sculptures, suddenly taking us through the looking glass, with Alice. Her research thesis – to prove the existence of an idea – retains its mystery and remains unresolved.

But Caruana has specific and personal experience of a *coup de foudre*: it happened to her. And, reader, she married him.

Untitled, 2011, Fairytale for Sale series

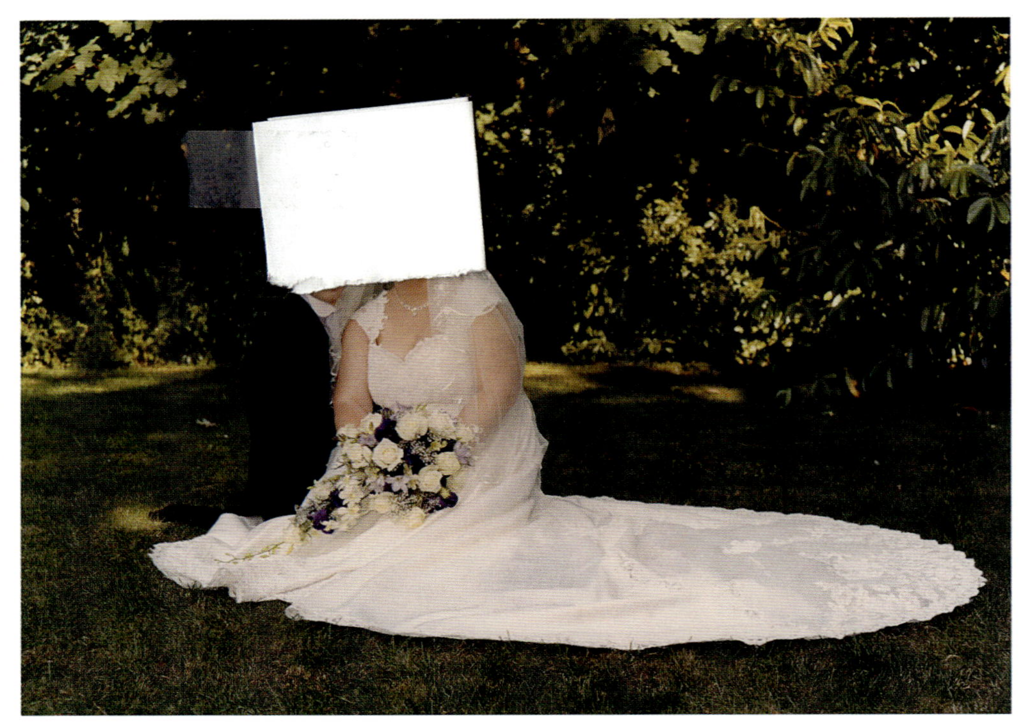

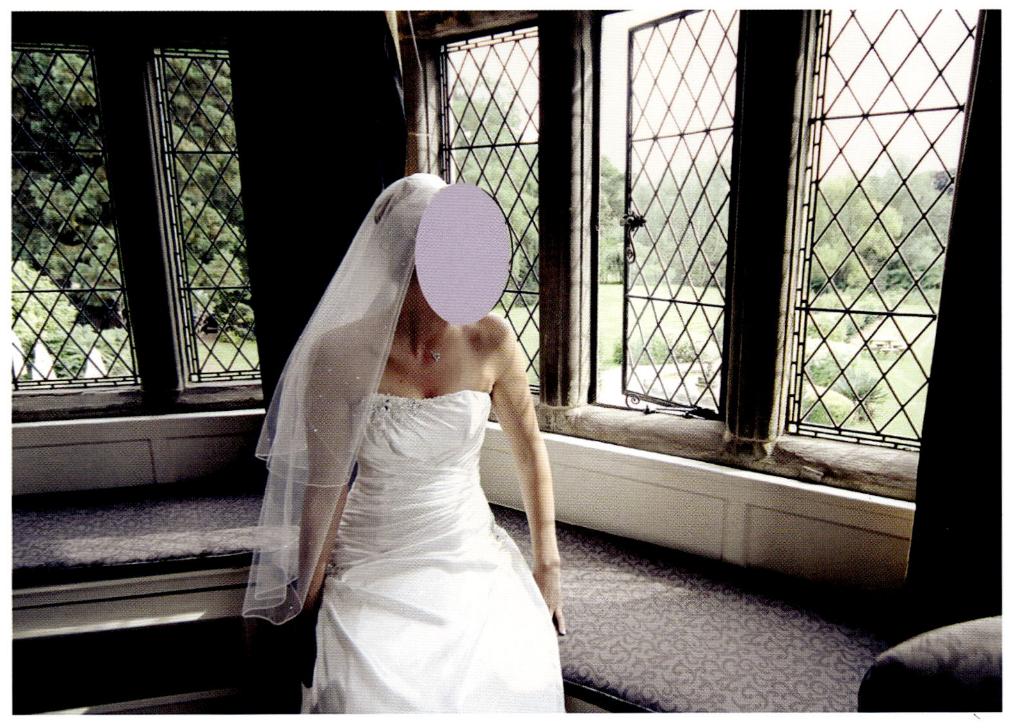

Untitled, 2011, Fairytale for Sale series

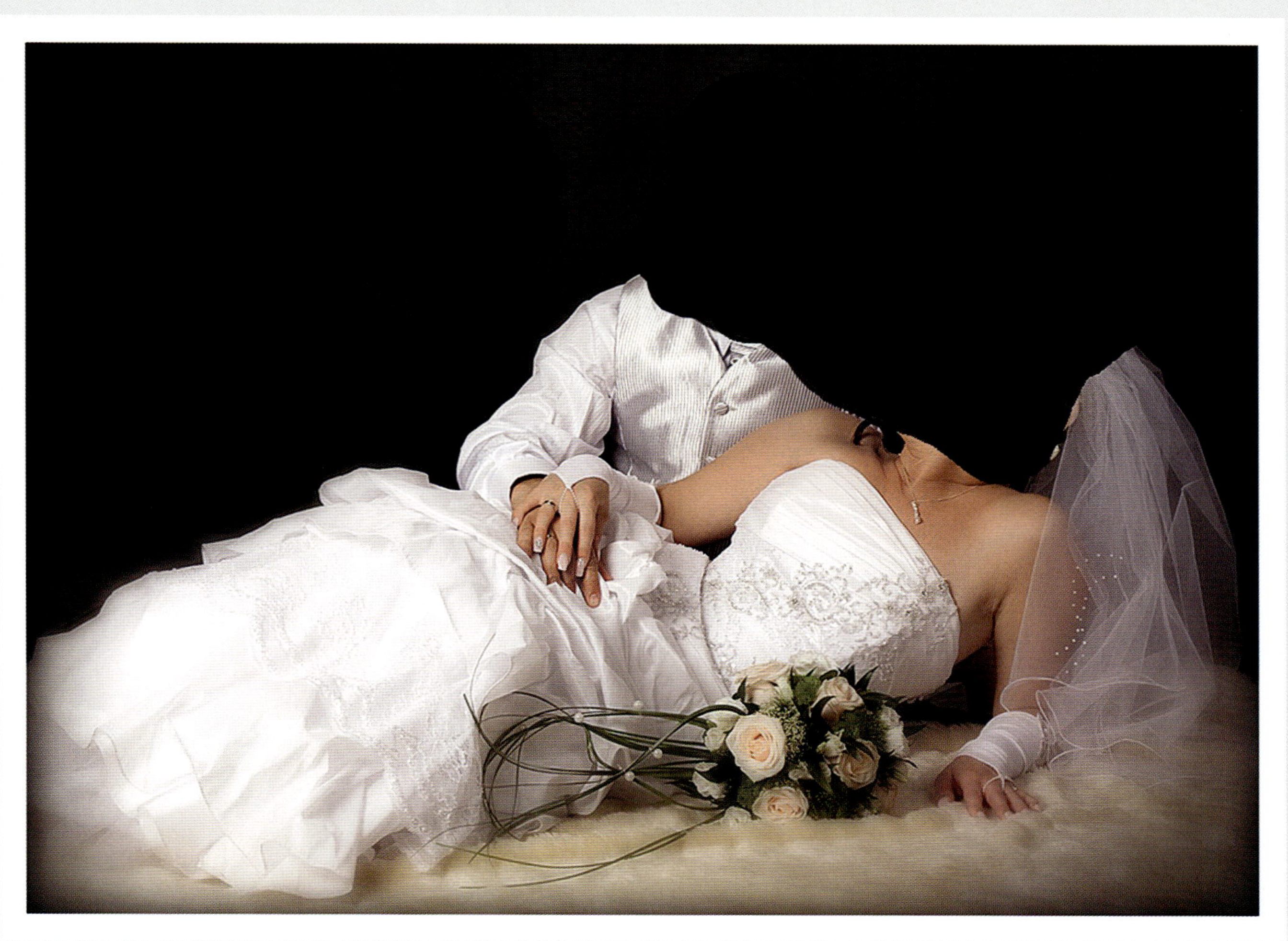

Untitled, 2011, Fairytale for Sale series

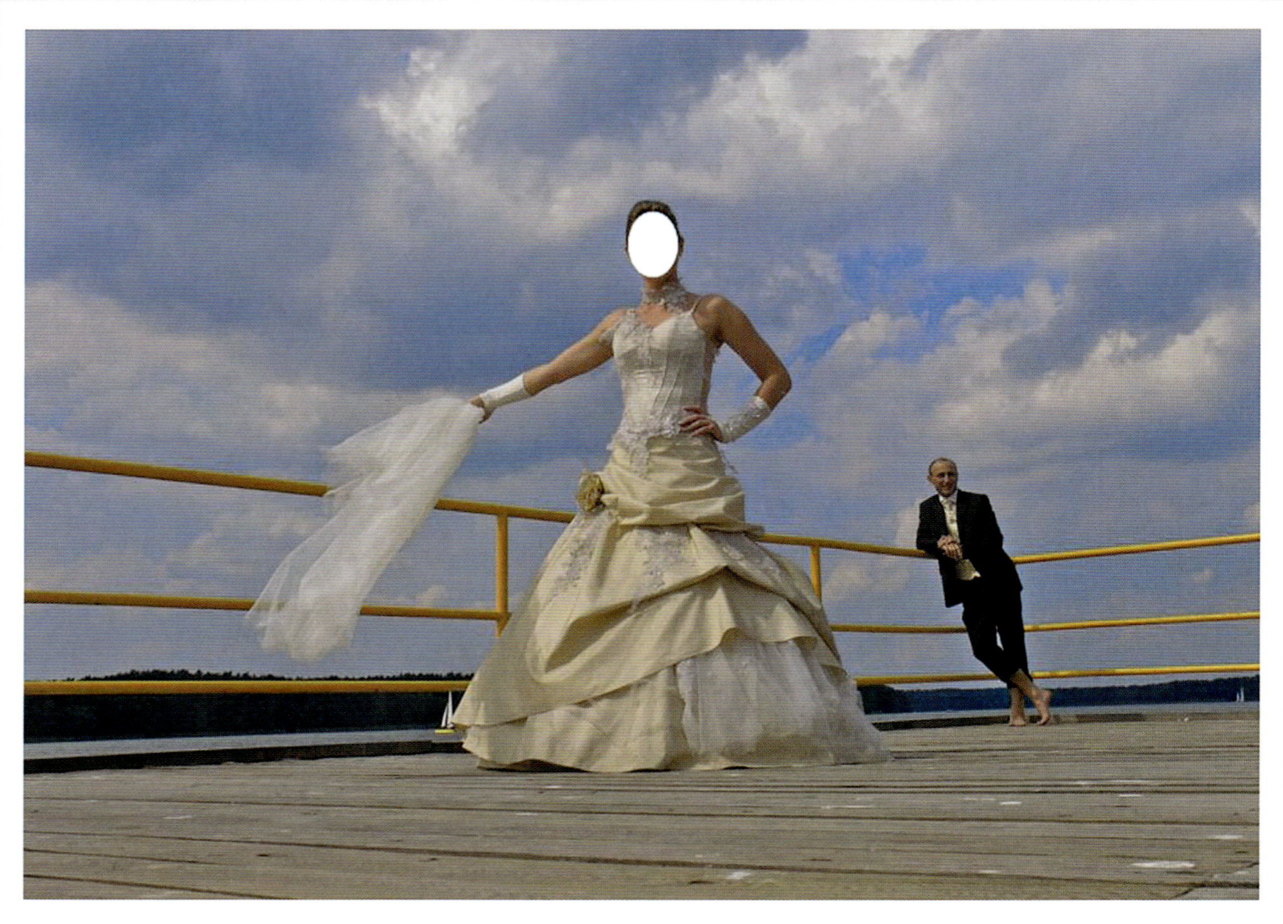

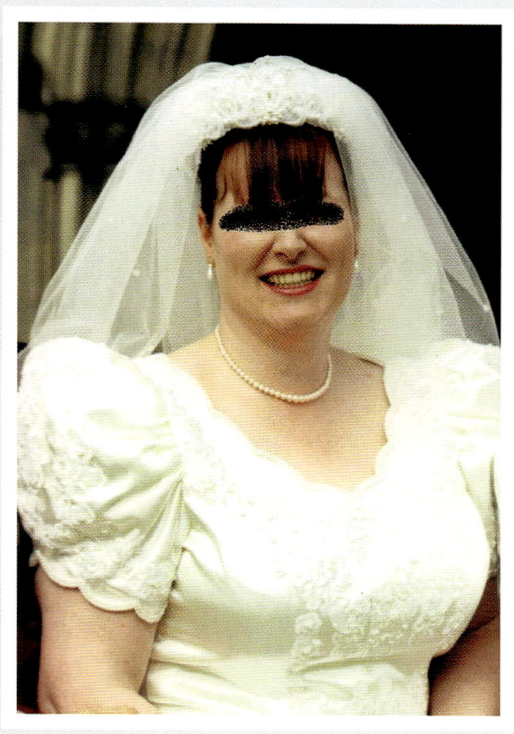 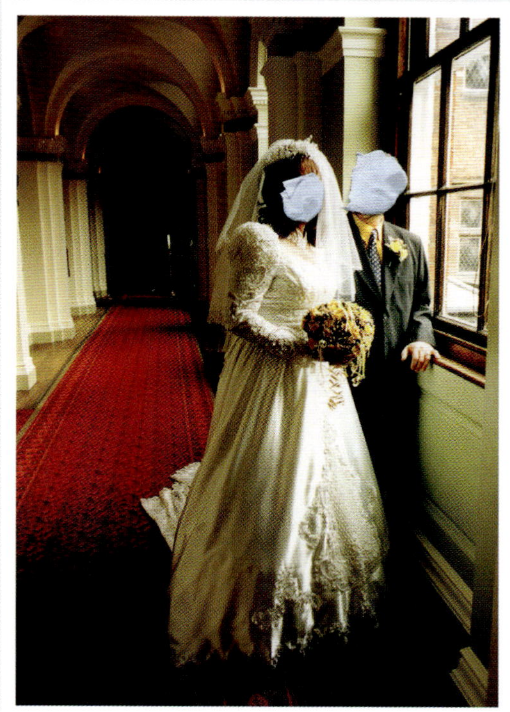 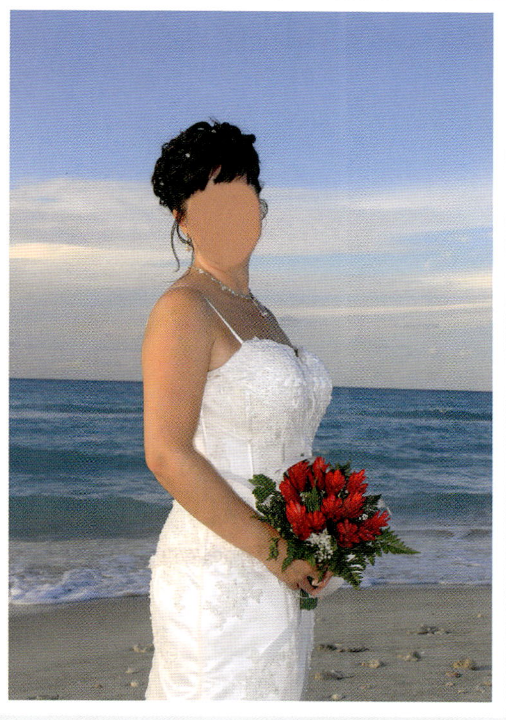

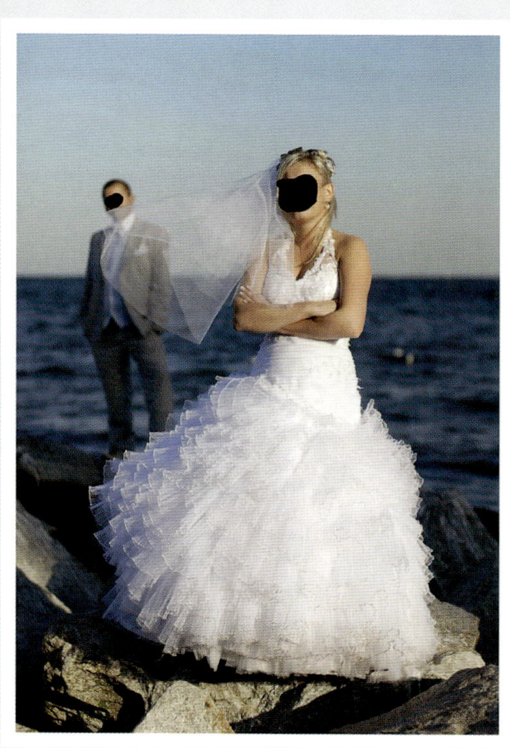 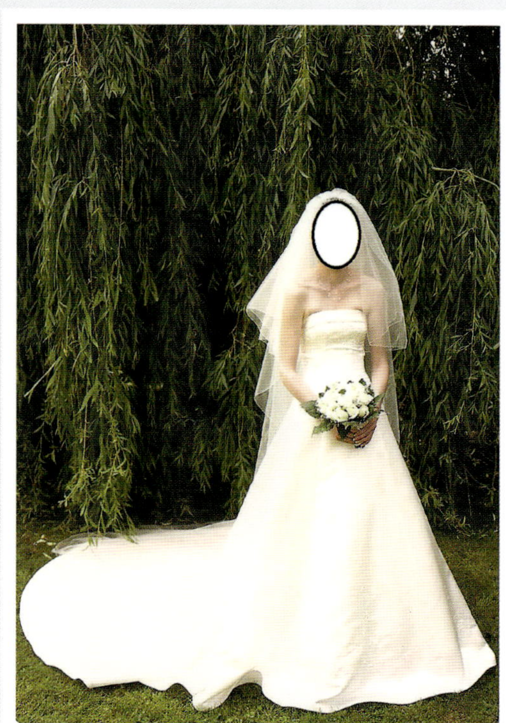 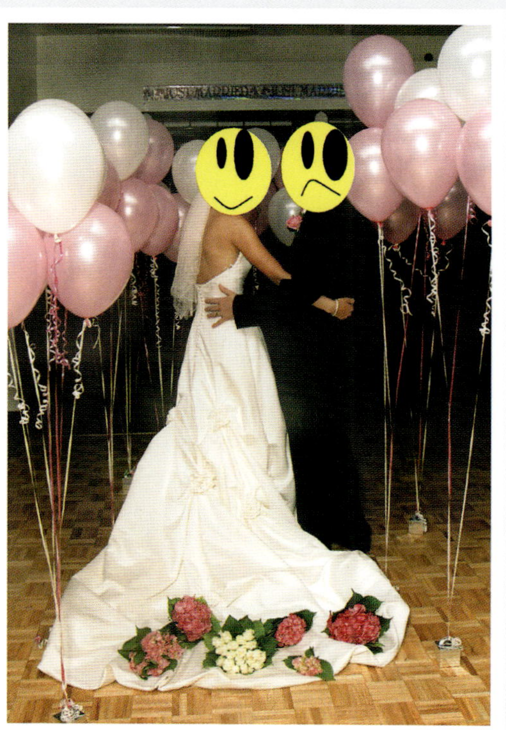

Natasha Caruana   59

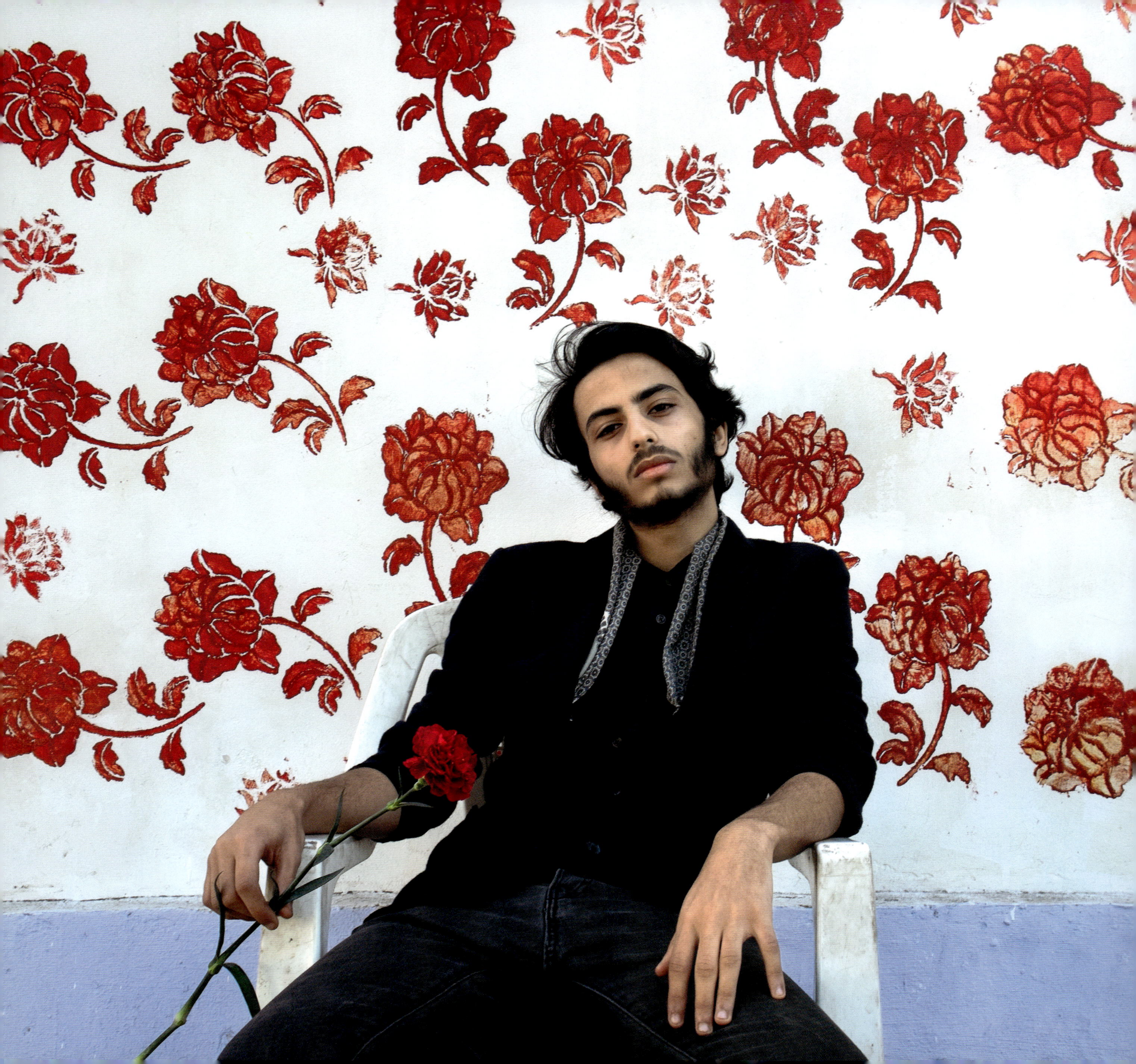

SCARLETT COTEN

'In countries where freedom is hidden, exposing oneself is an act of rebellion.' This observation underpins French photographer Scarlett Coten's work with young men in Egyptian and Moroccan cities. Coten invites men she sees on the streets to pose for her, and in doing so flips the convention of whose right it is to look at whom.

As well as their unusual subject matter – we are not often invited to stare at the male Arab body – a hallmark of Coten's work, especially the series *Mectoub*, is its vibrant colour. This is revealed in her choice of background: vivid reds and yellows command attention, but do not detract from the sensual imagery of the young men, who are styled by Coten to reveal an unexpected fragility, or even femininity. Her choice of backdrops – a derelict building, a wall of birdcages – offer discreet clues about the society she is penetrating, but never overwhelm the poise of the sitter.

Coten sees these staged portraits as a collaboration between cultures, a subject that influenced her choice for her post-graduation project at L'Ecole Nationale Supérieure de la Photographie, Arles. She spent months travelling through the Sinai desert with a Bedouin group and, eventually, the photographs culminated in *Still Alive*.

The title typifies the Bedouins' response to a world that is not necessarily sympathetic to their customs. Coten manages to capture their spirit of survival in her photographs, which, as in her other work, display an acute appreciation of the impact of colour. Her approach to representation in this early series carries with it a sense of freedom that is an essential part of Bedouin culture too.

The progression of Coten's work is particularly interesting, not necessarily because of the composition or form of her photographs, but because of how she pays ever-closer attention to the politics of seeing and being seen. For her work *Maroc Evolution*, she stayed in a small seaside town in Morocco, where she might best perceive the changes in the country. On the beach, itself an ever-changing location, she utilized the ingrained discomfort of being photographed to her advantage, playing with ideas of veiling, covering, hiding and thus making it clear it is never possible to see everything at once. It is noticeable how many – though by no means all – of the younger generation delight in showing off their bodies for the camera.

Coten's own fascination with cultural crossover is of course timely. Her use of the camera as a tool of inquiry seems pertinent when vexed questions of race, gender and religion are inextricably linked to how such topics are seen. Her vision is not bound by cultural constraints and her optimism is infectious.

Mectoub series

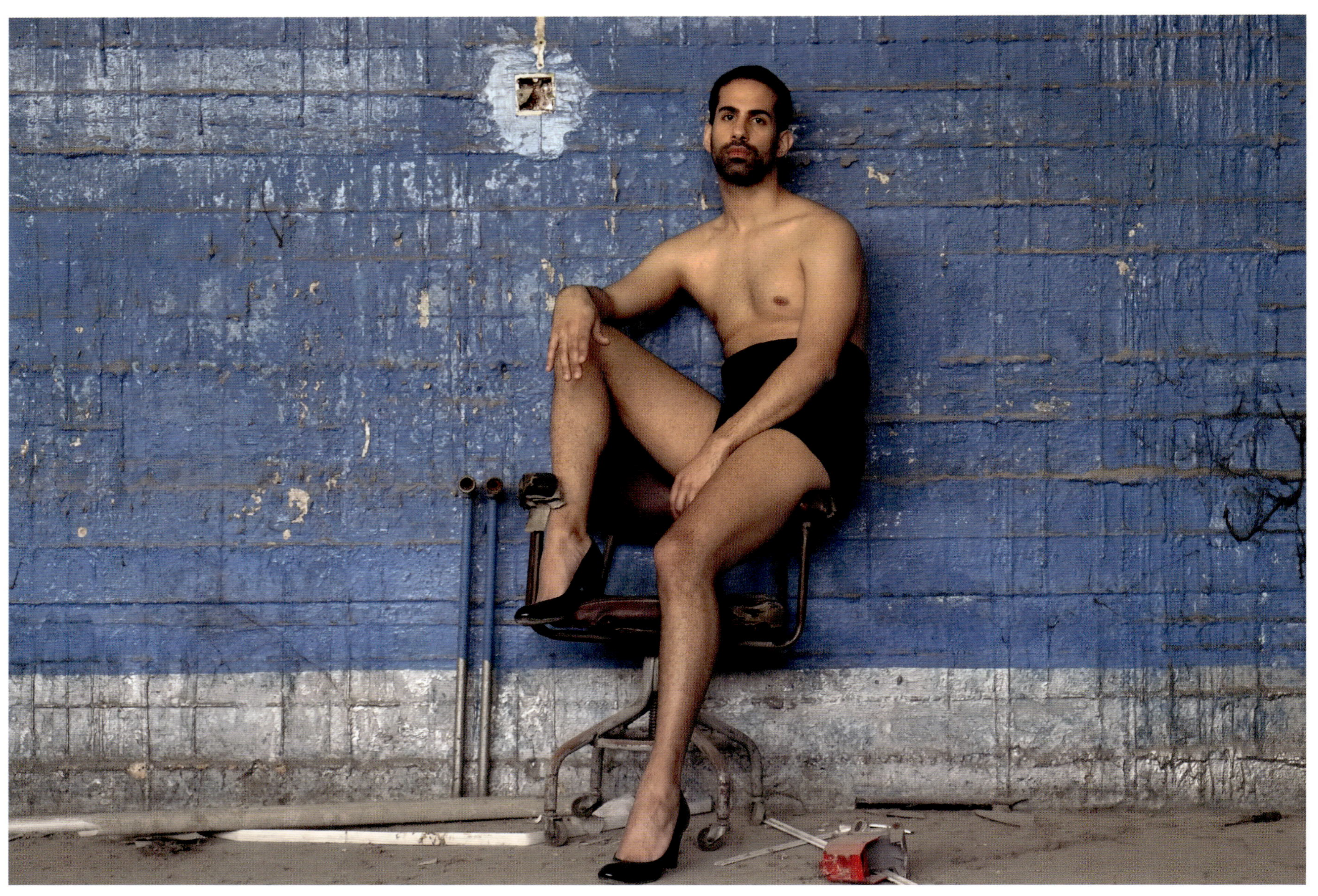

    Firecrackers

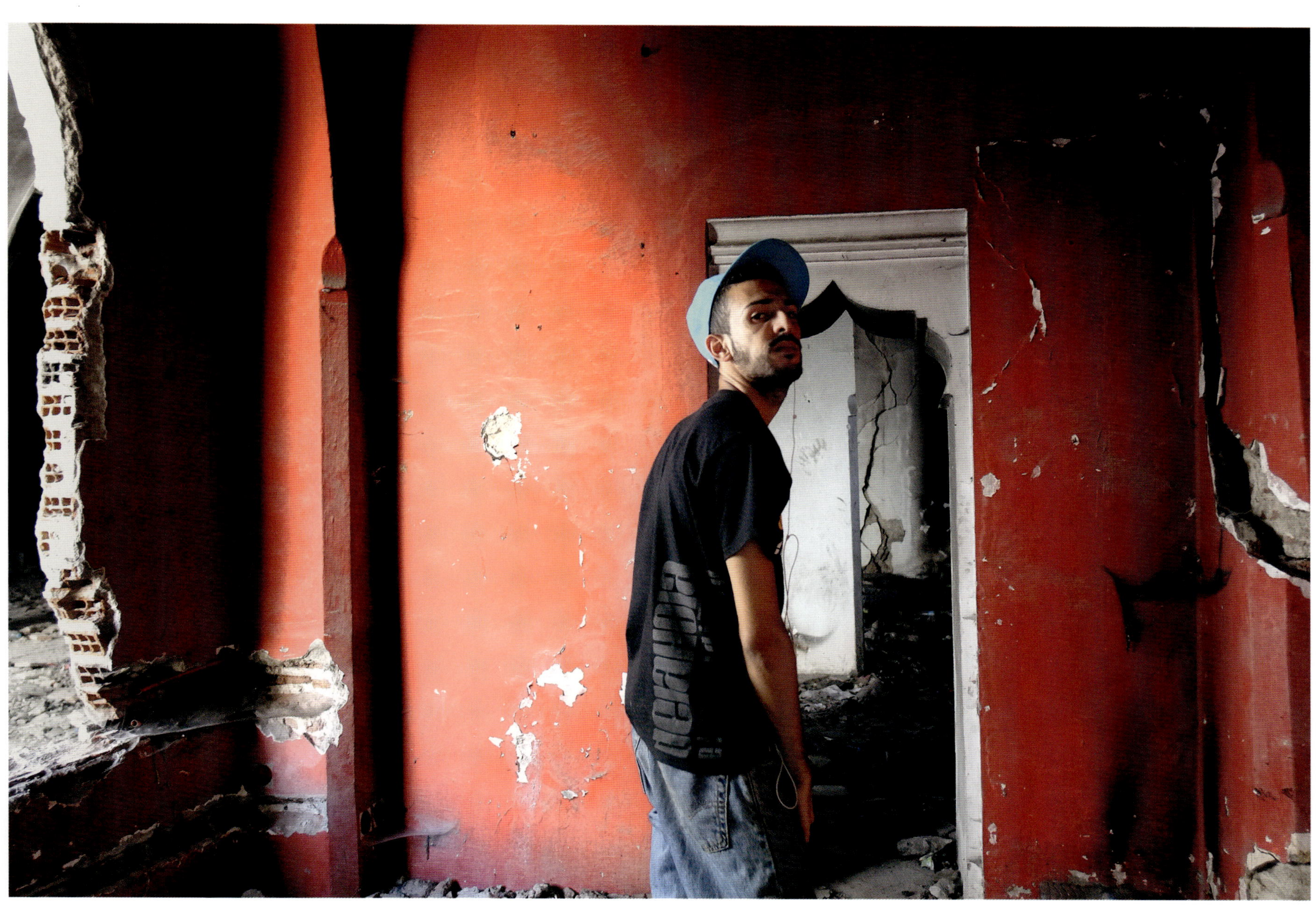

Scarlett Coten 63

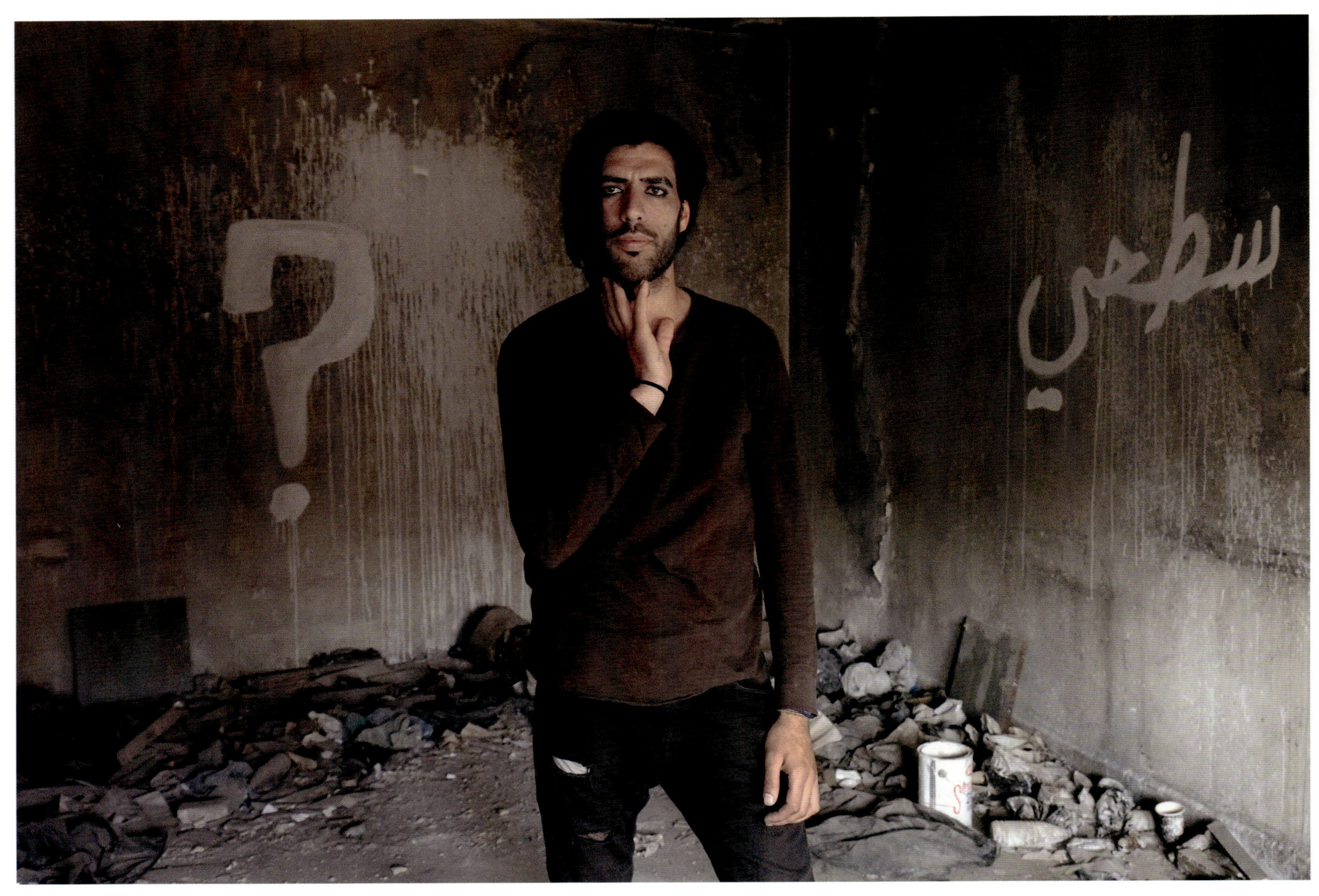

؟
سطحى

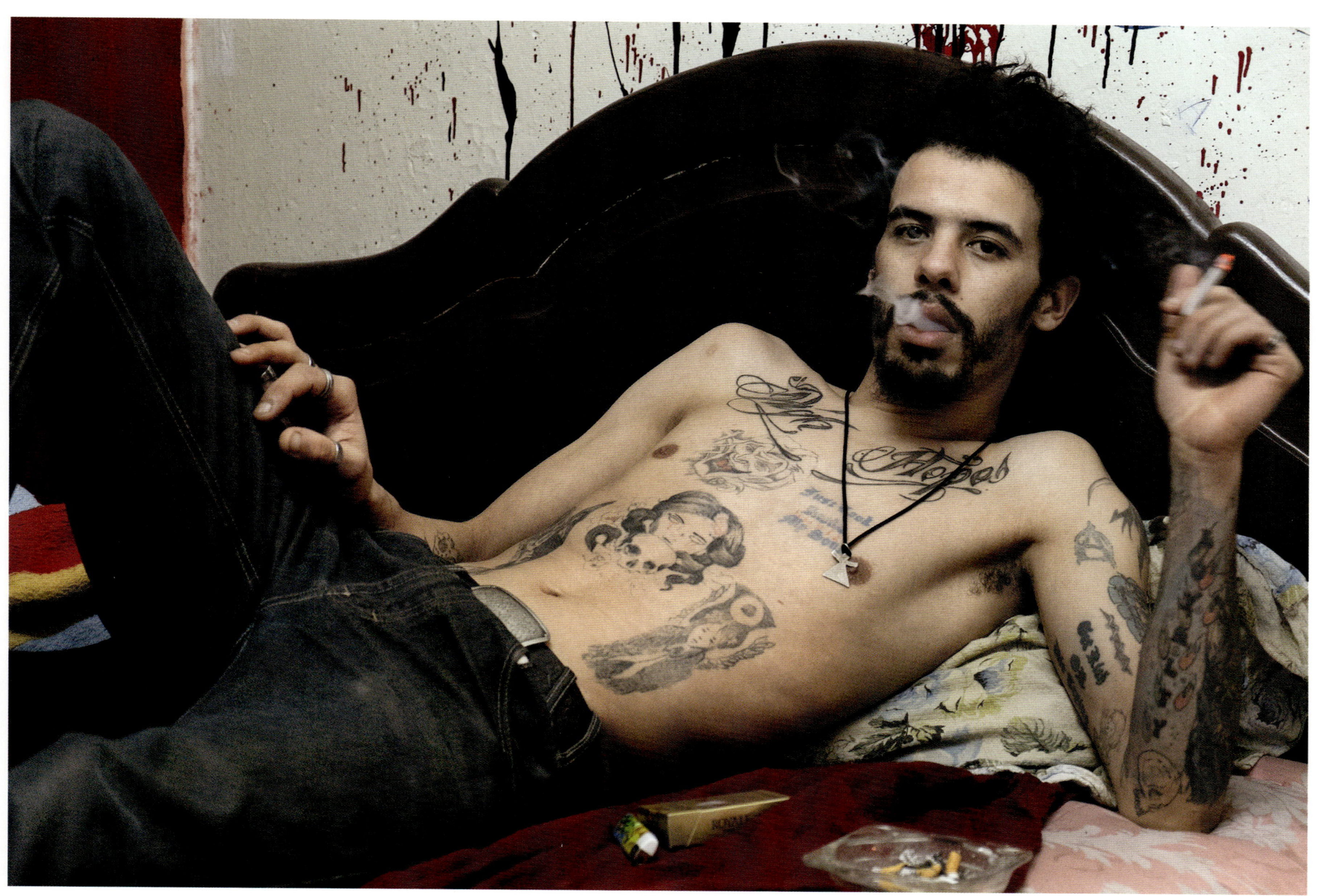

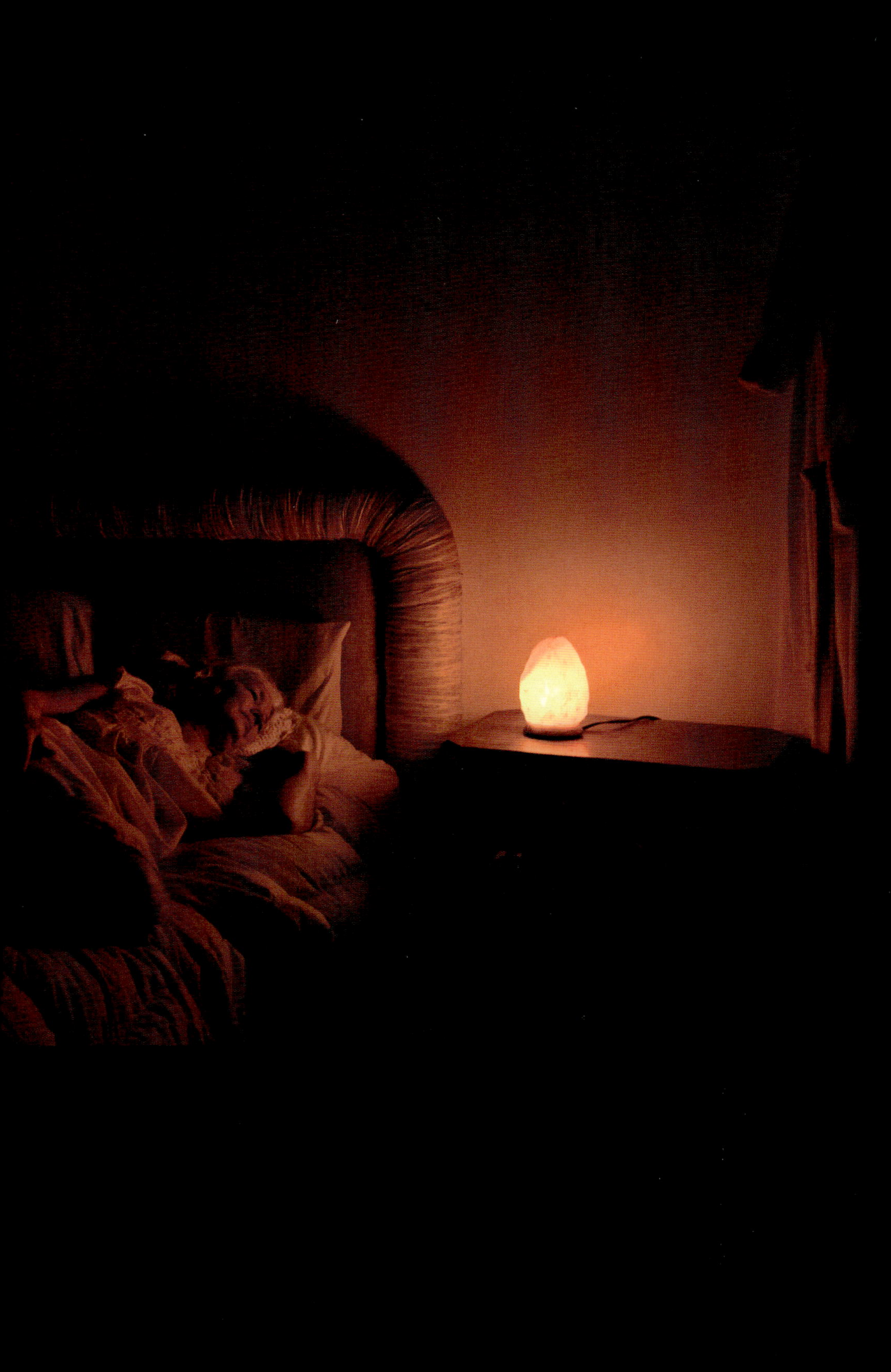

BIEKE DEPOORTER

…
Depoorter captures
a place where secrets
were whispered,
vulnerabilities shared
and unguarded, fleeting
moments captured
…

Belgian photographer Bieke Depoorter may just be one of the bravest photographers working today, and yet her work doesn't take her to the frontlines of conflict, but rather the frontiers of everyday life.

The most recent female photographer to become a full member of the Magnum Photo collective, Depoorter has spent most of her career photographing perfect strangers in their homes. After completing her masters at the Royal Academy of Fine Arts, Ghent in 2009, Depoorter travelled through Russia with little more than her camera and a note asking for a place to stay. Over three months she gained an unparalleled trust of the people she met, photographing, as an almost invisible entity, women as they bathed, children as they slept, men as they watched television. The work *Ou Menya* (which means 'with you') was published by Lannoo in 2011 and won the Magnum Expression Award, gaining the attention of the agency's photographers who would later become her peers.

Depoorter credits the success of *Ou Menya* to the separation of language and the comfort of shared silences, but was curious to see how the concept would play out in a country where she could speak the language. In 2010 she travelled to the US, where again, in less than twenty-four hours, people had opened up in a remarkable and surprising way – one woman even revealed a suicide note that she had hidden from her husband.

'I think part of people letting me in has to do with the fact that they know I'm going away the next day,' says Depoorter. 'It's sometimes a lot easier to share personal things if you know you'll never see this person again.'

Produced over four years, the resulting work became *I Am About to Call it a Day* (Hannibal and Edition Patrick Frey, 2014). The title is an acknowledgment of the transition between day and night when Depoorter believes she made her best work: a place where secrets were whispered, vulnerabilities shared and unguarded, fleeting moments captured. 'I like the atmosphere of the night,' Depoorter says. 'When people go to sleep, I think it's most real. No one is looking at us, and we become our true selves.'

Depoorter's work is a sophisticated exploration of the similarities that bind us rather than the differences that separate us. Part-documentarian, part-performer, her cinematic approach to capturing the quieter, perhaps mundane, aspects of everyday life results in a truthful empathy, revealing more in their stillness than a 'big moment' ever could. By entering into people's homes and spending the night with them, Depoorter finds a more honest and truthful way to investigate these ideas. Her photographs and experiences are visual accounts of an exchange between subject and photographer, and the impact that brief but significant moments can have on humanity.

Untitled, 2011, I Am About to Call it a Day series

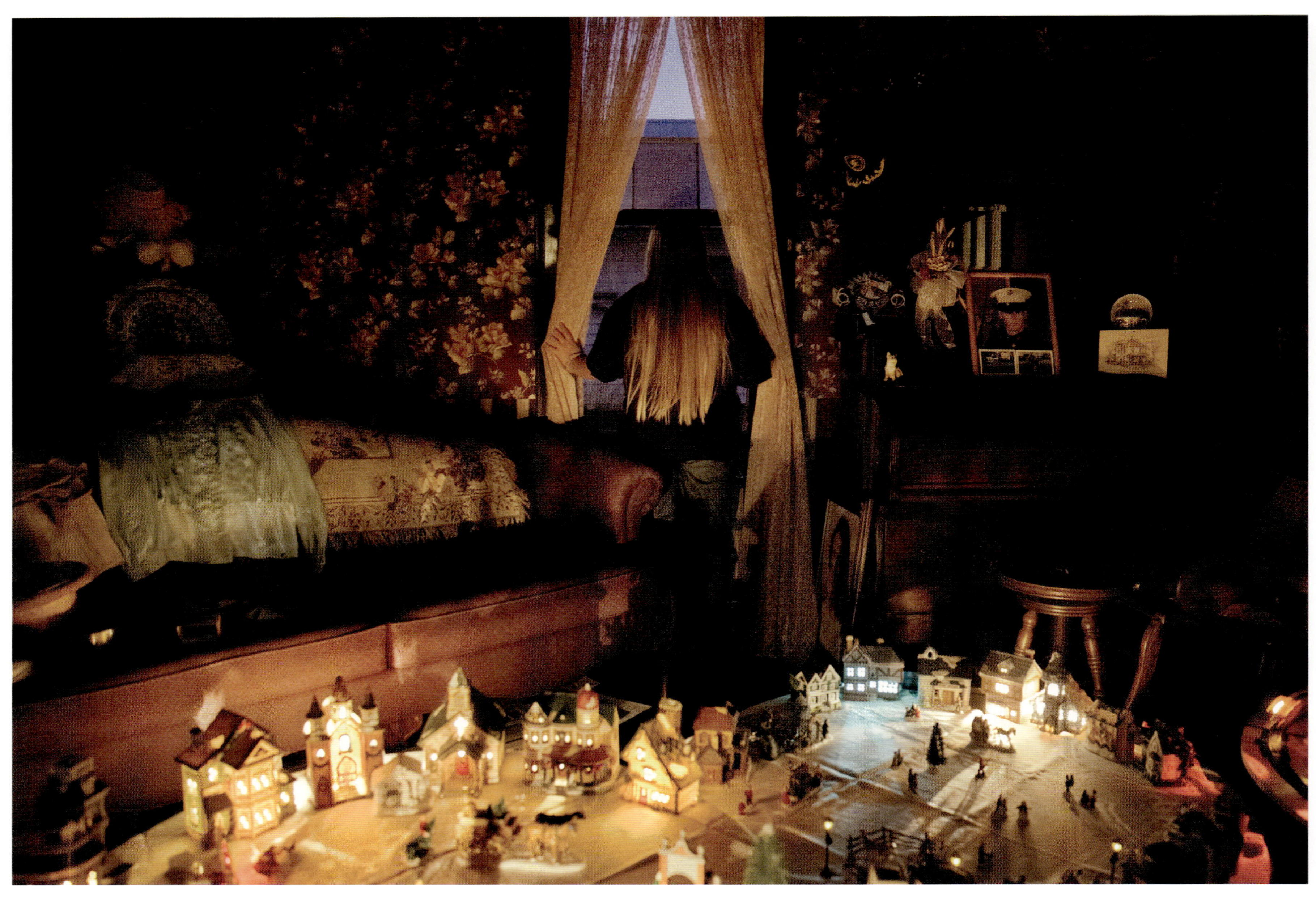

Untitled, 2012, I Am About to Call it a Day series

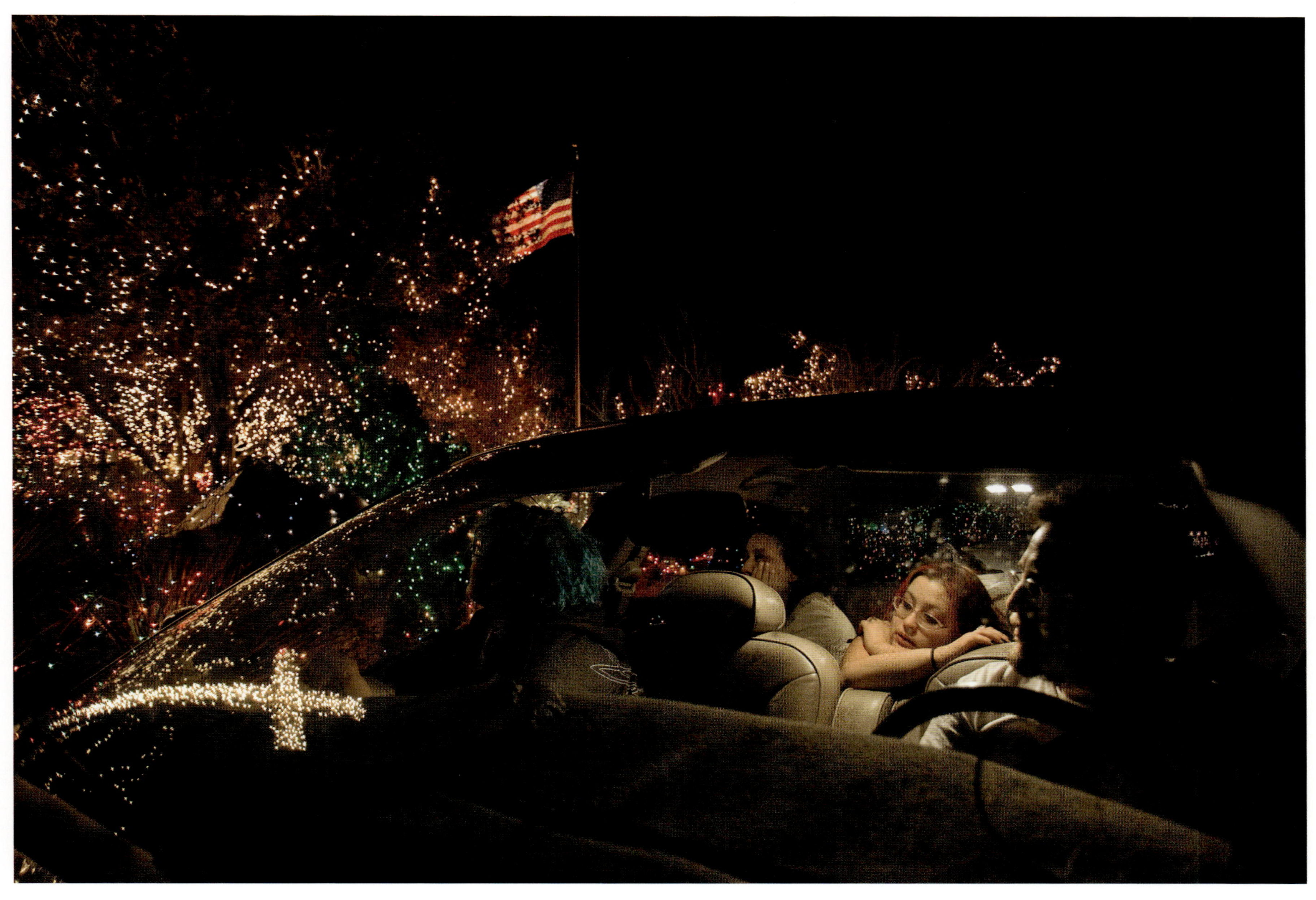

Bieke Depoorter   69

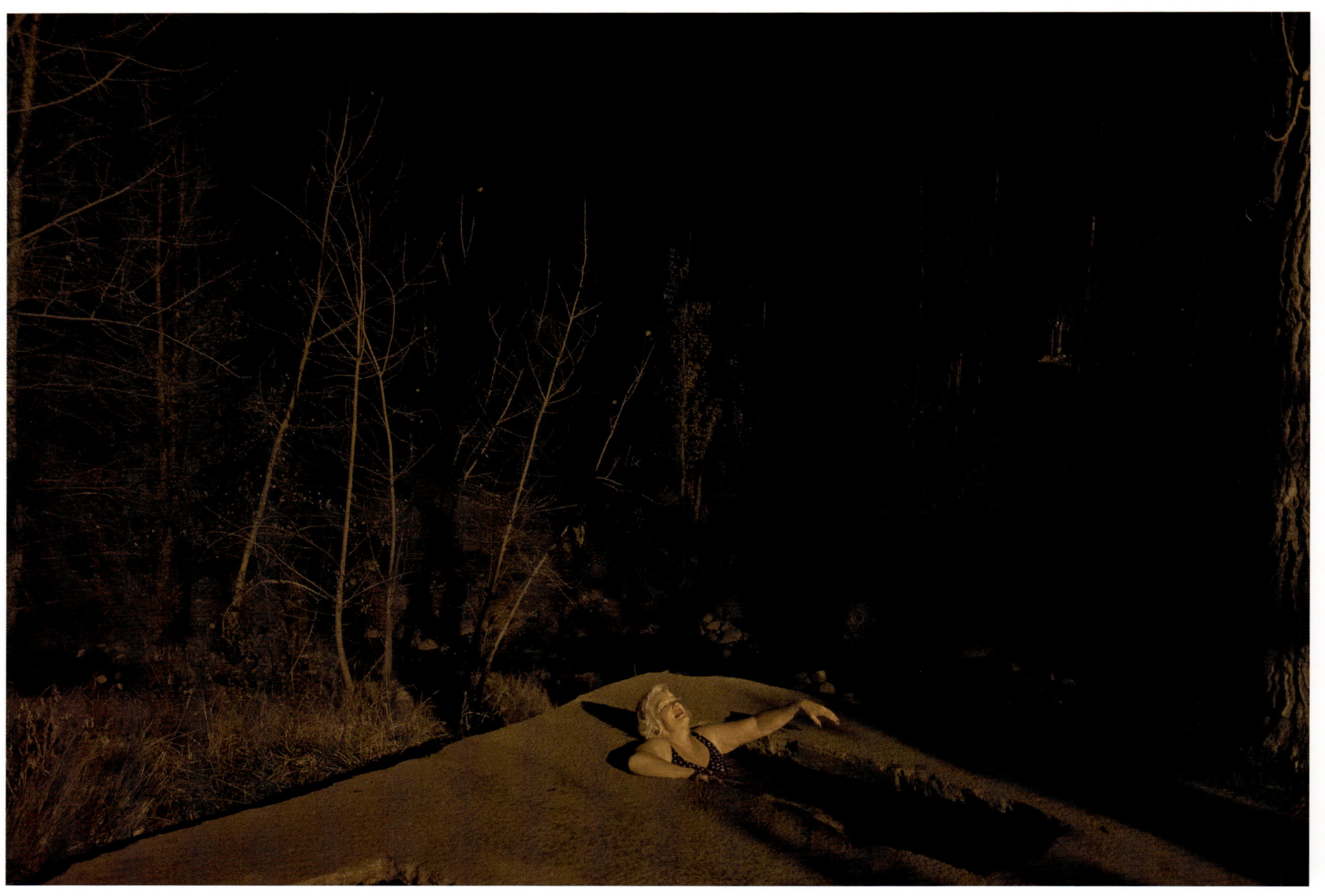

Untitled, 2011, I Am About to Call it a Day series

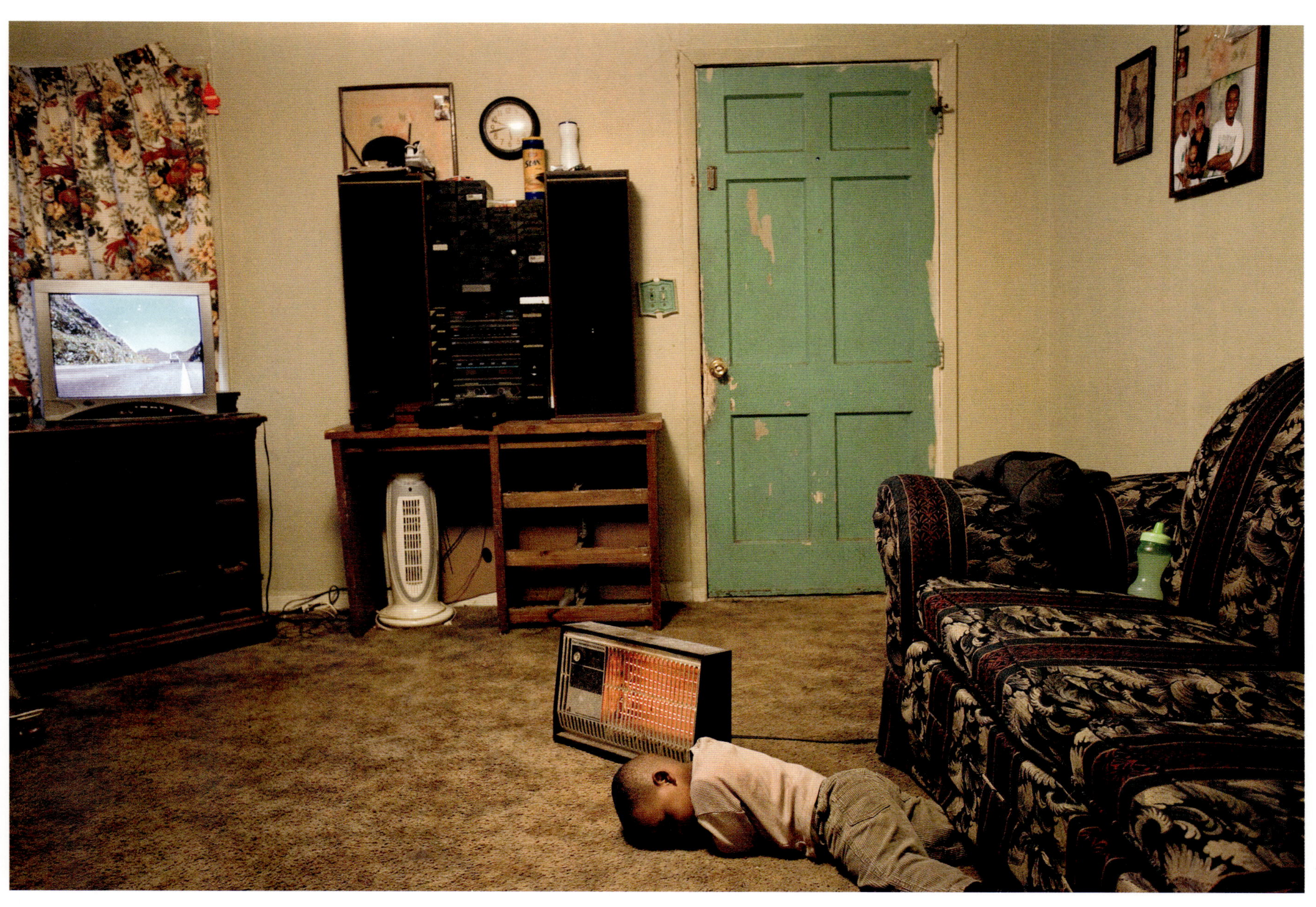

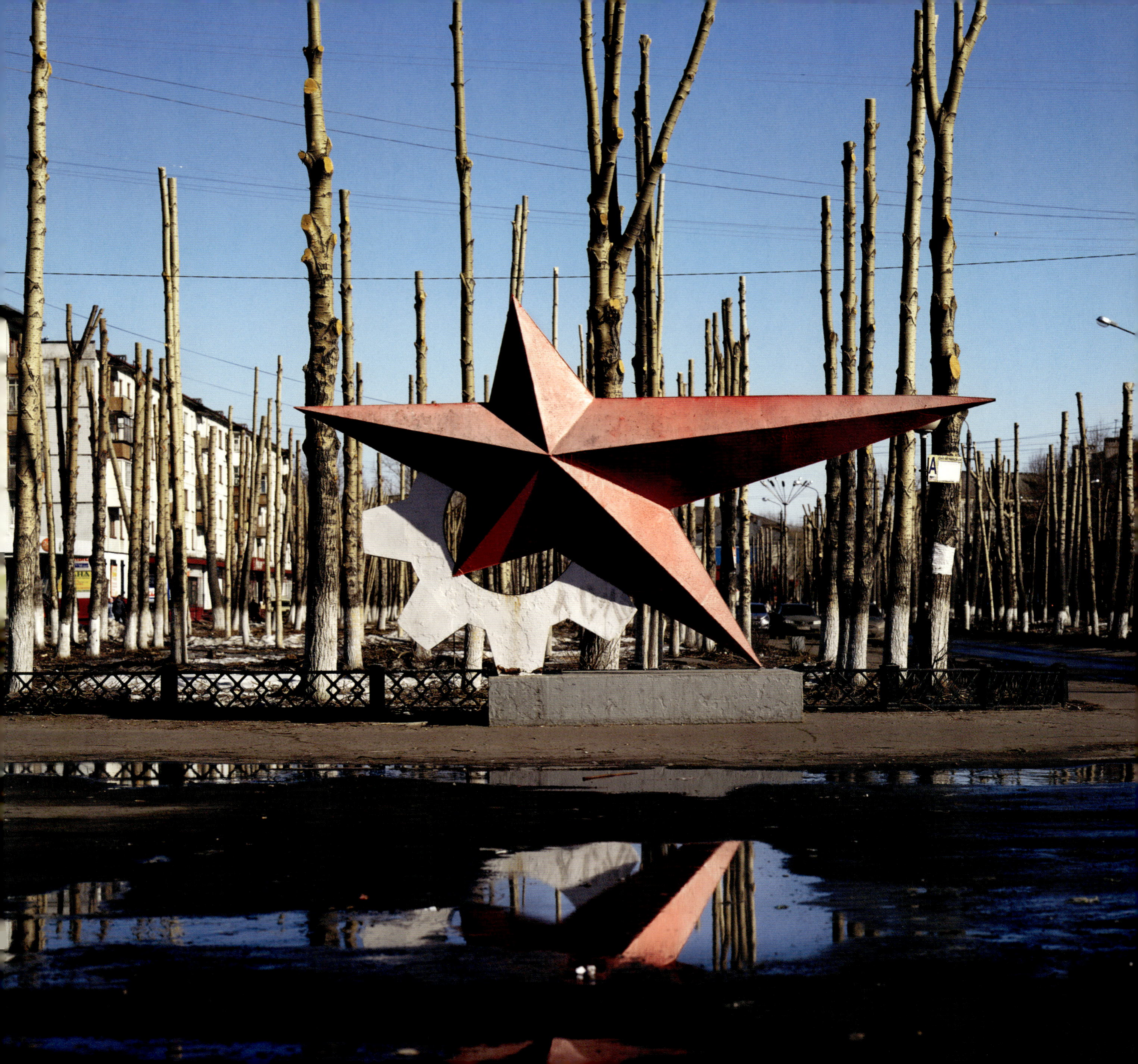

MARIA GRUZDEVA

…

Borders of Russia represents the tensions between contemporary and historic Russia: the country's ethnic heritage and its more recent conflicts
…

The vastness of Russia and its complicated, historic relationship with boundaries is the subject of Maria Gruzdeva's seminal work *Border: A Journey Along the Edges of Russia* (Schilt Publishing, 2016). The result of extensive research, the project is both an ethnographic study and a sophisticated visual essay exploring concepts of national identity, collective memory and the politics and culture of geography.

A graduate of Central Saint Martins School of Art and Design, London, Gruzdeva enjoyed early success with *Direction–Space!*, an analytical, visual and documentary photographic study of the Russian space industry (Dewi Lewis, 2011). She received a host of accolades including the IdeasTap Photographic Award with Magnum Photos and the Magenta Flash Forward for Emerging Photographers.

Gruzdeva was born in Russia in 1989 and her work *Borders of Russia* was inspired by the different perspective that she developed from being away from her birthplace later in her life. Having been born in the Soviet era and then living through its collapse in the early 1990s, the photographer began to reconsider Russia's territorial history and her own emotional response to it. Gruzdeva describes how border territories as 'the most distant and disturbed areas of the country

illustrate like no other the state of present-day Russia; how it is shaping its identity and its relationship with the Soviet consciousness, which it seeks to both outlive and preserve.' *Borders of Russia* takes us on a physical and metaphorical journey across 60,000 miles of Russian landscape, tracing the longest national border in the world, from the warm regions of the Caucasus to the icy extremes of the north, the exclave of western Kaliningrad Oblast and the Russian Far East. Sharing boundaries with sixteen sovereign states, its territory converges with more countries than any other state in the world, making its geographical, political and cultural make-up endlessly fascinating.

Symbolism is just one of the tools that Gruzdeva deploys in presenting us with a sense of place: fading communist structures are placed alongside desolate, snowy landscapes; people wearing traditional dress vie for visual attention with a man in a balaclava (a word derived from the Crimean War) wielding a Kalashnikov. The military, too, is omnipresent, evidence of the delicate negotiations Gruzdeva had to engage in to access many of these remote and secretive places, and a reminder that twenty-five years on geographical insecurity still pervades.

Borders of Russia represents the tensions between contemporary and historic Russia: the country's ethnic heritage and its more recent conflicts. Gruzdeva's photographs are a visual record that help to reimagine our perception of Russia. She reminds us too that her relationship with Russia is not simply ethnographic but personal and emotional as she presents her anecdotal experiences through the inclusion of sketchbook pages, intimate travel diaries and contact sheets.

In Gruzdeva's investigation into the hinterland of her native Russia we can see an anthropological journey unfolding before us, while being offered a glimpse into the photographer's own exploration of what it means to be Russian.

Red Star monument, Severodvinsk, Arkhangelsk Oblast, *Borders of Russia* series

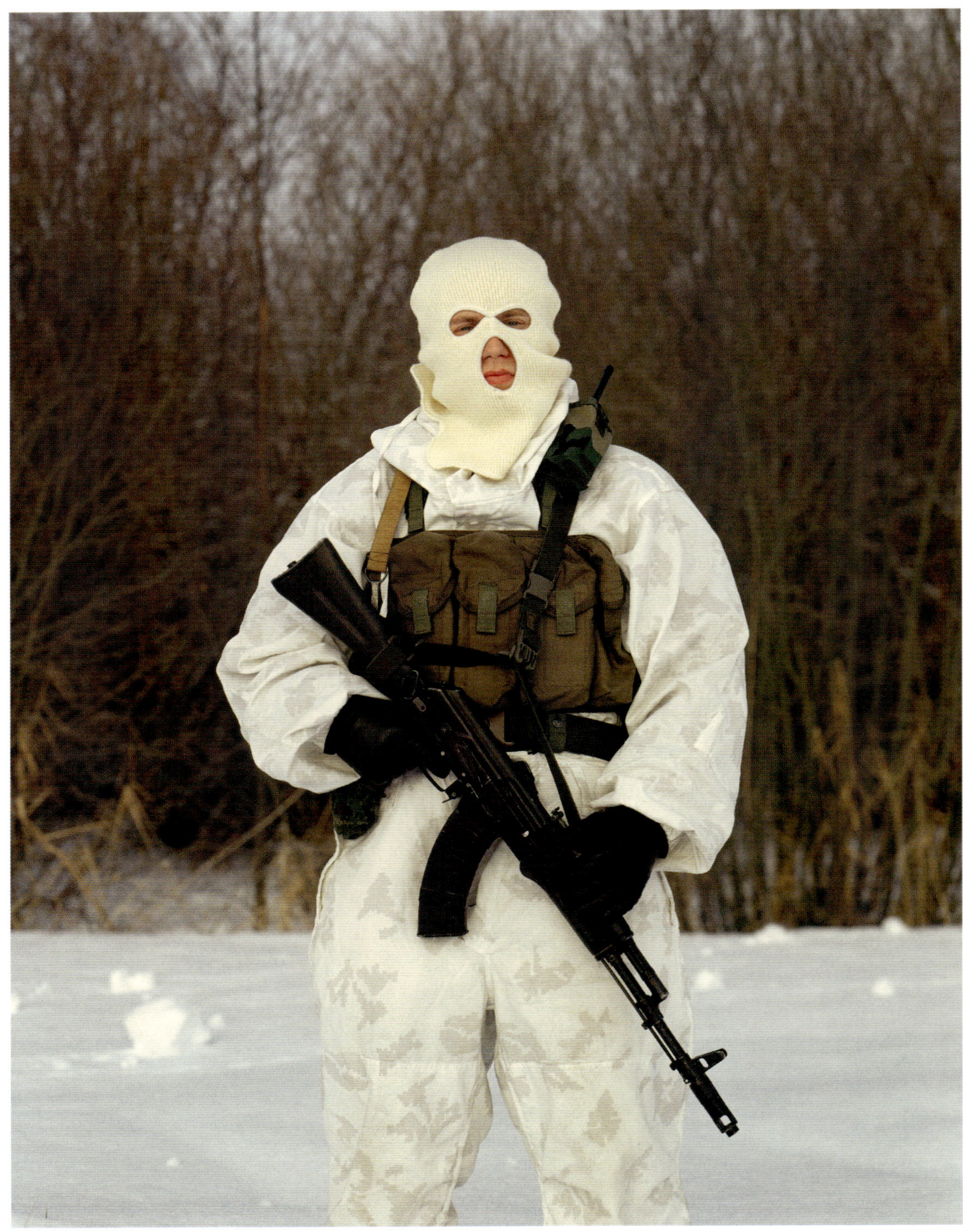

Man in mask, combatant of the Alpha group, *Borders of Russia* series

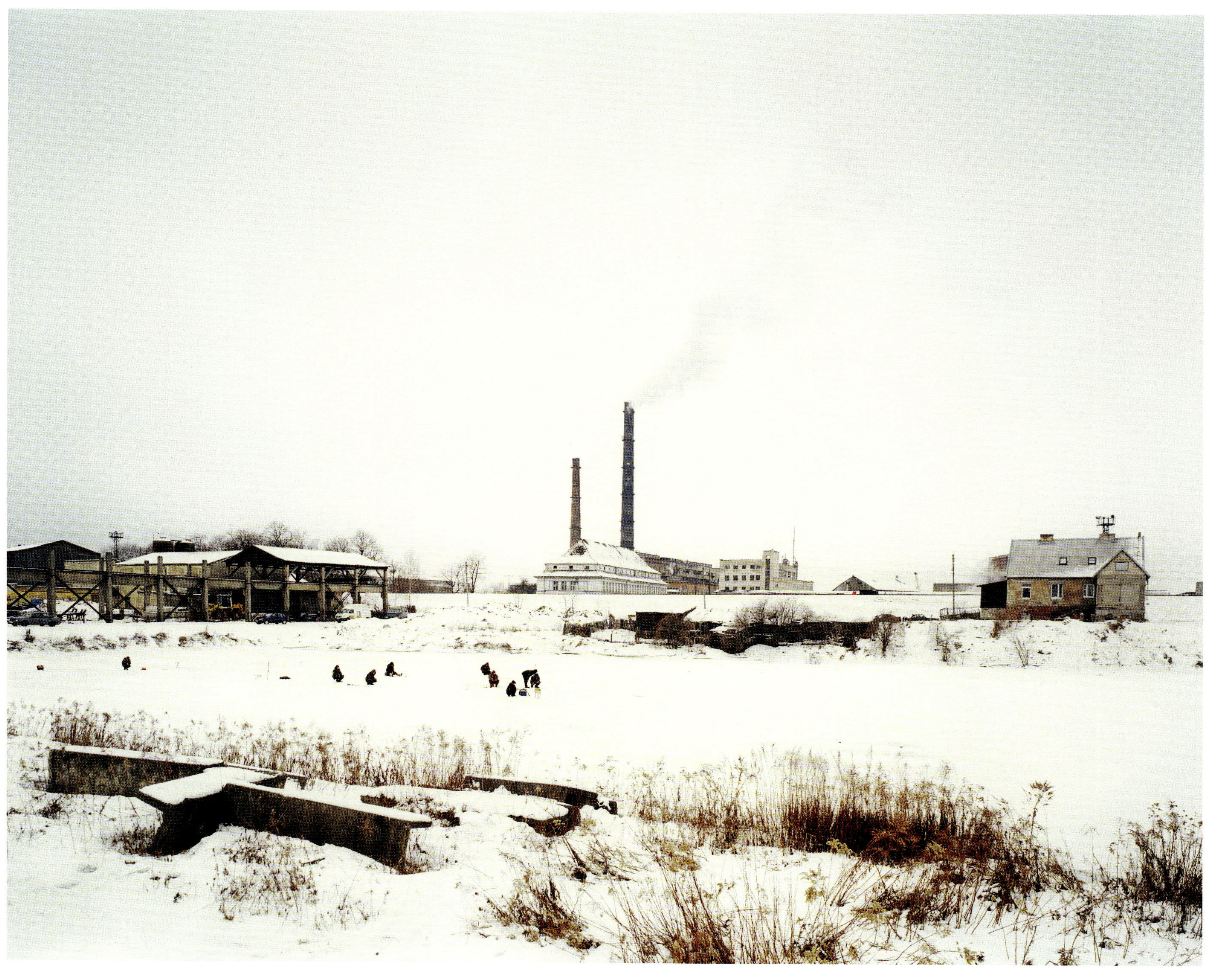

Cityscape, Sovetsk, Kaliningrad Oblast, *Borders of Russia* series

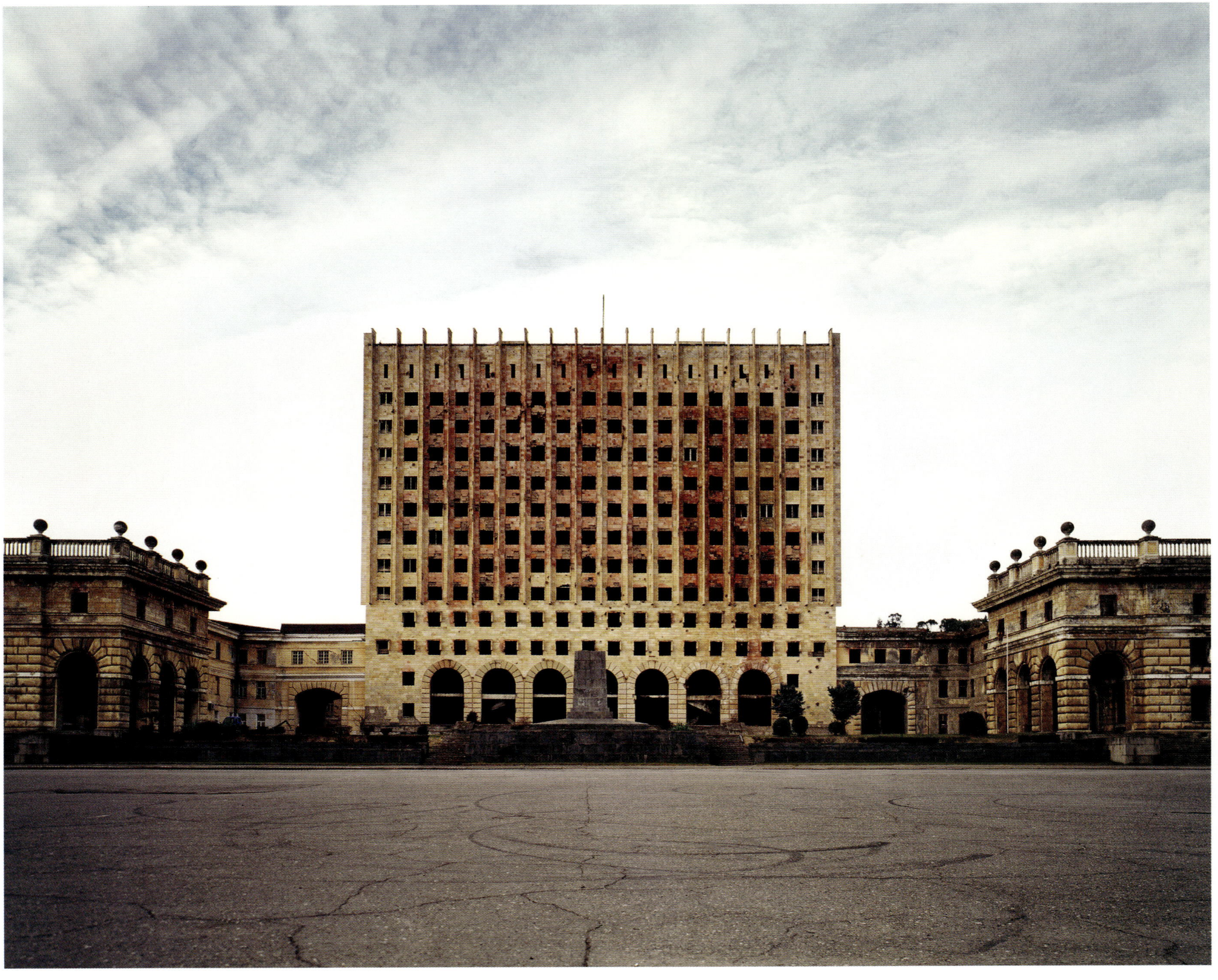

Building of the Council of Ministers of Abkhazia, Sukhumi, Abkhazia, *Borders of Russia* series

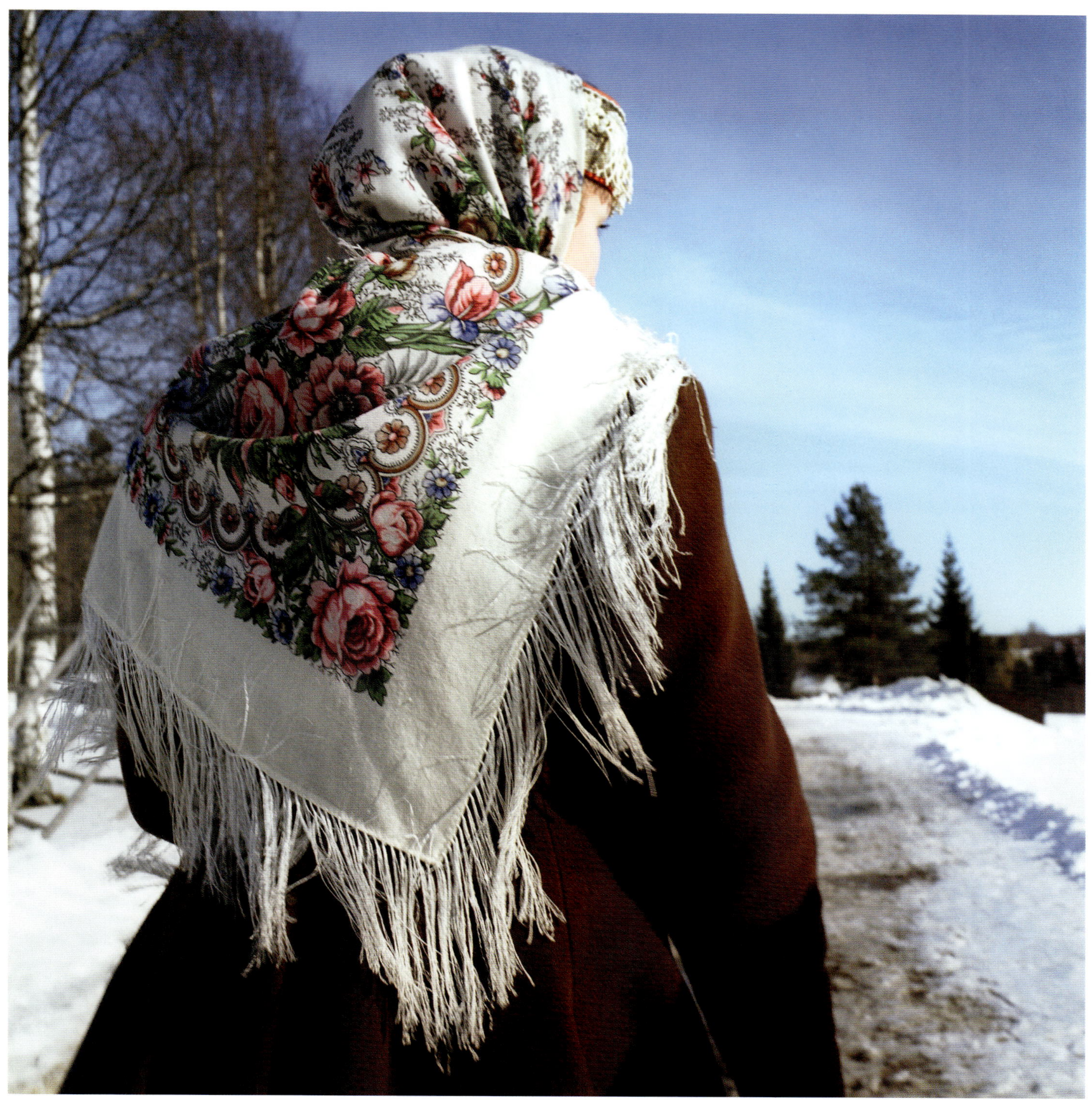

Natalia, Malye Korely village, Primorsky district of Arkhangelsk Oblast, *Borders of Russia* series

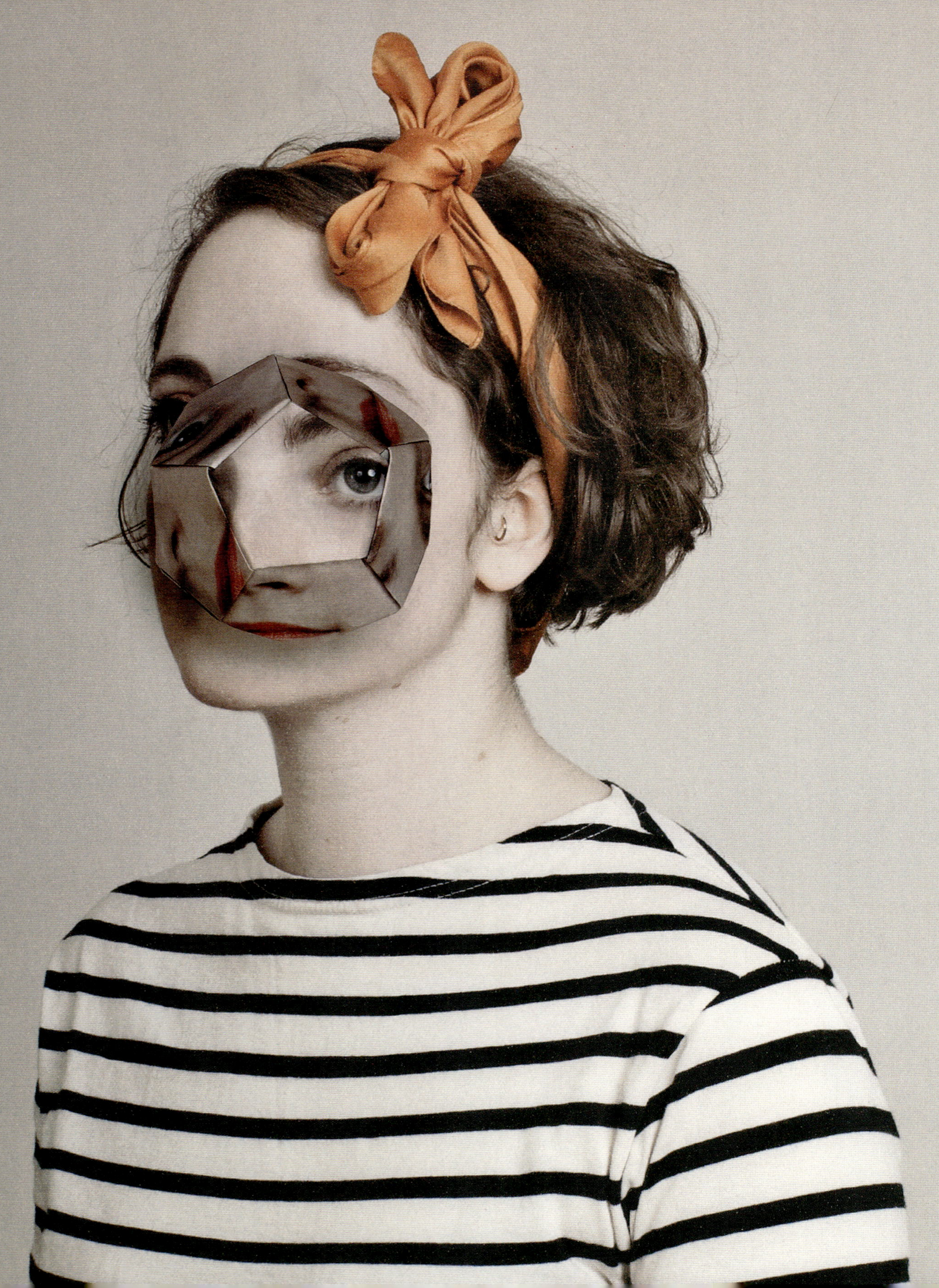

ALMA HASER

Alma Haser's memorable series *Cosmic Surgery* offers a peek into a future where there are so many versions of ourselves that our physiognomy has altered to fit. She has created a portrait series de nos jours. Born in Germany, she is now based in the UK.

The title *Cosmic Surgery* came about as the result of a slip of the tongue when Haser was explaining the idea to her family. Like many primarily visual thinkers, she is dyslexic and often uses a word that is similar to the word she is looking for. In this instance, she said 'cosmic' when she meant 'cosmetic': a happy accident here. For the series, Haser photographs the subject and then prints multiple copies of the face of the sitter. She folds the prints into intricate origami sculptures, places them onto the subject's face and re-photographs them, bringing her fine art training into her photographic work. The folding process is meditative; hours pass in a moment.

The haptic folding process requires meticulous care, enfolding a version of the self back into the self, over and over again. Haser takes the place of the surgeon, so frequently asked to reshape a natural face to render it clone-like, and instead creates an original work of art. The results are as unsettling as they are beautiful.

Haser makes her subjects blossom into uncanny futuristic flowers, in a style that has become her own.

Haser managed to embark upon a photographic journey with self-portraiture without necessarily revealing her identity. In *Ten Seconds Project* her camera is on a timer and, as in her own childhood game, she has ten seconds to conceal her body before she is discovered. With this work there is a disquieting similarity to Claude Cahun's *Self Portrait (in Cupboard)*, c. 1932, although Cahun's body-work is perhaps an unconscious antecedent here. We see the adult body, uncomfortably squeezed into a tight space, and we seek the face, but it remains hidden.

In another series Haser's fascination is directed at the concept of the automaton. A self-portrait with a wig allowed her to retain her anonymity; she then continued the work by photographing other willing models in the same wig and clothing, thus creating a cloning process. Interestingly, her other projects have included twins, in which two women are often pictured as conjoined, and the concept of ventriloquism. Such subjects dwell very deep in the psyche.

In her portrait *The Ventriloquist* a man is seated behind another man, whom he embraces. The man being embraced does not look at the camera. He is considerably smaller than the man who is holding onto him. The latter's gaze meets that of the viewer. Both men have severely cut fringes, an echo of the detail that Roland Barthes famously theorized as the punctum in *Camera Lucida*; the partial object that wounds and is entirely personal to the viewer as it smashes the codes of the studium. We learn from the accompanying text that James, the bigger man, used to bully Luke at school. Now they are the best of friends. Haser captures the tension of not only their specific embrace, but also of all embraces for eternity, with the precision of a markswoman. Who is holding and who is being held? Who is the beholder? Photography serves up such questions like a last supper.

Patient no. 01, 2013, Cosmic Surgery series

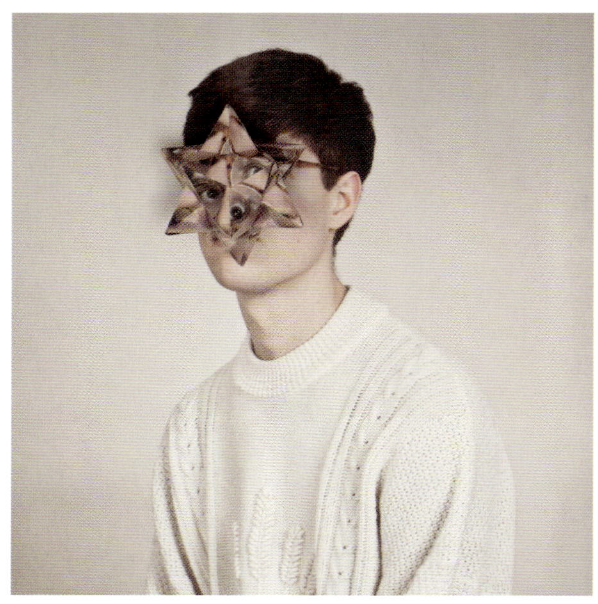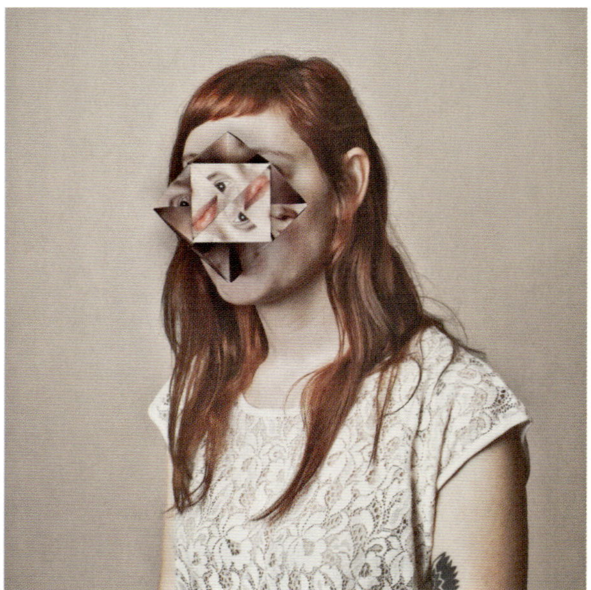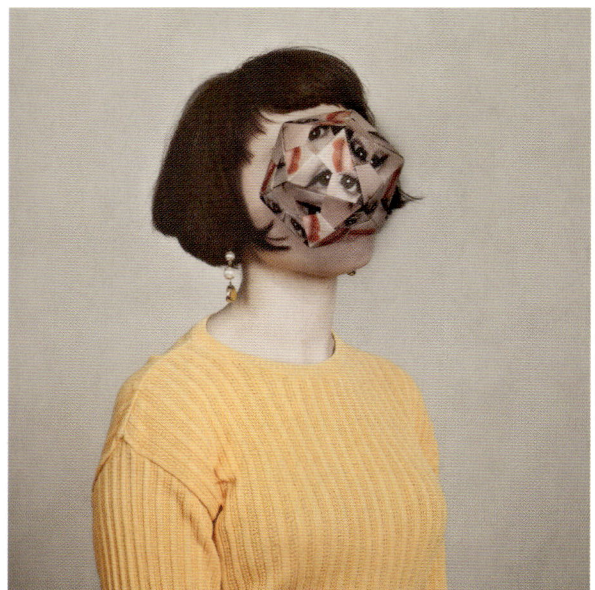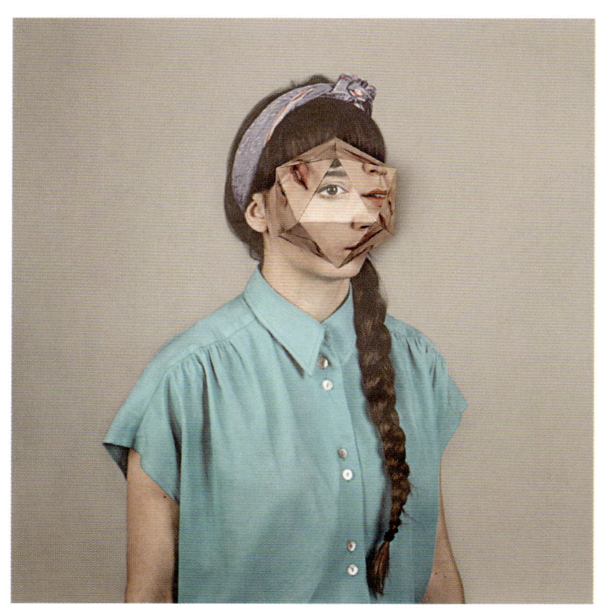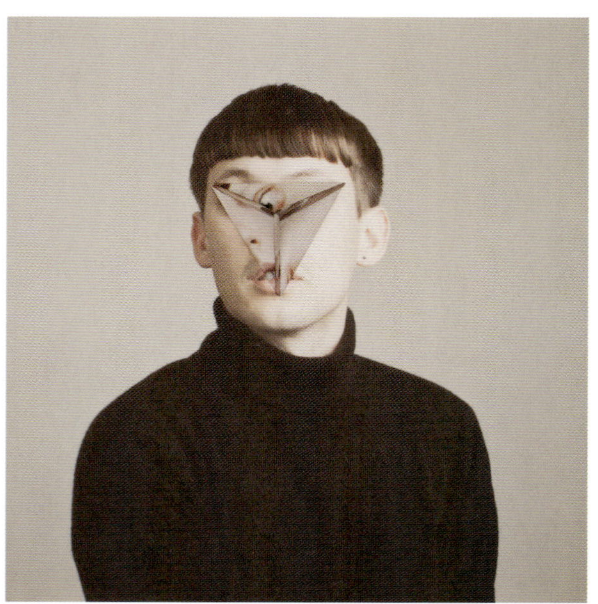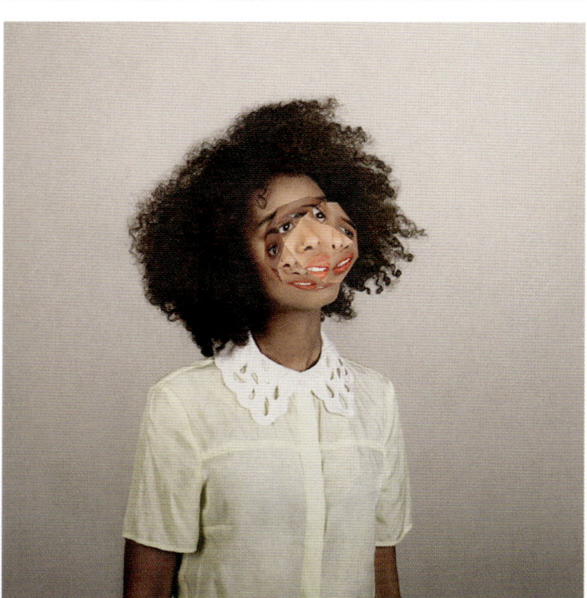

Top row, from left to right: *Patient no. 07, 2013; Patient no. 02, 2013; Patient no. 03, 2013;* second row, from left to right: *Patient no. 27, 2015; Patient no. 12, 2013; Patient no. 17, 2015; all Cosmic Surgery series*

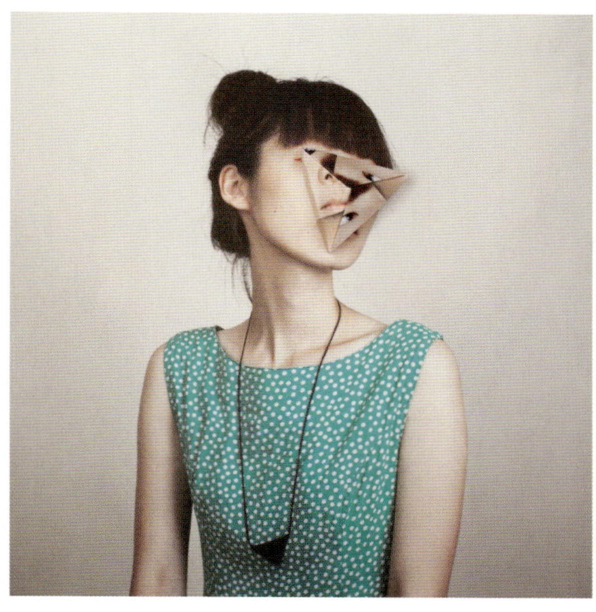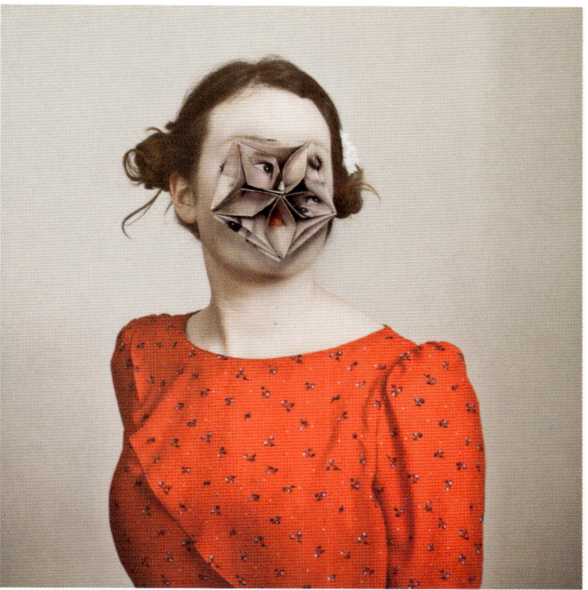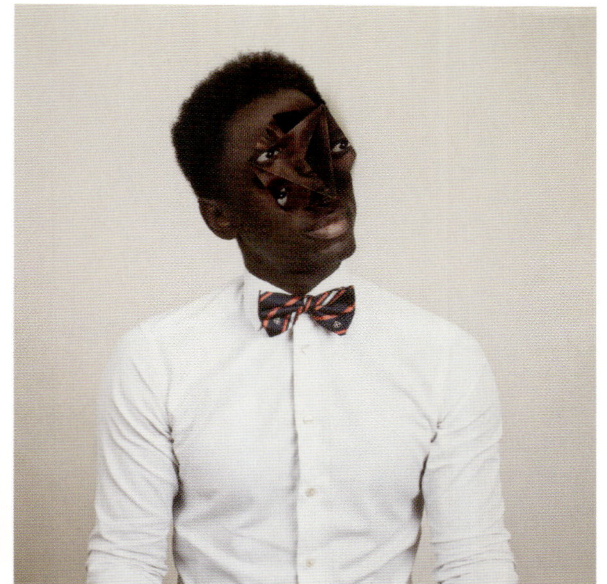
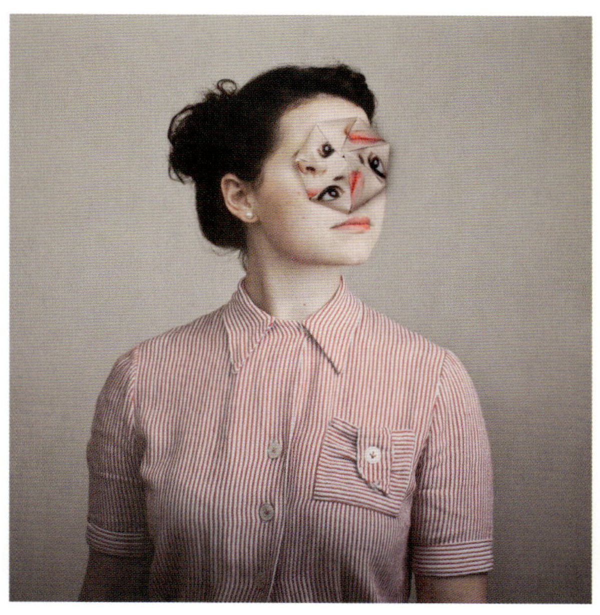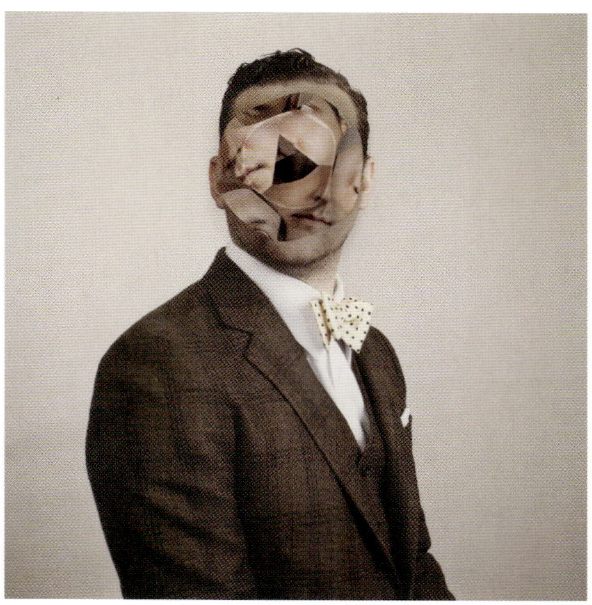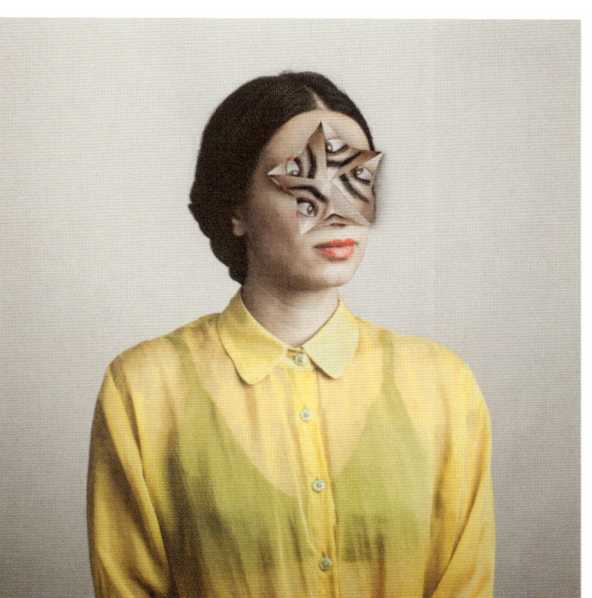

Top row, from left to right: *Patient no. 05, 2013*; *Patient no. 04, 2013*; *Patient no. 11, 2013*;
second row, from left to right: *Patient no. 09, 2013*; *Patient no. 14, 2013*; *Patient no. 15, 2013*; all *Cosmic Surgery* series

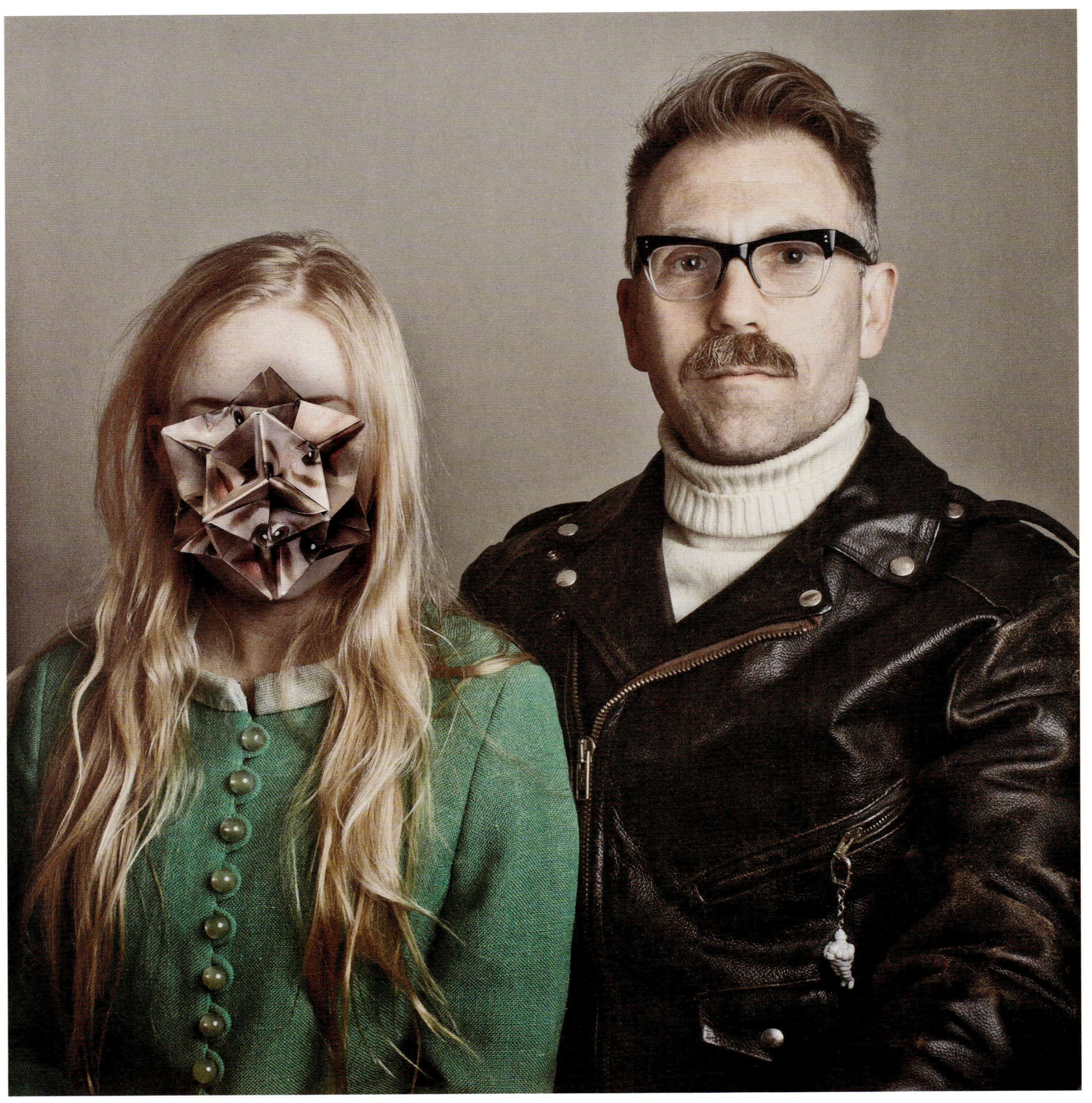

Patient no. Ø8, 2Ø13, Cosmic Surgery series

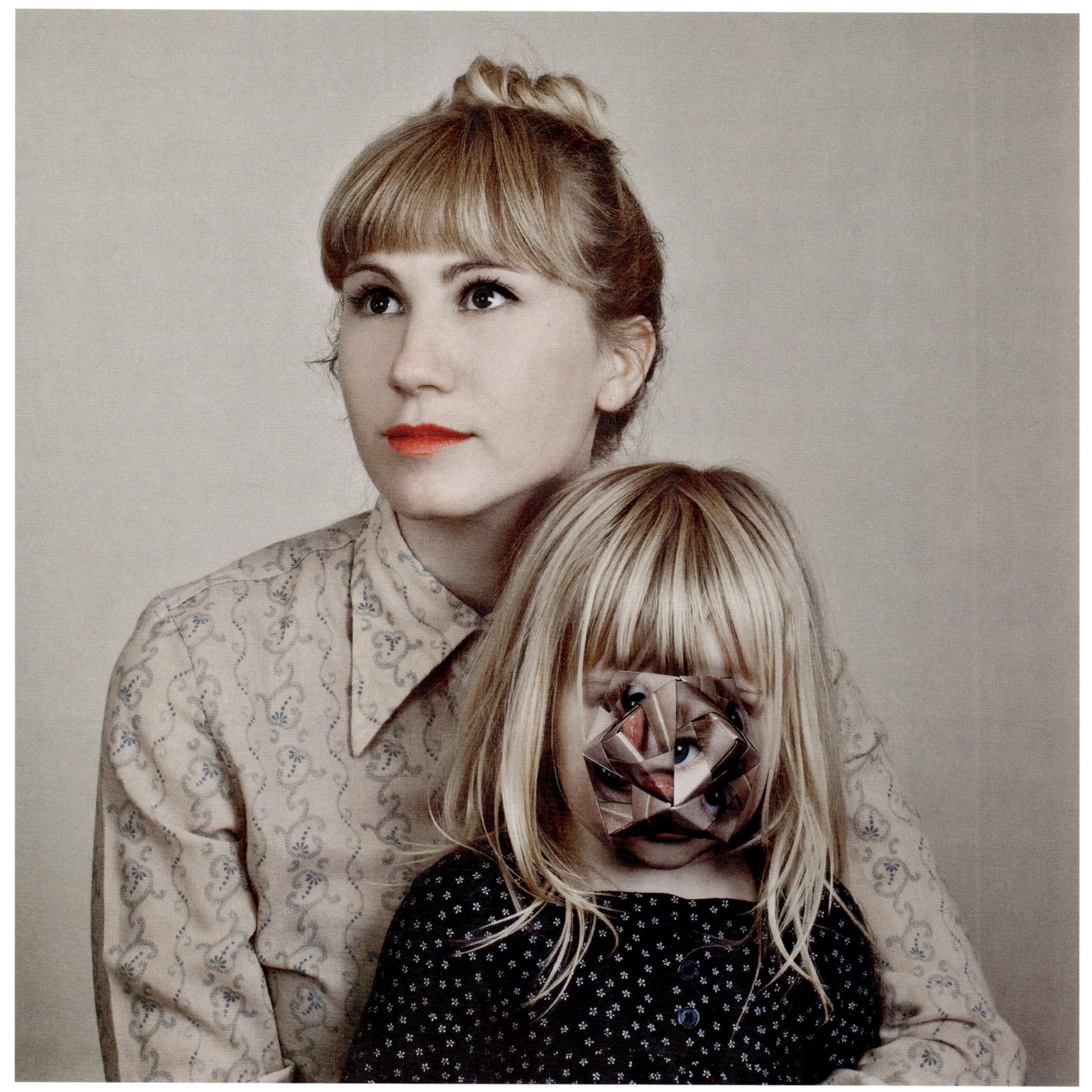

MAYUMI HOSOKURA

…

The beating heart of *Kazan* is the tightly clasped blue bird, carefully positioned in the frame to obscure the genitalia of the nude figure

…

The exquisite imagery of Japanese photographer Mayumi Hosokura can be found between snapshot and staged image, animal and mineral, rock and flesh, instant and eternal. Her meditation on youth finds its ideal medium in photography, which captures it and preserves it forever.

Her first series was called *Kazan*: all of her work that has followed blossomed from it and connects back to it. She photographs androgynous young bodies, her studies of the photographic nude asking us to consider the nature of our own gaze. Where is the tipping point between pleasurable looking and scopophilia? She enjoys the anonymity of the people in her photographs; specificity would be a distraction. And, anyway, there is already an overwhelming presence in the work: beauty itself. This has been much commented upon in relation to Hosokura's photographs: a surfeit of beauty. When the human form is juxtaposed with minerals from deep inside the earth, or with naturally occurring geographical formations, like waterfalls, which endures? Hosokura photographs the body as a work of nature, fully beautiful and perfect *in that moment*.

The beating heart of this series is the tightly clasped blue bird, carefully positioned in the frame to obscure the genitalia of the nude

figure in the background. It is a revealing substitution. This exotic symbol of ultimate freedom stands in here for sexuality. Its wings, however, are not yet unfurled. The moment of unleashing is, and will always be, yet to come.

This startling potency is everywhere at work in Hosokura's photographs. For her series *Transparency is the New Mystery* she elected to work solely in black and white, giving the images a hallucinatory, oneiric quality. Her subject remains youthful bodies and crystals, but photographically it is all about form, and how she can control it.

Crystal Love Starlight enters into different territory in that it was inspired by a criminal investigation into a restaurant in Gunma, Japan, which was being investigated for allowing prostitution to take place on the premises. By choosing this steamy story as a catalyst, Hosokura is now able to further her inquiry into contemporary mores. She utilizes the neon signage we might expect to see in work from Japan, but contrasts it with a tightly controlled cool blue tone, which she uses to continue her nudes series. It makes for a fascinating investigation of her own; and the question of 'whose gaze' that she began to explore in *Kazan* is thus neatly resurrected.

With influences from east and west, from Hiromix to Tillmans, Hosokura is creating a wildly original photographic language to explore those elements of her culture that might be taken for granted, or are hard to express in words. This most visual of approaches seems pertinent for a society so obsessed with looking at itself that it sometimes fails to see anything at all. The word 'kazan' means 'volcano' in Japanese…this natural phenomenon remains motionless for centuries, and then pours forth, fiercely. To borrow from the late John Berger, as 'brief as photographs'.

Untitled, 2009–11, Kazan series

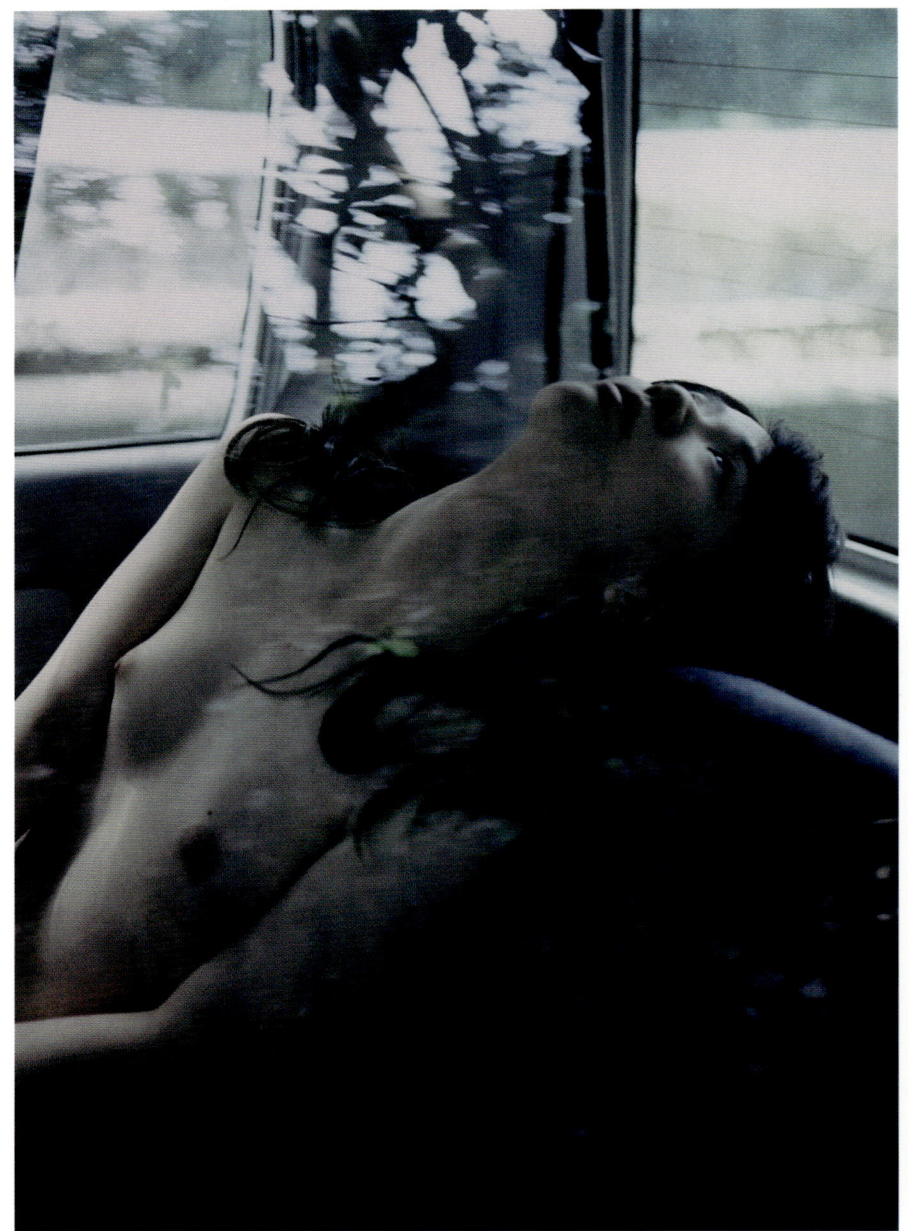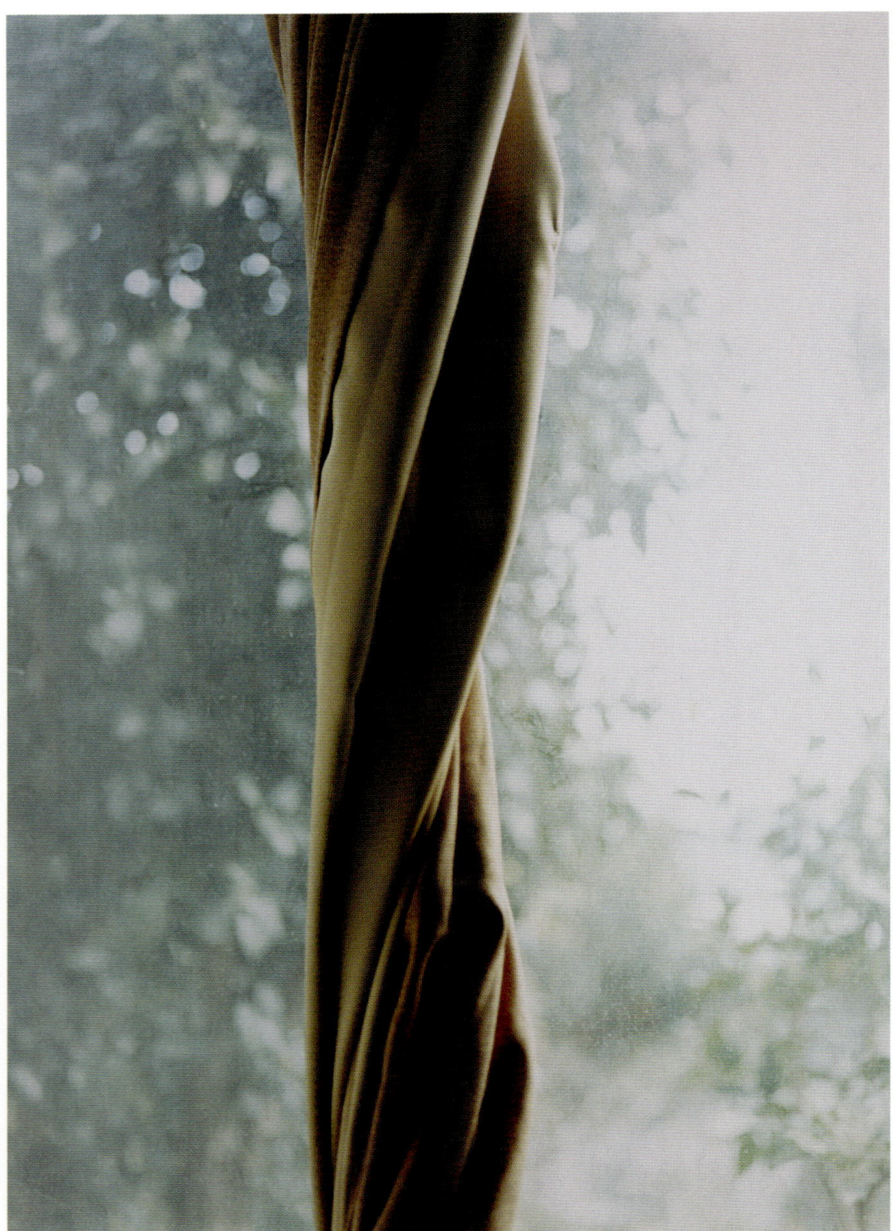

Untitled, 2009–11, Kazan series

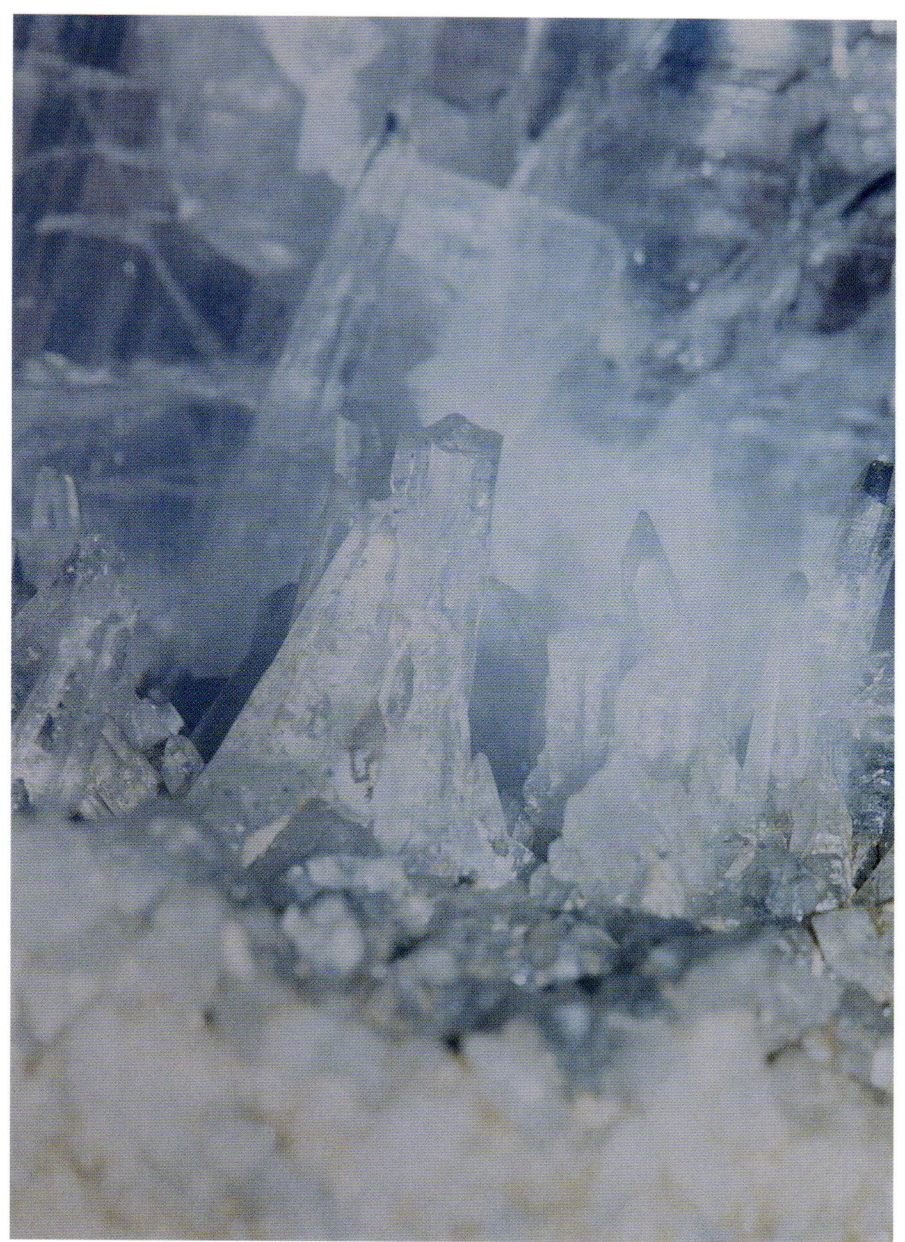 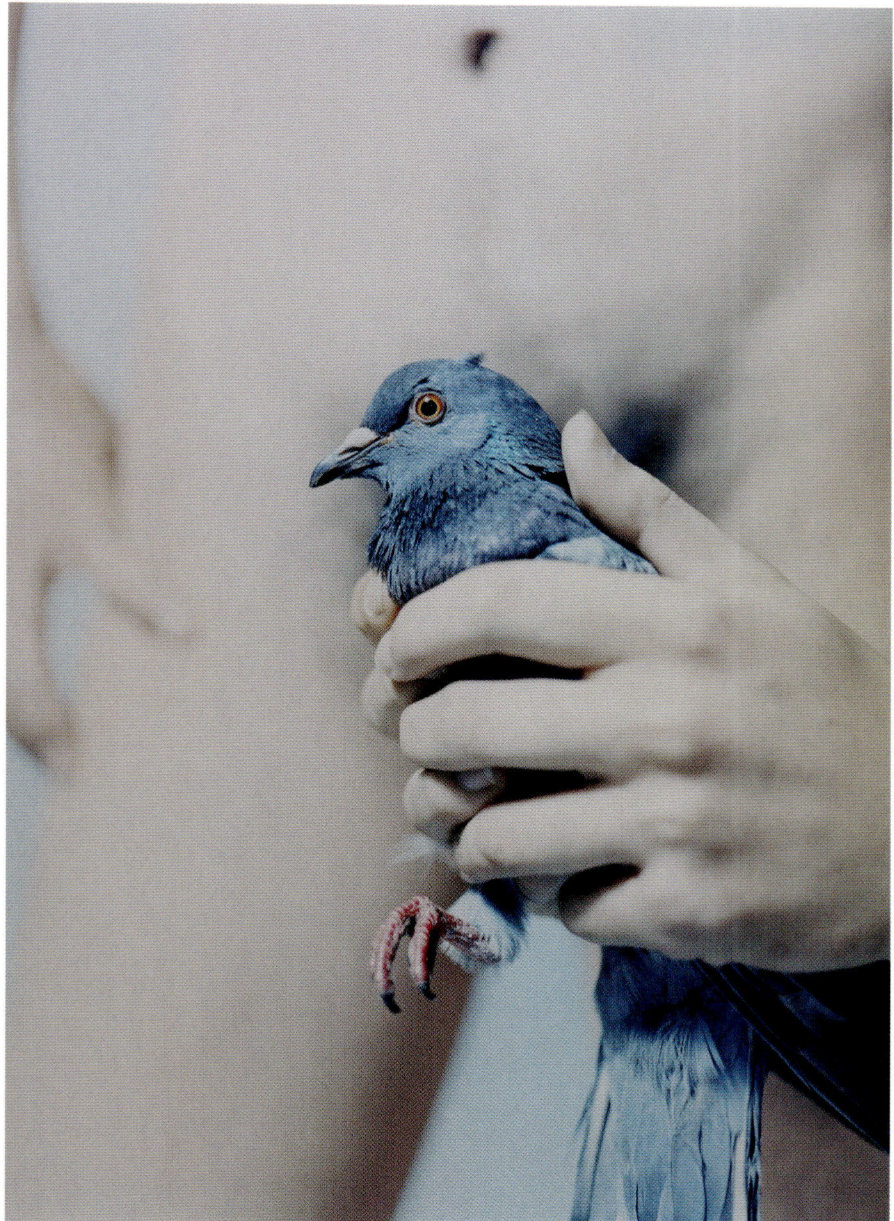

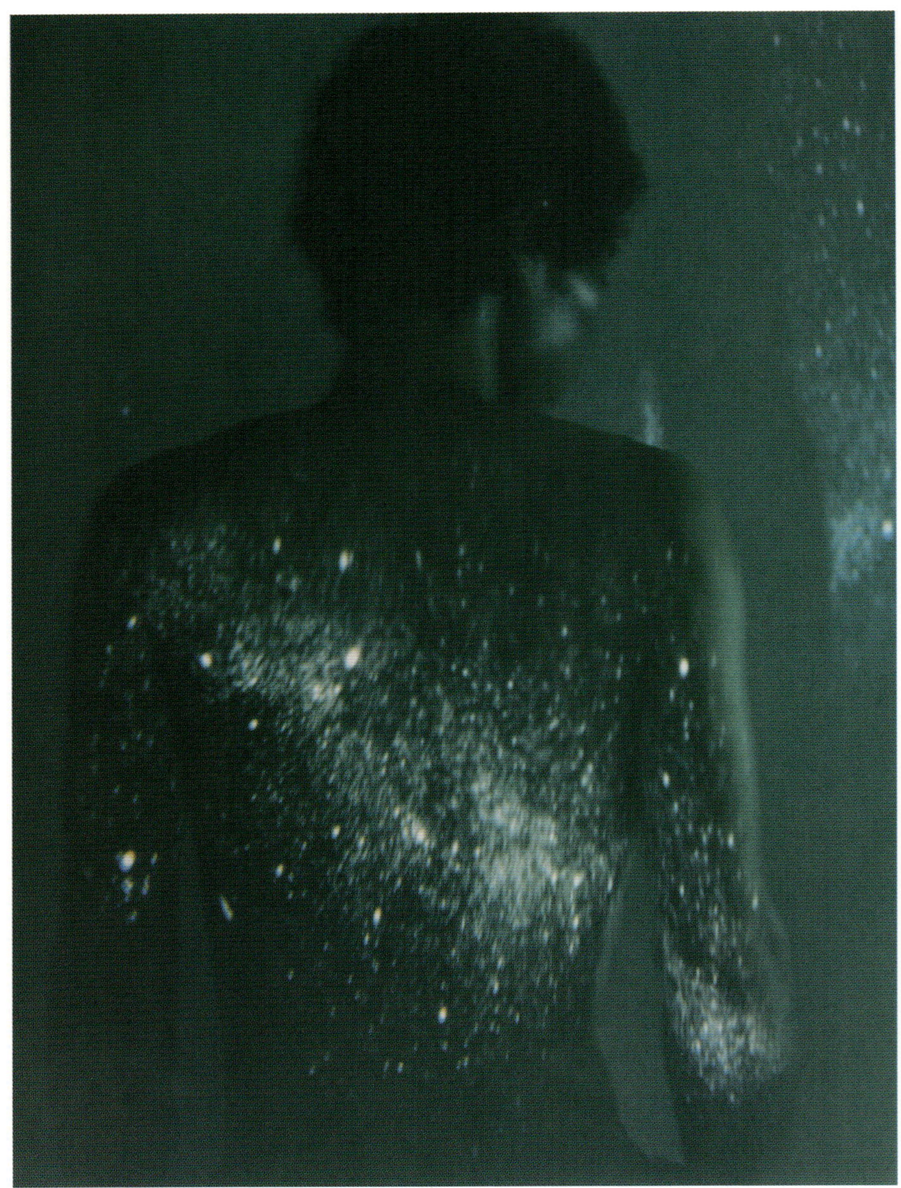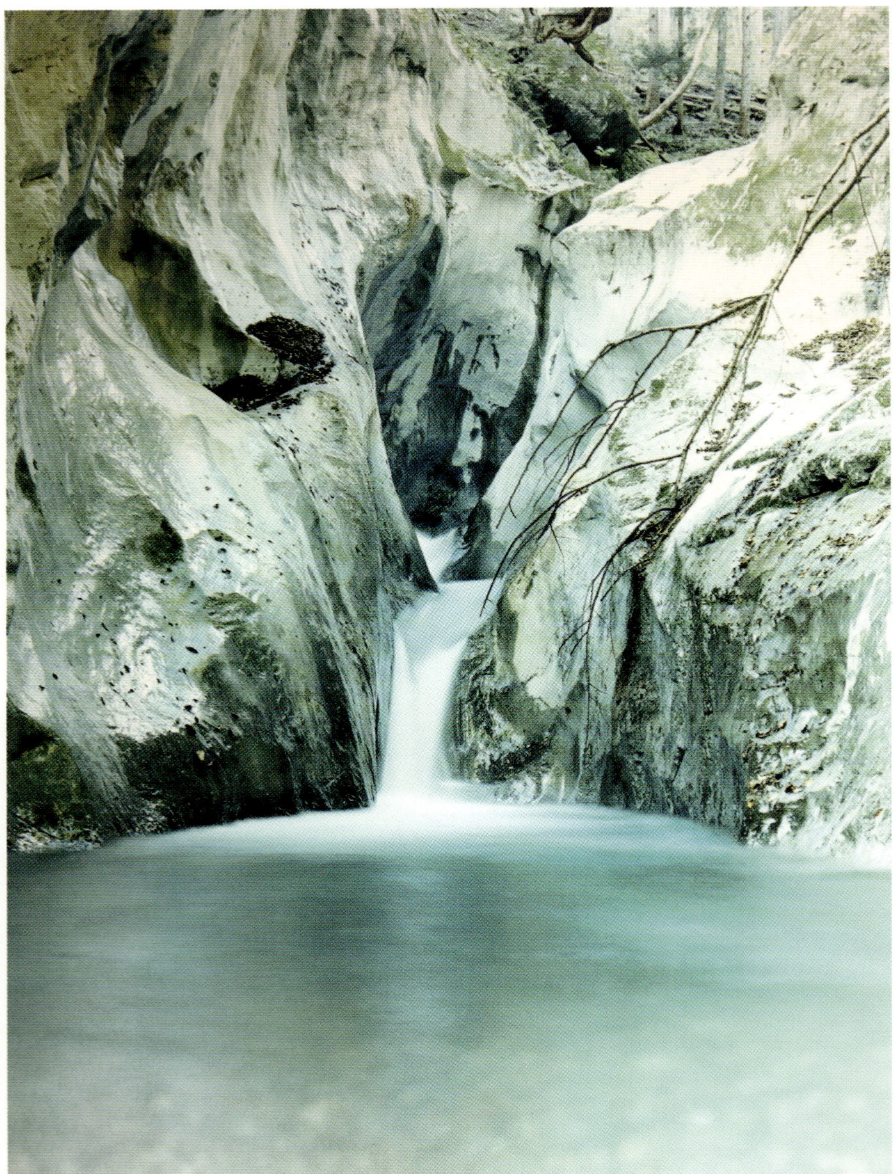

Untitled, 2009–11, *Kazan* series

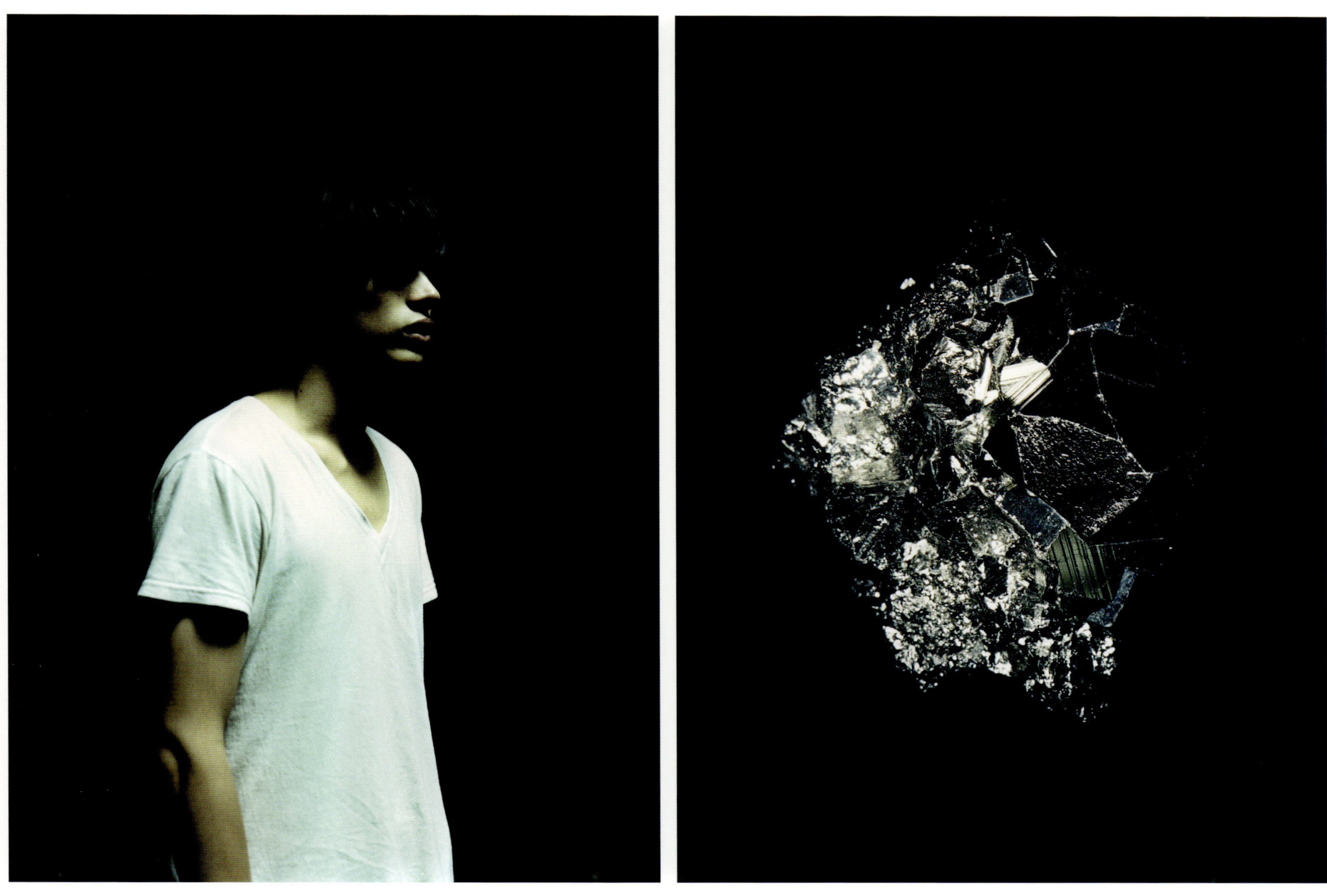

Untitled, 2009–11, Kazan series

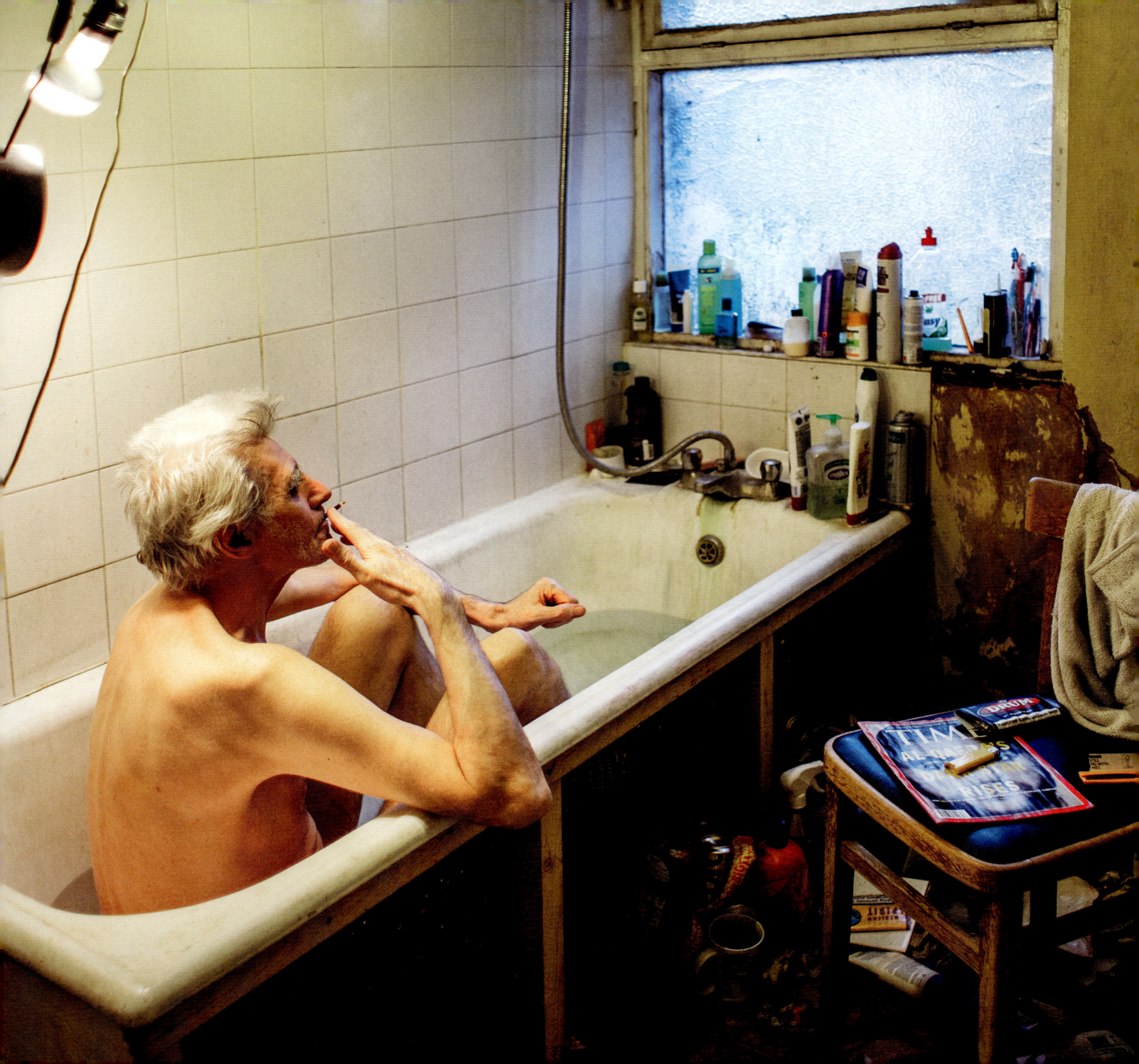
DRUM
TIME
AL-QAEDA'S
RISES

CORINNA KERN

…
'I wanted to blur the lines between neurotic compulsion, humanity and non-conformism'
…

After graduating from the University of Westminster, London in 2013, Corinna Kern quickly established a reputation as a first-rate photojournalist. She was signed up by Getty Images Reportage and her images have gained international recognition as well as many prestigious photography awards such as Pictures of the Year International, NPPA Best of Photojournalism and the International Photography Awards.

In Kern's first long-term project, *A Place Called Home*, which is about the London squatting scene, she made intimate connections with the people she photographed. Her inclination is towards the counter-cultural, or non-mainstream, and her vivid, bold and compassionate photography proposes a challenge to preconceived ideas.

Kern lived in Kentish Town with the inhabitants of a squat in a former design studio and visited many more such sites regularly, including The Castle, a five-storey former office block, during the summer of 2013. A legal amendment in September 2012 rendered squatting illegal in residential buildings and resulted in the concept of home being played out in unexpected places. Kern located these places and inhabited them too, witnessing moments of total relaxation in a frenetic city.

Remarkably, she also shared the home of seventy-two-year-old George Fowler for two months, while documenting the condition of hoarding, or 'an accumulated illness' as Mr Fowler refers to it. He has lived in the same four-bedroom house in London for thirty-three years, during which time he has acquired a vast amount of 'stuff' – picked up from the street, or out of dustbins – with the desire to repurpose it. As someone who experienced post-war rationing, his compulsive response to consumer society seemed logical to Kern. 'I wanted to capture the relation between his illness, his inner world and domestic environment and the outside world,' she says, 'and to blur the lines between neurotic compulsion, humanity and non-conformism.'

Kern's eye homed in on the bathtub as the nexus of her project. It was the only place in the house that was in a state of constant flux. While the other rooms sat silently, weighed down by years and tons of accumulated matter, the bath played host to crockery (for washing), laundry (ditto), bikes (for repair), and also served as a reading room, and a place to take coffee and contemplate the day. Kern photographed it as a kind of sanctuary.

After two years in London, Kern moved to South Africa, where, typically, she sought to tackle under-represented subjects such as how different racial identities – people of mixed race are now in the most marginalized of the country's ethnic groups – find expression post-apartheid. Kern also worked with South Africa's traditional healers, sangomas, having gained privileged access. She immersed herself in a documentary project with transgender women in communities where such non-conformity is considered 'un-African' and created a highly theatrical series of images of the vivid AfrikaBurn festival in the Tankwa Desert.

Kern is working on a long-term project that looks at the little-discussed subject of female masking. Kern has been meeting people from all genders who are united by a desire to transform into a female alter ego by wearing a mask. This is fast becoming a compelling portrait series, which continues her philosophical focus on the paramount importance of mental and spiritual wellbeing and freedom in a world that often champions the opposite.

George's World, 2013

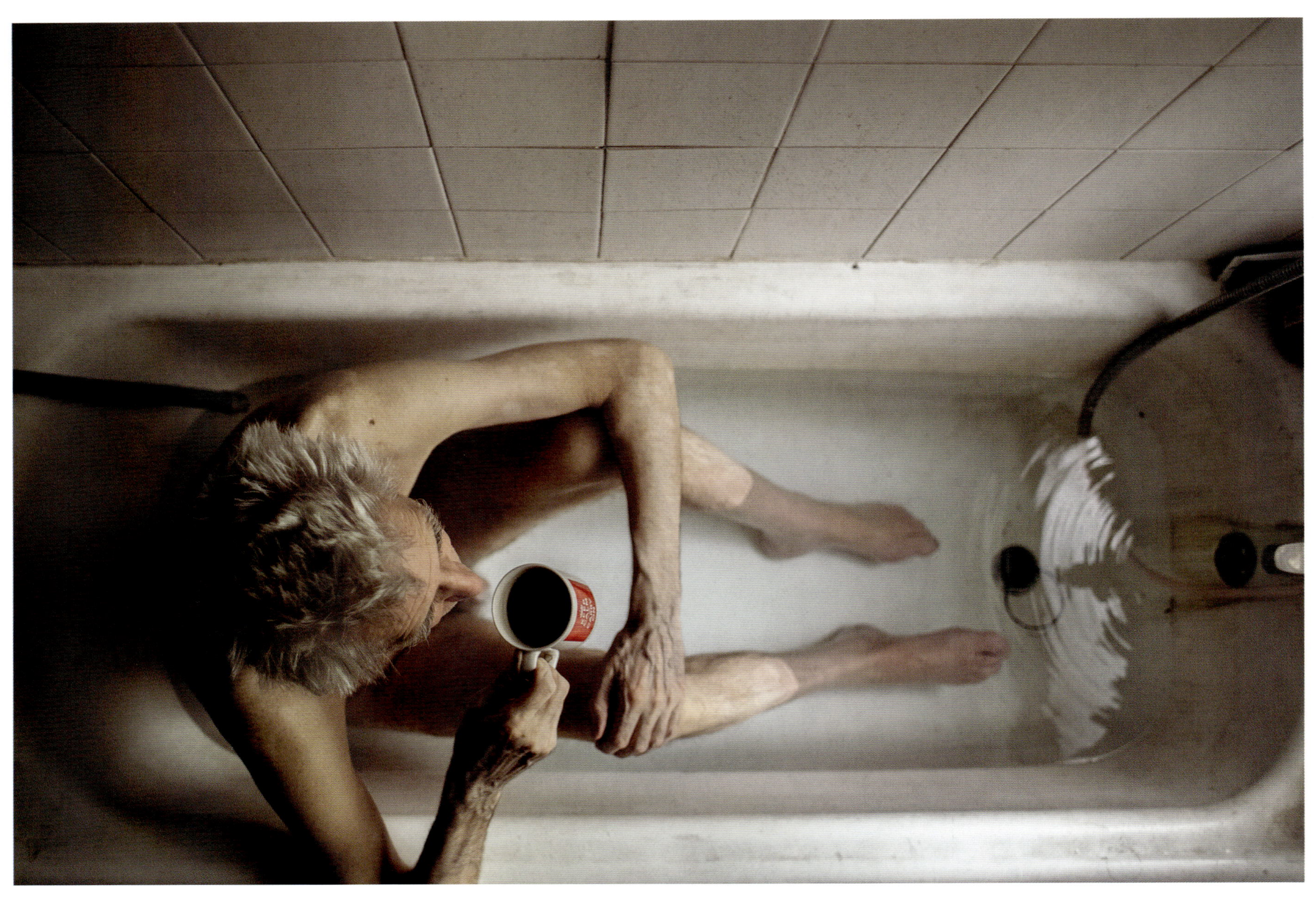

George's Bath, 2014

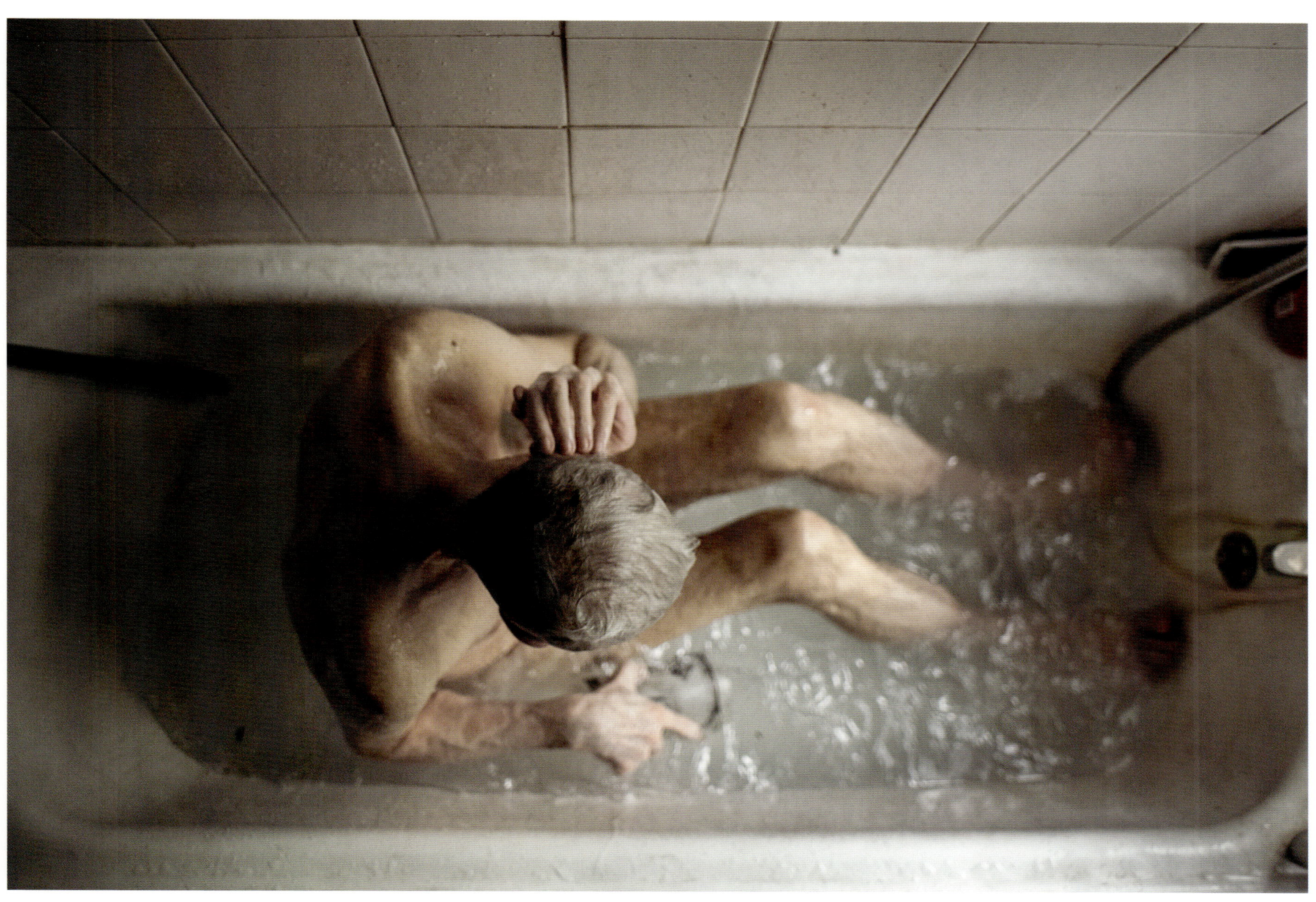

George's Bath, 2014

Corinna Kern　93

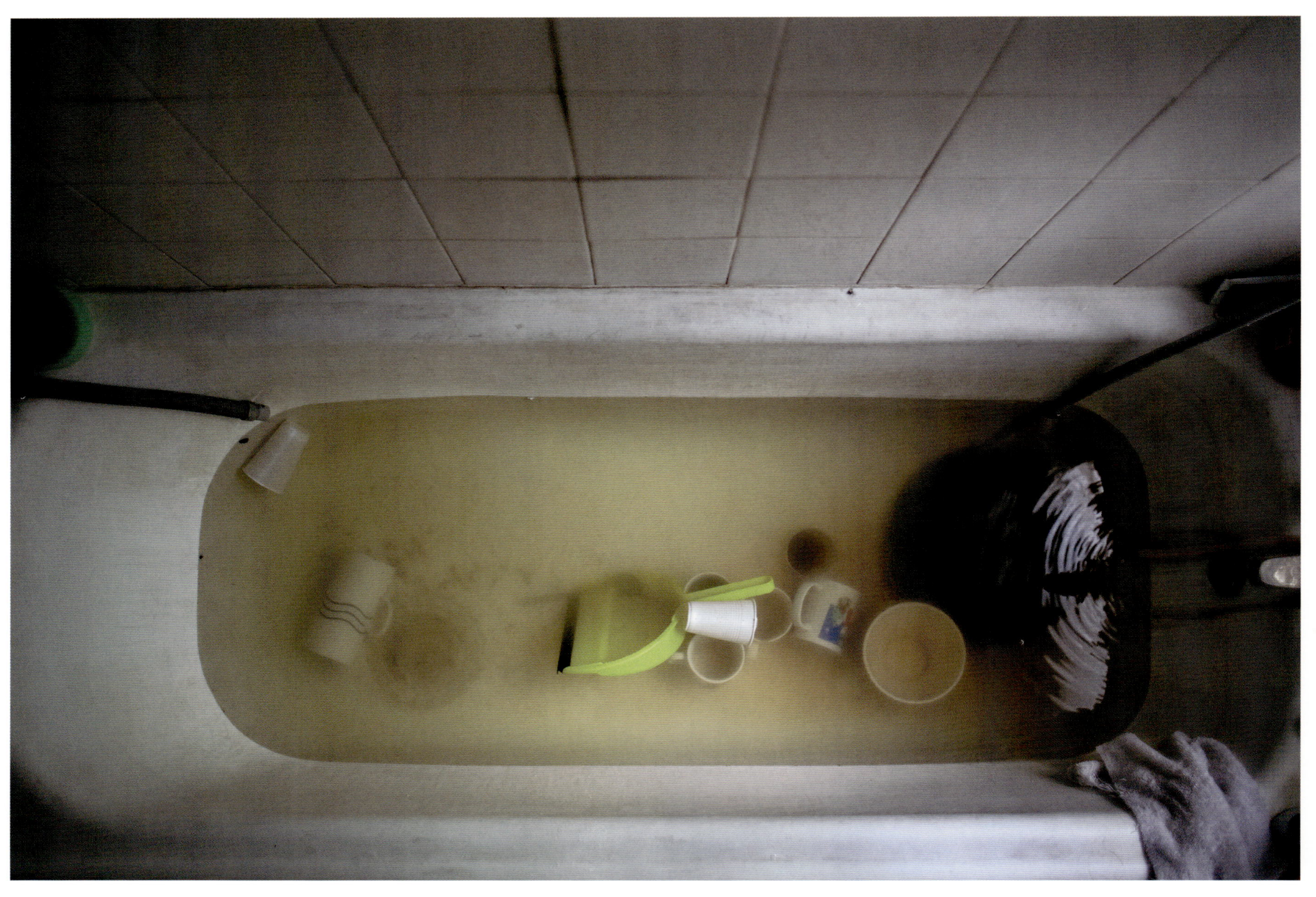

George's Bath, 2014

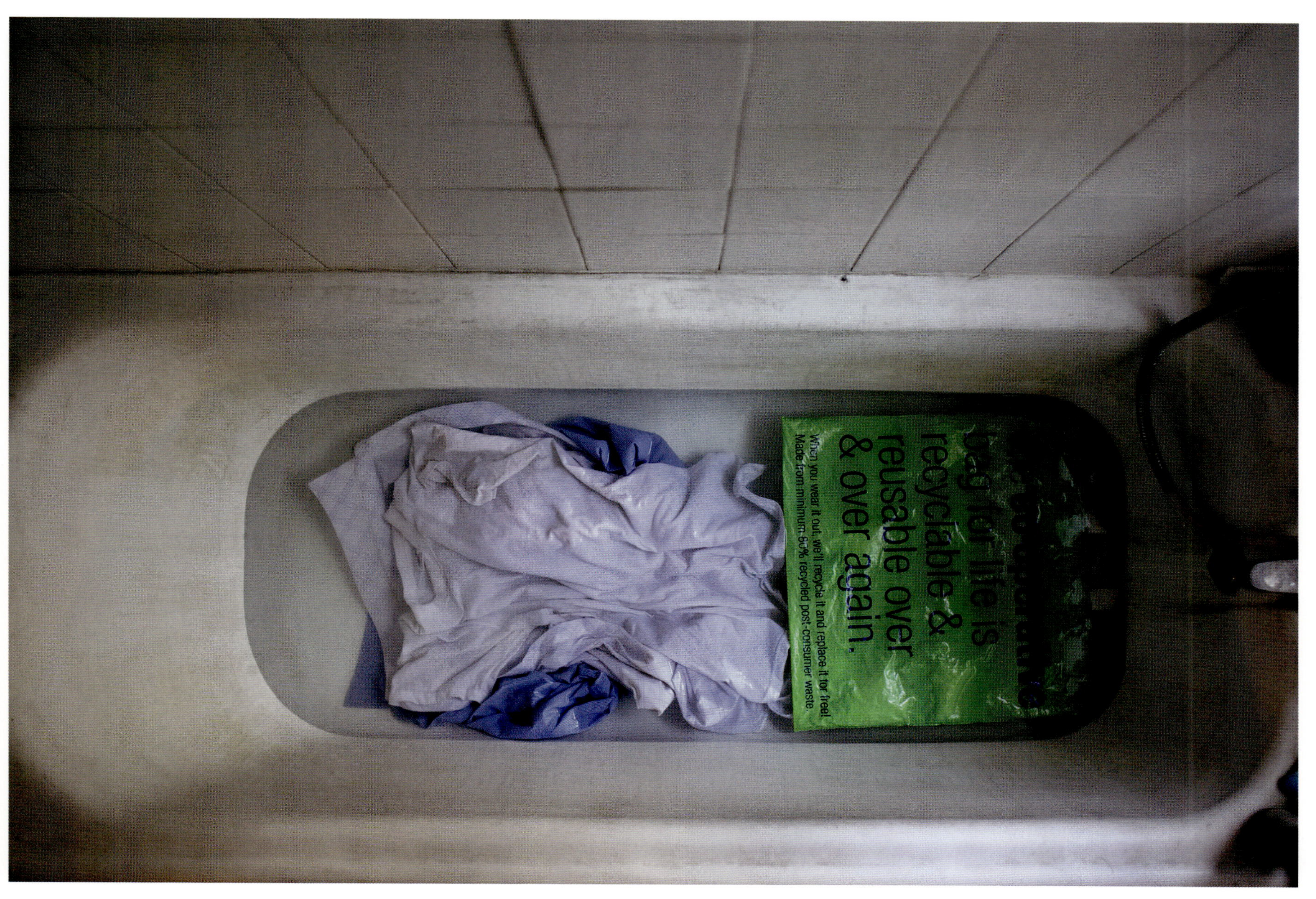

George's Bath, 2014

Corinna Kern   95

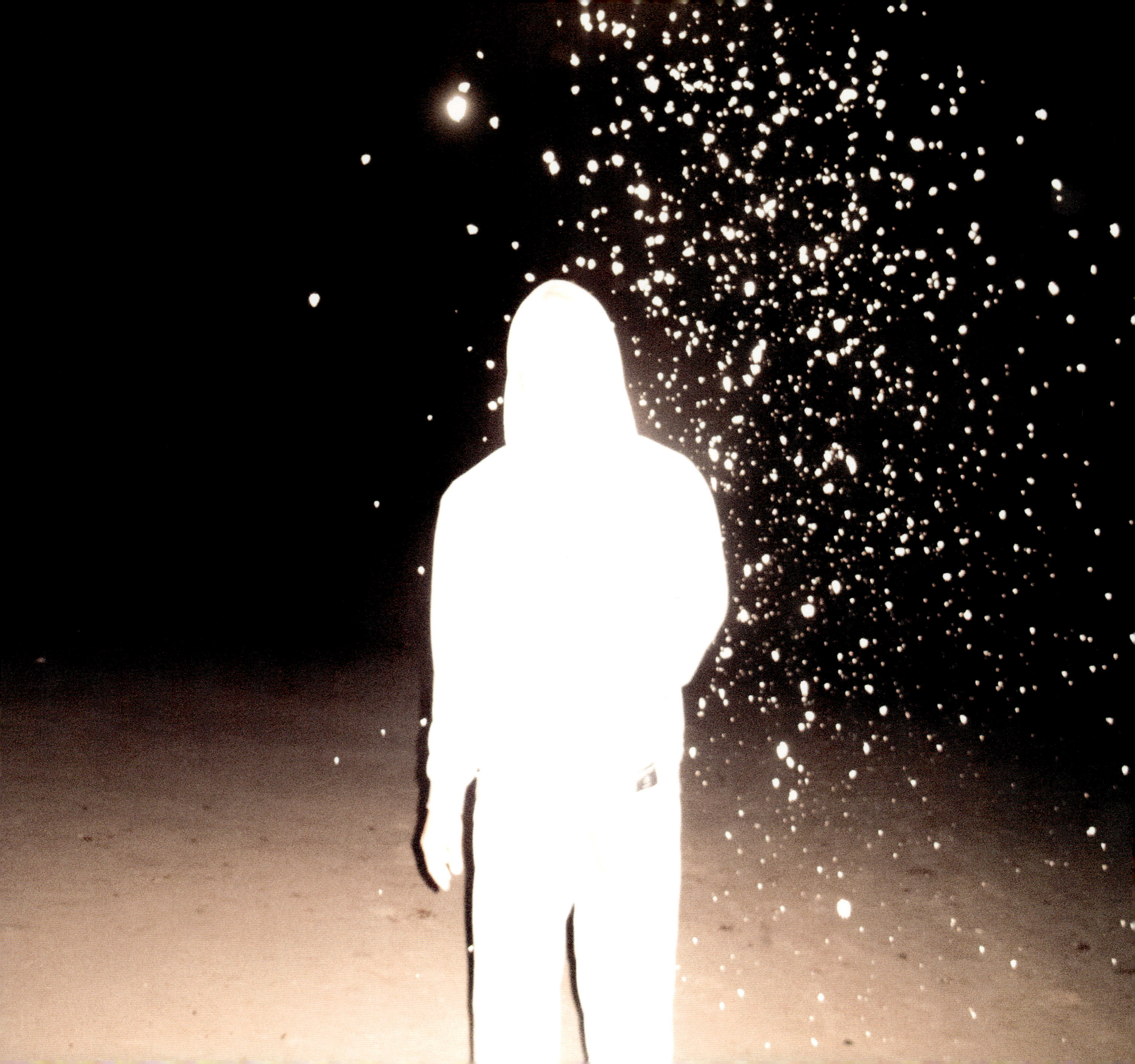

KATRIN KOENNING

…
**In Koenning's metaphysical world,
location is an unnecessary concept**
…

Katrin Koenning finds the extraordinary in the ordinary. Through her highly autobiographical work she explores notions of love, light and distance, and the invisible ties that bind us.

Koenning was born in Germany and migrated to Australia at the age of twenty-five. In 2015 she won the Daylight Photo Award; she has had notable exhibitions in several countries and has garnered particular attention for her ethereal Instagram account, named by Alec Soth as one of his favourites. In 2016 she published her first photobook, *Astres Noirs* (*Black Stars*, Chose Commune), an innovative 'visual conversation' between Koenning's phone photography and the work of Bangladeshi photographer Sarker Protick.

Koenning's series *Indefinitely* (2007–15) draws upon the photographer's personal migratory experiences to investigate universal emotions and connections with place and belonging. Shot over eight years and in three different countries (her native Germany, Australia and New Zealand), the project developed out of an earlier body of work, *Near,* in which Koenning documented her family across the four corners of the world.

Indefinitely is a poetic record of the inbetween space created by distance. She describes 'the notion that this space, removed from nationality or border, is not a vacuum or a void. Rather it is the curator of new narratives: a space of the imaginary, holding the world.' Her photographs evoke notions of transience, loneliness and the persistent sense of longing, but also consider the opportunity this may present for new experiences.

Koenning's photography is celestial and transcendent, but also factual and scientific. Nature is ever-present; images of the sky, the woods and the sea are presented alongside the otherworldly. Koenning deploys her signature overexposure technique (much lauded, particularly on her Instagram account) to create alien life forms, constellations of matter and dream-like states where reality and fiction can collide. *Indefinitely* stands as a sophisticated testament to the pervading question: how do we document something that isn't visible?

Her meditative musings ebb and flow ambiguously between the three locations and it is not clear which location we are in from one photo to the next. In Koenning's metaphysical world, location is an unnecessary concept. Light appears as a metaphor for filling emotional voids, and overall the series feels like a supernatural dialogue between day and night, or the sun and the moon.

The subject of migration has been a preoccupation of artists for centuries and, with the recent global migration crisis hitting headlines, has been widely documented both artistically and journalistically. Koenning's intensely beautiful photography offers a very different perspective to an often difficult and depressing subject. Through her own personal emotions and explorations, she observes experiences of transience and separation, and provides a counterpoint.

Relative Distances #2, 2015, Indefinitely series

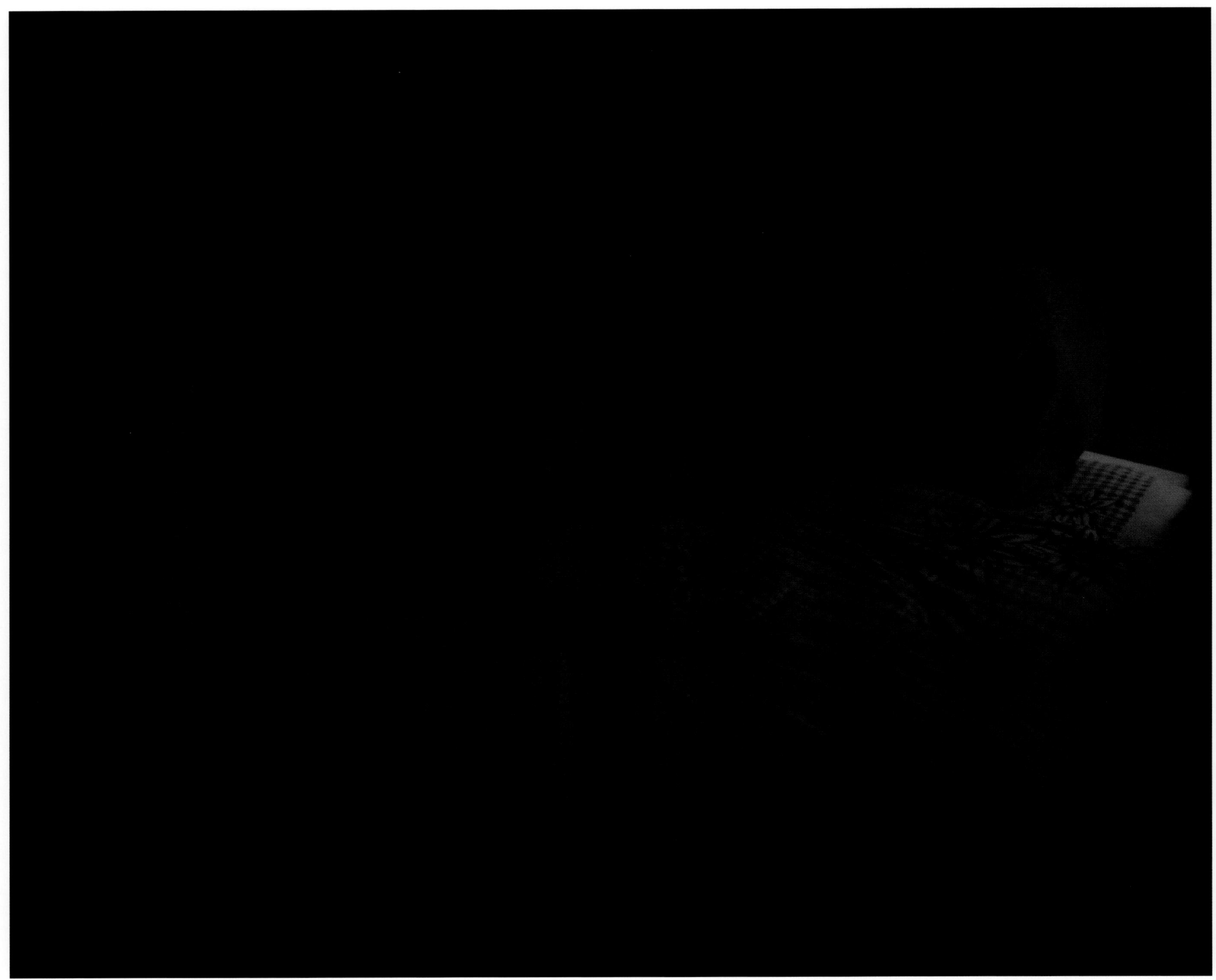

K Sleeping #2, 2013

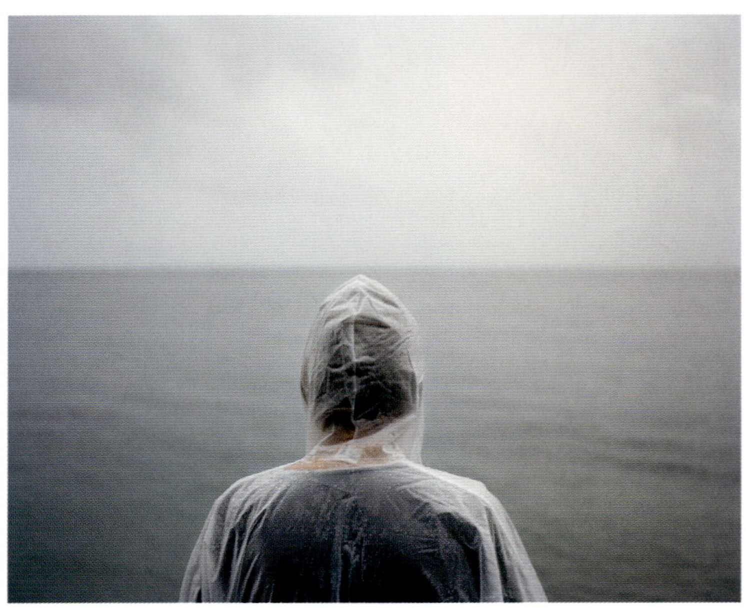

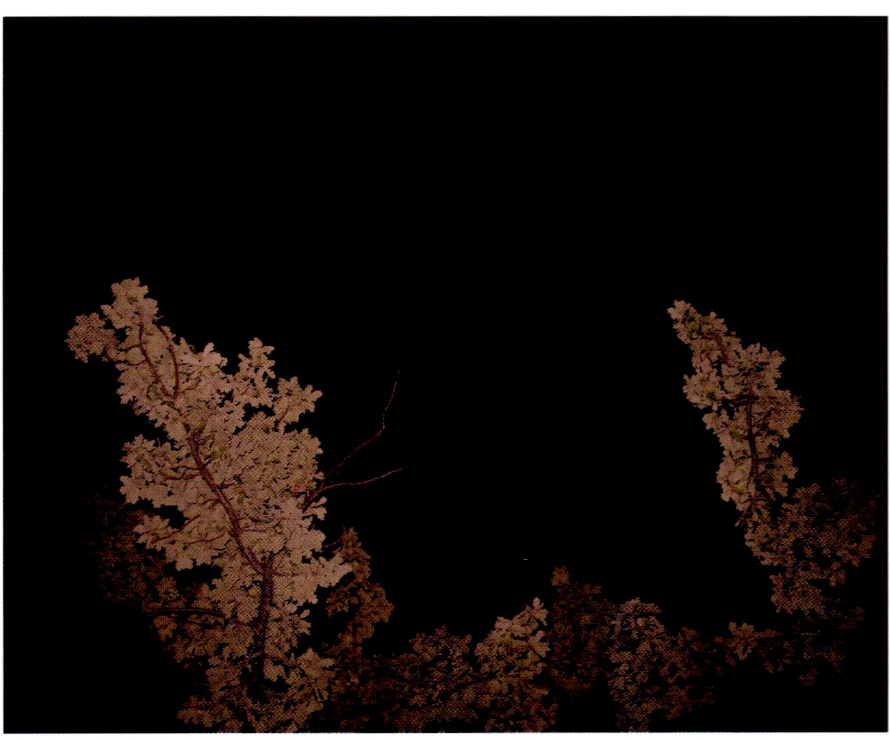

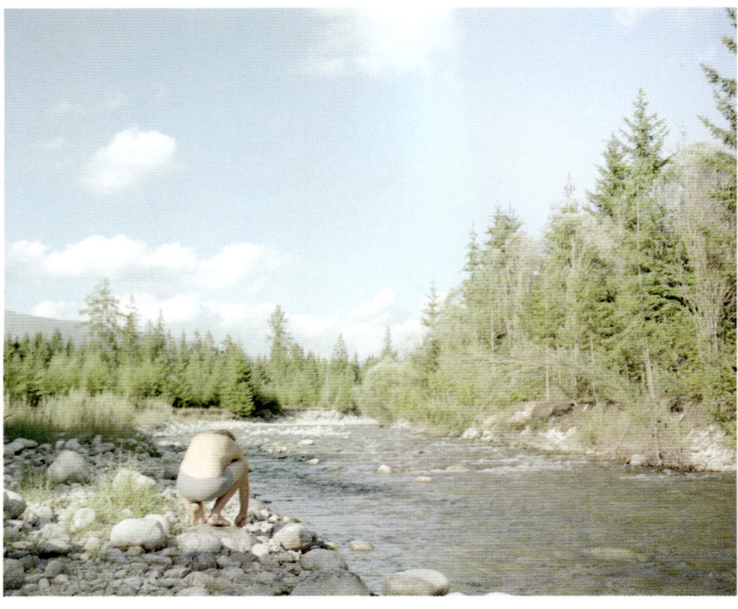

Top left: *View over the Pacific Facing West from Amity Point*, 2013;
left: *Constellation #4*, 2014;
above: *Keke by the River #1*, Slovakia, 2013

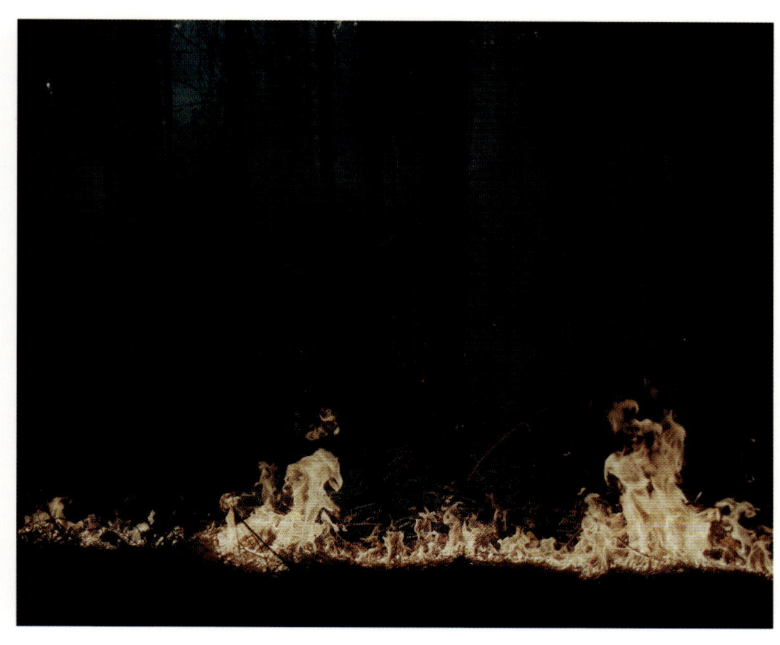

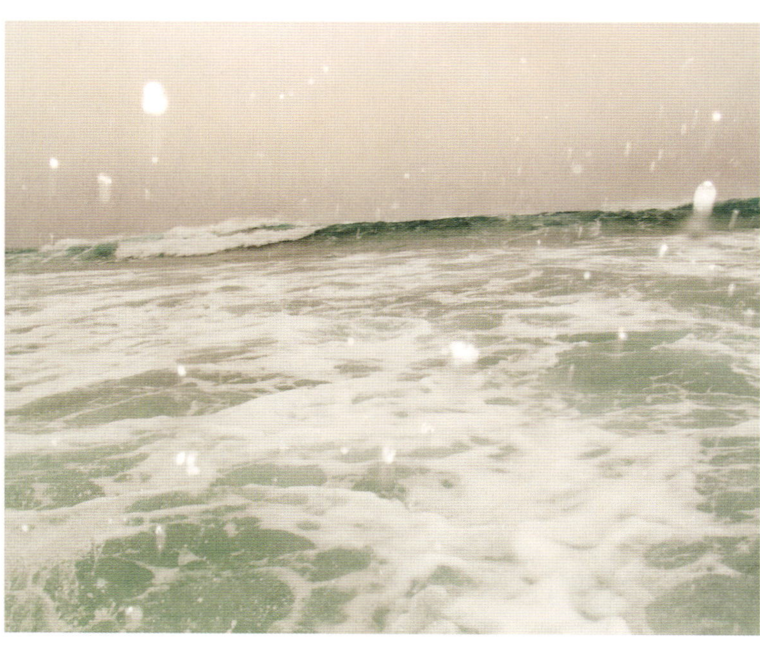

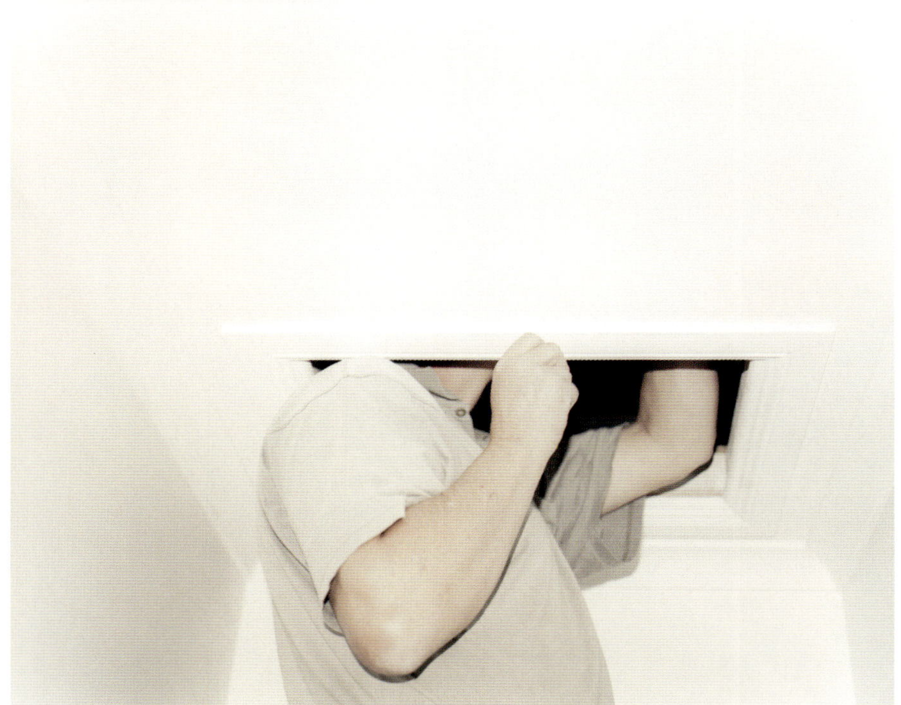

Top left: *Fire in the Forest #1*, 2013; above: *Pacific View #1*, 2013;
above right: *My Father Looking for Something*, 2012

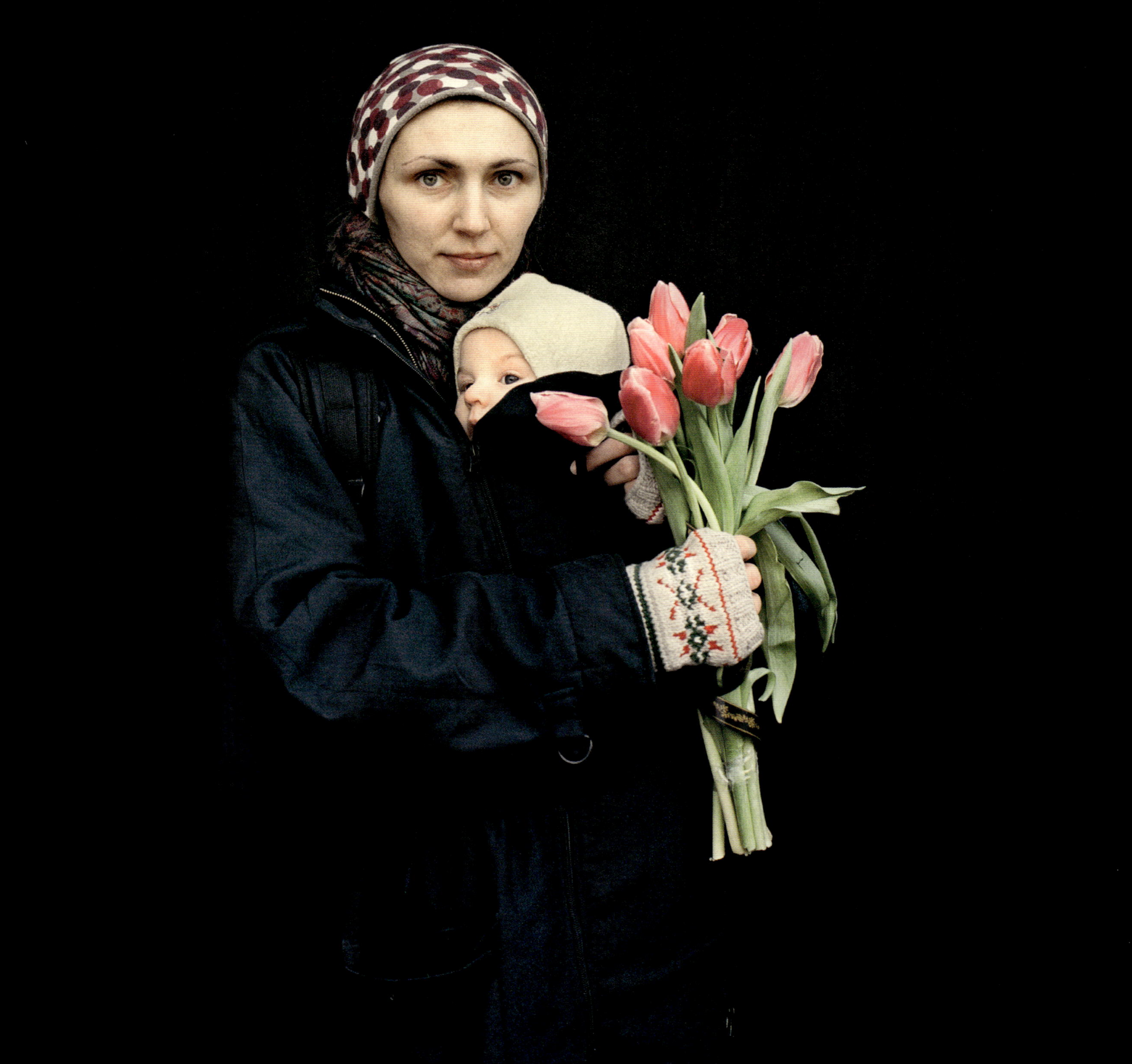

ANASTASIA TAYLOR-LIND

...

Taylor-Lind's eye was drawn to the women who brought flowers to commemorate the fallen

...

Anastasia Taylor-Lind embarked on her photographic career in 2004 after graduating in documentary photography from the University of South Wales, Newport. Her first story after she graduated was *No Friends but the Mountains: Women of the PKK*. She travelled to the autonomous region of Iraqi Kurdistan to photograph female guerrilla fighters along the Turkish border. Their story of resistance in the face of human rights atrocities towards Kurds captivated Taylor-Lind, and seeds were sown for her future work.

Taylor-Lind went on to photograph crucial subjects, which included Nagorno-Karabakh's *Birth Encouragement Programme*, women of the Cossack resurgence and, rather more unexpectedly, Siberian supermodels. She sought out isolated female communities surviving within deeply patriarchal societies. Her work has appeared in newspapers and magazines all over the world.

In 2014, Taylor-Lind travelled to Ukraine to continue a long-term project, *Negative Zero*, about Europe's declining populations. En route to Donetsk she encountered the growing dissent and protest movement in Kiev, just as the government collapsed and the nation later erupted into war. She stayed in the capital for a month, setting up a makeshift studio in the square that became the stage for the uprising, and after which her subsequent book was named: *Maidan: Portraits from the Black Square*.

Her photographs of Ukrainians wearing home-made body armour, with weapons crafted from table legs and metal rods, came to signify the conflict. Bloody Thursday, 20 February 2014, saw the worst day of violence, with up to seventy people killed in the space of a few hours. President Yanukovych fled to Russia two days later, and after this the square was filled with thousands of mourners joining the protestors. Taylor-Lind's eye was drawn to the women who brought flowers to commemorate the fallen. In her words, 'Men fight wars; women mourn them'.

Taylor-Lind also created a series of videos on her iPhone, shooting through the viewfinder of her Bronica camera, and filming fascinating vignettes of the photographer/subject exchange, which at first she shared via Instagram. On reflection, she realized their creative potential, and created an installation, alongside the portraits, at Four Corners Gallery in London. She continued her social media collaboration with a series called *Welcome to Donetsk*. She bought a cache of touristic Ukrainian postcards and used them to commemorate individuals killed in the war by sending the name of someone who had died to a complete stranger. Recipients responded by sharing images of the postcards inside their homes, lighting candles at shrines and by researching the victim.

Ironically, it was this experience of war in Ukraine, as well as perhaps the near-fatal experience of her close friend, the photographer Guy Martin, who was seriously injured in the mortar blast in Libya that killed Tim Hetherington and Chris Hondros, which helped Taylor-Lind to understand, or recalibrate, her own boundaries. The frontline would not be a target for her, though her desire to work with people living in conflict would endure. Her decision to focus on how people dressed during this turbulent time in Ukraine, as a significant detail of a much larger story, pointed towards a new direction in her work.

The publication of *Maidan: Portraits from the Black Square* (GOST, 2014) propelled Taylor-Lind into a different league, professionally. In December 2014, she became a TED fellow, and the following year she received a 2016 Nieman Journalism Fellowship from Harvard University, and is now a Logan non-fiction fellow at the Carey Institute for Global Good in New York where she is writing about war, photography and picturing contemporary conflict.

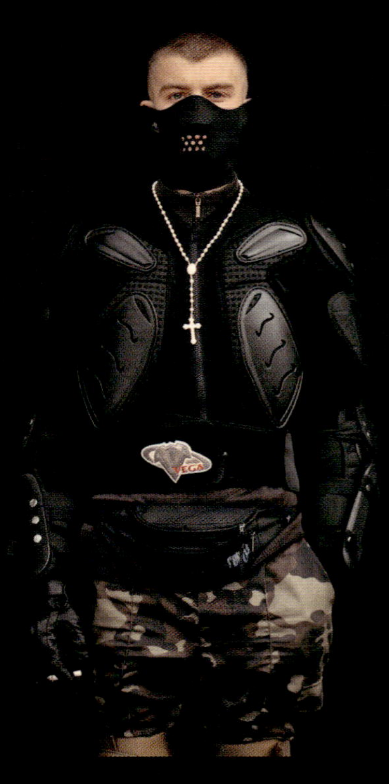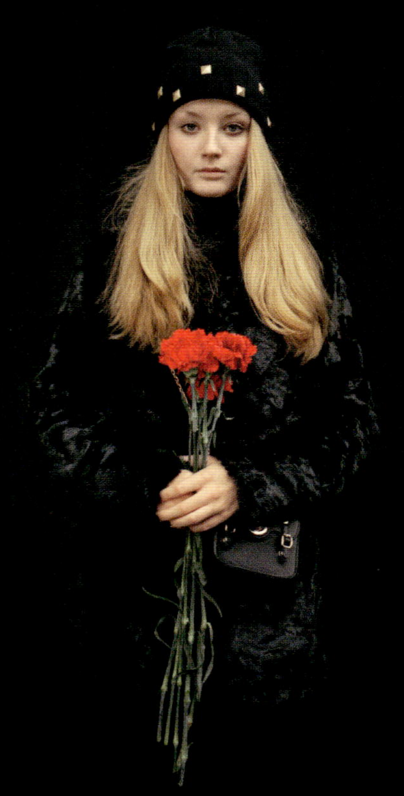

Left: *Eugene*, 2014; right: *Anastasia*, 2014; both *Maidan* series

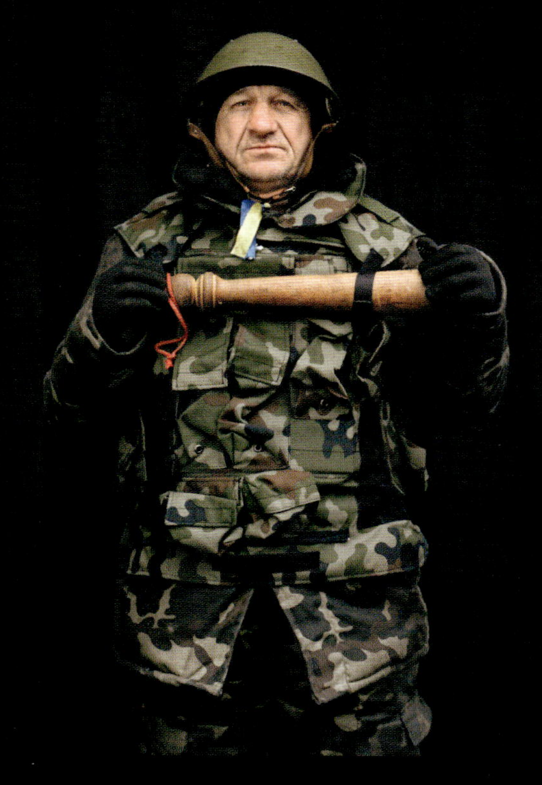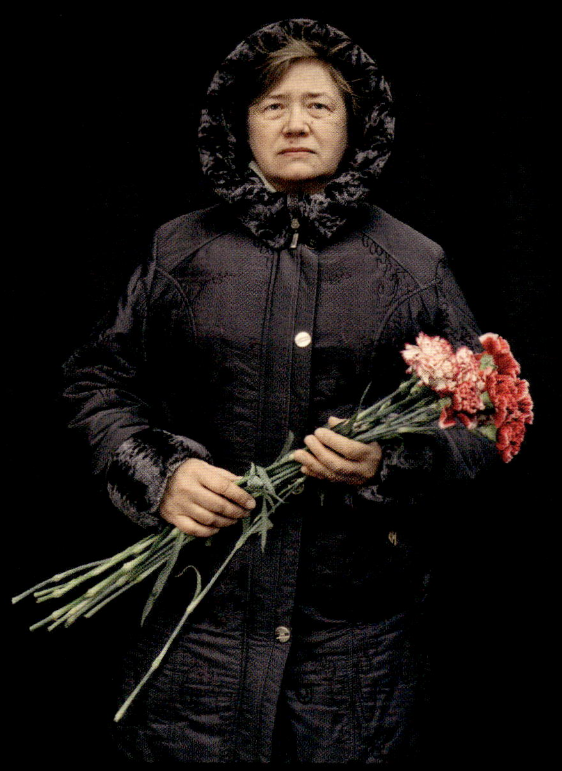

Left: *Ivan*, 2014; right: *Elena*, 2014; both *Maidan* series

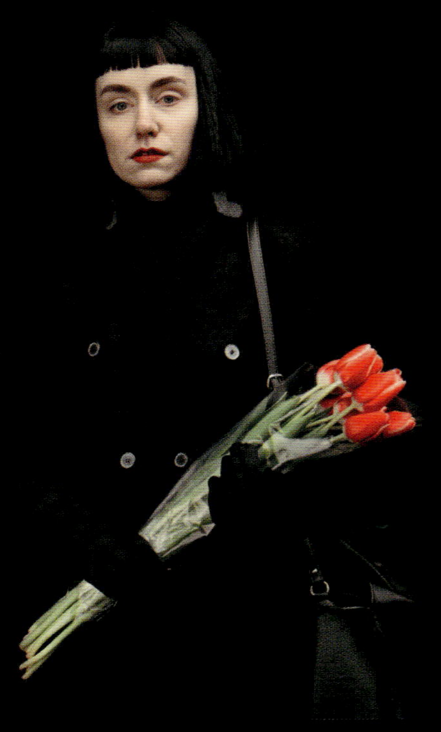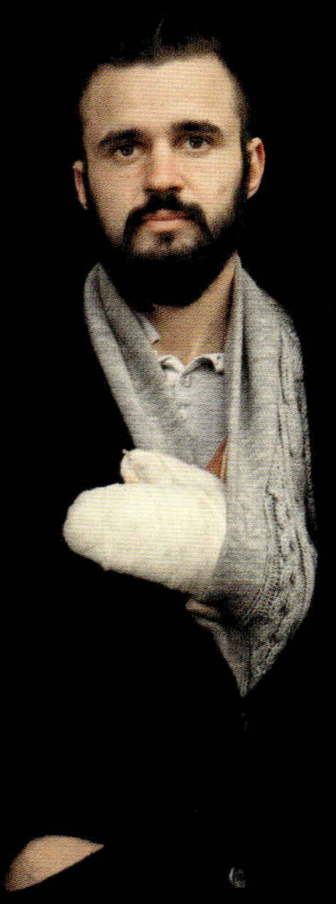

Left: *Hanna*, 2014; right: *Maxim*, 2014; both *Maidan* series

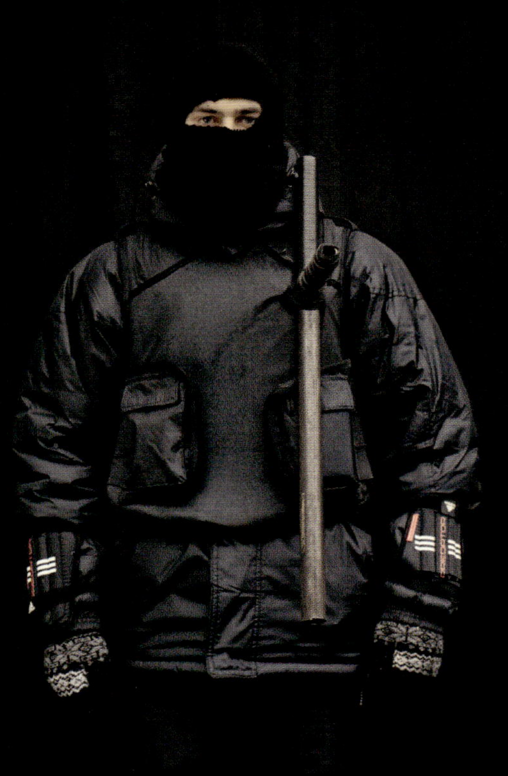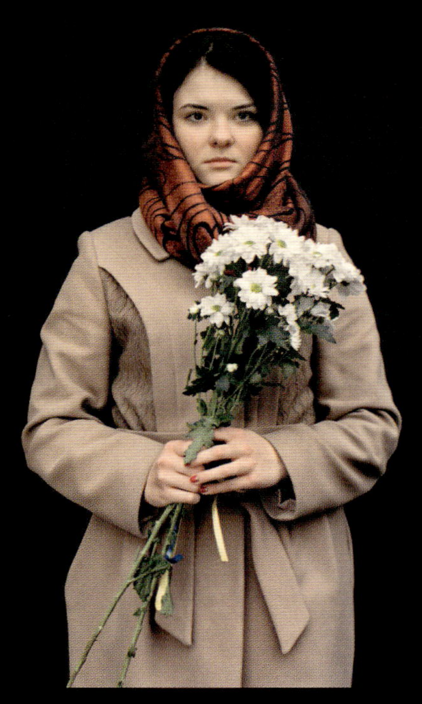

Anastasia Taylor-Lind   107

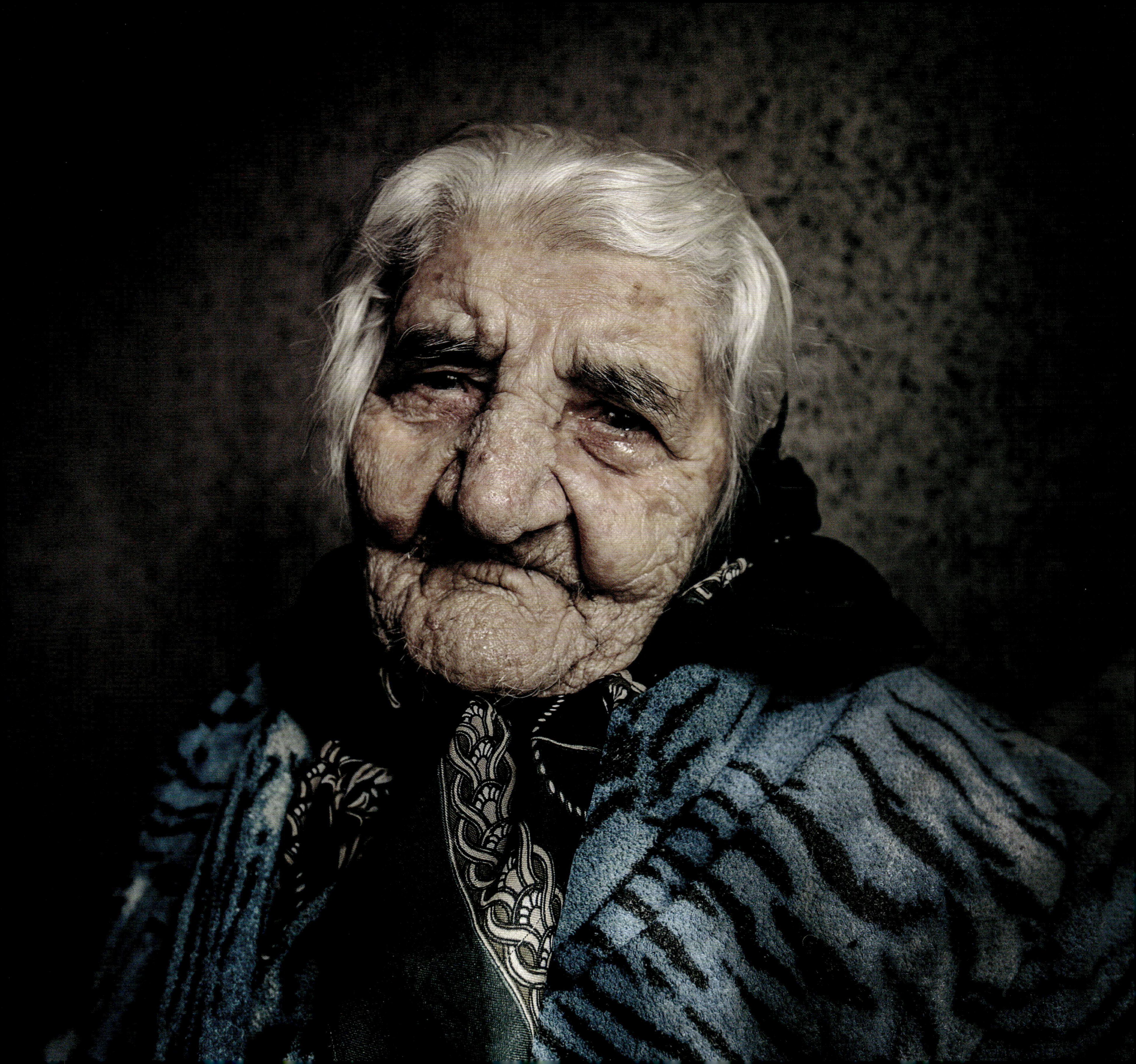

DIANA MARKOSIAN

...
personal experiences of loss, separation, memory, time and healing ebb and flow through Markosian's work
...

Diana Markosian's project *1915* documents Armenian survivors of the controversial genocide of the Christian minority carried out by the Ottoman empire in 1915. During a presentation of the work in 2015 a man in the audience was visibly tearful and the room was charged with emotion. He spoke passionately about his parents' struggle to come to terms with their experience and diaspora, and how Markosian's work was both a timely and important reminder of a conflict infrequently discussed.

It is this power to affect people deeply that underscores Markosian's short but illustrious career as a storyteller. The emotional complexity of the work belies her age, encompassing a maturity and depth in its research and conception which is both admirable and startling. From documenting Chechen girls coming of age in a country growing increasingly conservative, to commemorating the atrocities of the 2004 Beslan school massacre, her work is charged with tangible empathy, acute attention to detail and compassion.

Markosian's approach to photography is inextricably linked to her own background and heritage. Born in the former Soviet Union to Armenian parents, Markosian's mother fled to the US with her two young children, severing ties with her husband. Markosian was seven years old. Fifteen years later, she travelled to Armenia, where her father had resettled, in an attempt to rebuild a relationship; the moving results of which were widely acclaimed and won the Firecracker Photographic Grant in 2014.

Personal experiences of loss, separation, memory, time and healing ebb and flow through Markosian's work; the perfect prelude to dealing with the sensitive issues of *1915*. Using voter registration records, Markosian found ten survivors scattered across varying parts of Armenia. She located three of them, Movses, Mariam and Yepraksia, and asked them to describe their homeland. She photographed the regions they talked about – places they hadn't seen since they were fleeing as frightened children 100 years ago.

Borrowing notions of site specifics, a strategy utilized by Susan Meiselas in her seminal work from Nicaragua, Markosian enlarged the landscapes to ten-foot-wide billboards so her subjects could immerse themselves in their birthplace once more. These huge prints still hang in the bedrooms and living rooms of these survivors and Markosian continues to support the community, her role now shifting from documentarian to active participant. She says, 'For me this isn't a casual interaction. Very little is about photography now, it's about being with them.

I wanted to establish a relationship where I was more than a photographer – I really wanted to give back.'

This project is far more than just a visual document; it's brought necessary closure to a number of victims. Woven together with dispatches from the consulates, who tried to alert the government to the unfolding atrocities, newspaper clippings, archival images, hand-drawn maps and the survivors' powerful experience of seeing their birthplace again for the first time, Markosian finds her role as an accomplished storyteller.

The experience has been a spiritual journey for Markosian too, an opportunity to connect with her Armenian heritage and to articulate a personal response to the genocide. It has been said that it's impossible to make a body of work which isn't in some way a personal reflection of the artist. This is certainly true in Markosian's case.

Yepraksia, now 109, escaped by crossing the river to present-day Armenia, 2015, 1915 series

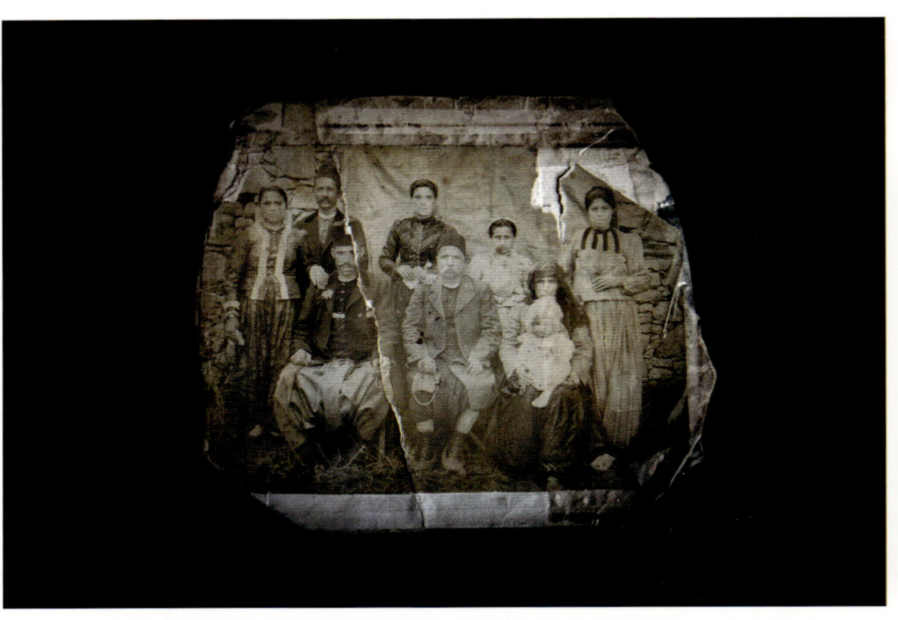
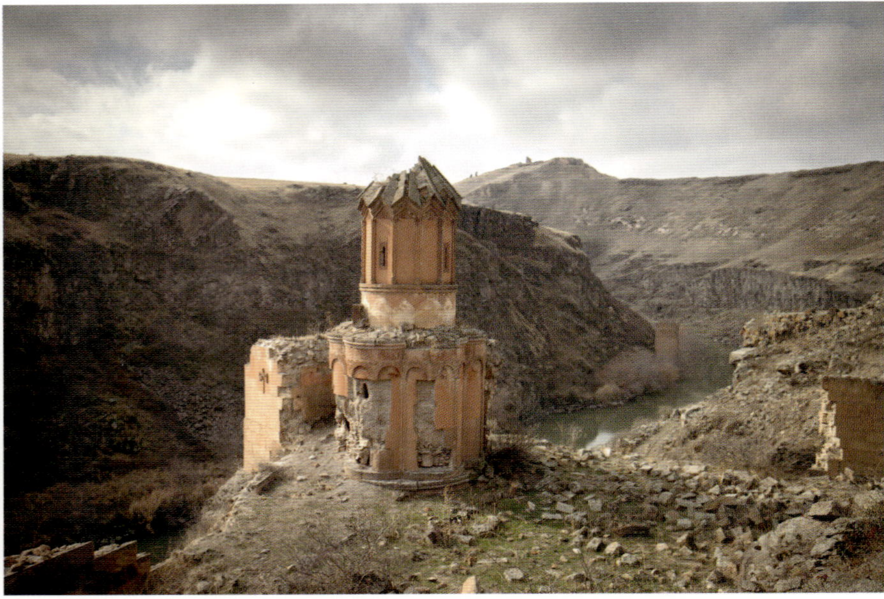
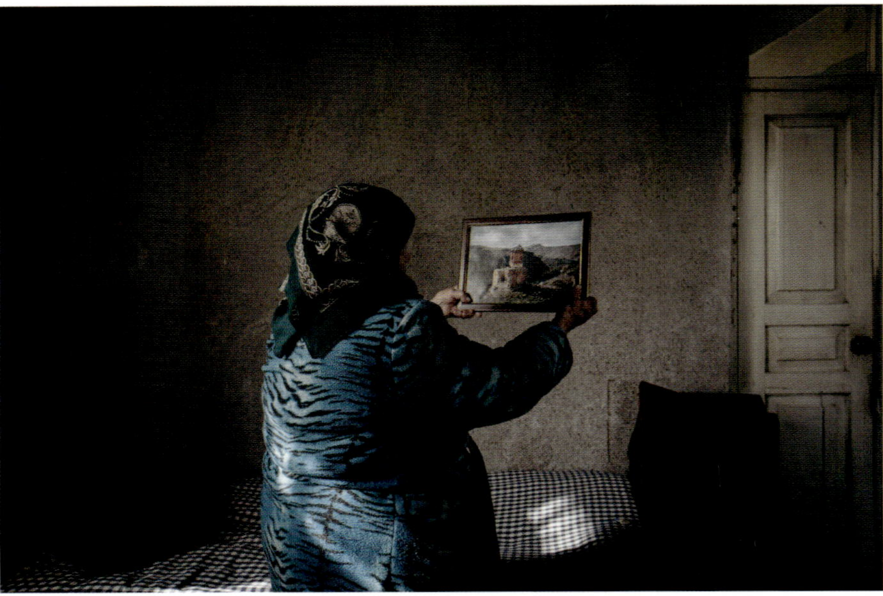
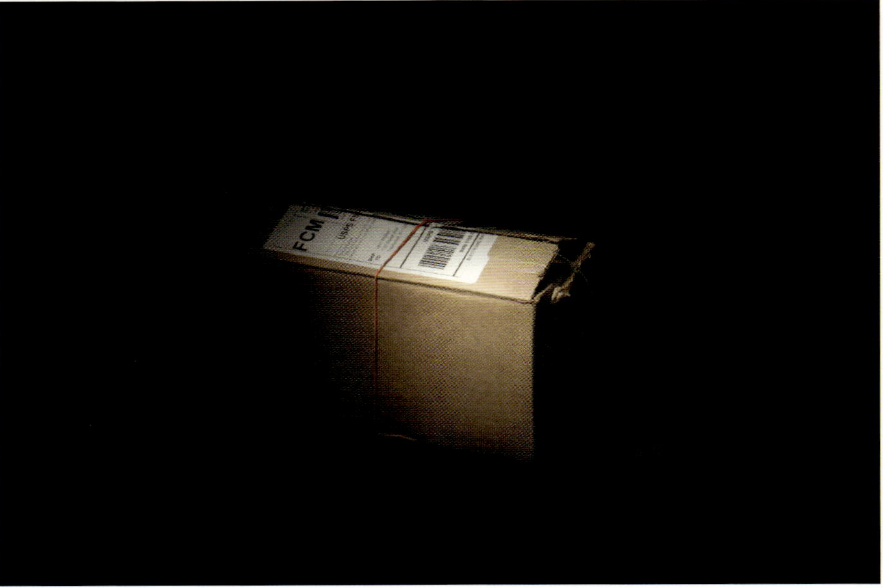

Top left: A portrait of the Sargsyan family in Kütahya, Turkey, before they were deported in 1915, 2015;
top right: The waters of the Akhurian River trace the border between present-day Turkey and Armenia, 2015;
above left: Yepraksia holds an image of the place she recalls escaping from with her family, 2015;
above right: A box containing the remains of Armenians from Der Zor, Syria, 2015; all *1915* series

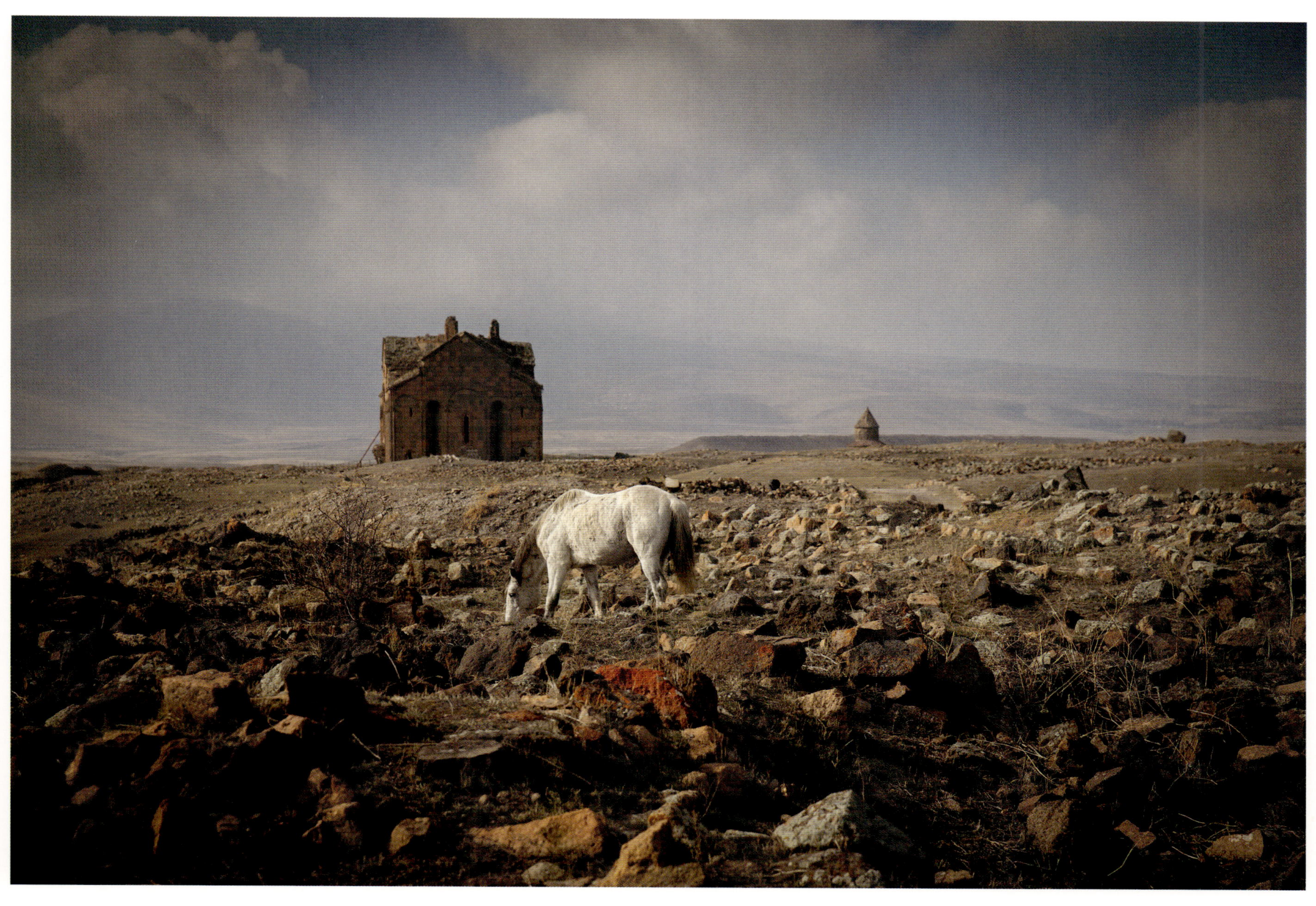

Once the capital of an ancient Armenian kingdom, Ani was known as the 'city of 1,001 churches', 2015, *1915* series

Diana Markosian   111

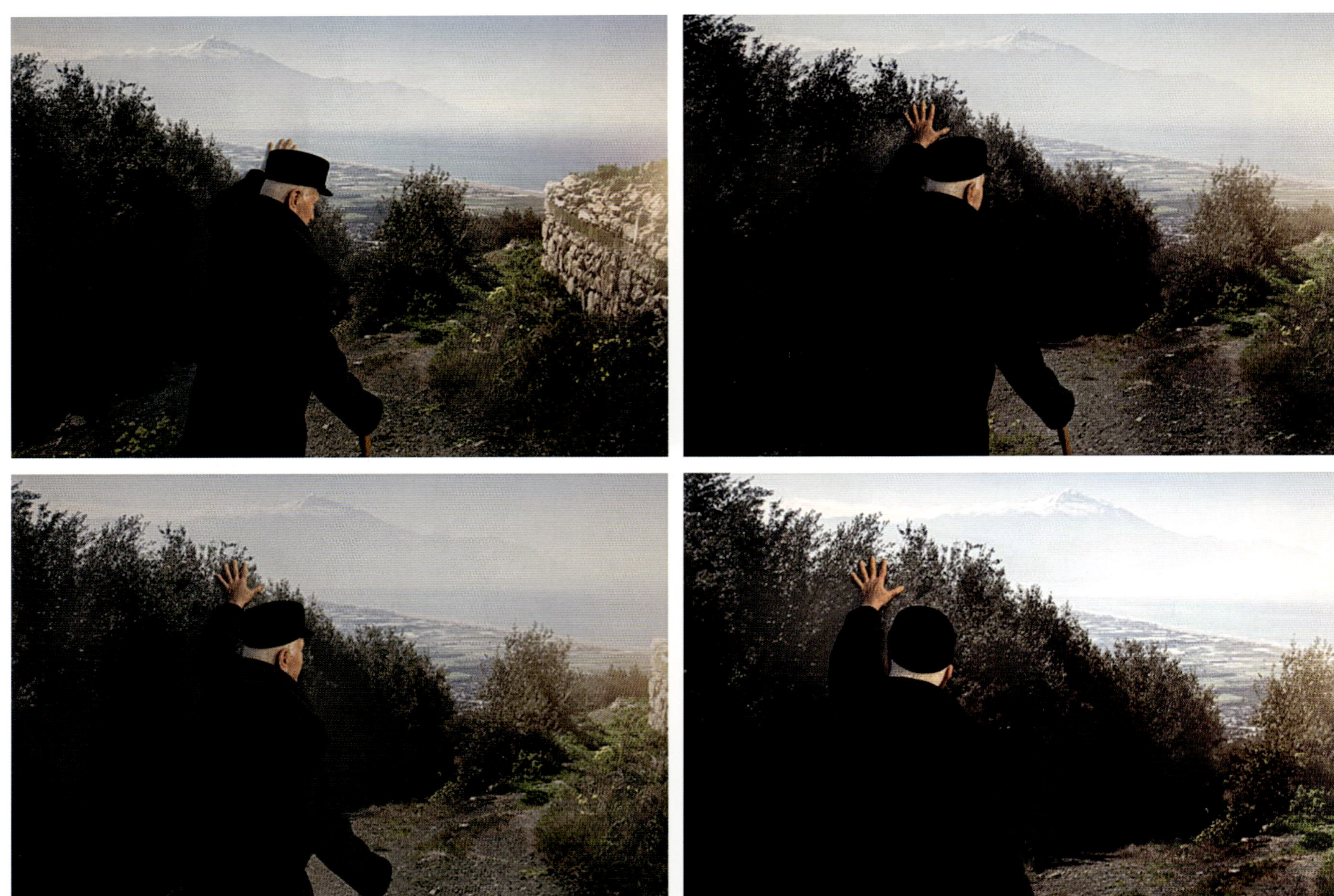

     Firecrackers

Movses and his father fled from the village to Syria in 1915. A century later, he asked me to go back to find
his church, and to leave his image there. A century later, a part of Movses found it too, 2015, *1915* series

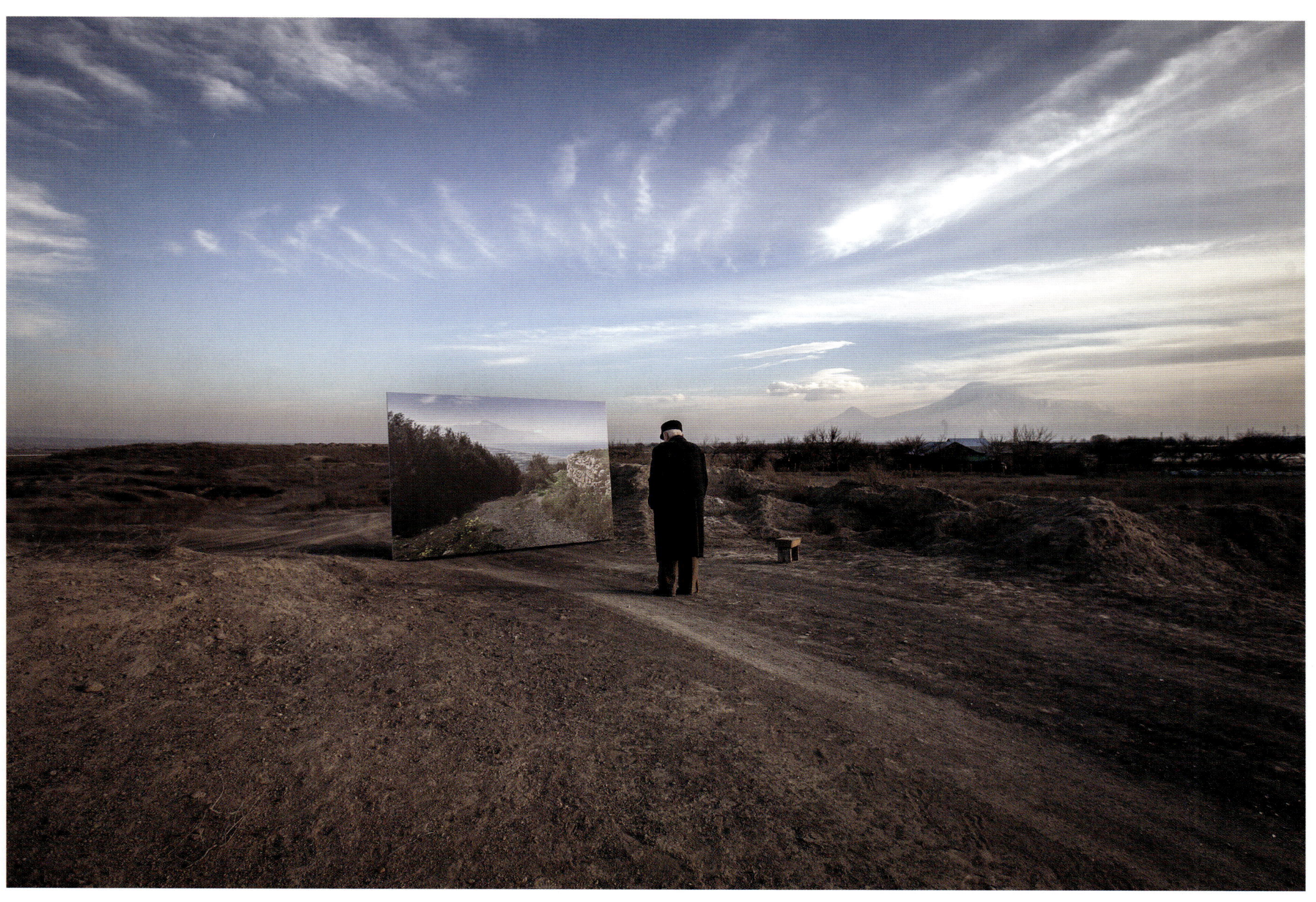

Movses, aged 105, slowly approaches a life-size landscape. He pauses, looks at the image,
and begins to sing: 'My home... My Armenia', 2015, 1915 series

Diana Markosian   113

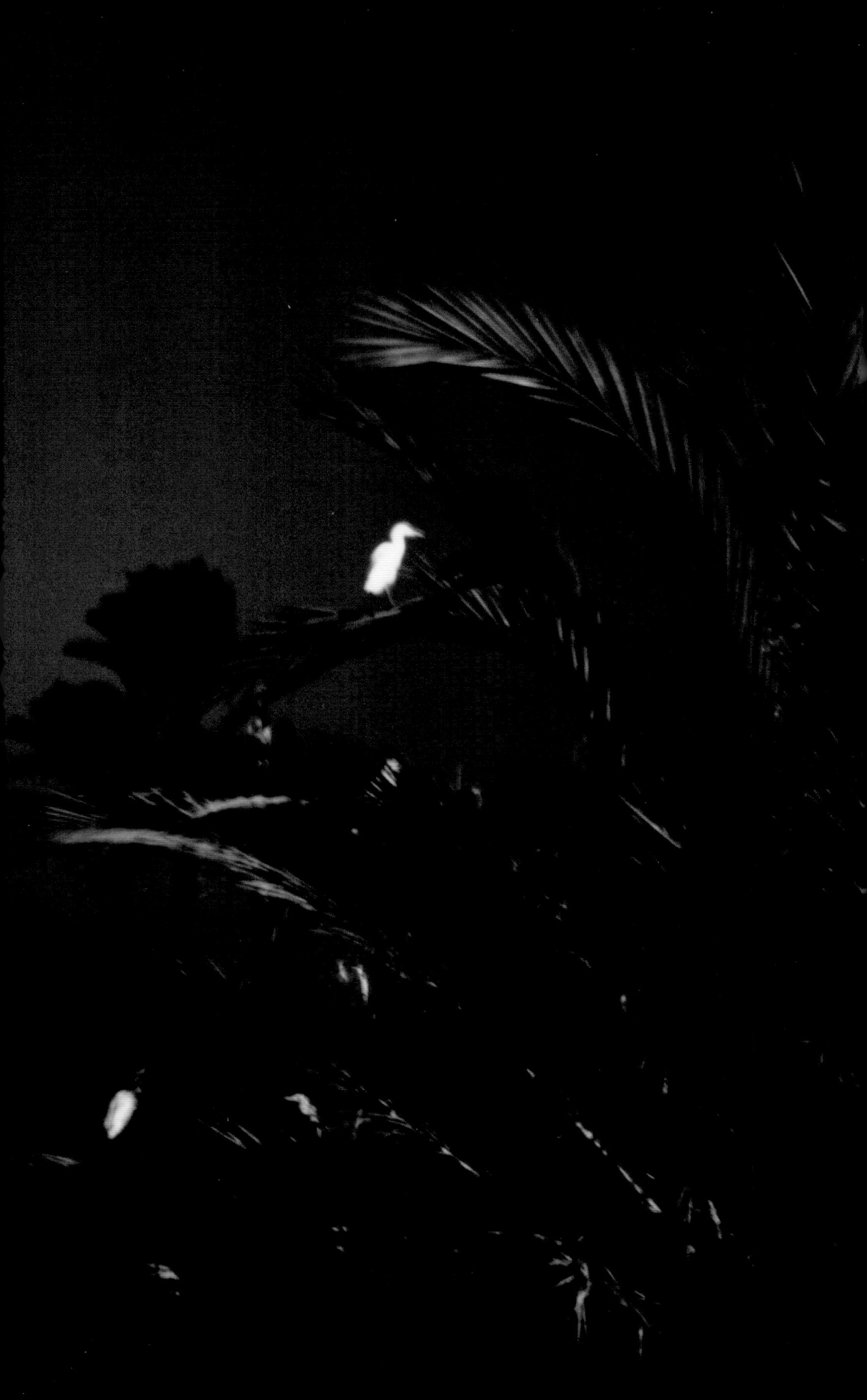

DIANA MATAR

...
Matar inhabits night time,
when anxiety peaks,
when the day's certainties
disappear, when nothing
can be seen clearly
...

The question of how to photograph something that cannot be seen was the beginning of Diana Matar's photographic practice for her work, which ultimately became a book, *Evidence*. The ongoing answer has involved creating a new language of loss and absence with her camera. Working exclusively with film, Matar uses predominantly black-and-white imagery to invoke a state of perpetual mourning.

Her quest for the invisible is borne out of a political disappearance. Her father-in-law, Jaballa Matar, was a Libyan opposition leader during Gaddafi's regime. He was abducted in Egypt, where the family lived, and taken to the notorious Abu Salim prison in Tripoli. He was never seen again. This missing haunts every image. Fabric spread out on a street could wrap a corpse, should one materialize. A chair, dappled with pools of light, will support only a ghost, since it has no seat. Trees that always grew together can now only be pushed further and further apart, blowing in the wind. Her photographic language is laden with sorrow, yet its rhythm is fluid, carried along by birds in the night.

The book *Evidence* (Schilt, 2014) uses archival images and text, as well as colour photographs, as it moves out of the specifics of the family's loss and into the horribly abstract realm of political assassination. Matar makes images of trees or plants as witnesses to known killings; these living things are all that remain. In this way, she travels to Rome, to dark alleys in Tripoli, silently collecting evidence. She also uses very long exposures, sometimes as long as an hour, as she stands, watching, waiting. The mode is night time, when anxiety peaks, when the day's certainties disappear, when nothing can be seen clearly. The story was born in darkness and continues to dwell there. As the words at the end of the book remind us: Jaballa is still missing.

Matar has been working on a new project, continuing her pursuit of invisible human rights violations, on different territory. She is locating sites in the US where citizens were shot by police in 2015 and 2016. For *This Violent Land*, Matar is focusing on California, Texas, Colorado, New Mexico, Arizona and Oklahoma; almost half of all killings by police in the US during this time occurred in these six western states. Here we see in her imagery signs of separation, obfuscation and entanglement. Matar enters vast landscapes and bigger skies, and seizes fragments. In her pieces of sky, her remnants of desert, we become witness to the American dream turned sour. The images, though mute, pulsate to the rhythm of a protest song. We become passengers on a long road trip, in that great photographic tradition, watching as another America unfolds before us. As Jack Kerouac said of Robert Frank, Matar got eyes.

Taken as a whole, Matar's beautiful photographs pursue a kind of aesthetic justice. By creating a visual language for the invisible, her work makes an important contribution to how we remember contemporary conflict and iniquity, and those whose bodies, one way or another, were caught in the crossfire.

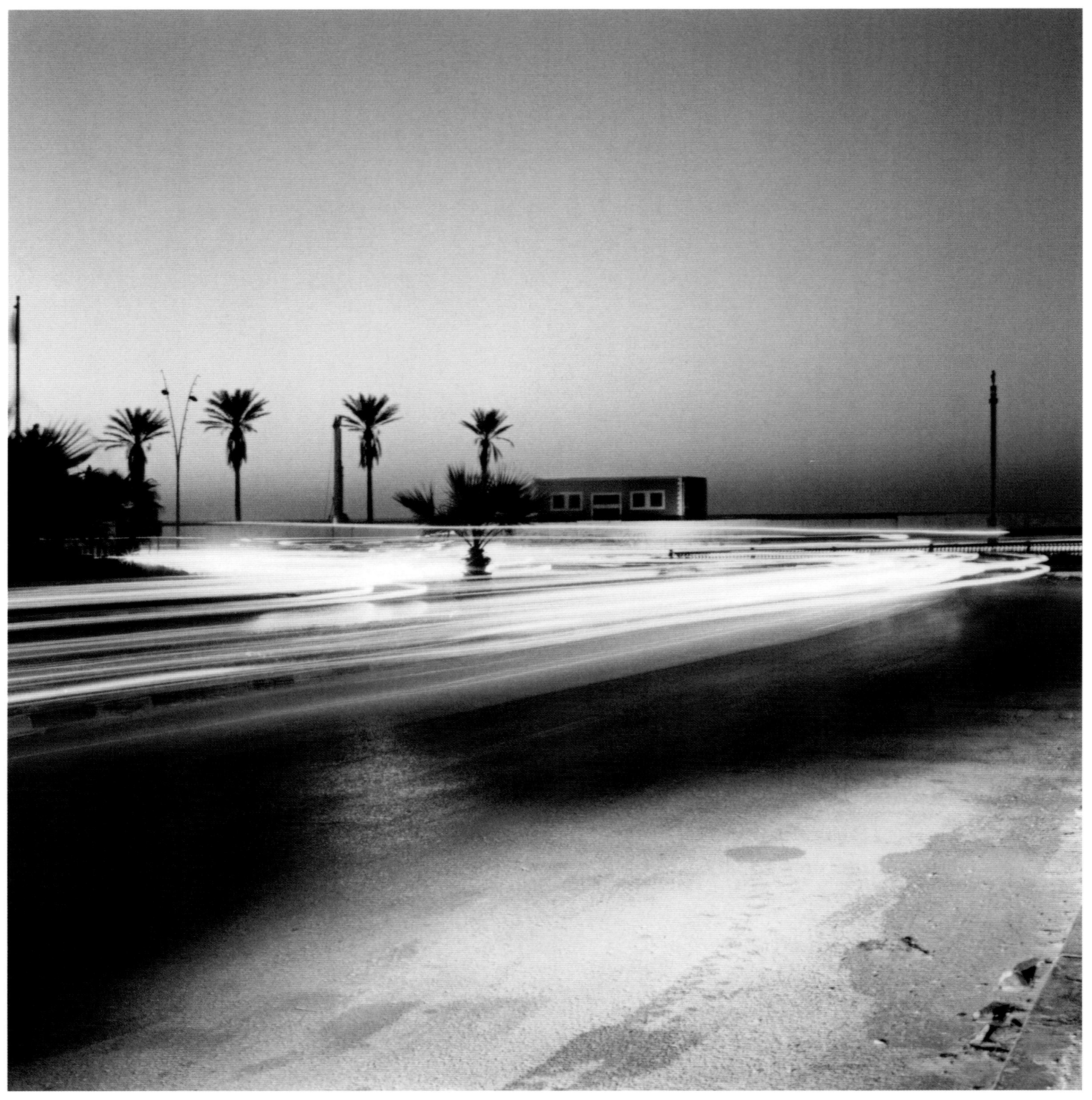

Evidence 5, 2012, Benghazi, Libya

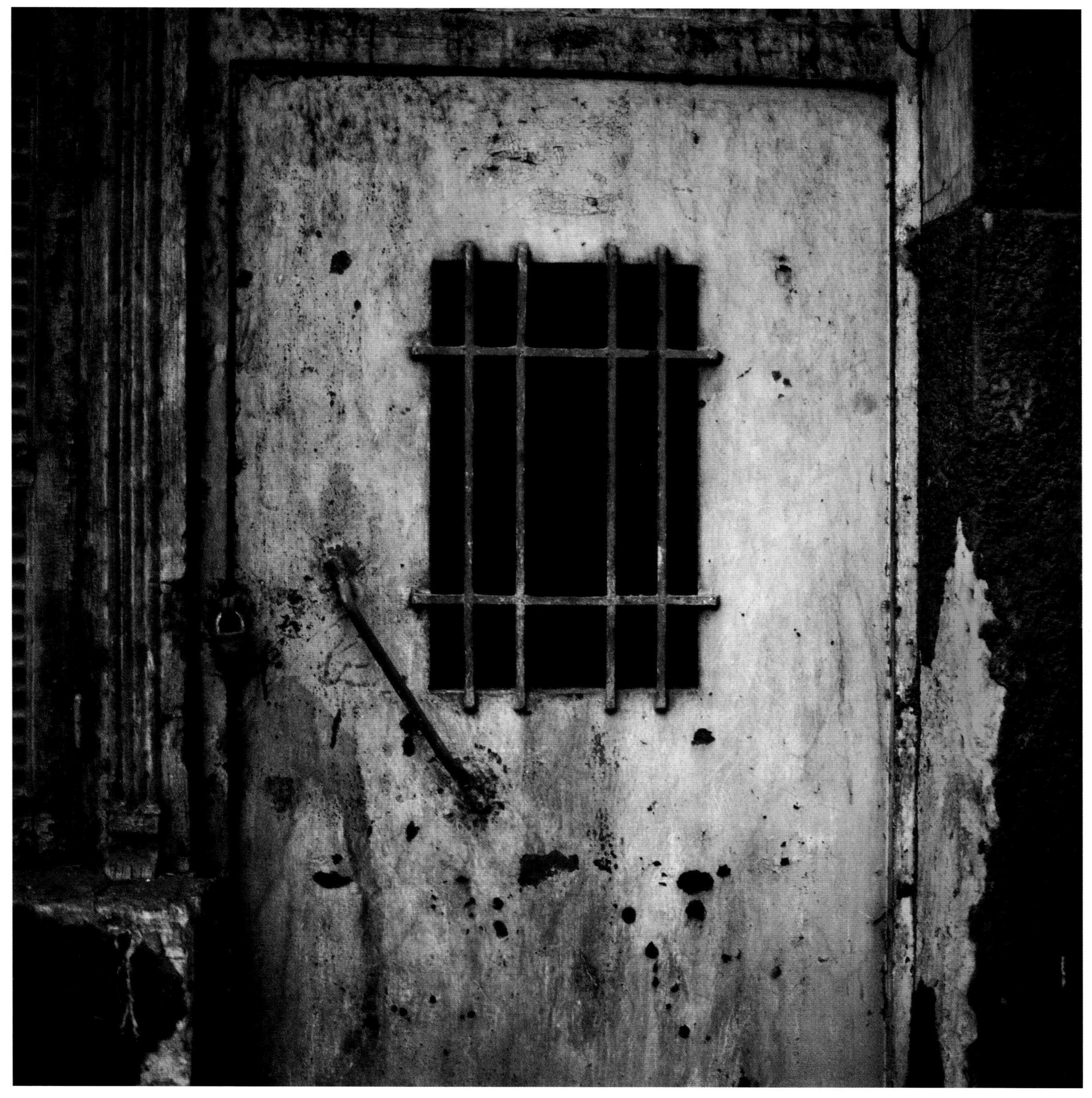

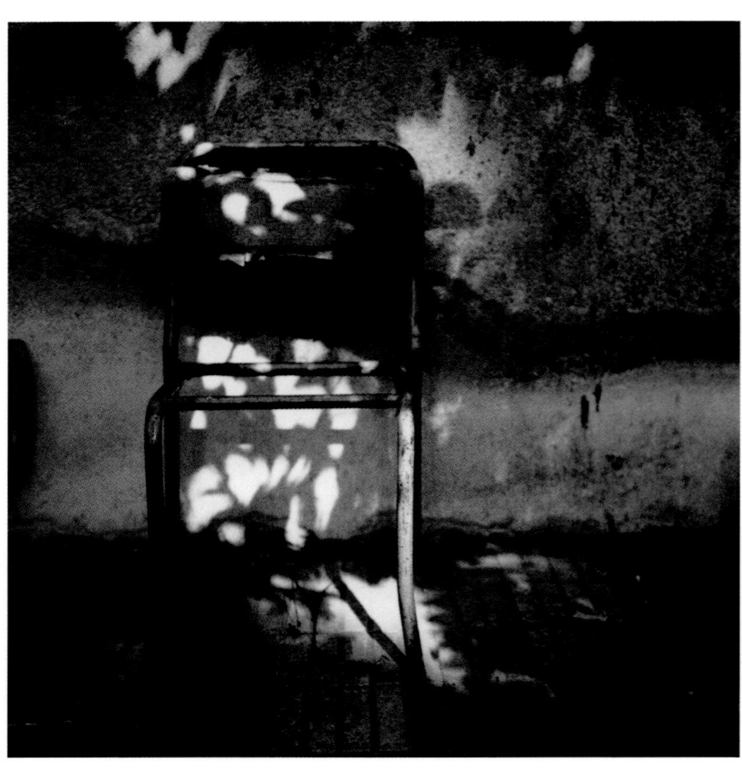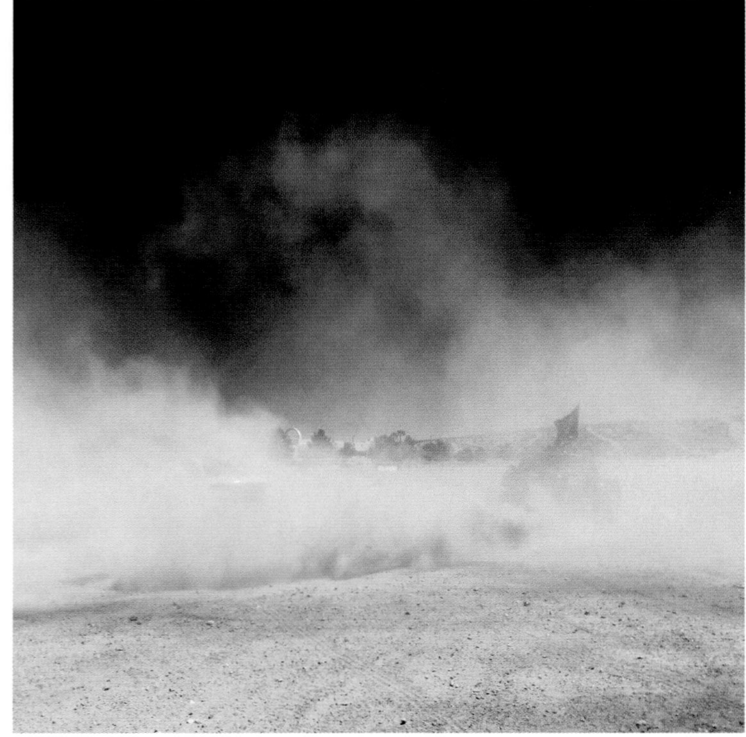

Above left: *The Chair*, 2010, Cairo, Egypt;
above right: *Wild Wild West This Violent Land 8*, 2016, California, USA

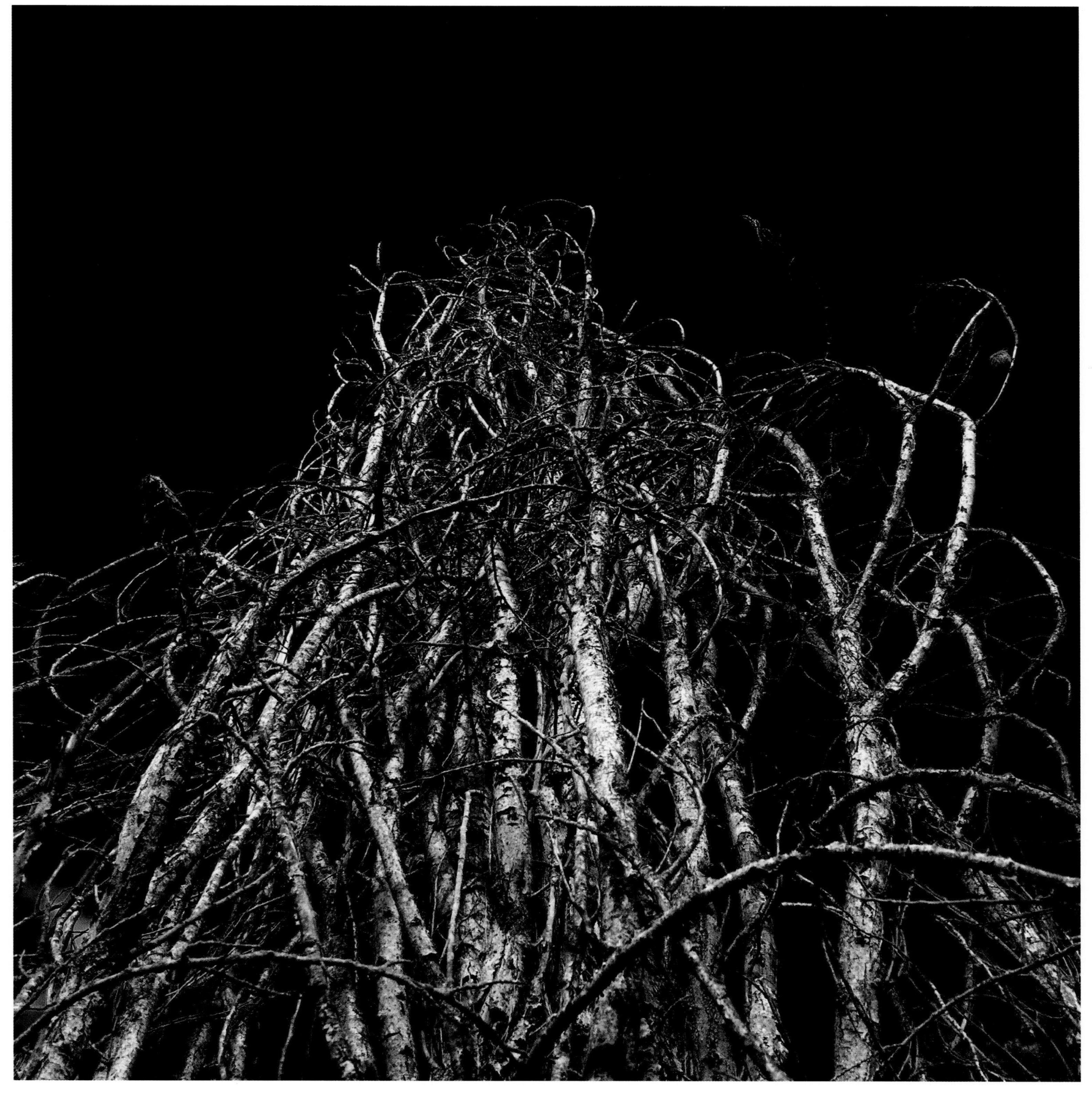

Wild Wild West This Violent Land 9, 2016, California, USA

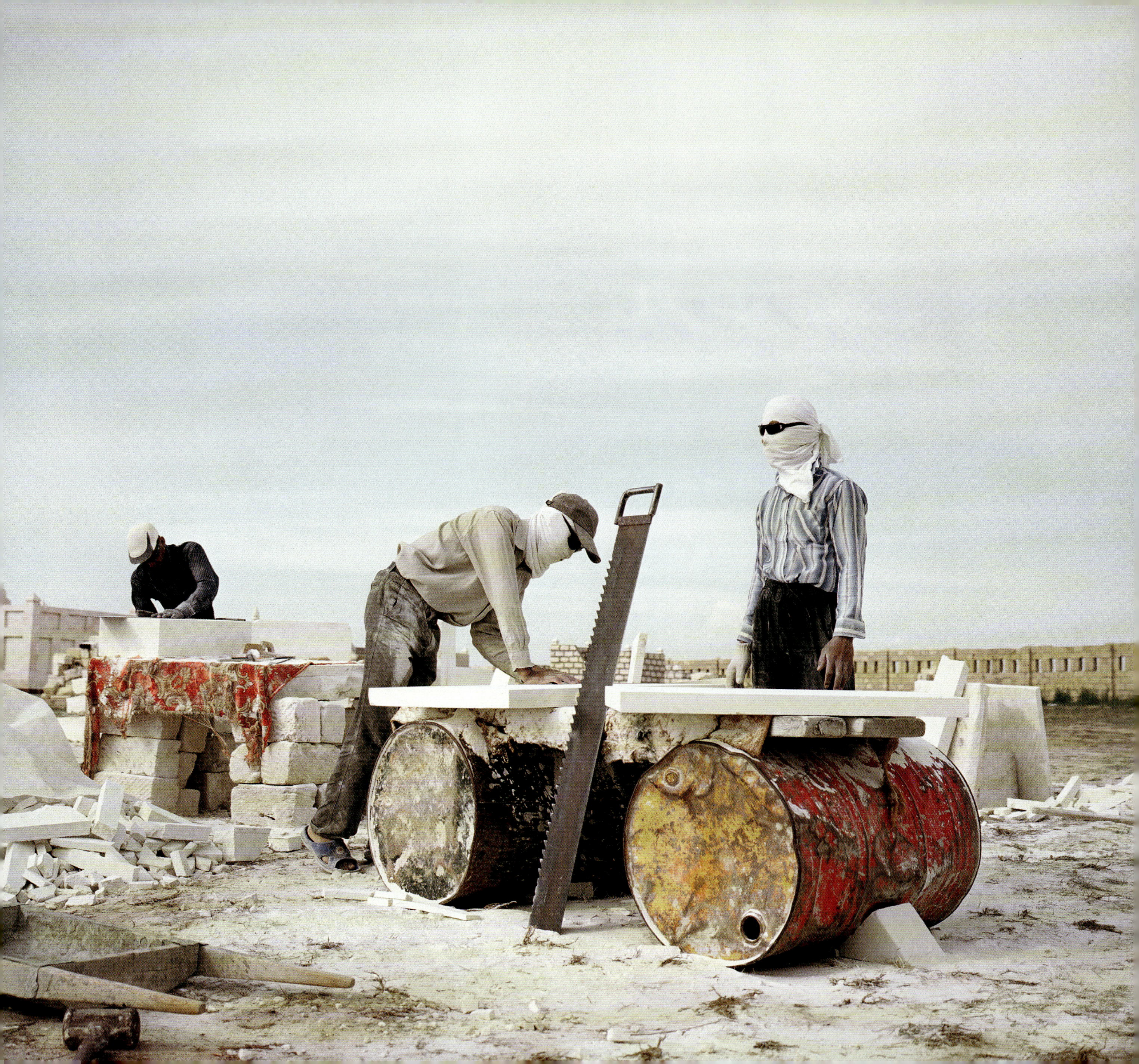

CHLOE DEWE MATHEWS

...

It is as though her work is snatched from
a dream, at once macabre and celestial
...

Chloe Dewe Mathews' rich engagement with people and place is what situates her work in the genre of documentary photography, but also in the great British tradition of landscape artists.

Dewe Mathews studied at the Ruskin School of Art, Oxford. She travelled to the Caspian region after graduation and the body of work she made there was inevitably seen through an outsider's eye, but her gaze was not fleeting. She has found herself compelled to return, and her continued insights make for a profound body of work, which is also hugely visually appealing. Her understanding of the myriad ways in which people are linked to the land offers an original commentary on a little-explored and much-contested region.

Her photographs pose questions of ownership, such as who owns the Caspian since the dissolution of the USSR in 1991. Is the Caspian a sea or a lake? These are important questions because they determine its potential division, which, in turn, is significant because of the wealth of the region's resources such as oil, gas, salt and uranium.

Dewe Mathews has made connections between geology and geography, which collide exquisitely in the arresting image of Uzbek migrant workers along the Caspian coast of Kazakhstan constructing

mausoleums for the newly oil-rich middle class. As she notes, 'Even the landscape of the dead is transforming as a direct result of the nearby oil industry.' It is as though this particular image is snatched from a dream, at once macabre and celestial. Another image, of a body bathing in oil, seems to transcend everyday activity. Perhaps Dewe Mathews has captured the timelessness of the practice – the therapeutic properties of the oil in Naftalan, Azerbaijan, were mentioned in the 13th-century diaries of Marco Polo.

The kinds of pictures made by Dewe Mathews are those that command a longer look. Her aesthetic is the antithesis of the snapshot, as was most evident in her body of work *Shot at Dawn*, shown as part of Tate Modern's *Conflict, Time, Photography* exhibition in 2014, alongside work by Sophie Ristelhueber and Diana Matar. Dewe Mathews researched sites where as many as a thousand British, French and Belgian soldiers were executed for cowardice or desertion in the First World War. Working with historians, her aim was to be as meticulous as possible in finding the exact location of each killing. She describes it as the opposite of war photography, in that it is the landscape itself that is the witness. Widely acclaimed as a haunting body of work, *Shot at Dawn* was an important addition to cultural memory,

and served to honour men murdered by their own battalions, for the most part because they were so traumatized by the atrocities of war that they could no longer function as soldiers themselves.

Most recently, Dewe Mathews has been documenting the River Thames in the UK, from its source to its mouth. With *Thames Log* she has continued her documentation of ritual, and once again brings her watchful eye to documenting the very essence of community through a sense of place.

Koshkar-Ata 'City of the Dead', Kazakhstan, 2010, *Caspian* series

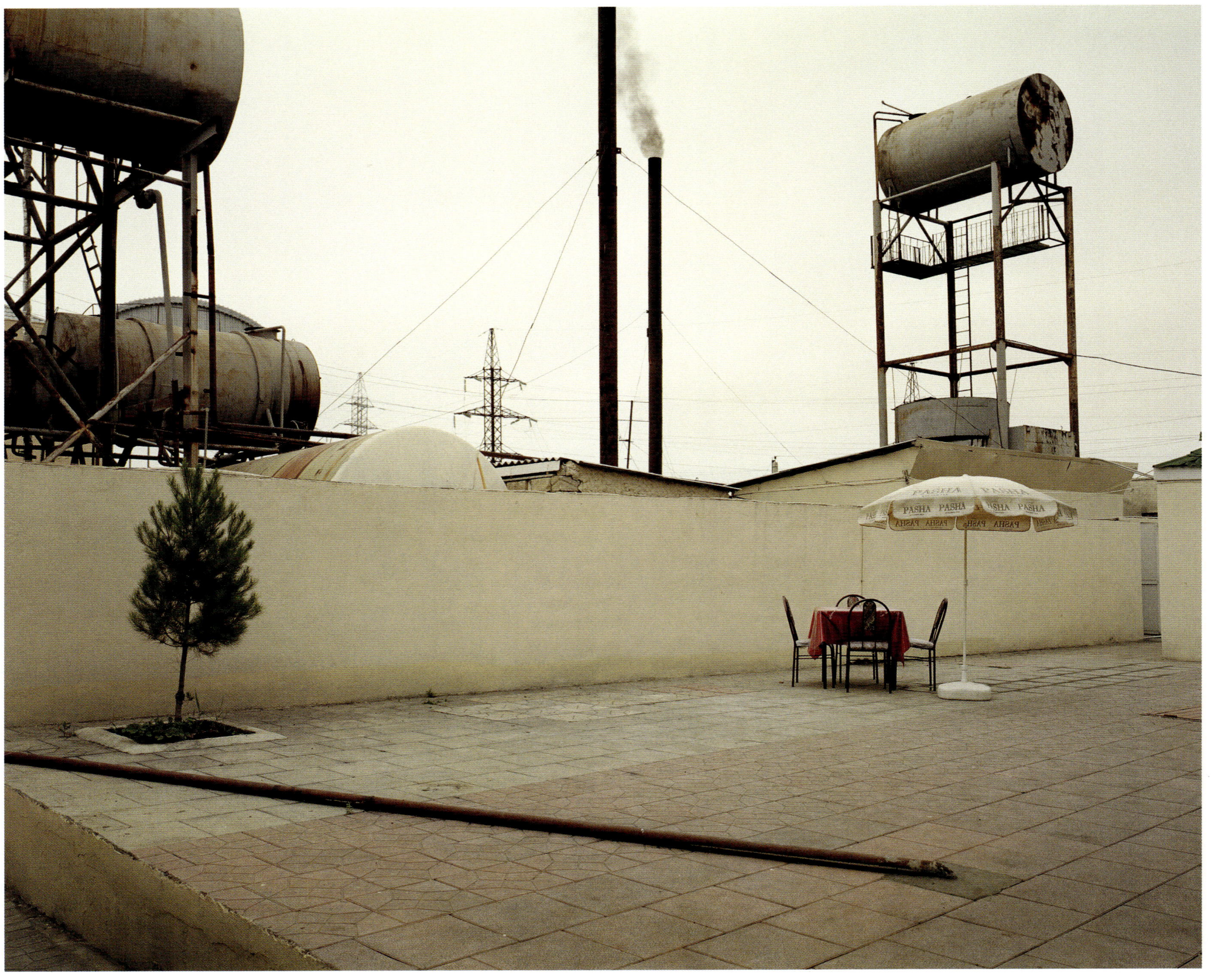

Café at the Shafa Sanitorium, Azerbaijan, 2010, *Caspian* series

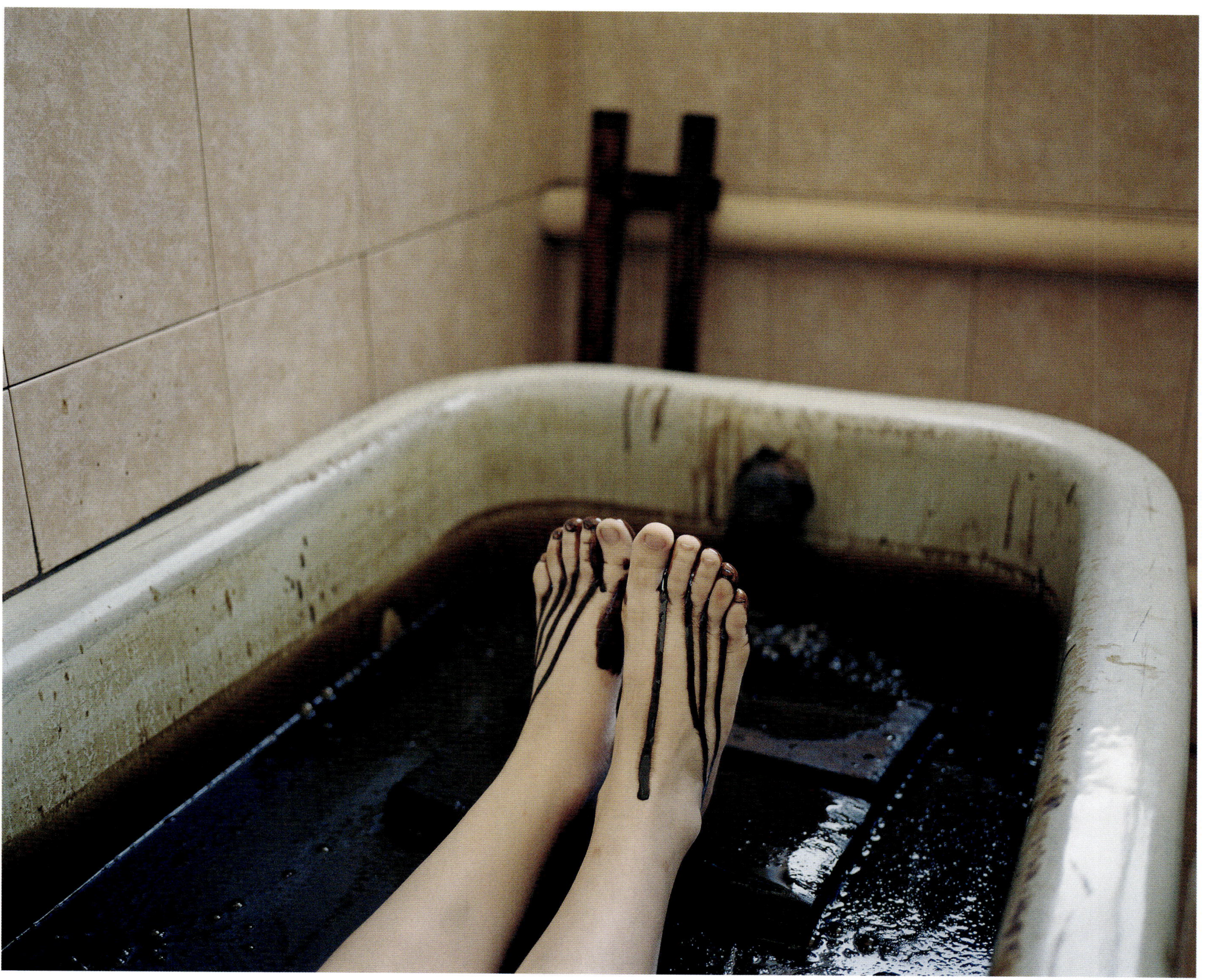

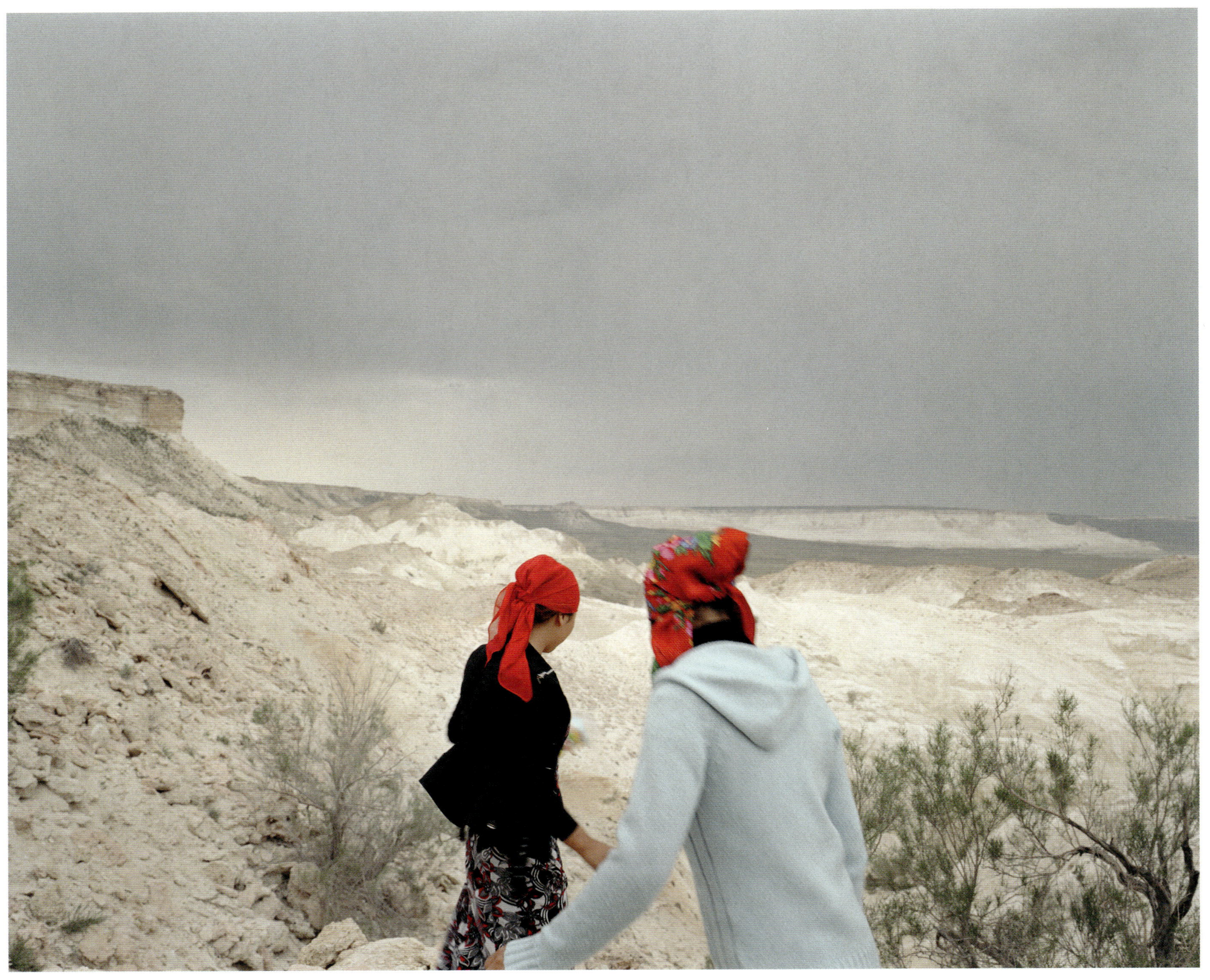

Beket-Ata Necropolis, Kazakhstan, 2010, *Caspian* series

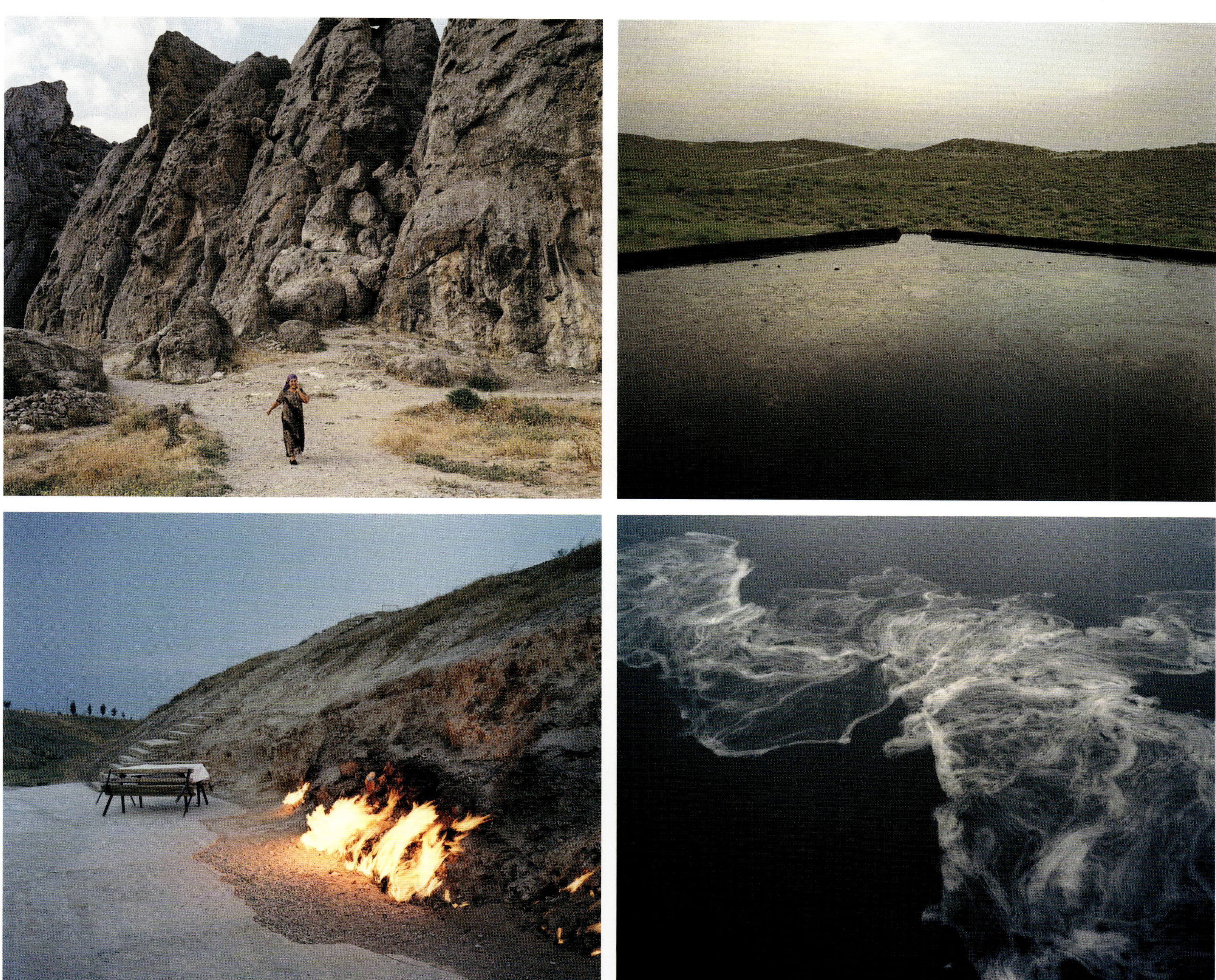

Top left: Beshbarmaq holy mountain, Azerbaijan, 2012;
top right: reservoir for the 'miracle oil', Azerbaijan, 2010;
above left: Yanar Dag, the 'burning mountainside', Azerbaijan, 2012;
above right: water turns to ice on the Epiphany, Russia, 2012; all *Caspian* series

Chloe Dewe Mathews

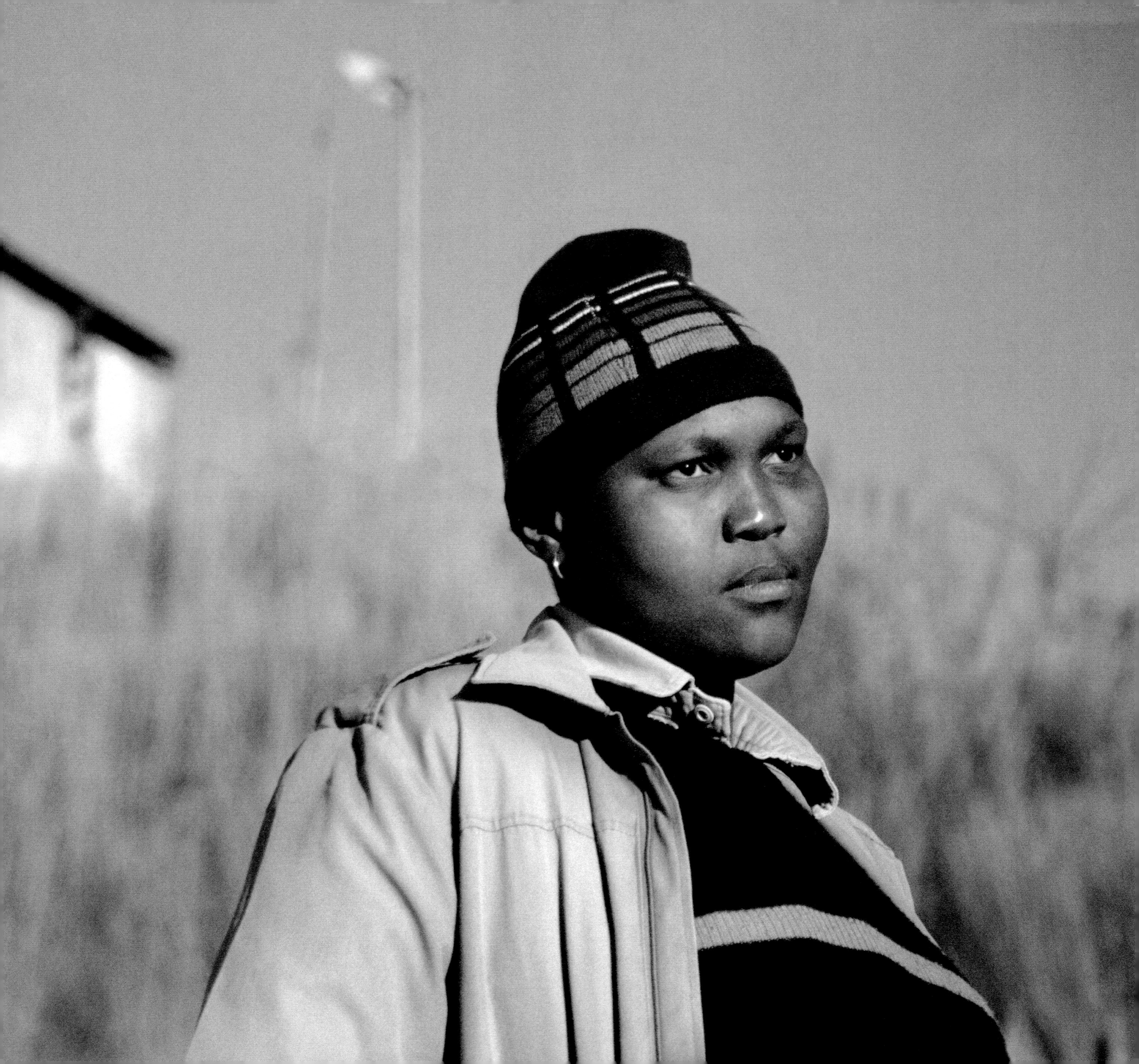

ZANELE MUHOLI

... Her subject matter has not become less urgent, and because Muholi's evolution as an artist – as well as a visual activist – is profound ...

The statement 'I am a visual activist before I am an artist' defines the practice of Zanele Muholi, who began documenting the community of LGBTI people in South Africa in 2002.

On winning the International Center of Photography (ICP) Infinity Award for Documentary and Photojournalism in 2016, Muholi said that she was on the brink of suicide when she realized photography was a way in which she could effect change. Her compelling black-and-white portraits, *Faces and Phases,* which are at once tender and direct, have played a vital role in the representation of a relentlessly marginalized community, subject to the most brutal and horrific violence as a consequence of their gender identity and sexual orientation. Muholi dedicates her work to 'black lesbian survivors and victims of hate crimes'. Despite greater constitutional protection, attacks remain frequent and deadly.

Although Muholi has been creating work for over a decade, and is now recognized and honoured internationally, we feel it is essential to include her in this book because her subject matter has not become less urgent, and because Muholi's evolution as an artist – as well as a visual activist – is profound and hugely influential. She brings to South African gay culture a 'queer black visibility', which is otherwise lacking.

Faces and Phases is underpinned by such questions as, 'What does an African lesbian look like?' and 'Can you identify a rape survivor by the clothes she wears?' Muholi's approach to direct portraiture has echoes of the essential identity photograph black people had to carry under the apartheid regime, the brutal system of racial segregation enforced by the governing National Party since 1948, into which the artist was born, and which continued until 1994. Over the years, she has amassed an archive of people who, if they even survived, might have been erased from history.

Her decision to include herself in her work as a sustained endeavour (she had published a self-portrait in her 2006 book *Only Half the Picture*) came after a burglary at her home in Vredehoek, a suburb of Cape Town, in 2012. It was a targeted attack, a hate crime on art, in lieu of the body, and served to extinguish five years' worth of work. It was only through reflecting on the physical harm inflicted on so many friends and neighbours that Muholi found the strength to continue working at all. Through her self-portraits, Muholi has been able to experience a dialogue with herself, perhaps for the first time. She was always 'inside' the work, but now, perhaps, the work is inside her too.

Another vital aspect of her work is Muholi's desire to 'reclaim blackness'. The practice of art and documentary photography has been predominantly a Western one, and a wealthy one, and, to quote Muholi, black people are usually photographed by 'the other', which inevitably causes further 'othering'. Muholi's gaze upon the people who share her life and beliefs is as gentle as it is powerful. It's an unusual combination. She describes the photographic process as 'healing', enabling her to move away from the pain that has informed her life. What is transmitted to the viewer of her photographs is how the potency of one woman's sustained gaze has enshrined the positive legacy of a generation.

Busi Sigasa, Braamfontein, Johannesburg, 2006, *Faces and Phases* series

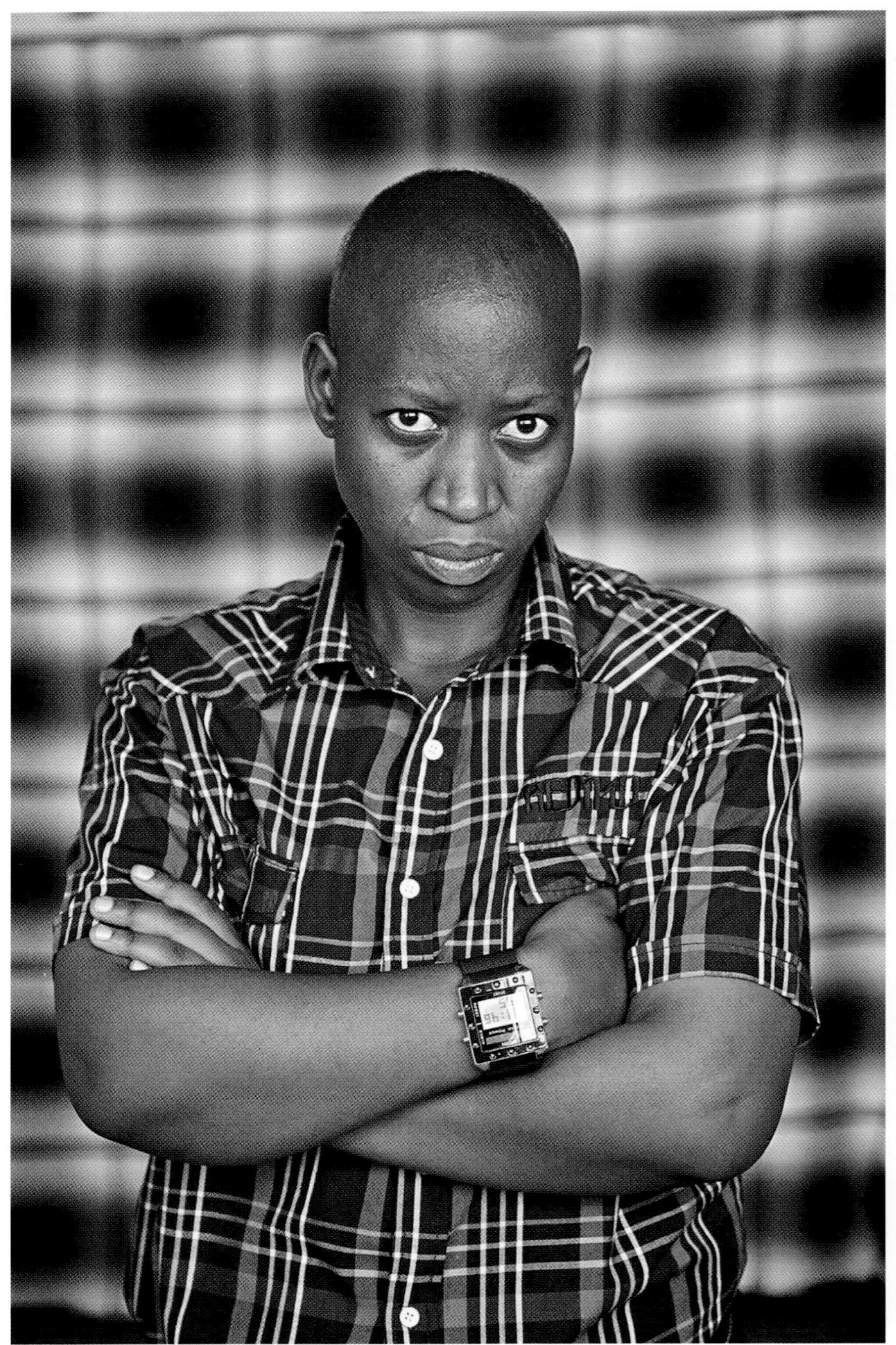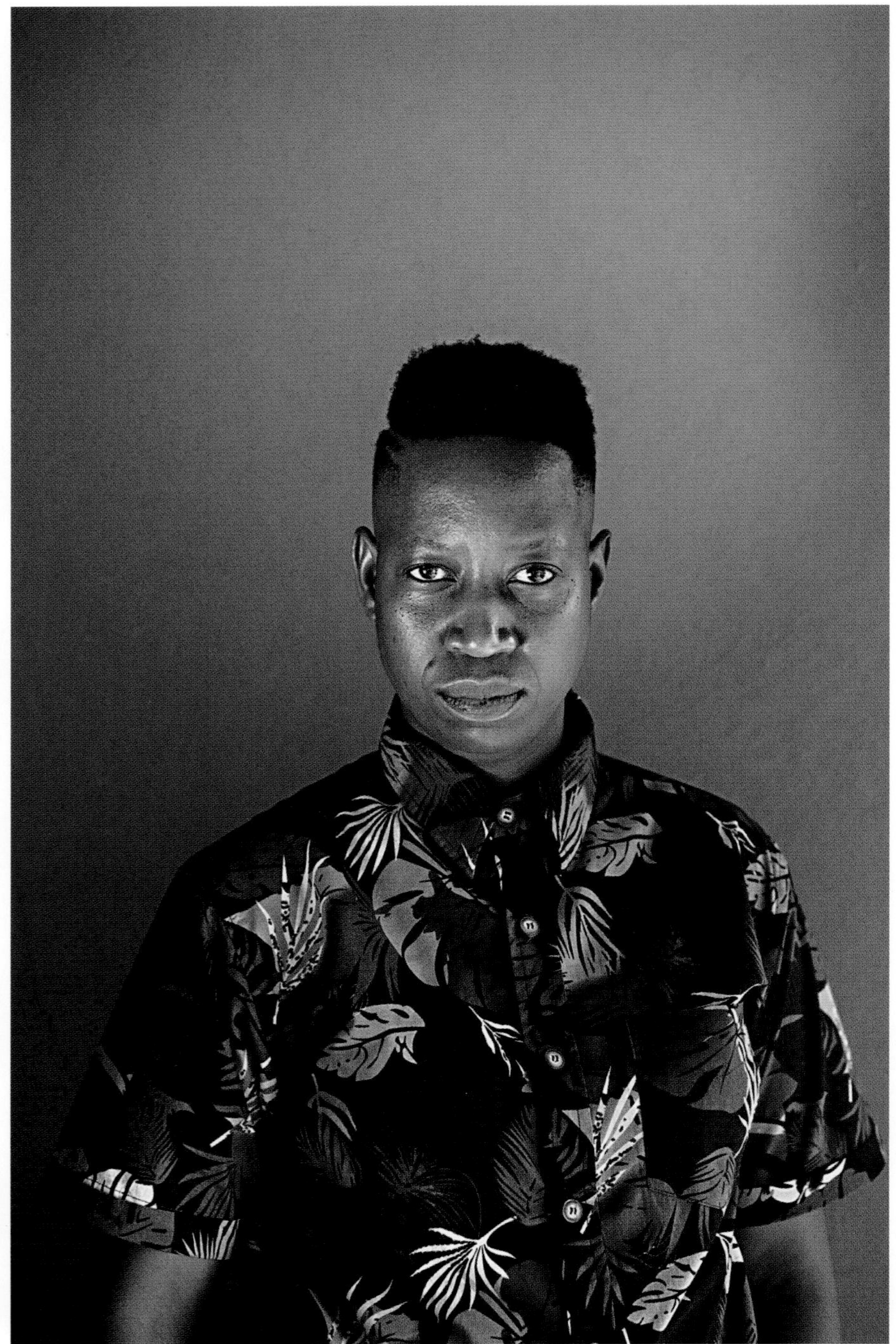

Above left: Ntobza Mkhwanazi, BB Section, Umlazi township, Durban, 2012;
above right: Ntobza Mkhwanazi, BB Section, Umlazi township, Durban, 2016;
both *Faces and Phases* series

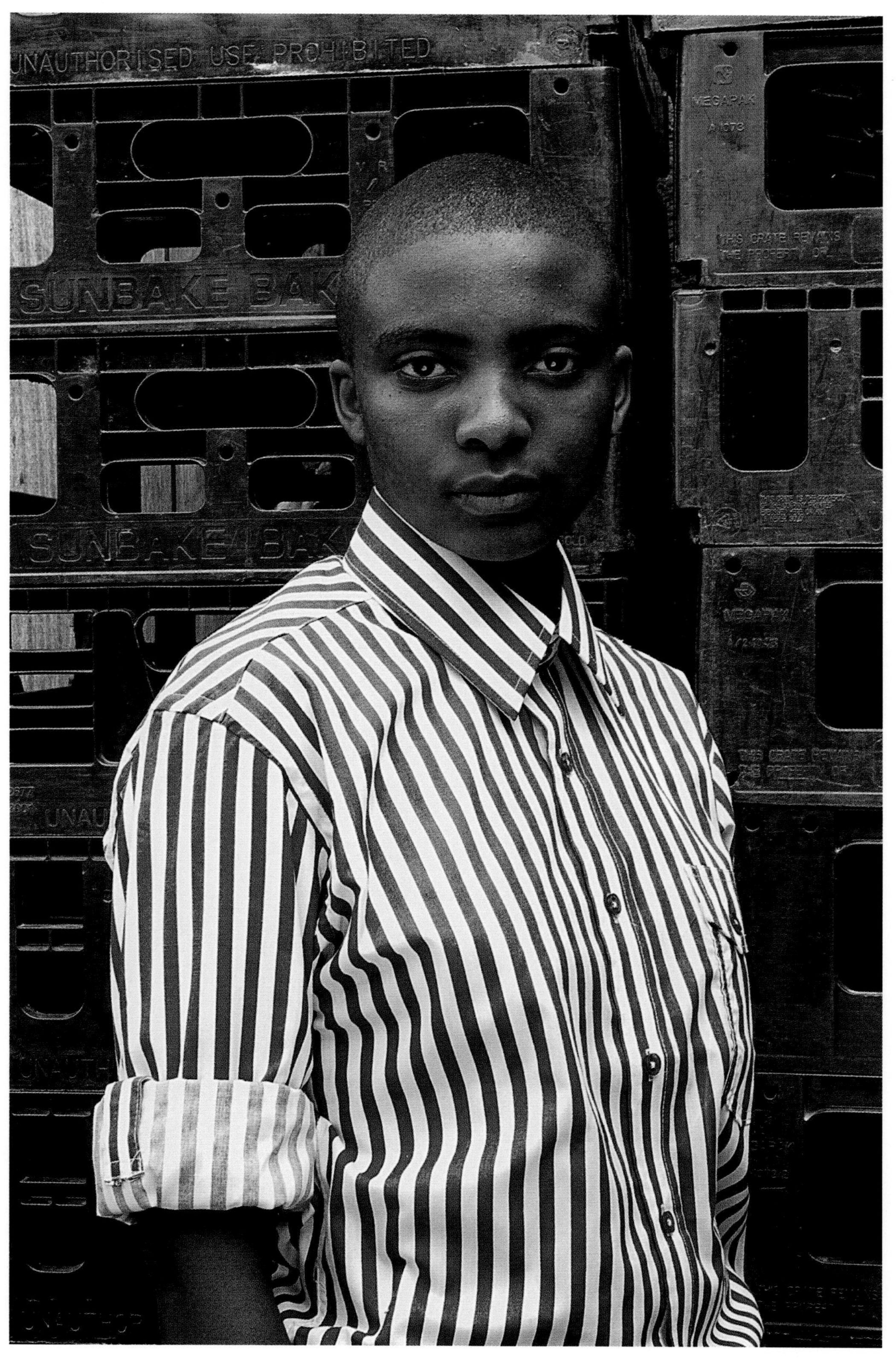

Lerato Dumse, KwaThema, Springs, Johannesburg, 2010, *Faces and Phases* series

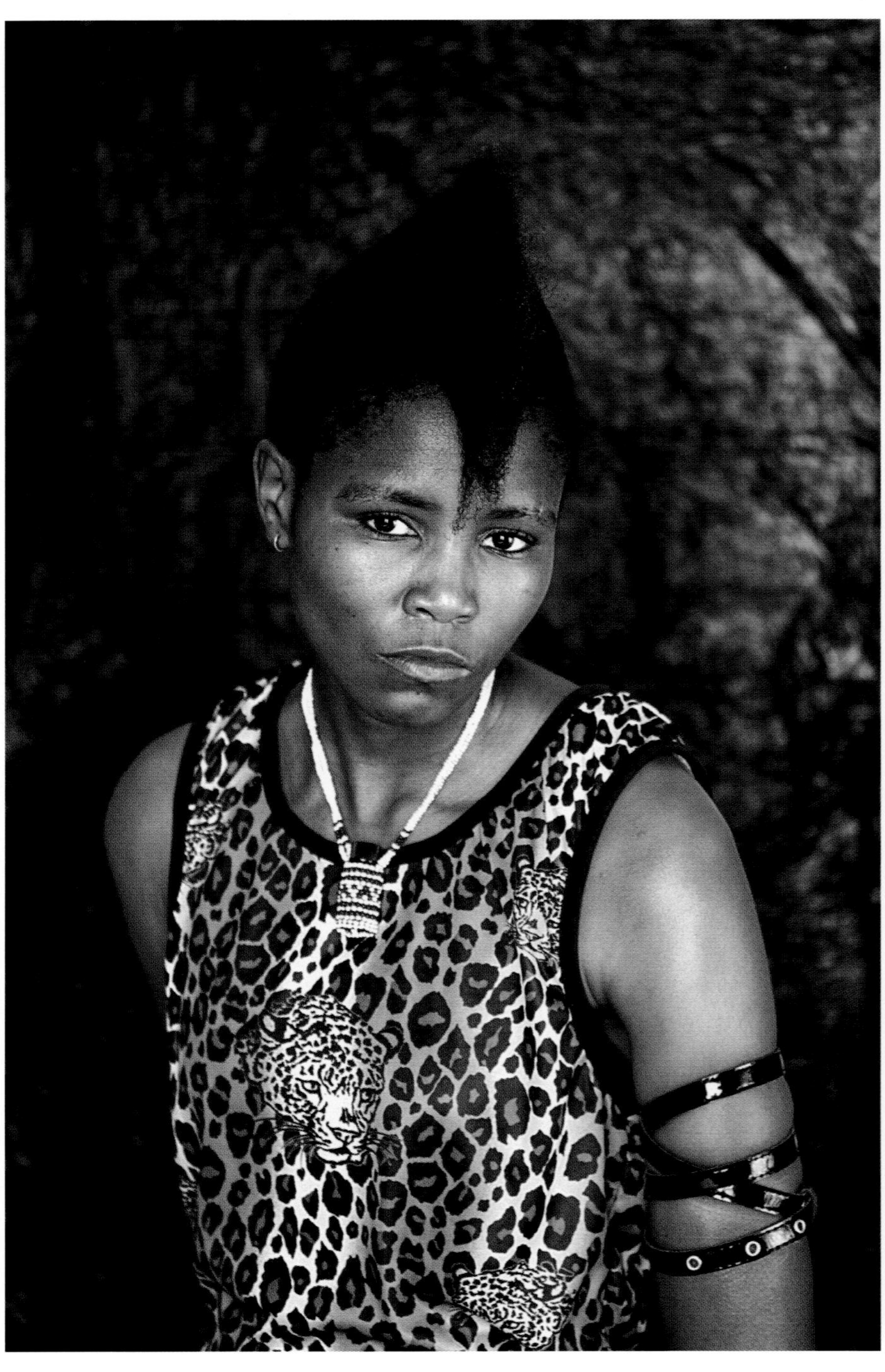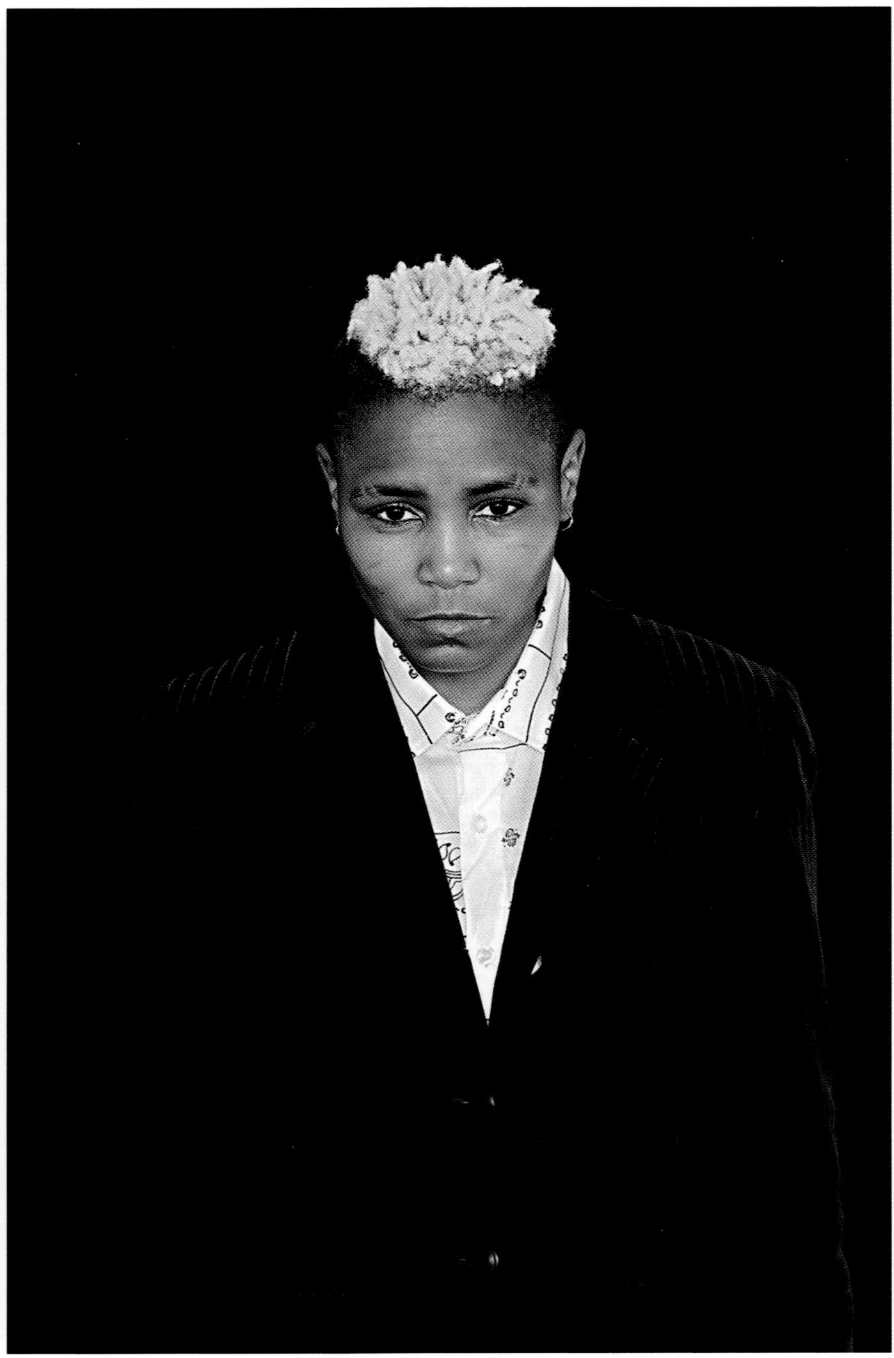

Above left: Thembela Dick, Vredehoek, Cape Town, 2012;
above right: Thembela Dick, Parktown, Johannesburg, 2016;
both *Faces and Phases* series

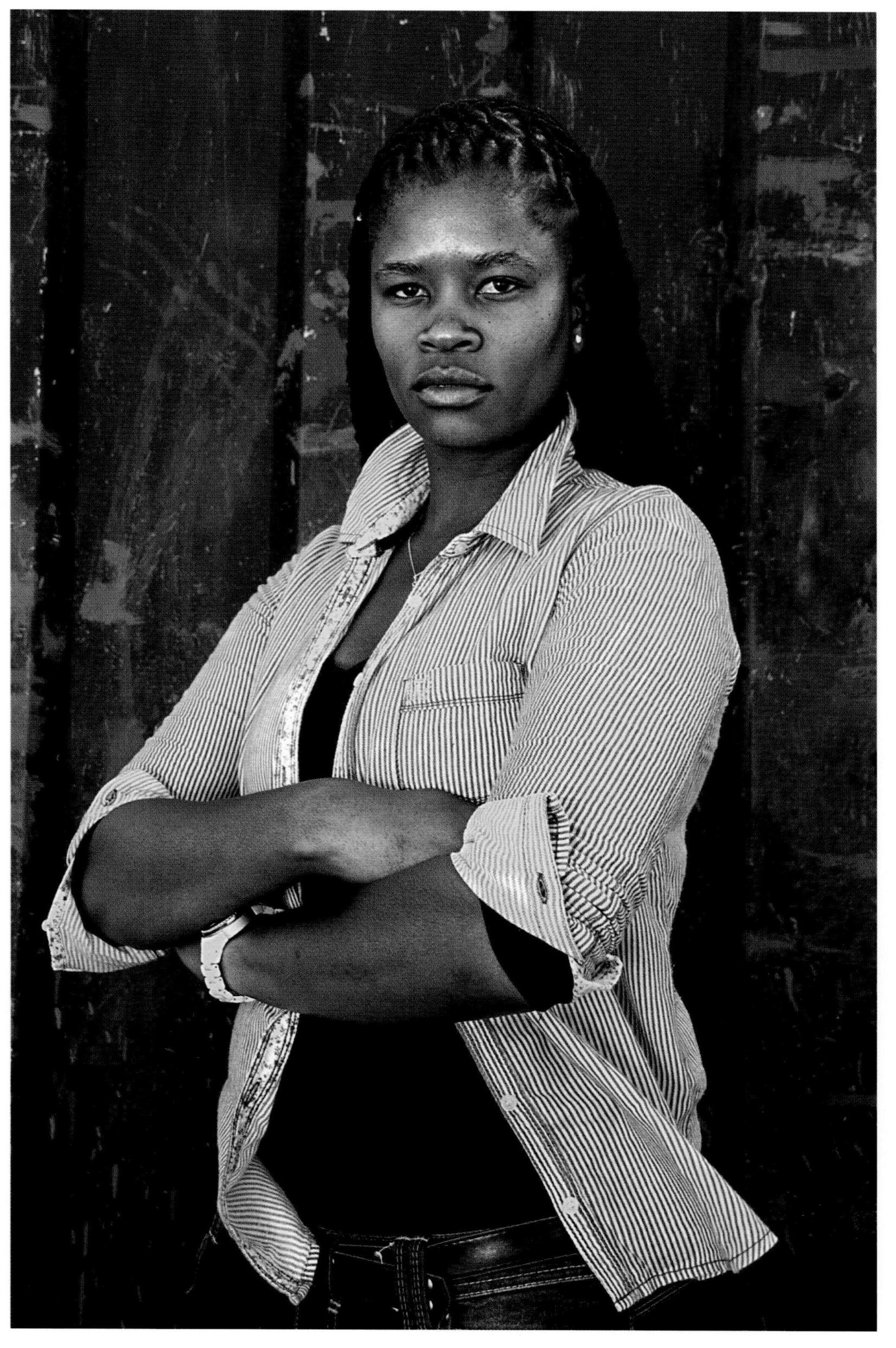

Bathini Dambuza, Tembisa, Johannesburg, 2013, *Faces and Phases* series

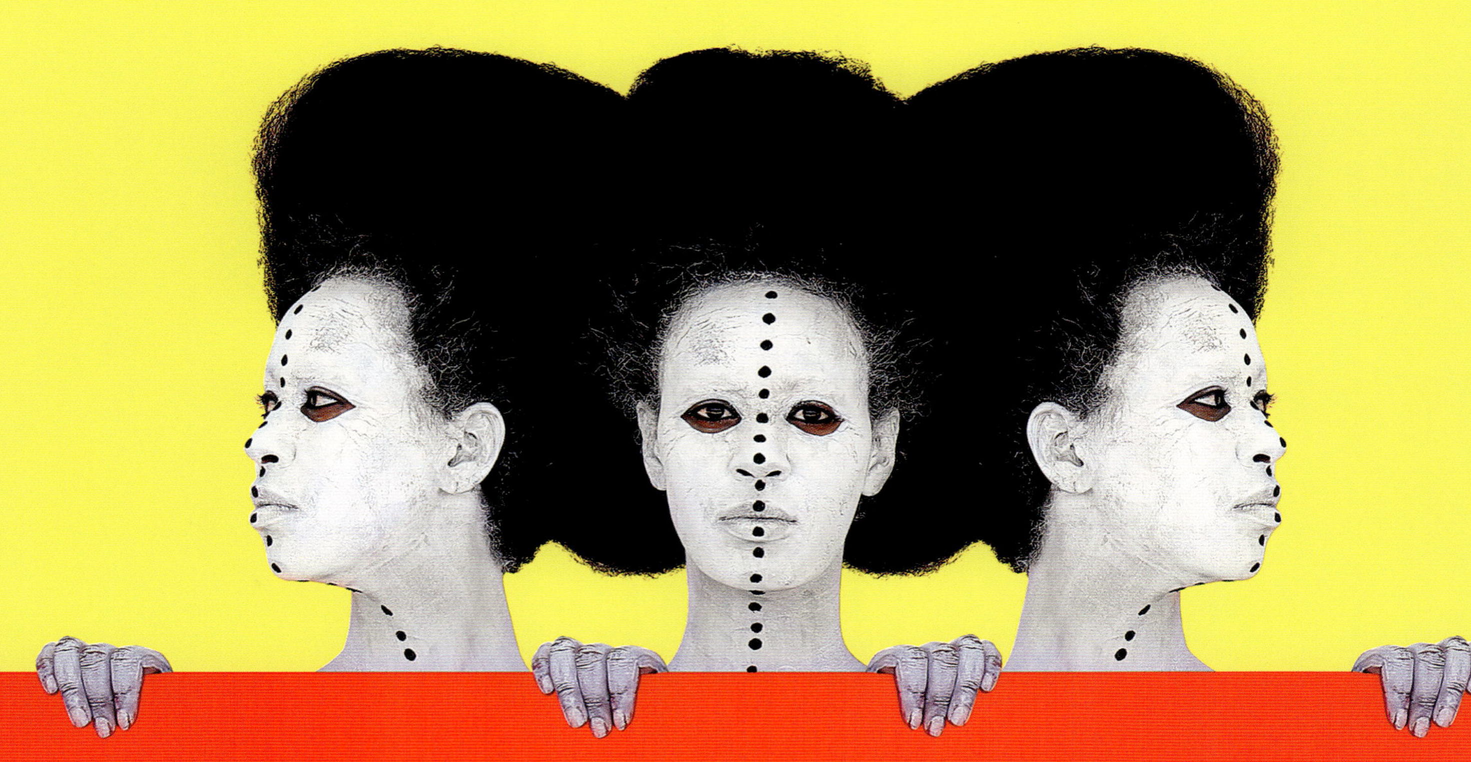

AIDA MULUNEH

...
Muluneh has crafted an unforgettable visual style that is very much her own – renegade, disruptive and bold
...

Aïda Muluneh is one of an exciting and growing number of African photographers reclaiming the cultural ownership of their native countries. She was born in Ethiopia and returned ten years ago, after living in Yemen, the UK, Canada and Cyprus. Her repatriation has spawned a new interest in reconnecting with her land and, in the process, interrogating and presenting Africa in a different way.

Having started her career as a photojournalist for the *Washington Post*, where she shot mostly black-and-white photographs, Muluneh's recent visual language is a more artistic form of expression. Using bold and bright colour, she finds the creative freedom to distort reality and creates a surreal environment in which she can provoke questions about life and love.

Her series *The World is 9* is inspired by an expression from her grandmother: 'The world is 9, it is never complete and it's never perfect'. There are connotations of infallibility, expectation, dissatisfaction and the balance we must strike between the imagined fantasy and imperfect realities of life to find our own inner equilibrium. The inspiration for her homecoming, the idea of making a photographic project testify to how Muluneh felt when she visited Ethiopia from Canada and found it too dynamic

a place to be imagined only from afar. She says, 'We are idealists seeking perfection but living in a reality which does not afford us that balance. Life is unpredictable and imperfect – we must conquer these challenges with strength and endurance.'

Drawing on the significant cultural symbolism of African body-painting techniques, *The World is 9* features elaborately staged theatrical portraits of highly decorated women – blank canvases on which the artist can project her conceptual ideas. Black skin is painted chalky white or bright blue, black dots adorn the face and hands, and bodies are wrapped in swathes of colourful cloth. Muluneh's practice acknowledges the studio greats of her historical African counterparts, including Malian artist Malick Sidibé, while maintaining an unforgettable visual style that is very much her own – renegade, disruptive and bold.

Through her own practice Muluneh has developed a new-found pride for Ethiopia. Coming home has provided not just a cultural outlet, but, as she writes, 'a lesson in humility, and a lesson in what it means to return to a land that was foreign to me'. Not content to contribute to the dialogue around African art solely with her own photography, Muluneh is an avid supporter of emerging African artists and a strong voice in the retrieval and

reinterpretation of national identity. As the founder of DESTA (Developing and Educating Society Through Art) and through serving as the director/curator of the first Ethiopian international photography festival, Addis Foto Fest, Muluneh successfully combines her role as both practitioner and advocate in order to provoke new thought about Africa, its art, and how it is seen in the wider world.

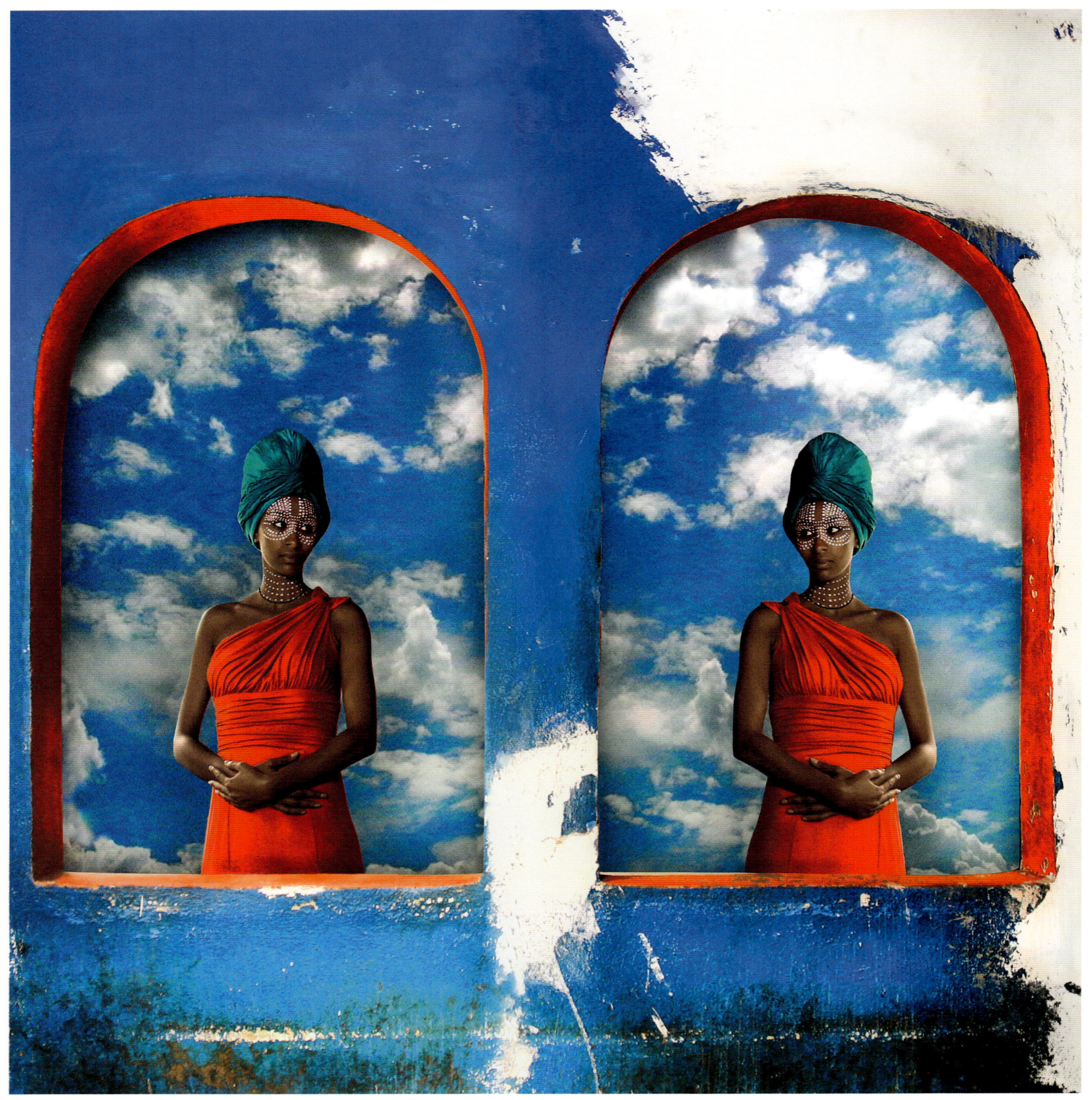

Age of Anxiety, 2015, The World is 9 series

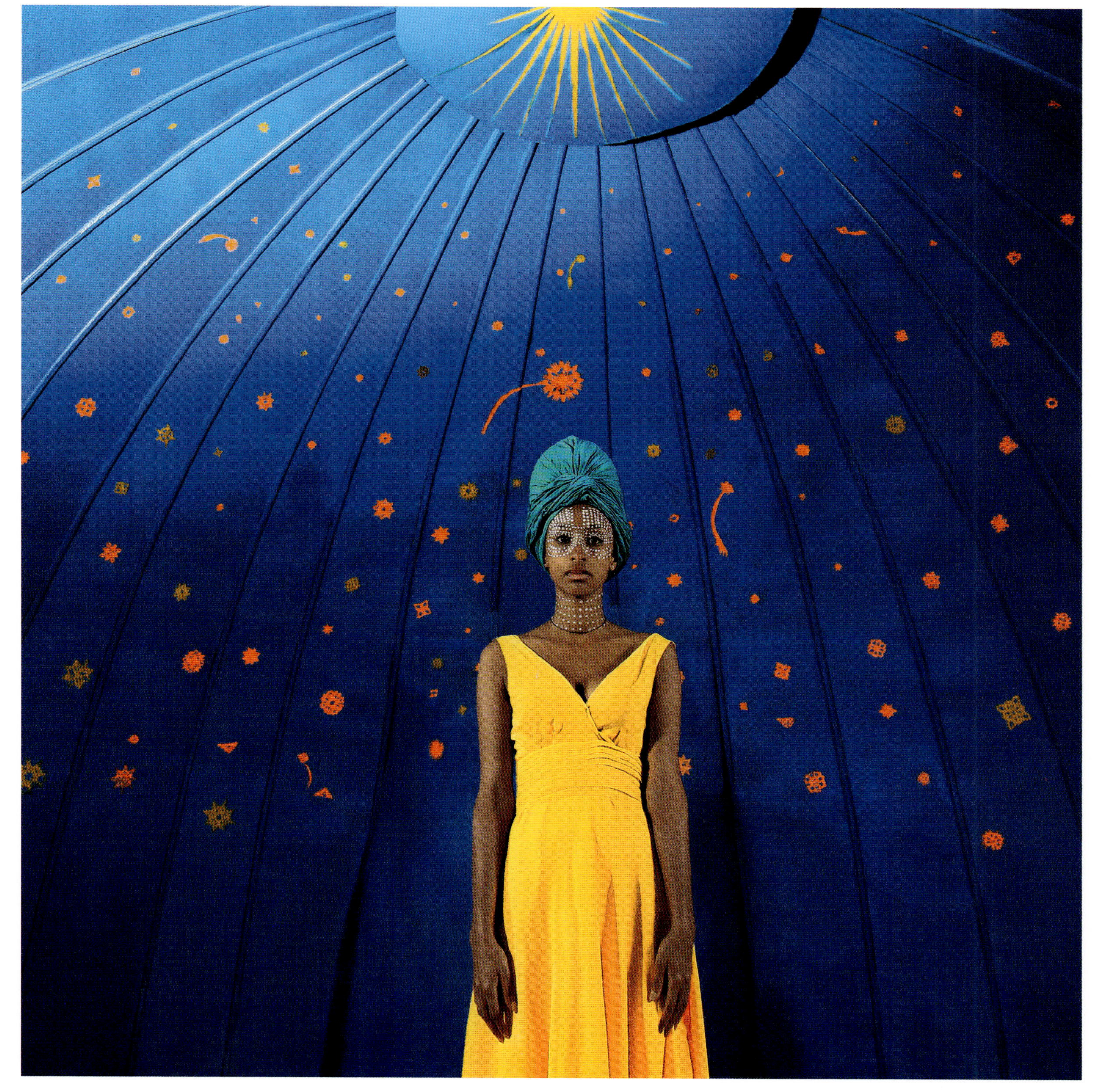

For All they Care, 2015, The World is 9 series

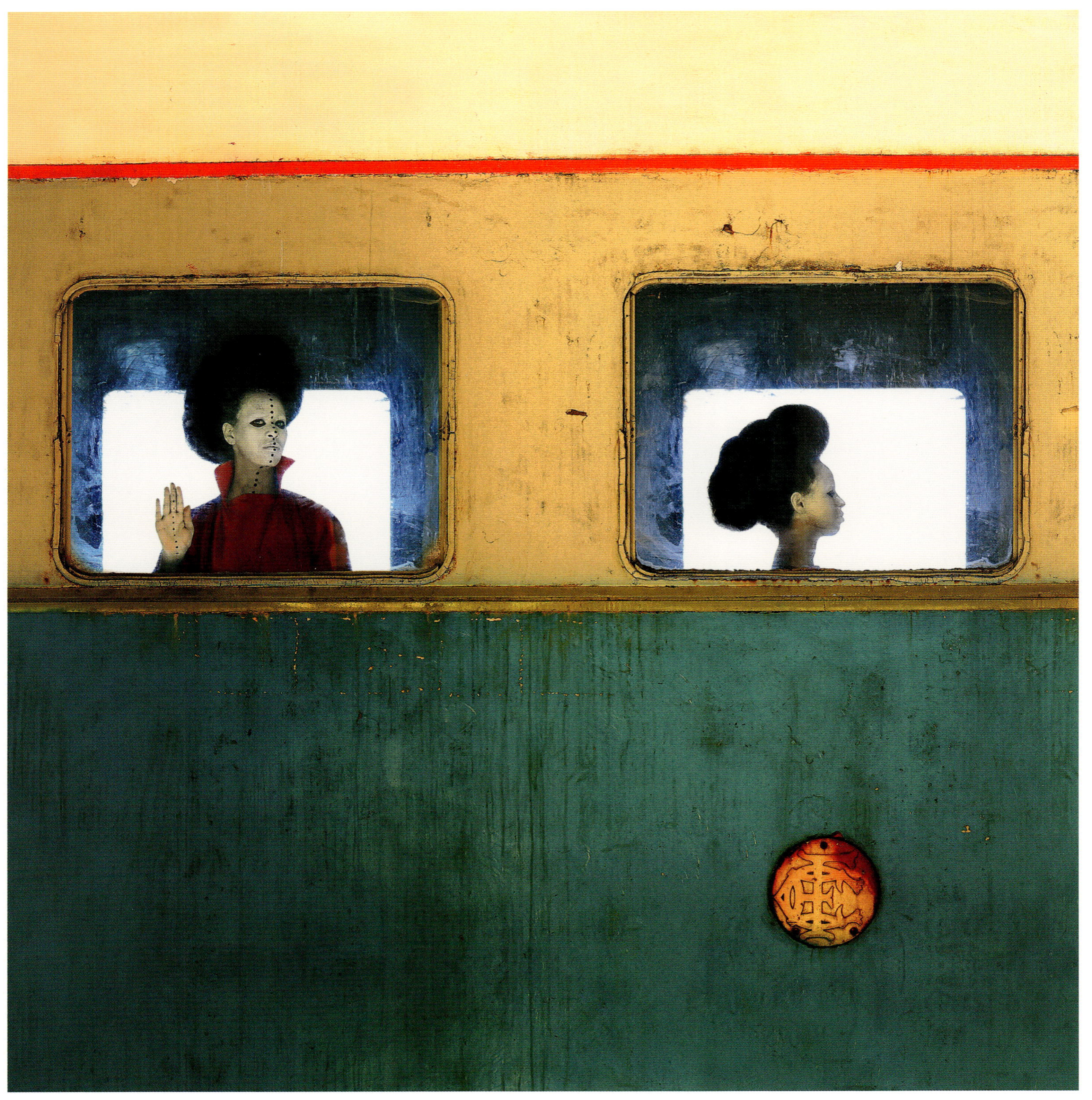

The Departure, 2016, The World is 9 series

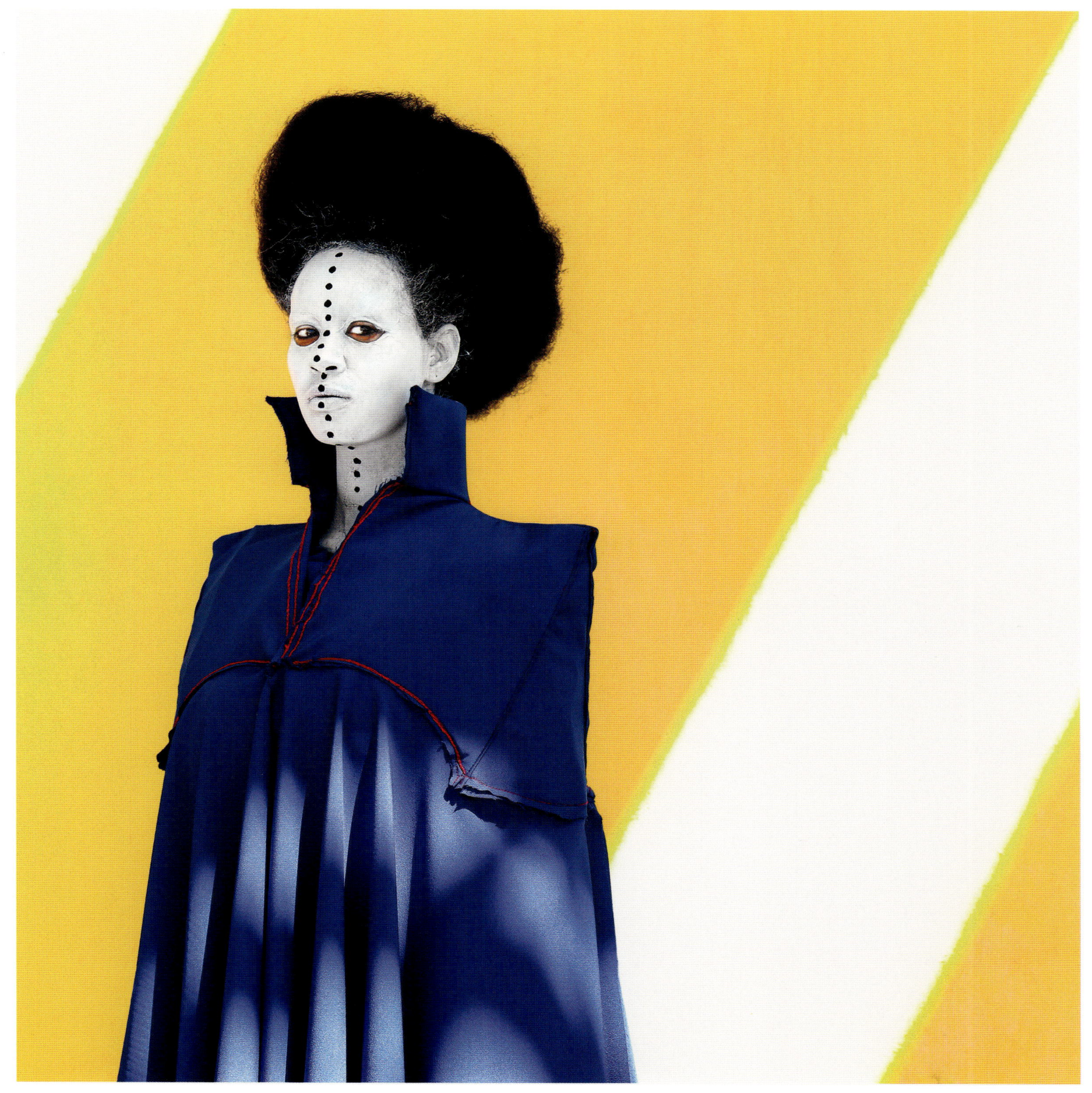

Fragments, 2016, The World is 9 series

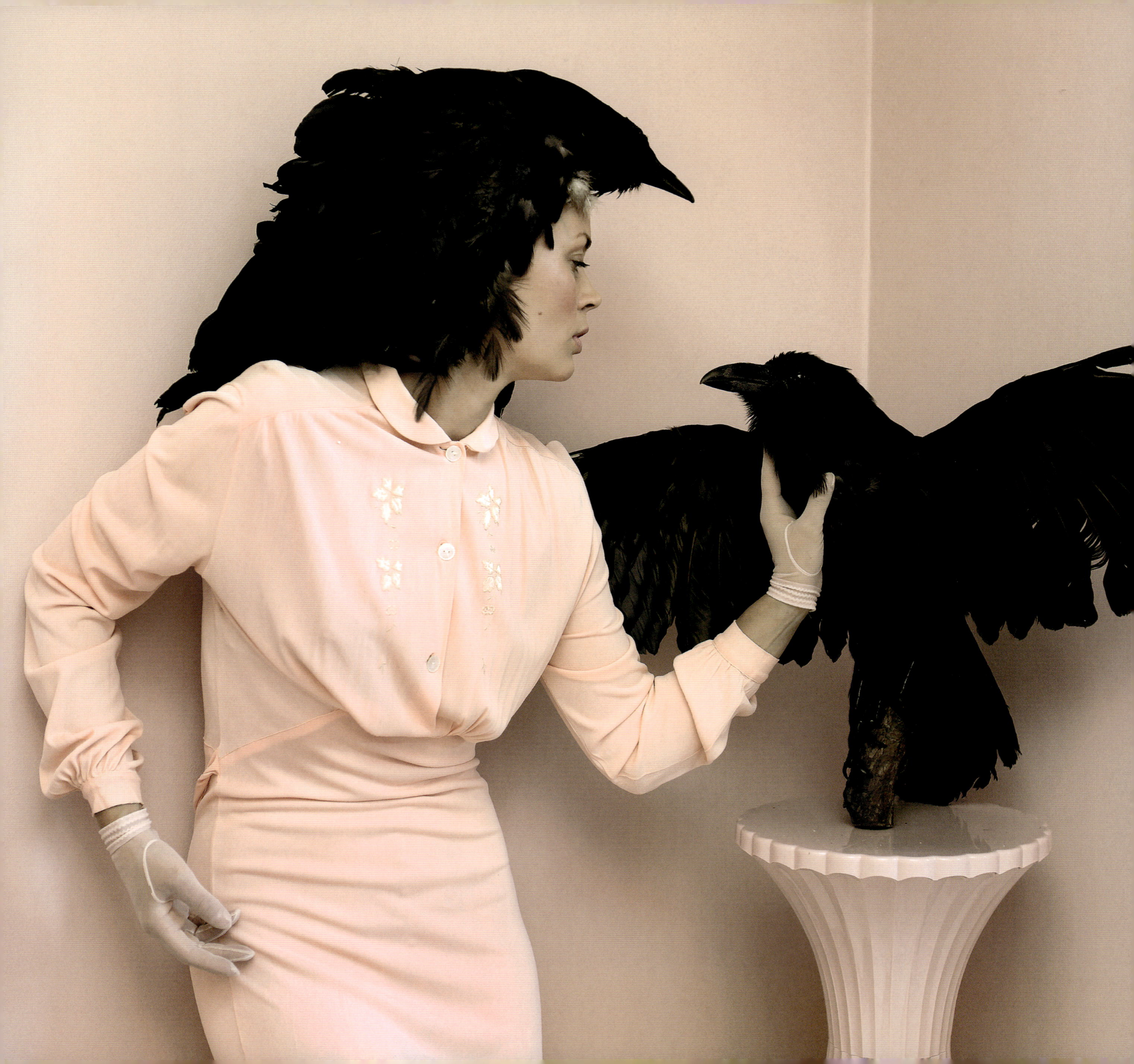

ANJA NIEMI

When Anja Niemi arrived on the London photographic scene it was as though Alfred Hitchcock had undergone a cryonic rebirth, a gender reassignment and retrained as a stills photographer.

With her purposeful mise-en-scènes, Niemi, using endless incarnations of herself, invites us to consider the construction of the female both in society and in its mirror image – film. The excessive femininity of her women, with coiffed hair and pristine dresses, poses as many questions as statements. Are they vulnerable or powerful, desirable or deadened, real or illusory, bride or showgirl?

While making seductive use of the tropes of film, Niemi traps the viewer inside a single frame, where all is at once familiar and deeply unsettling. The costumes and sets are so elaborate that the viewer cannot help but judge by appearance. The flat plane of the photograph is the perfect vehicle for this apparent superficiality. Overwhelmed by sight, we see everything at once.

In *Starlets* Niemi uses the device of doubling in many images. Otto Rank theorized the concept of the double as a representation of the ego in a 1914 essay that Freud drew upon heavily in his 1919 work *The Uncanny*. While the double can assume various forms, such as a shadow, or a reflection, or the superego as observer of the self, in Niemi's work the double is always an exact replica, often assuming a contradictory position to its twin. 'The Wife', for example, in *Starlets* is engaged in an act of potentially fatal domestic violence: the double on the verge of obliteration. Both women remain without expression, yet are so sartorially immaculate that they could themselves be automata. Similarly, 'The Bride' strikes a pose, barefoot, shoulder exposed, white furs immaculately draped. Yet beneath her, under the chair, inscrutable, lies the double. The way we look, and the ways in which we assume authority, or even authorship, are all thrown into sharp relief in this work, at once deeply complex and scintillatingly skin-deep.

In Niemi's own words, 'I do often multiply myself, sometimes to look at inner conflicts or to show the contrast between what we show and who we are. We have a tendency to cover up our flaws and decay, hiding all the ugliness of life and I try to have a bit of humour about it.'

The darker side of her imagery follows a thread back to Surrealism, with its obsession with fragmented body parts, but her most vivid antecedent is surely the film-maker David Lynch. 'Maybe it's that severed ear found in the grass in *Blue Velvet*. It's an image that just never left me. I love the way David Lynch blends the surreal into mundane everyday life.'

As photographer, model, stylist and director, Niemi retains an exacting control over her imagery, which in turn grants her creative freedom. With a mind brimming with stories, photography has turned out to be a useful medium for a dyslexic perfectionist to create exquisite fictions, which at the same time remind us of what might be crawling just beneath the surface.

The Taxidermist, 2013, *Starlets* series

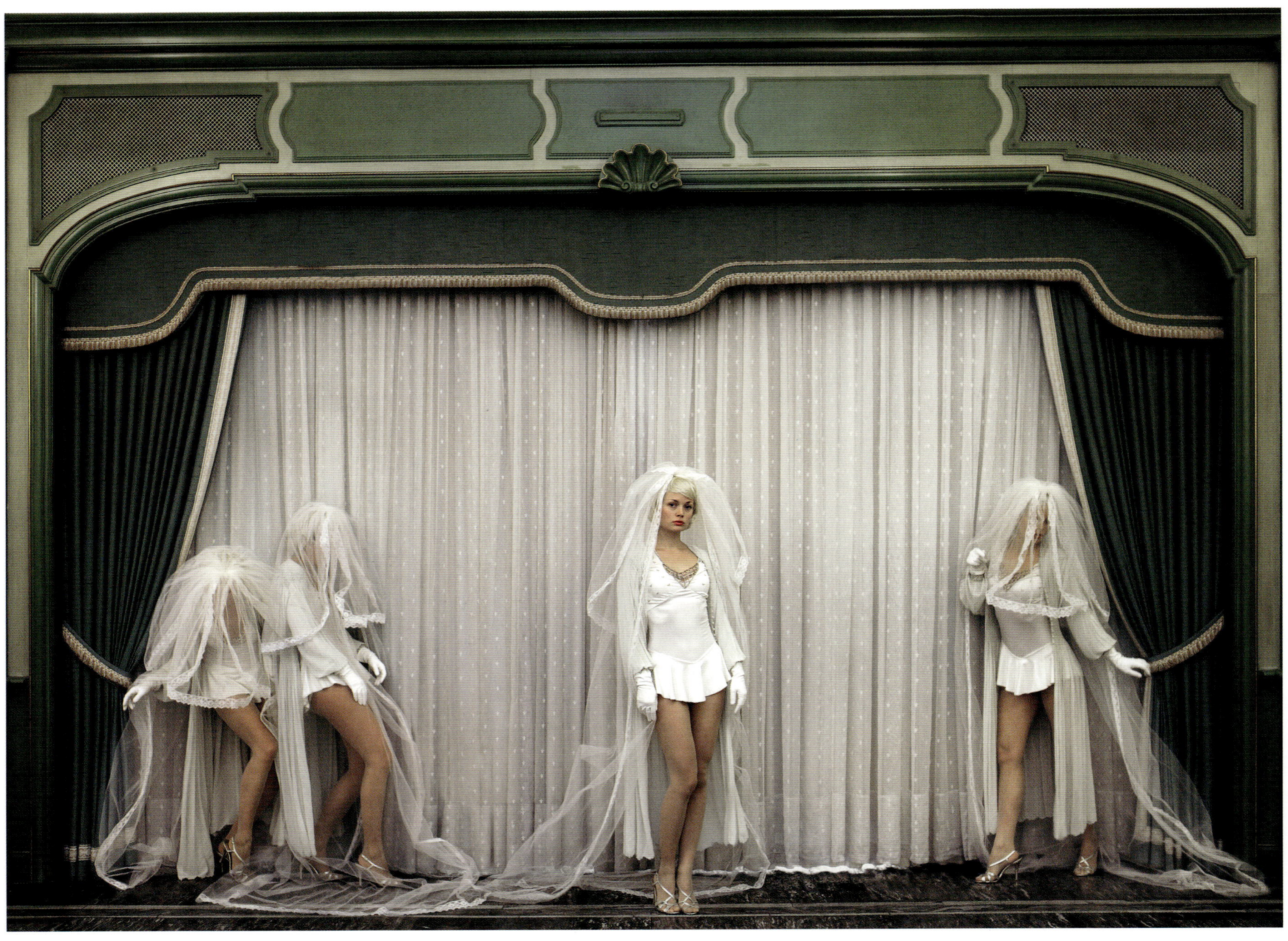

The Showgirl, 2013, *Starlets* series

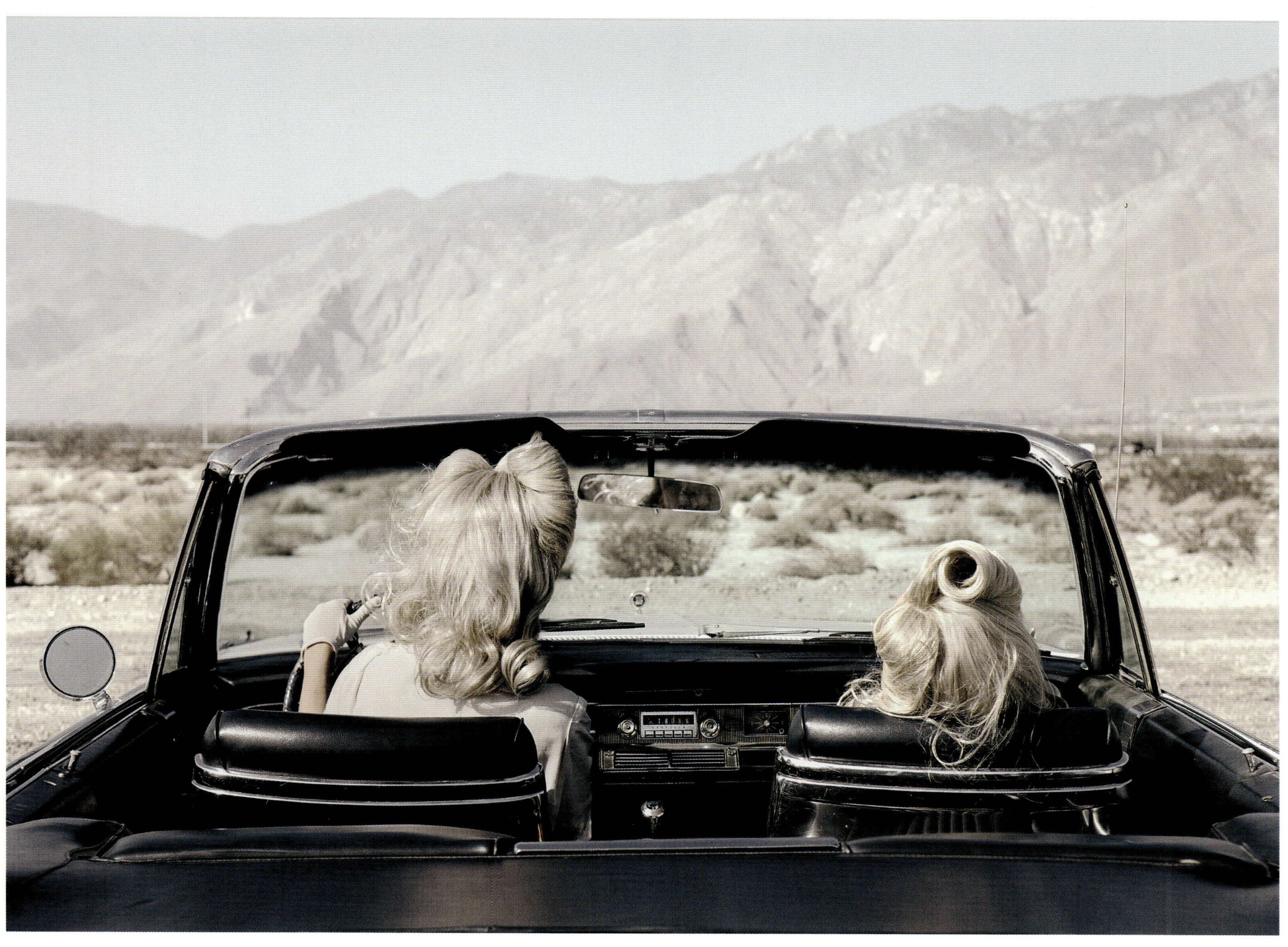

Chrysler, 2014, Darlene & Me series

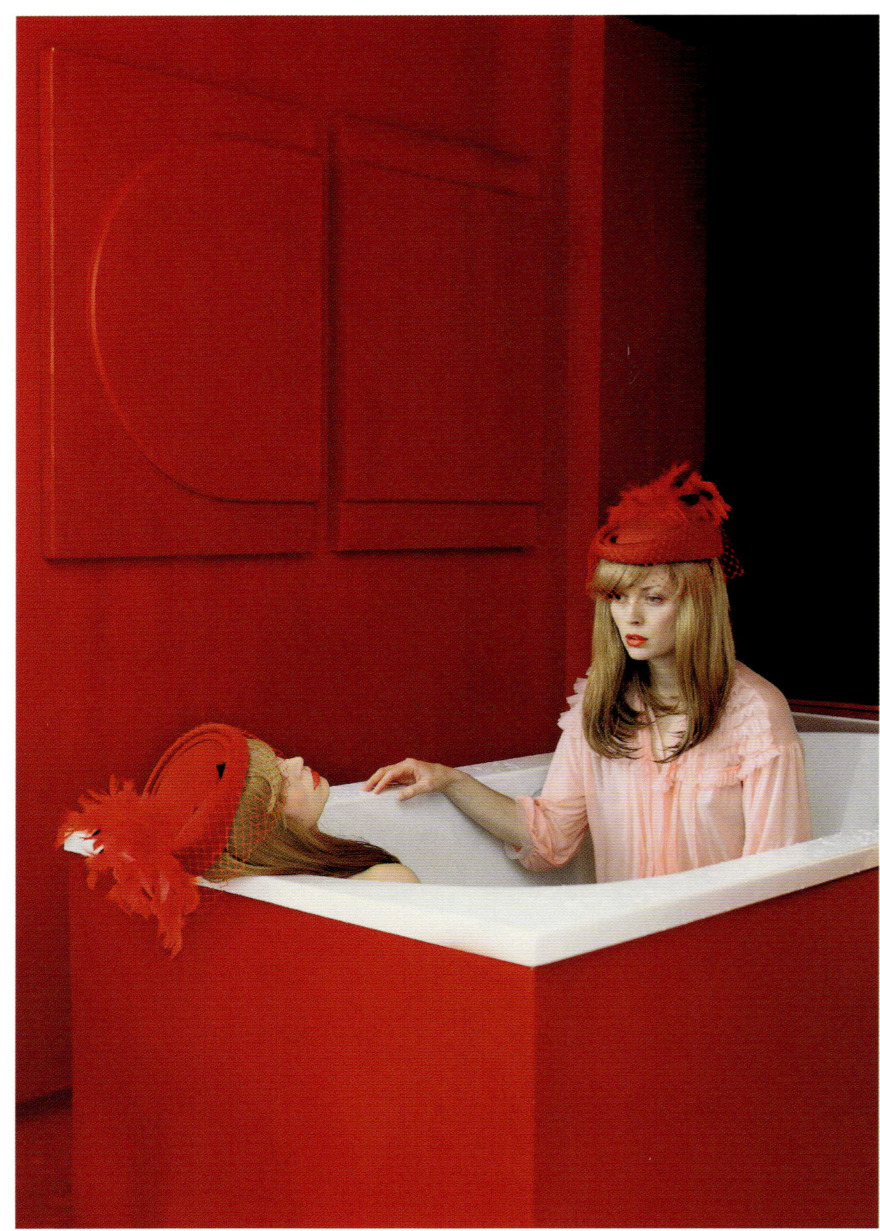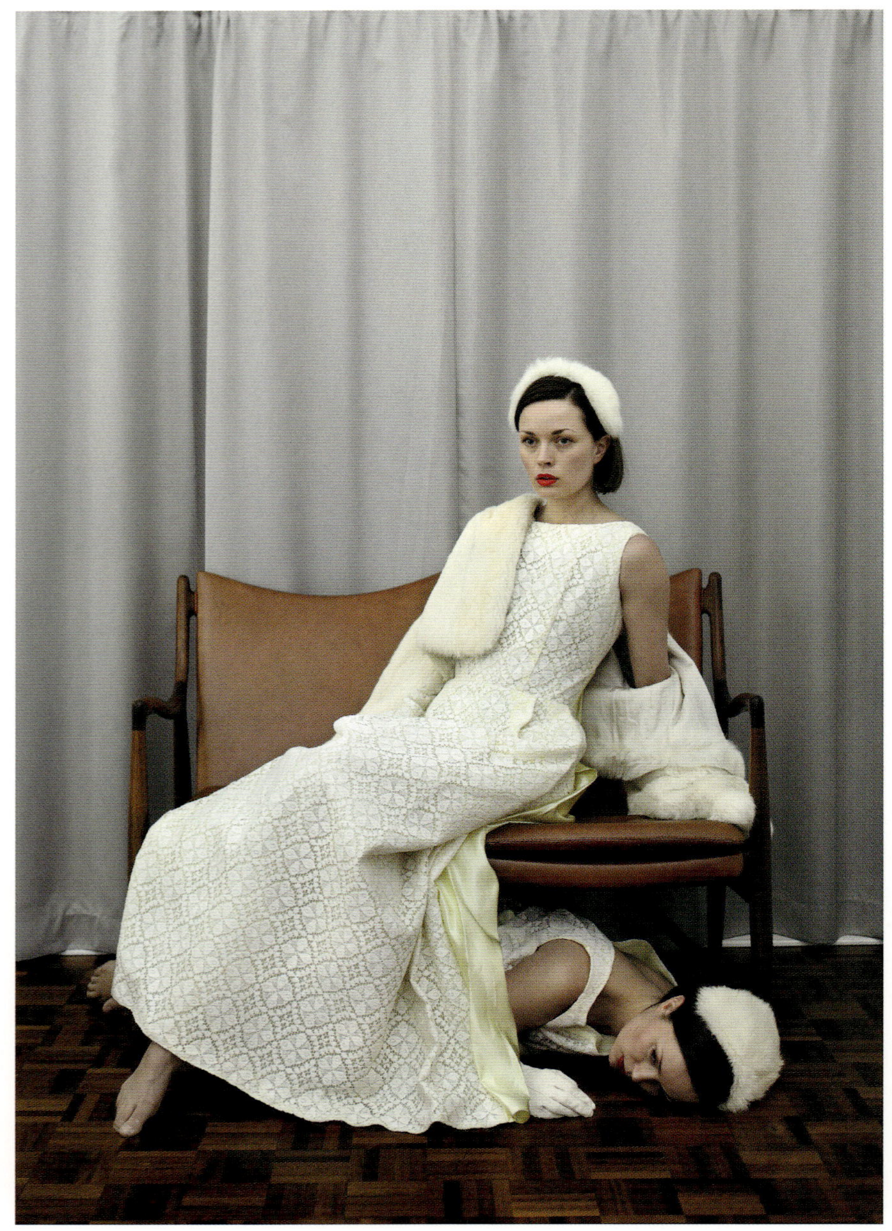

Left: *The Socialite*, 2013;
right: *The Bride*, 2013; both *Starlets* series

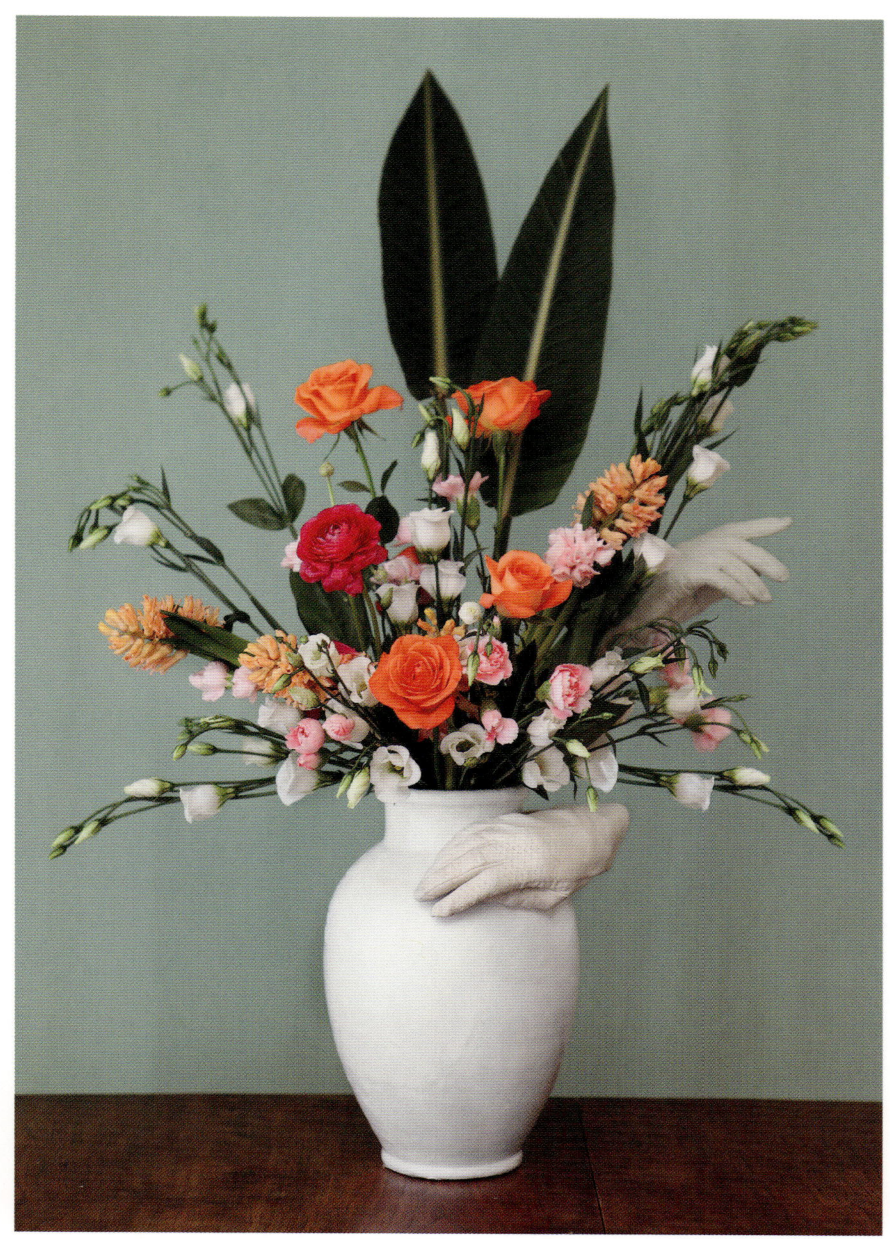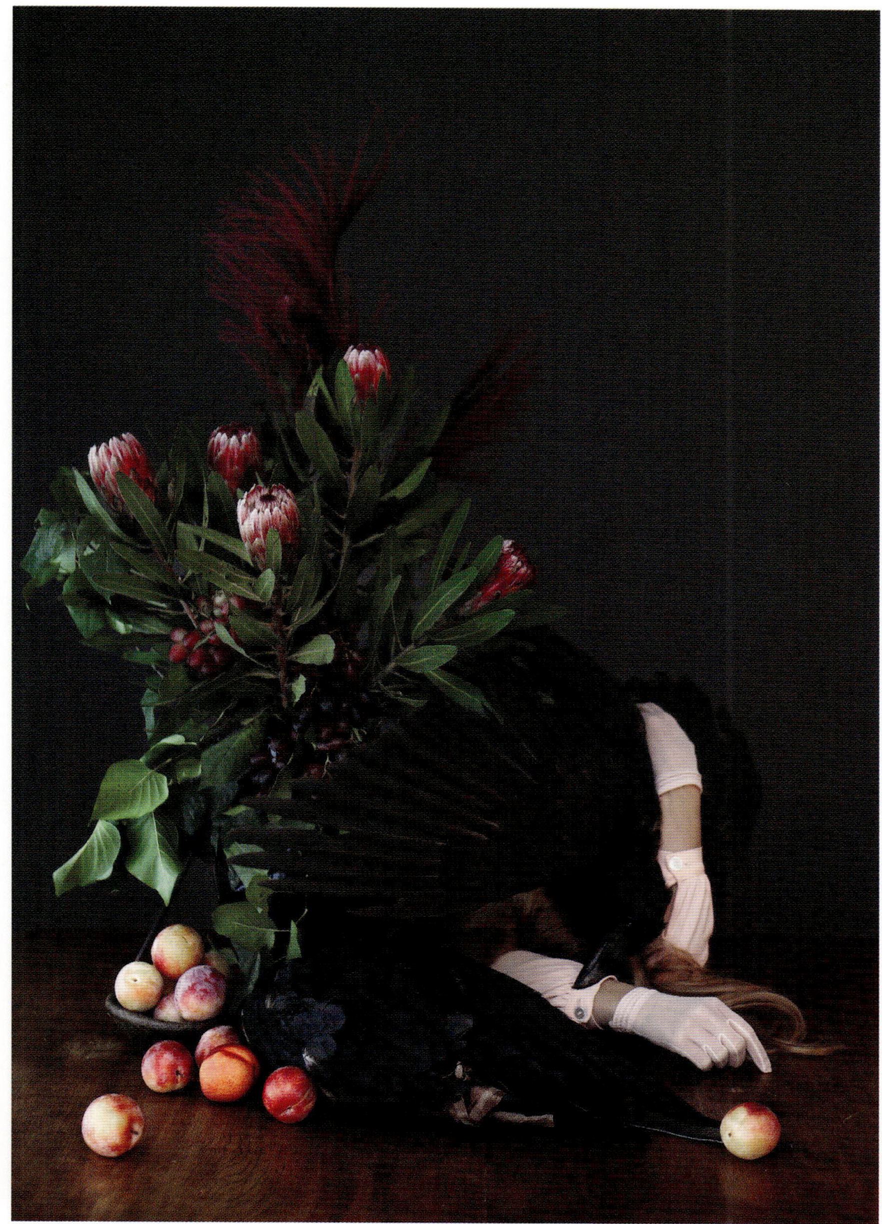

Anja Niemi   143

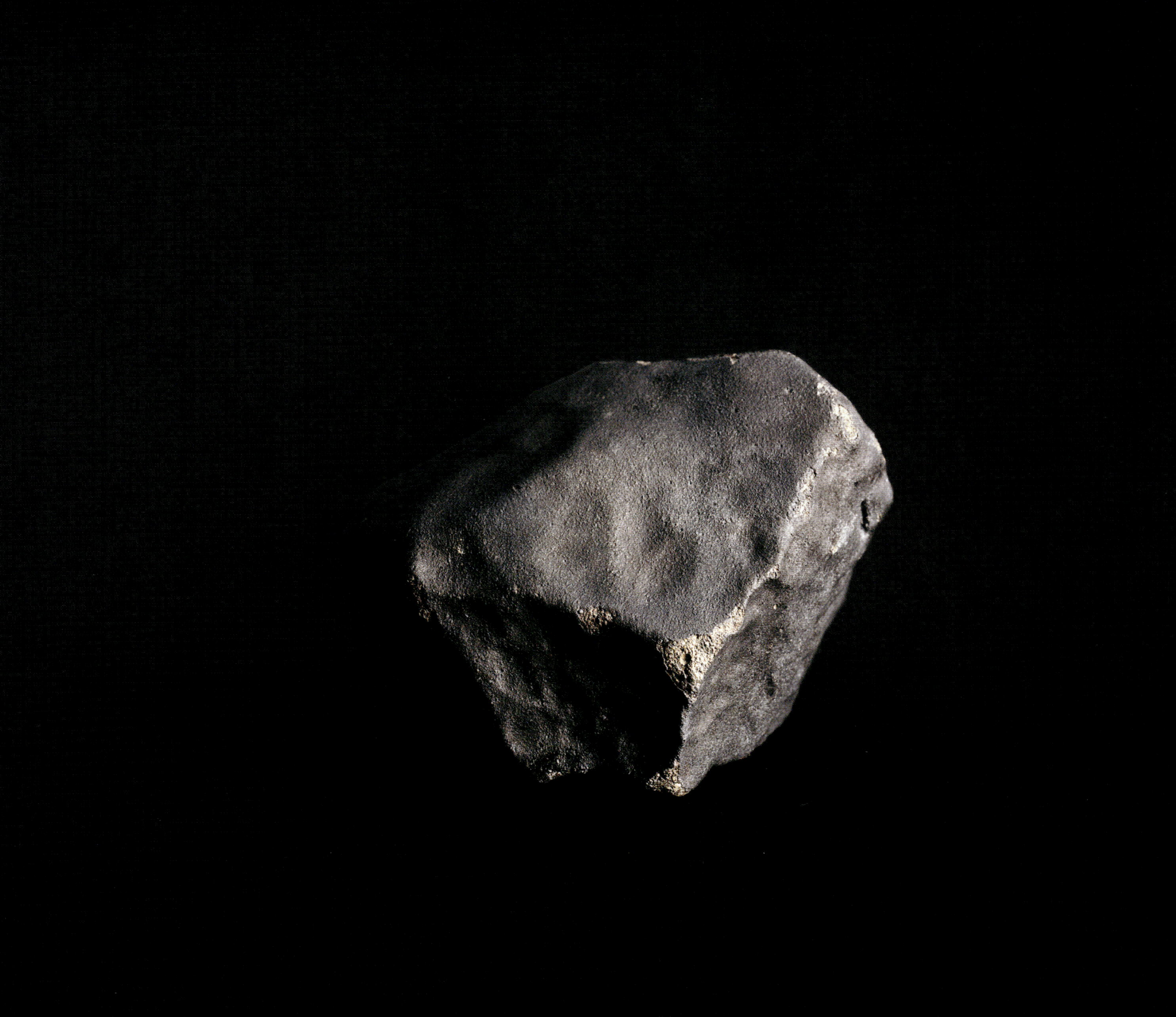

REGINE PETERSEN

...

Petersen's subjects look quizzically through half-smiles, as if they know something we don't

...

Suggestive, poetic and otherworldly, the work of German multimedia artist Regine Petersen spans notions of time, history, memory and myth. Petersen graduated from the Royal College of Art, London, in 2009 and has won international acclaim, notably as recipient of the 2010 National Media Museum bursary and in her nomination for the prestigious Discovery Award at the Rencontres d'Arles in 2012.

Petersen's most celebrated body of work is a collection of three chapters, all exploring the phenomenon of meteorites. *Find a Fallen Star* (Kehrer, 2015) was inspired by Petersen's chance encounter with a photograph of Ann Hodges, the first person to be officially recorded as being hit by a meteorite in modern times. In the photograph we see Hodges, eyes downcast, surrounded by two police officers inspecting a large hole in her ceiling. One is holding a black rock, the size of a grapefruit, and no one seems to know what's going on. Petersen says, 'I had to know how the meteorite changed her life, and what became of her.' Hodges was to become the subject of a Special Forces investigation, a media frenzy, a bidding war and a lawsuit; divorce and a breakdown ensued. She died in 1972, having gifted the troublesome meteorite that unquestionably changed her life to the Alabama Museum of Natural History.

The fascination with Hodges' photograph and story propelled Petersen to an 'investigation' into two extraordinary, and somewhat similar, events. She travelled to Kanwarpura, a village in India, where a 6.8 kg meteorite fell close to an atomic plant in 2006, and to Ramsdorf in Germany, where in 1958 local children uncovered a meteorite, which they broke into smaller pieces as individual keepsakes, and subsequently argued over for decades to follow.

For Petersen, the meteorite embodies a contradictory physical entity, both a scientific object and a heavenly apparition; a 'time capsule' from another era. There are parallels to be drawn between the meteorite as a historic cache of information and photography's ability to communicate the same. Petersen uses the medium to weave effortlessly between historic and contemporary narratives, science and superstition, and reality and mythology.

Find a Fallen Star becomes a playground for Petersen's artistic imagination: her fragile, ethereal photographs are interspersed between scientific reports, newspaper clippings, transcripts and archival photographs. She documents the meteorites themselves, photographing them as curiosity pieces and artefacts of the uncanny and unknown. Landscapes are seen in half light, as if unearthly creatures are scanning the scenery before them. In her portraits, Petersen's subjects look quizzically through half-smiles, as if they know something we don't.

The book includes eyewitness accounts of events, but these are often misremembered, exaggerated or forgotten. Her research and collection of ephemera are impressively thorough and somehow amplify the bizarre nature of the stories she presents to us, stories that are so outrageous and unusual that they couldn't possibly be made up.

Sylacauga, 1954, 2010-15, 'Find a Fallen Star' series

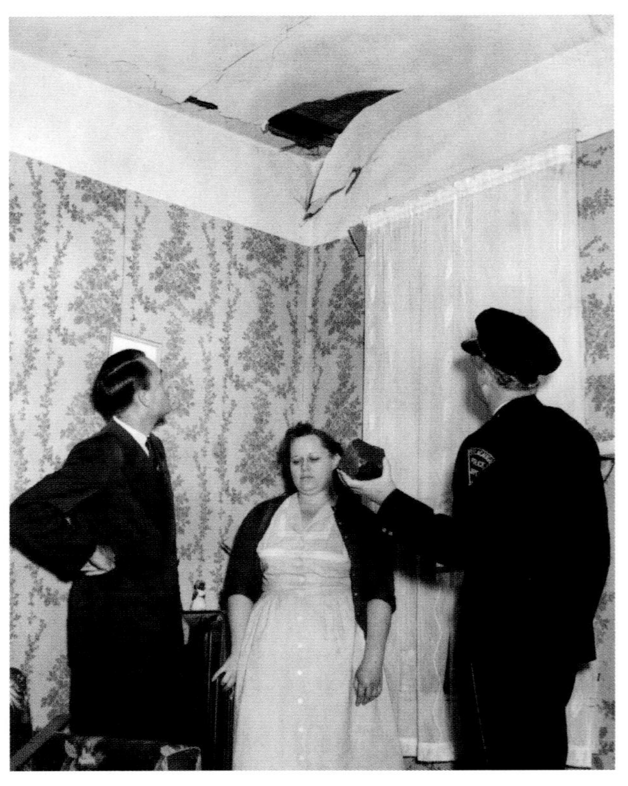

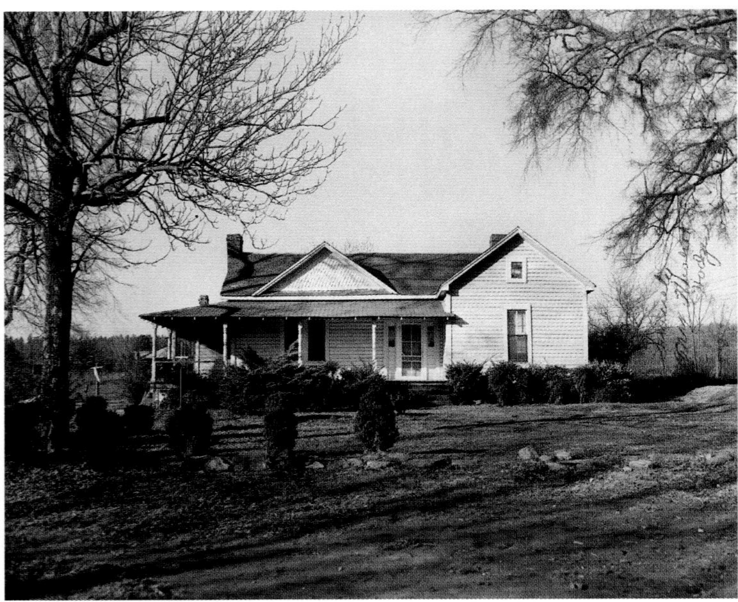

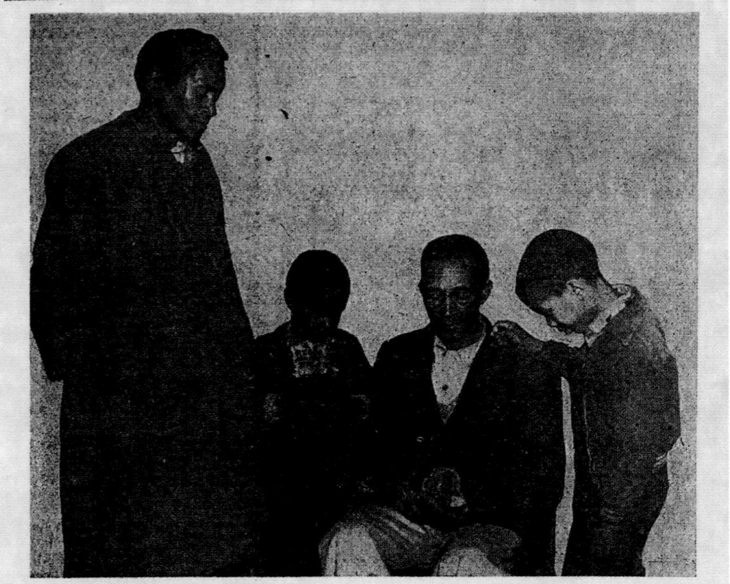

McKinney explains his possession of his piece of 'black pearl' by saying: "I think the Lord gave it to me— but my mule found it and showed it to me." He further

ed into the army during W came home where he began dale Mills between farming

McKINNEYS MIGHTY PROUD of meteo-rite found near their home on December 1st. They examine the black colored pearl in their house near Sylacauga, Ala.

Above left: Ann, 2010–15; above right: Hodges House, 2010–15;
above: Black Colored Pearl, 2010–15; all from the *Find a Fallen Star* series

DETINUE BOND   (Box 618-2)   MARSHALL & BRUCE

The State of Alabama, ___TALLADEGA___ County

CIRCUIT COURT

Know all Men by these Presents, That we, ___Hulitt Hodges___

are held and firmly bound unto ___Ed J. Howard___

in the sum of ___Five Hundred & No/100 ($500.00)__________________ Dollars,

for which payment, well and truly to be made, we bind ourselves and each of us, our and each of our heirs, executors, and administrators, jointly and severally, firmly by these presents.

Sealed with our seals, and dated this_______________day of_______________________, 19___

The Condition of the above Obligation is such, That whereas, the above bound ___________________

___Hulitt Hodges___

ha_S_ this day commenced ___a___ suit in the Circuit Court of ___Talladega___ County, against the said

___Ed. J. Howard___

for the recovery of the following property, to wit: ___(1) One sulphide variety meteor,___
___weight about ten (10) pounds, six (6) inches in diameter,___
___black satin color___

and having made affidavit that the property sued for belongs to ___him___, and entering into this bond, has obtained an order

requiring any Sheriff of the State aforesaid to take the said property sued for into his possession:

Now, if the said ___Hulitt Hodges___________________________________shall fail on said

suit, and pay the Defendant all such costs and damages as he may sustain by the wrongful complaint, then this obligation to be void; otherwise to remain in full force and effect.

Hulitt Hodges (L. S.)

Billy Jack Walker (L. S.)

Mitchell Brown (L. S.)

_______________________ (L. S.)

Approved this_______________day of_______________________, 19___

_______________________, Clerk.

Code 1940, Title 7, Sec. 918.

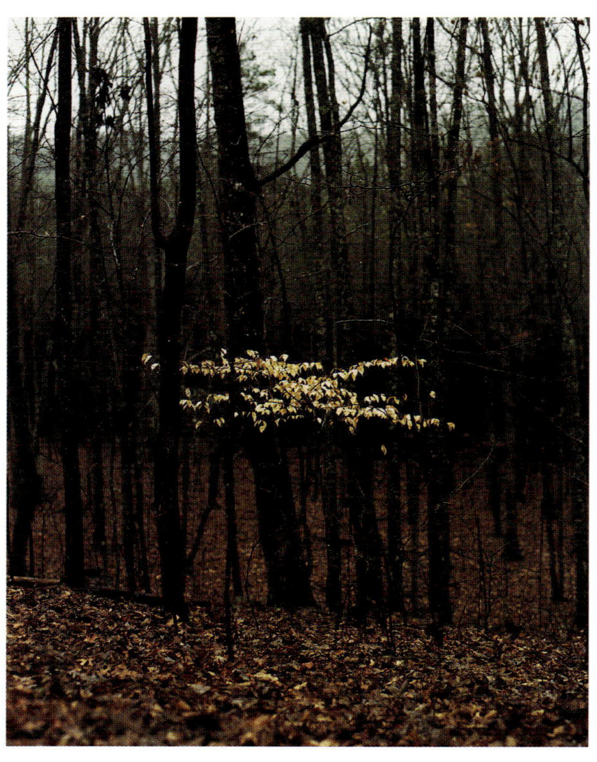

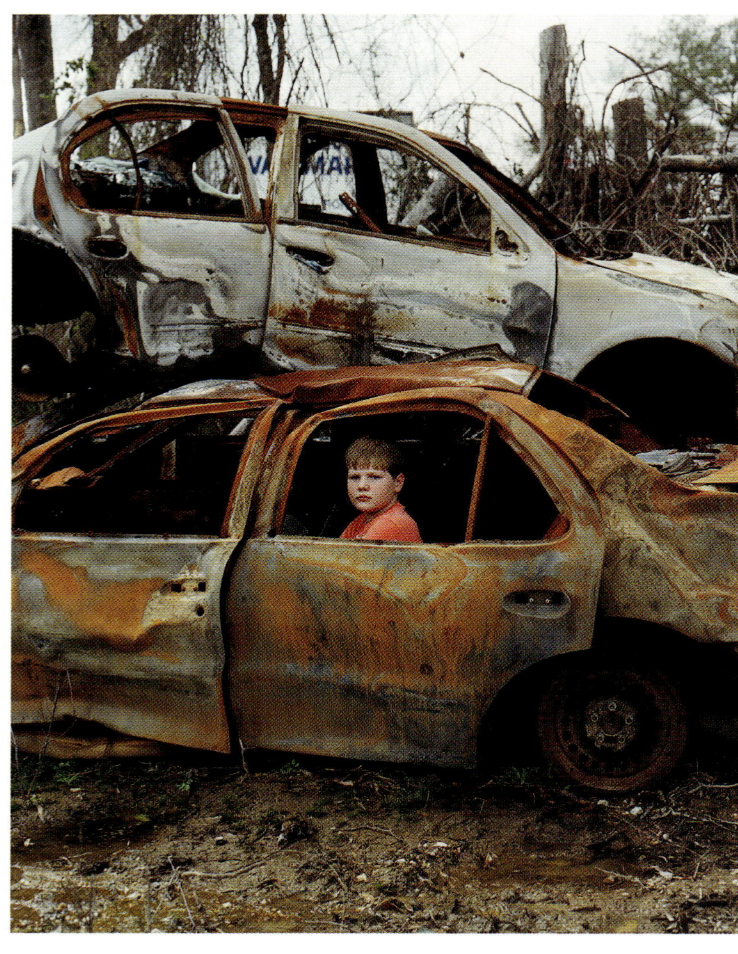

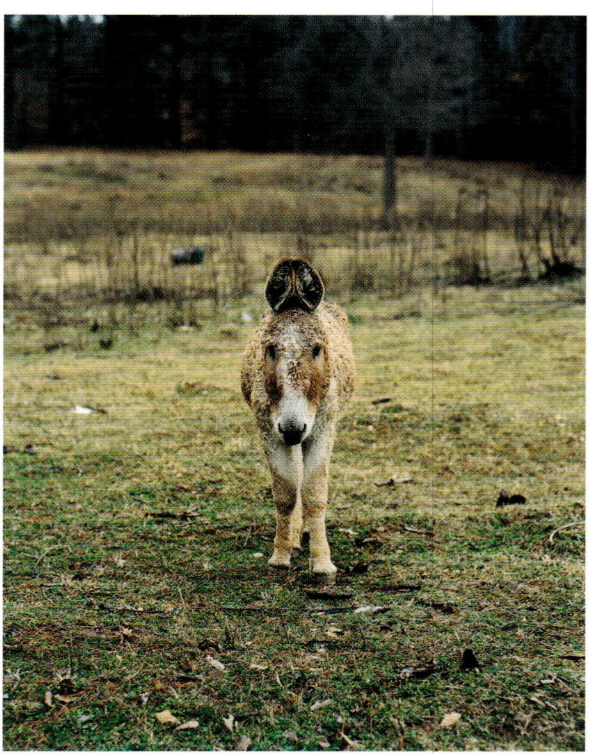

Above left: Talladega, 2010–15; above right: Merkel's Junkyard, 2010–15;
left: Mule, 2010–15; all *Find a Fallen Star* series

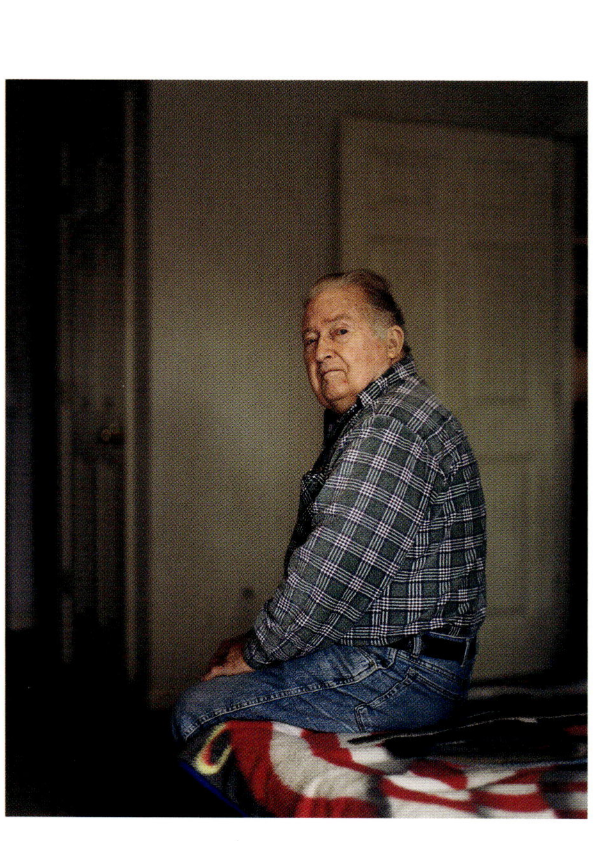

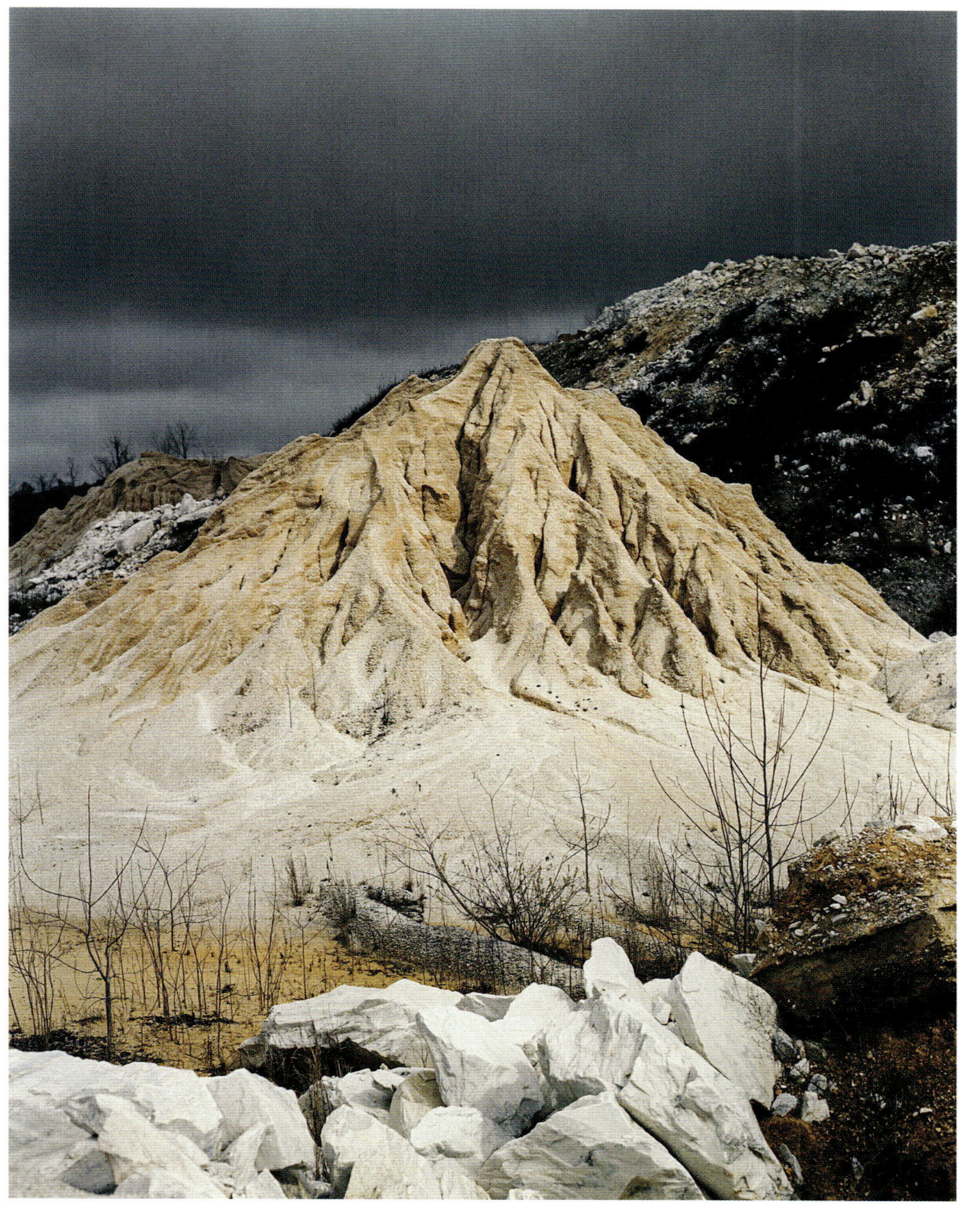

Above left: Ed, 2010–15; above right: Sylacauga Marble City, 2010–15;
both *Find a Fallen Star* series

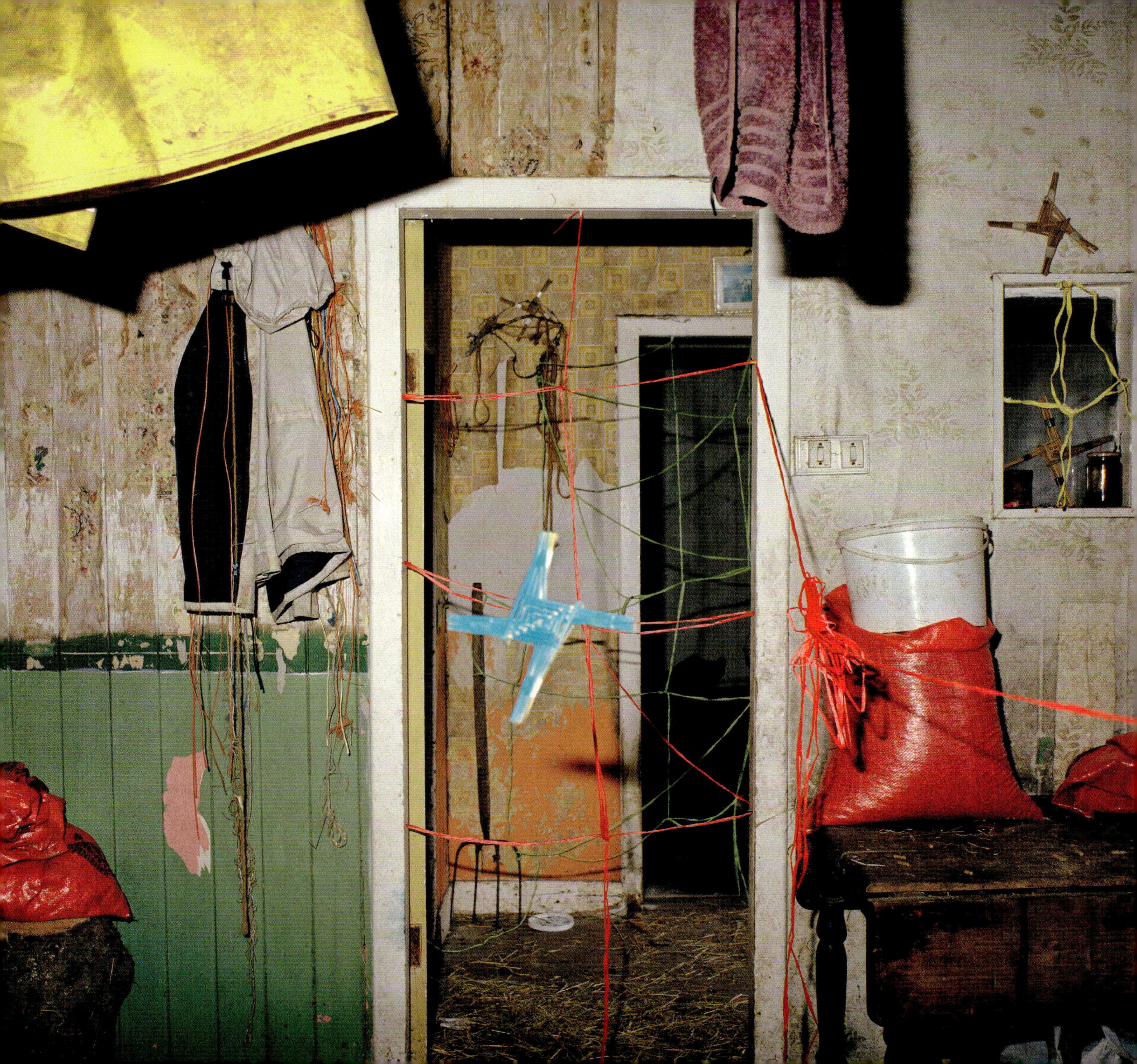

JILL QUIGLEY

... Part-performer and part-documentarian, Quigley injects colour, movement and modernity into these appropriated spaces ...

Born in rural County Donegal, Ireland, Jill Quigley now resides in Belfast. Her work questions contemporary pastoral life and our often nostalgic or romantic preconceptions of traditional culture and heritage. She graduated from Ulster University, Northern Ireland, in 2014. She has received nominations for the MACK First Book Award and the Prix Pictet for 'Space'. She has been highlighted as one of the *British Journal of Photography*'s 'Ones to Watch'.

In her widely lauded project *Cottages of Quigley's Point*, she stages disruptive and colourful acts to abandoned rural farmhouses, subverting notions of sentimentality, re-contextualizing the derelict space and celebrating these dwellings in the context of the contemporary landscape.

Quigley began working on *Cottages of Quigley's Point* while doing her MFA research: she wanted to find a way of engaging with and utilizing her familiarity with rural Donegal, while avoiding introspection. The abandoned cottages are plentiful and well known in the region, a representation of quintessential Ireland and its bygone era, and a decaying result of regional housing booms.

The dwellings have been quietly left to rot: an obvious and convenient subject matter for the native Quigley, but one she had originally rejected as 'romanticized ruin porn'. This was, however, until she thought of the idea of making her mark – literally – on the landscape and experimenting with her locality in a highly unconventional and artistic way.

Part-performer and part-documentarian, Quigley injects colour, movement and modernity into these appropriated spaces, staging her artistic 'interventions' with explosions of paint, fabric and textures. She steals her moments (occasionally trespassing) and conducts her clandestine performances in private – filling the desolate, empty interiors with temporal life in a colourful clash of past and present.

Brightness contrasts with the fading palette of decomposition. There is a chaotic sense of joy, freedom and fantasy; a neon rainbow arcs over a dusty stove. Balls of coloured wool bounce towards a crumbling fireplace, a splash of paint stains the corner of a dilapidated bedroom, and bits of twine barricade a doorway. Quigley describes it thus: 'The process of intervention subverts a wistful reading of a disappearing way of life, and provides the opportunity to take a fresh and playful approach to familiar subject matter.' Collectively the photographs become the record of her staged acts and evidence that someone was there, before Quigley herself re-abandons the space.

Though there is no namesake connection to the place of Quigley's Point and the artist herself, a misunderstanding of this helps to hint at whether this fantastical project is real or the work of fiction. Quigley's methodology, process and aesthetic are tools with which she successfully navigates cliché, and are how she provokes ideas of sentimentality, heritage and the passage of time. We are left wondering if the spaces are still smeared with signs of life, if Quigley's mark is omnipresent, as the buildings continue to crumble in the landscape.

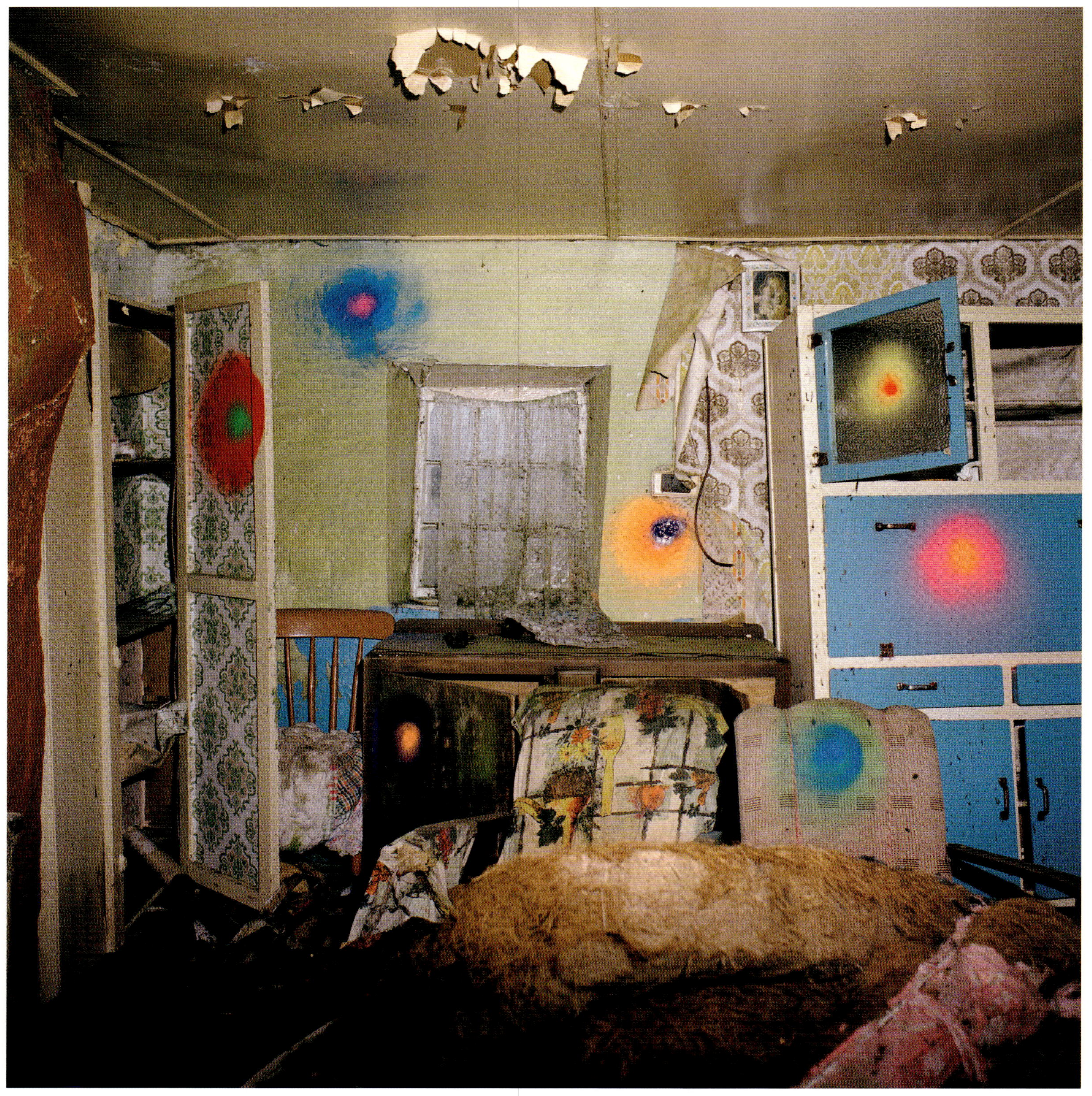

Magowens I, 2013, Cottages of Quigley's Point series

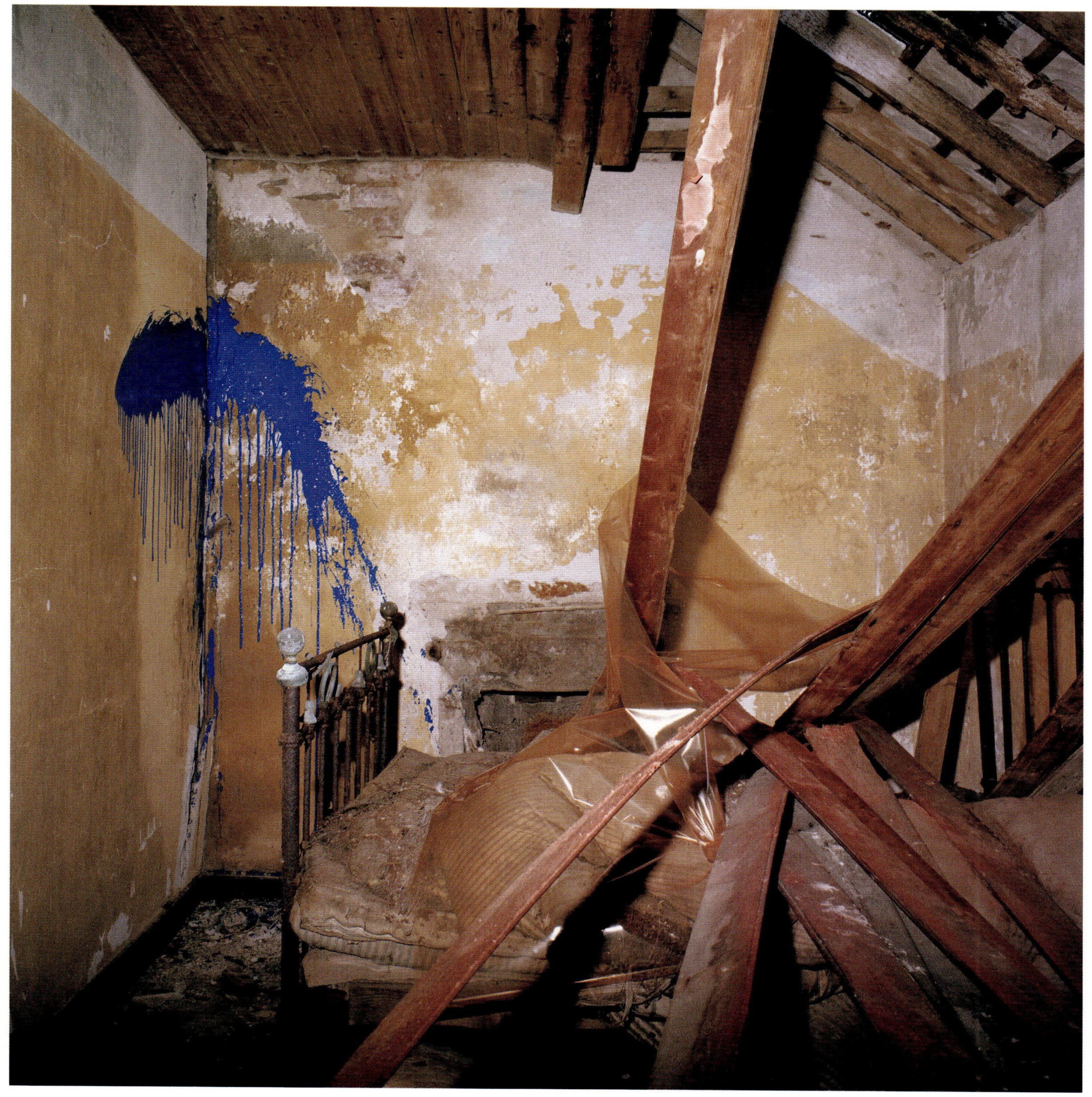

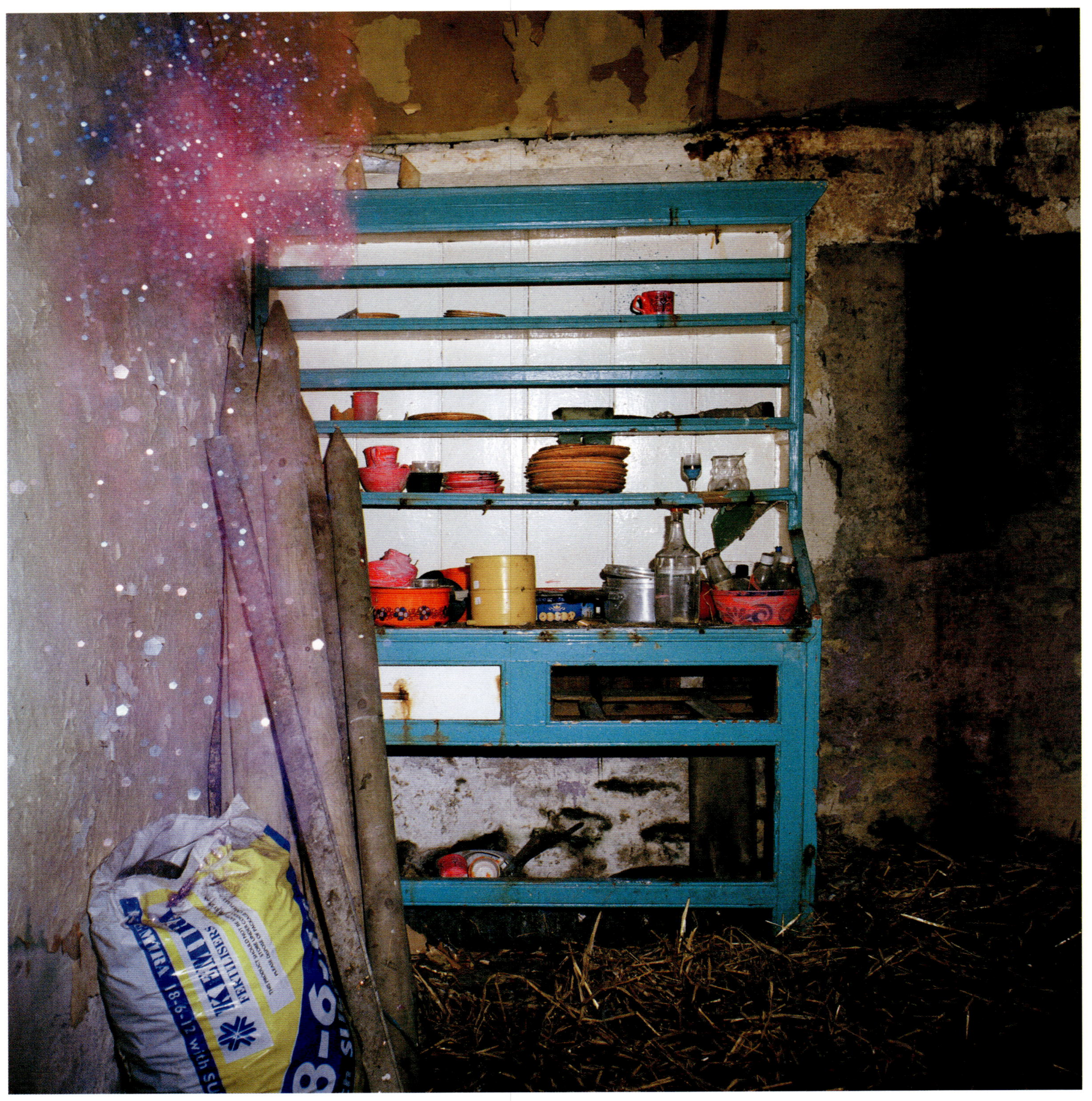

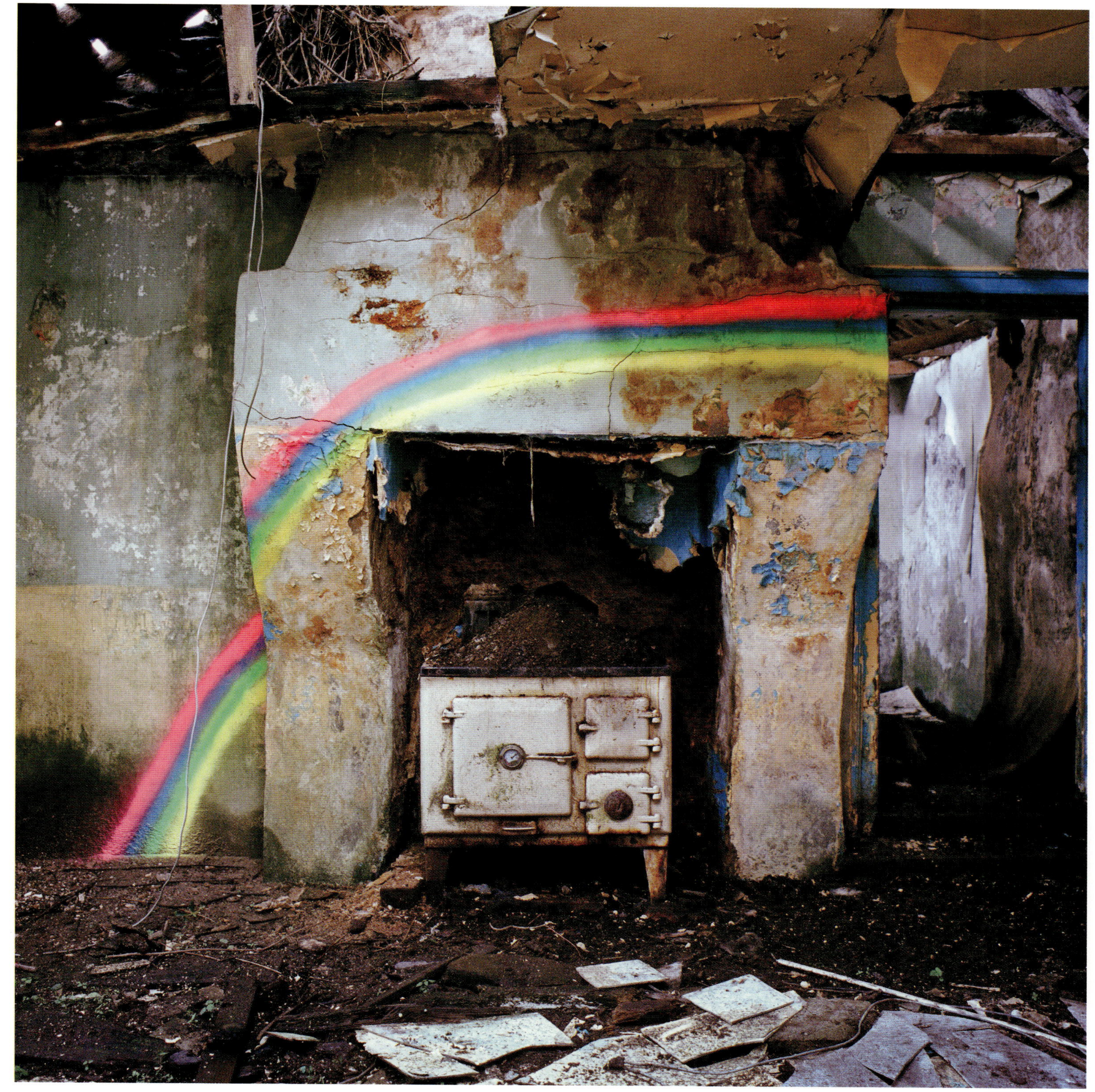

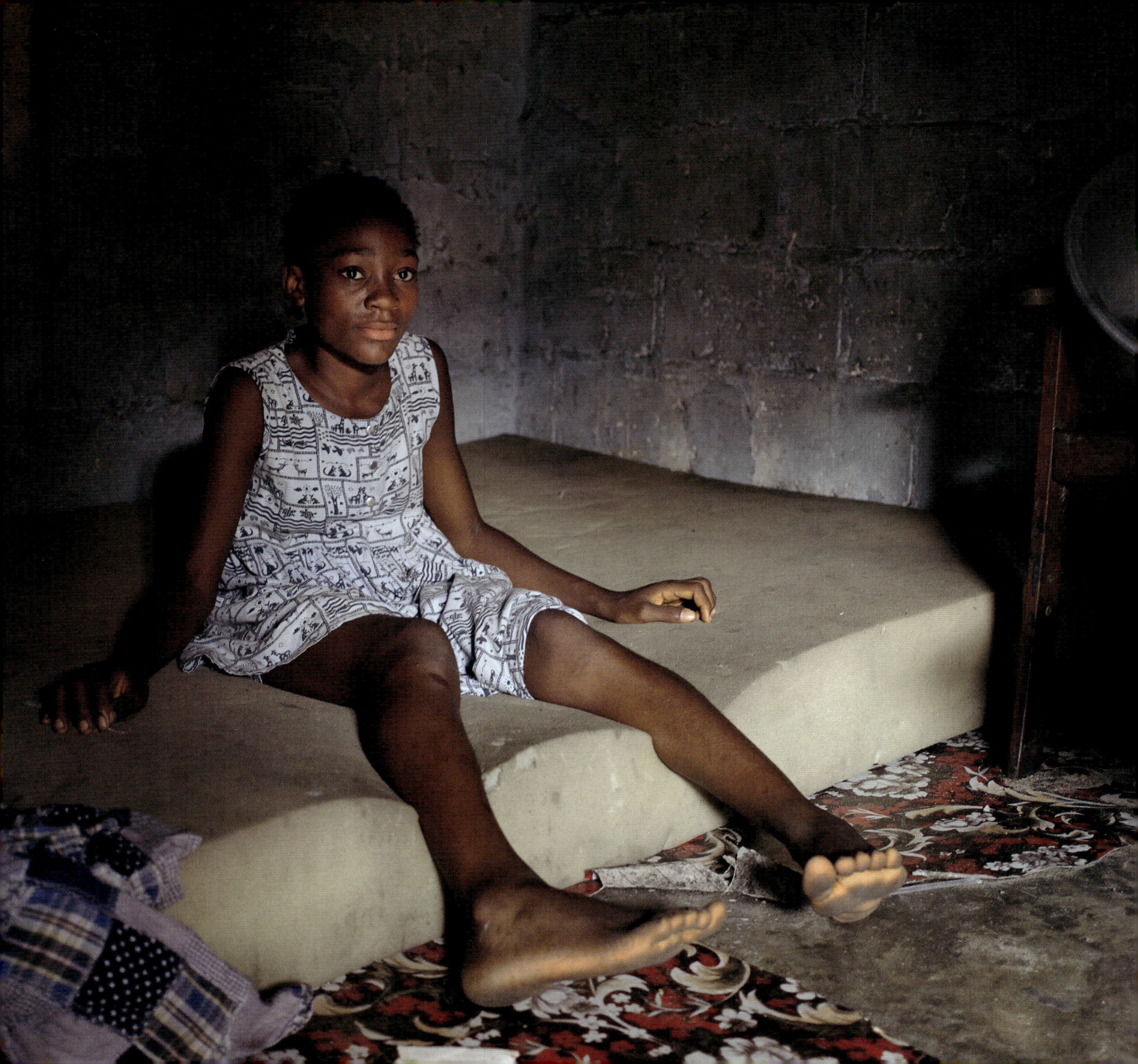

MAGDA RAKITA

...

Rakita's photographs reveal life's fragility as something to be embraced and understood, rather than feared

...

Magda Rakita's documentary practice is unflinching in the subject matter with which she chooses to engage. Although her professional focus since graduating from London College of Communication in 2013 has been NGO work, Rakita has been gradually compiling a portfolio, both photographic and multimedia, which tackles under-discussed subjects.

Her graduation project was memorably titled *God Made Woman then he Jerked*, which was a piece of graffiti Rakita noticed, and photographed, in Liberia. She visited the country, one of the poorest in the world, in 2013, on the tenth anniversary of peace. Her intention was to explore the experience of girls growing up with the legacy of the brutal civil war, and the disproportionate burden of its aftermath on girls and women.

As Rakita says, 'Relatively few girls are able to attend school as they find it difficult to reconcile their obligations towards their families with the demands of schooling. Many struggle to afford the obligatory school uniforms and registration fees despite education being (at least in theory) free. Sexual- and gender-based violence remain major concerns, including in Liberia's educational system, and it is not uncommon for students to be subject to sexual harassment when it comes to exchanging favours for grades.' In 2013, all 25,000 candidates failed the entrance exam to the University of Liberia, which prompted President Ellen Johnson Sirleaf to brand the education system 'a mess'.

Rakita's photographs belie the strident title, and instead depict, with gentleness and soft colour, a young population coming to terms with gender-based violence: finding a path to a different life via education and with the help of organizations that provide scholarships. Rakita's photographs reveal life's fragility as something to be embraced and understood, rather than feared. She understands well the play of light and shadow, and the use of symbolic imagery to reinforce her narrative. We see balloons and bubbles, swollen with potential; a discarded typewriter; a brutalized doll. Together this narrative arc offers an untypical representation of a group of young women on the threshold of a different future.

After the outbreak of the deadly Ebola virus, Rakita returned to Monrovia. She felt compelled to do so, to reconnect with the people who had shared their time and lives with her. She made a series of portraits of young people wearing masks, as part of an art therapy project, through which self-expression is possible. In her wider work, she has found her own methods to encourage self-expression in people whose voices we might otherwise not hear. Two multimedia projects made in 2015 continue the focus on underexposed subjects. In *The Past is Another Country* the viewer observes the possibility of remaining a sexual being into one's eighth decade and in *Cosmo was Murdered that Night* we hear the raw testimony of being a victim of male-on-male rape.

What shines through in Rakita's work is her involvement with the people she photographs, her ability to facilitate people's own storytelling, and her instinctive and profound humanitarianism.

Untitled, Monrovia, Liberia, 2013, *God Made Woman then he Jerked* series

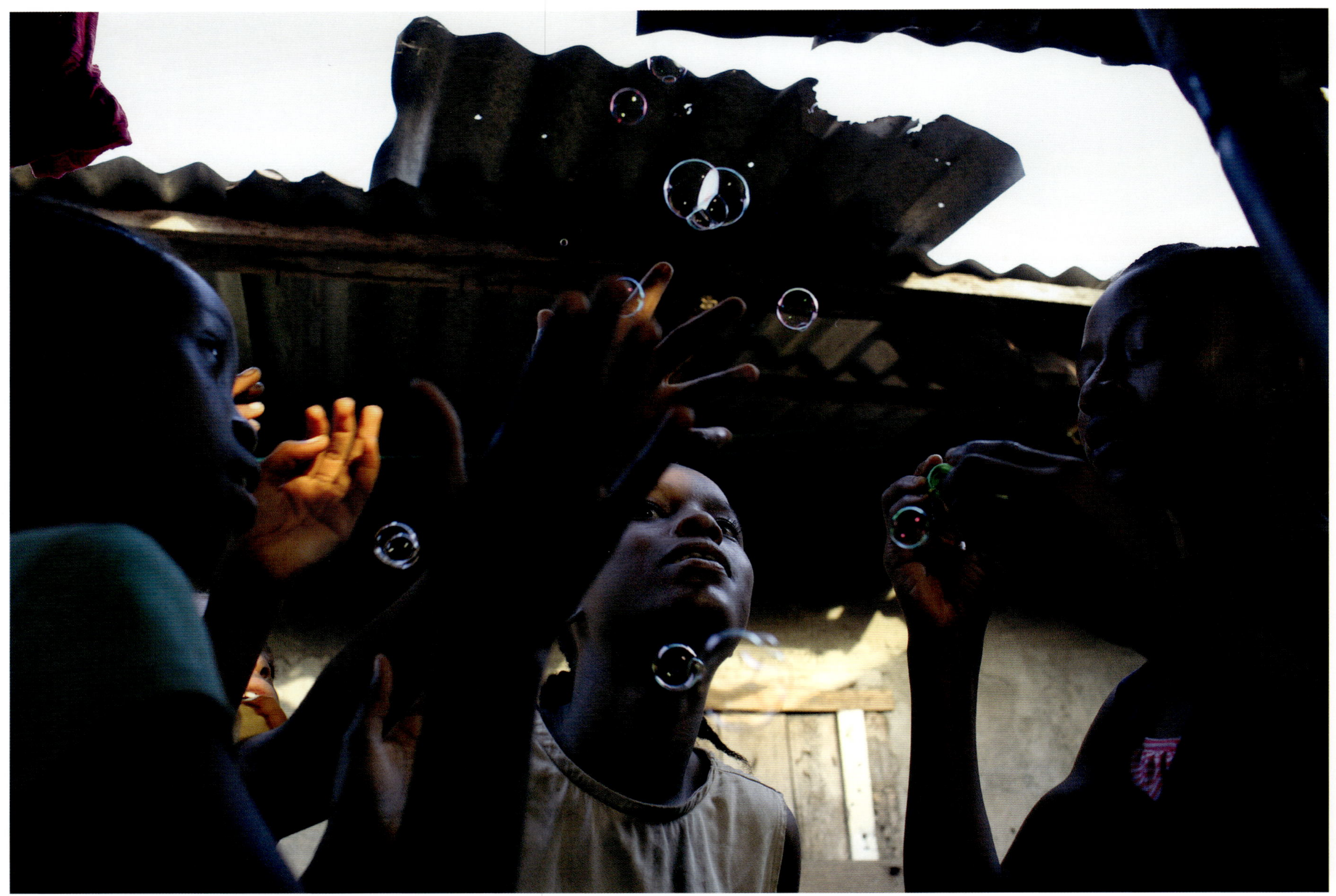

Untitled, Monrovia, Liberia, 2013, *God Made Woman then he Jerked* series

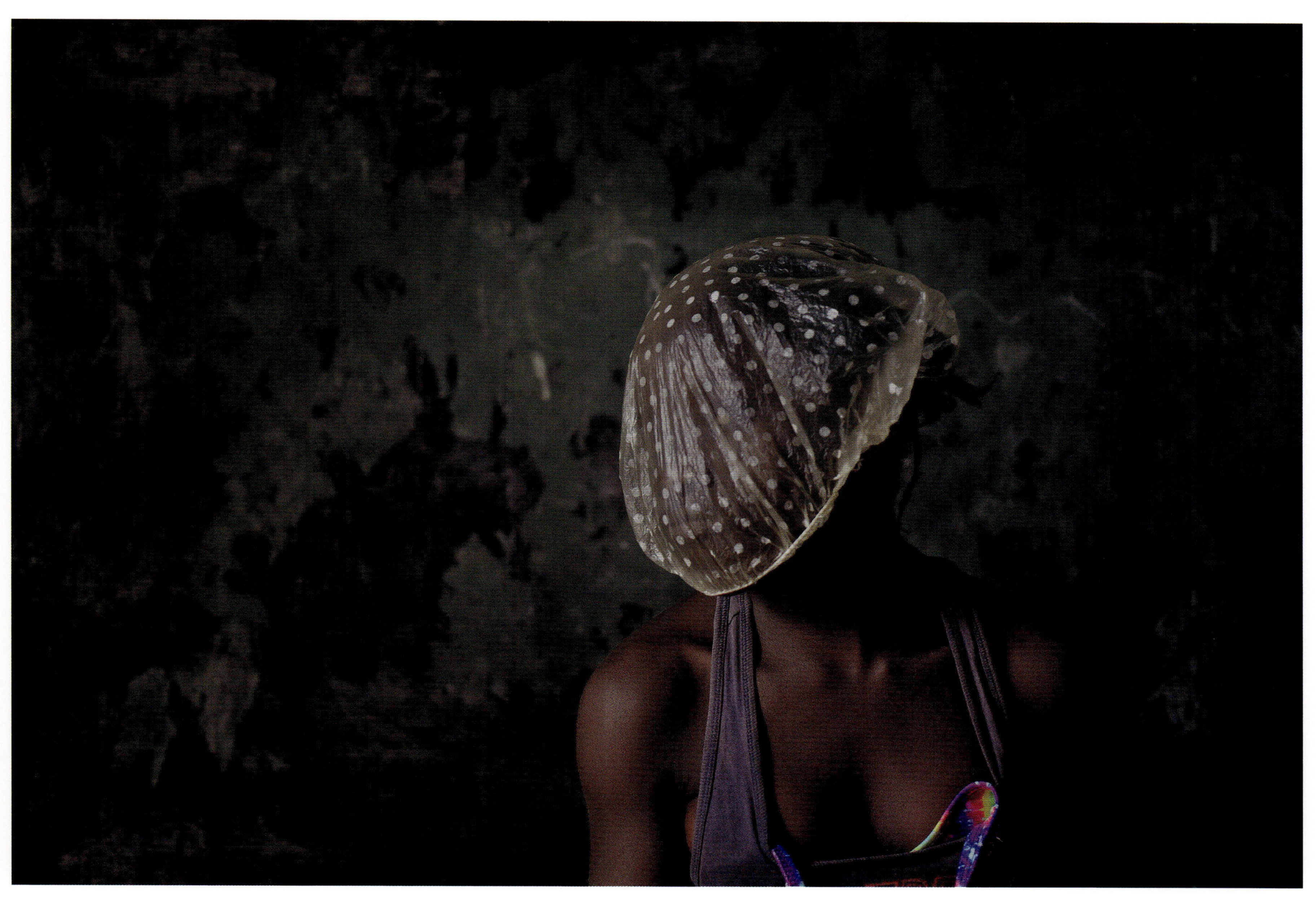

Untitled, Monrovia, Liberia, 2013, *God Made Woman then he Jerked* series

Magda Rakita　159

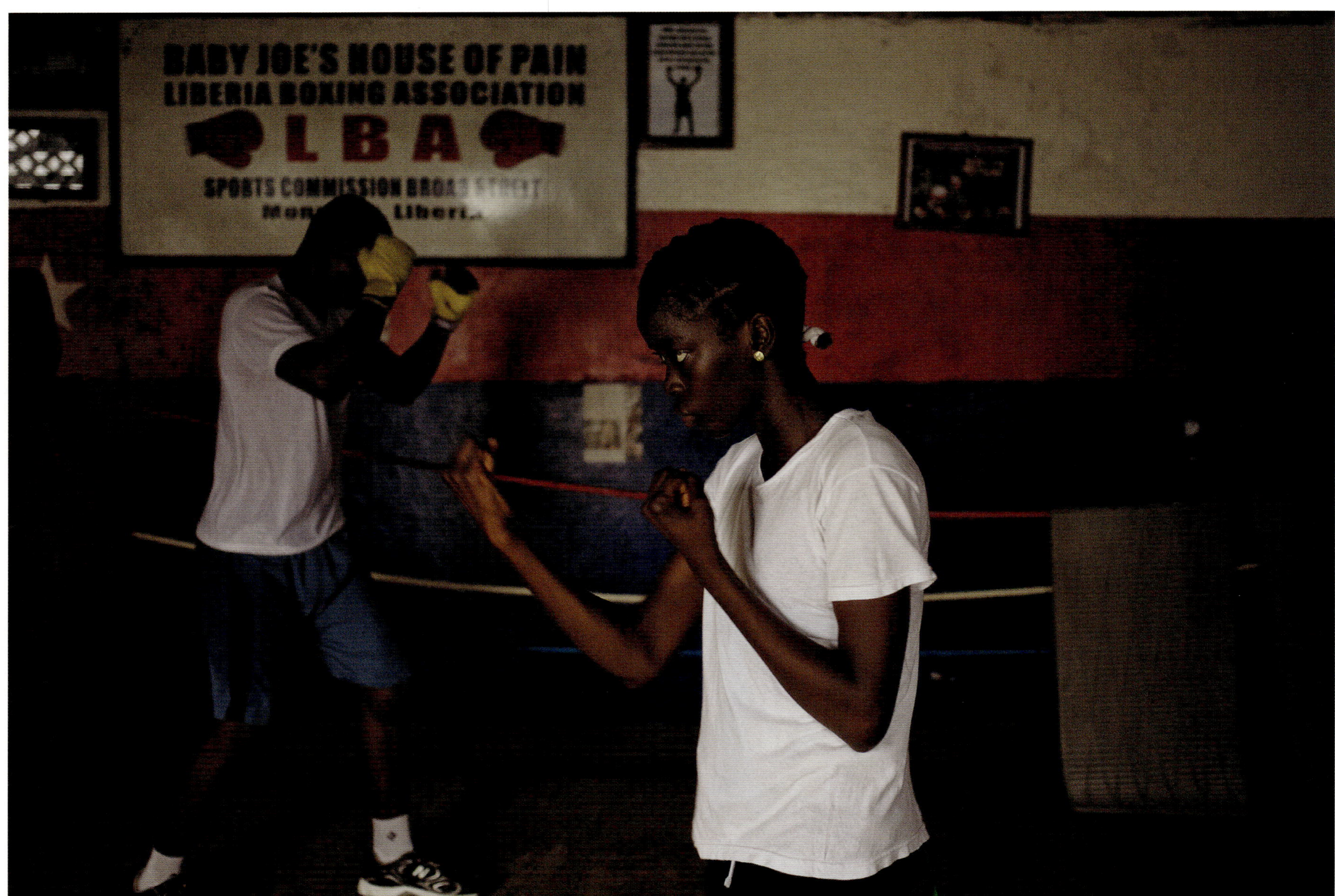

Untitled, Monrovia, Liberia, 2013, *God Made Woman then he Jerked* series

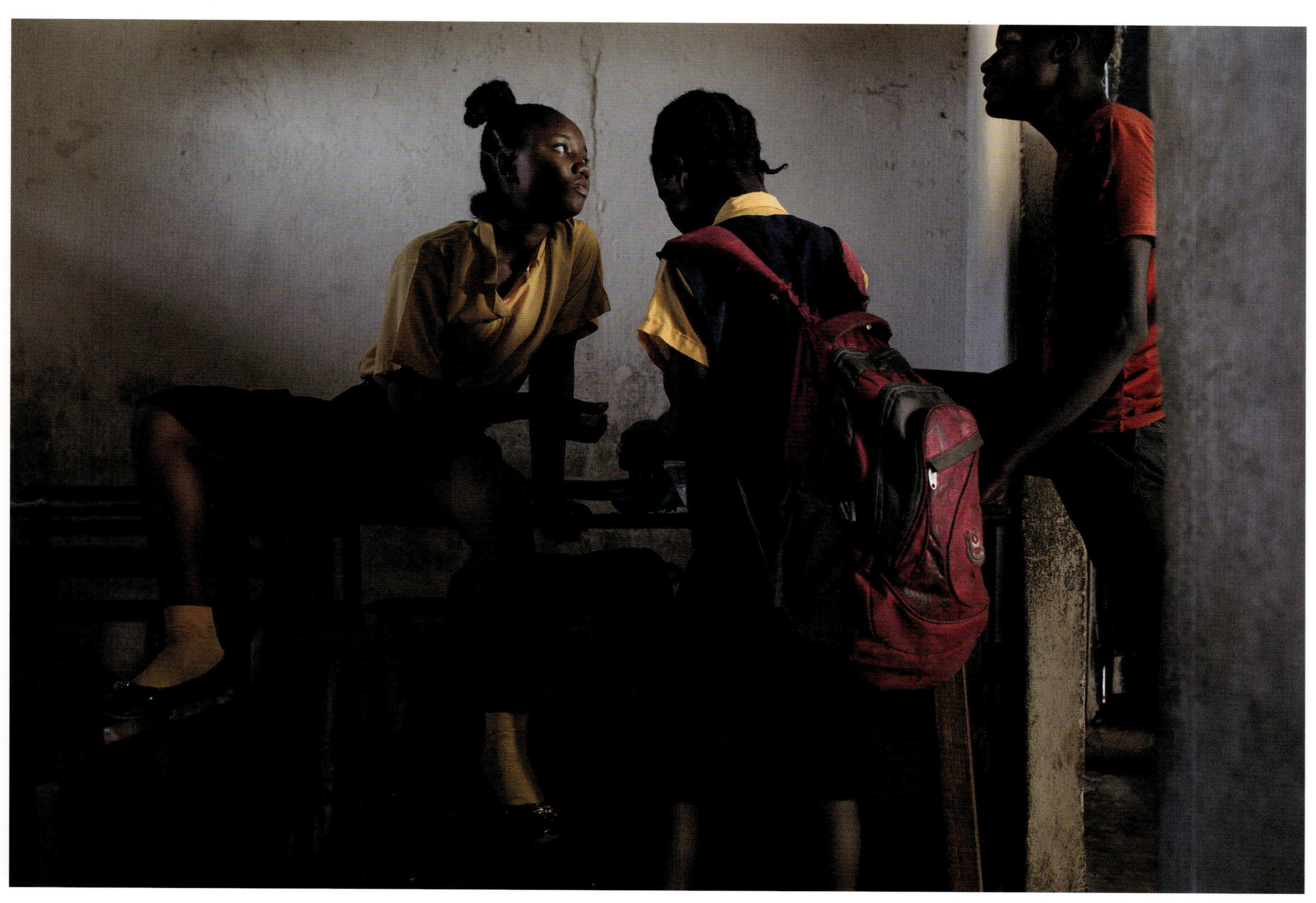

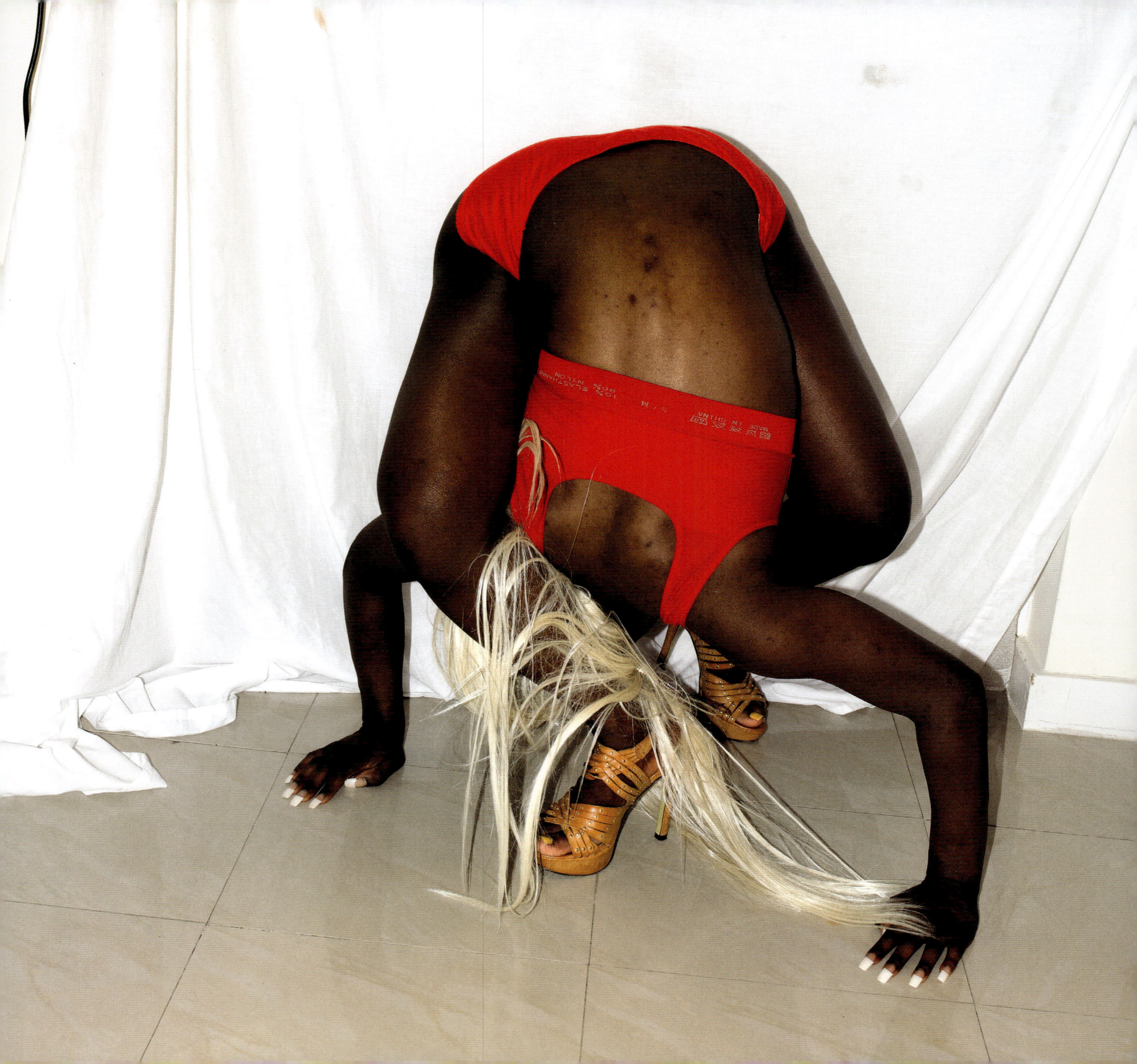

LUA RIBEIRA

Spanish photographer Lúa Ribeira is perhaps one of the most exciting new artists to arrive on the photographic scene in the last few years. A recent graduate of the acclaimed BA in documentary photography at the University of South Wales, Newport, Ribeira creates work that injects vibrant colour, visually and metaphorically, into a contemporary photographic aesthetic often dominated by the poetic and the pastel.

Her ongoing project *Noises in the Blood* does not so much speak to you – it grabs you by the collar, slaps you in the face and demands to be noticed. In 2015 the work was awarded a Firecracker Photographic Grant.

The excitement generated by Ribeira's work is not only attributed to her undeniable ability as an artist, but also to her chosen subject matter. Jamaican Dancehall culture is at once exotic, theatrical and noisy, as well as complicated, subversive and ritualistic. An important part of post-colonial, post-slavery culture, Dancehall has transcended its origins of music and dance to become folklore, encompassing style, language and societal practice.

The title *Noises in the Blood* is borrowed from a book by West Indian author and scholar Carolyn Cooper, who critically examines the dismissed discourse of Jamaica's vibrant popular culture and reclaims it as a powerful cultural expression. Ribeira, too, visually explores misconceived notions of sexuality versus feminism, and presents her protagonists as indisputably feminine and unquestionably in charge.

Challenging perceptions and subverting preconceived notions are key to this work. Despite the overwhelming tropical sensibility of *Noises in the Blood*, the work is predominantly shot in Birmingham, UK. Ribeira captures her collaborators in a tantalizing, hyper-real universe and provides a futuristic space in which to perform. Female gender is displayed as a highly sexualized and flamboyant version of itself. Pre-ritual, the women embark on a radical transformation of their appearance, using wigs, ornaments, colour and provocative clothing, like birds of paradise, to heighten their sexuality. On the dancefloor this voluptuousness is further expressed with gyrating pelvic motions but we are in no doubt as to who owns their sexuality.

It is the women that you notice in Ribeira's work. The men are almost absent, and when they are present they are passive, seemingly a tool used to highlight the fabulousness of the female leads further. This concept is reinforced by Ribeira's addition of exotic plants, a metaphor for the rich and the heady, the fertile and the primal. Ribeira invites us into a universe where usual rules and social codes do not apply. There is a sense of the familiar, but it is wrapped in an energetically charged, surrealist landscape.

It is easy to draw parallels of 'the other' in Ribeira's work, but this is collaborative, performance-based art at its best and Ribeira revels in the subversion and the stereotype. By accepting that, as a Spanish woman, she can never fully understand or interpret a culture so different from her own, she frees herself by creating a super-sized and fantastical representation. Through the vibrancy of *Noises in the Blood* everyone can celebrate the diaspora of Jamaican culture and its proud resistance to global homogeneity.

Untitled 1, 2016, Noises in the Blood series

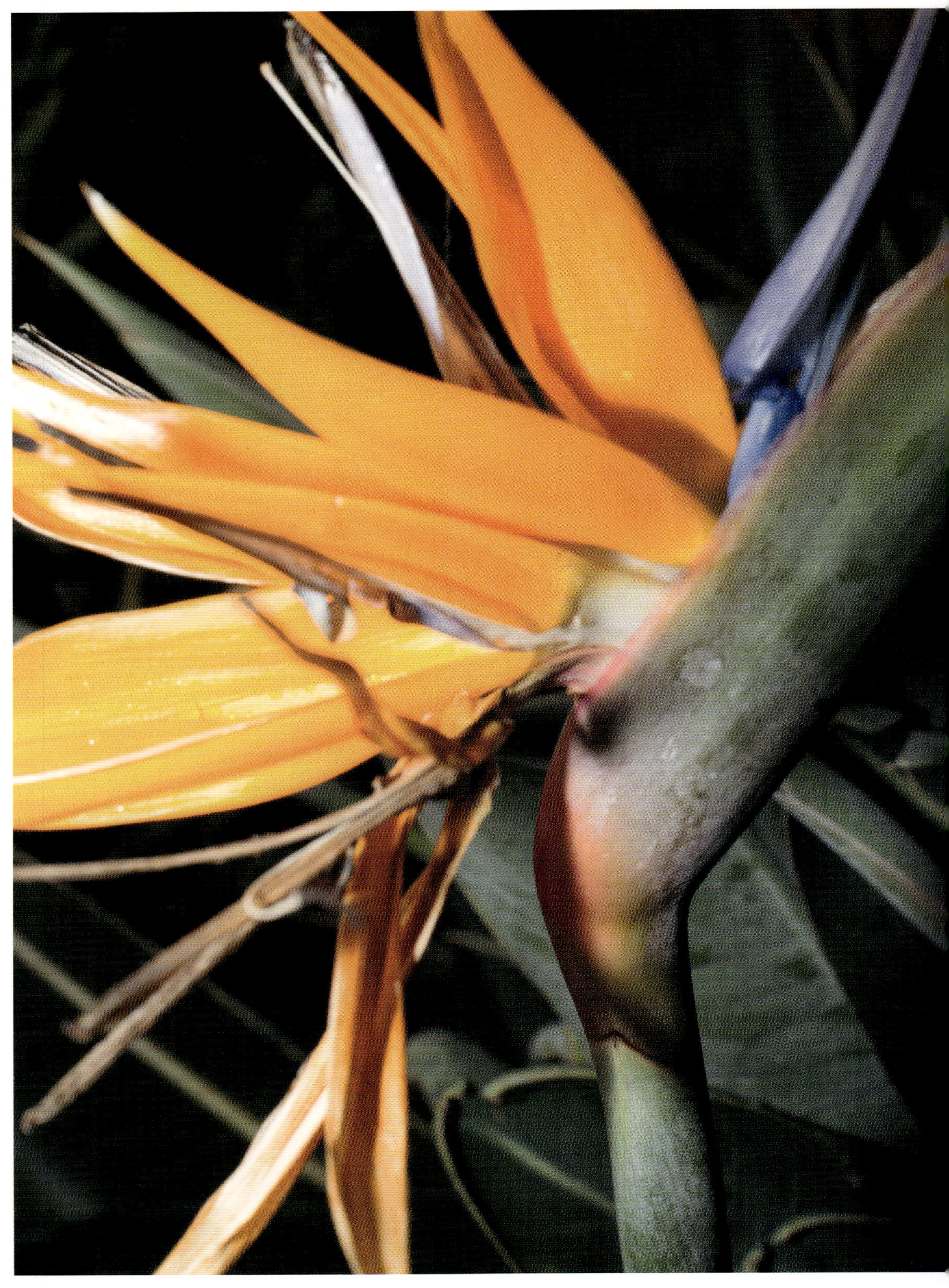

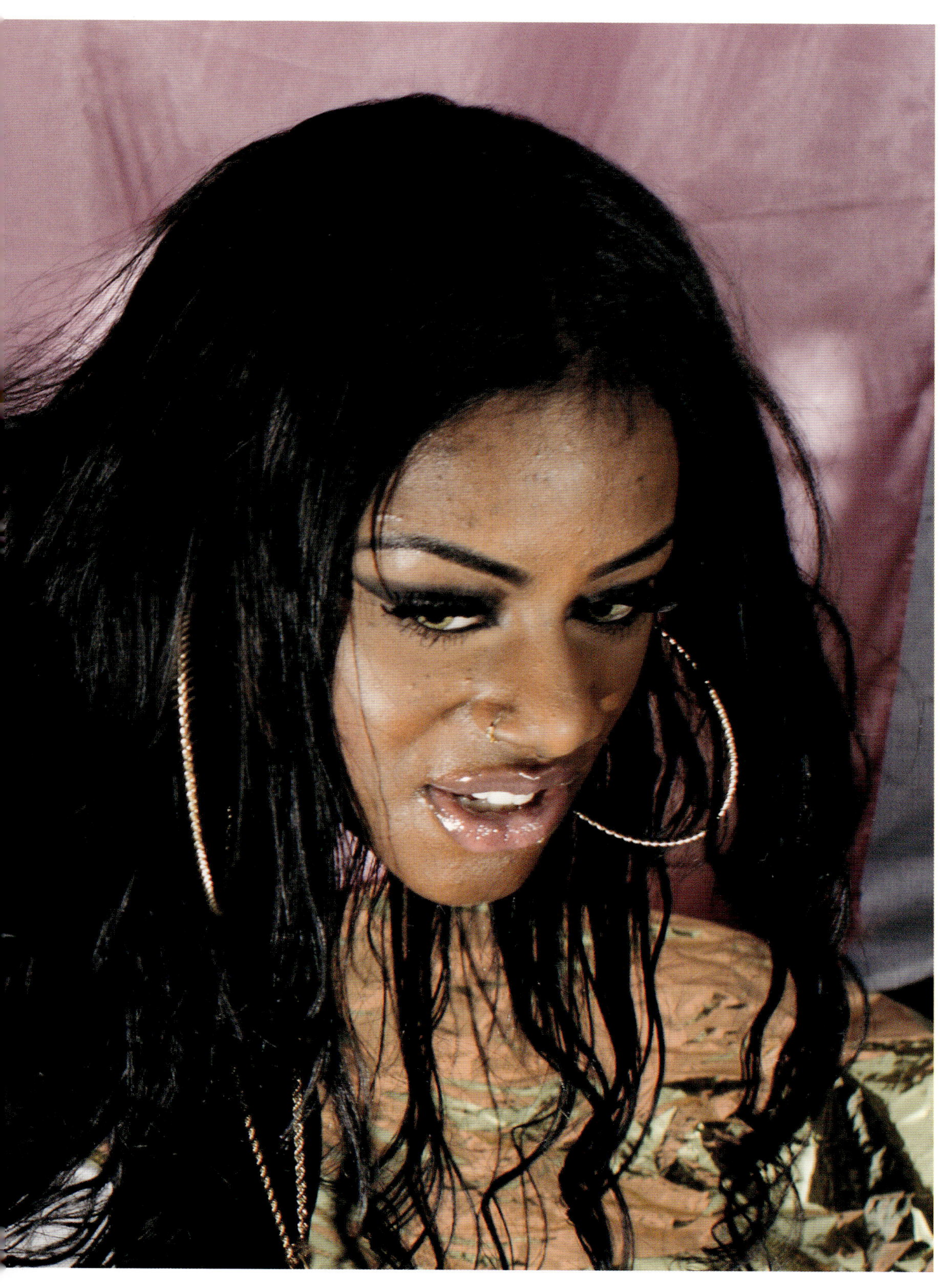

Lúa Ribeira   165

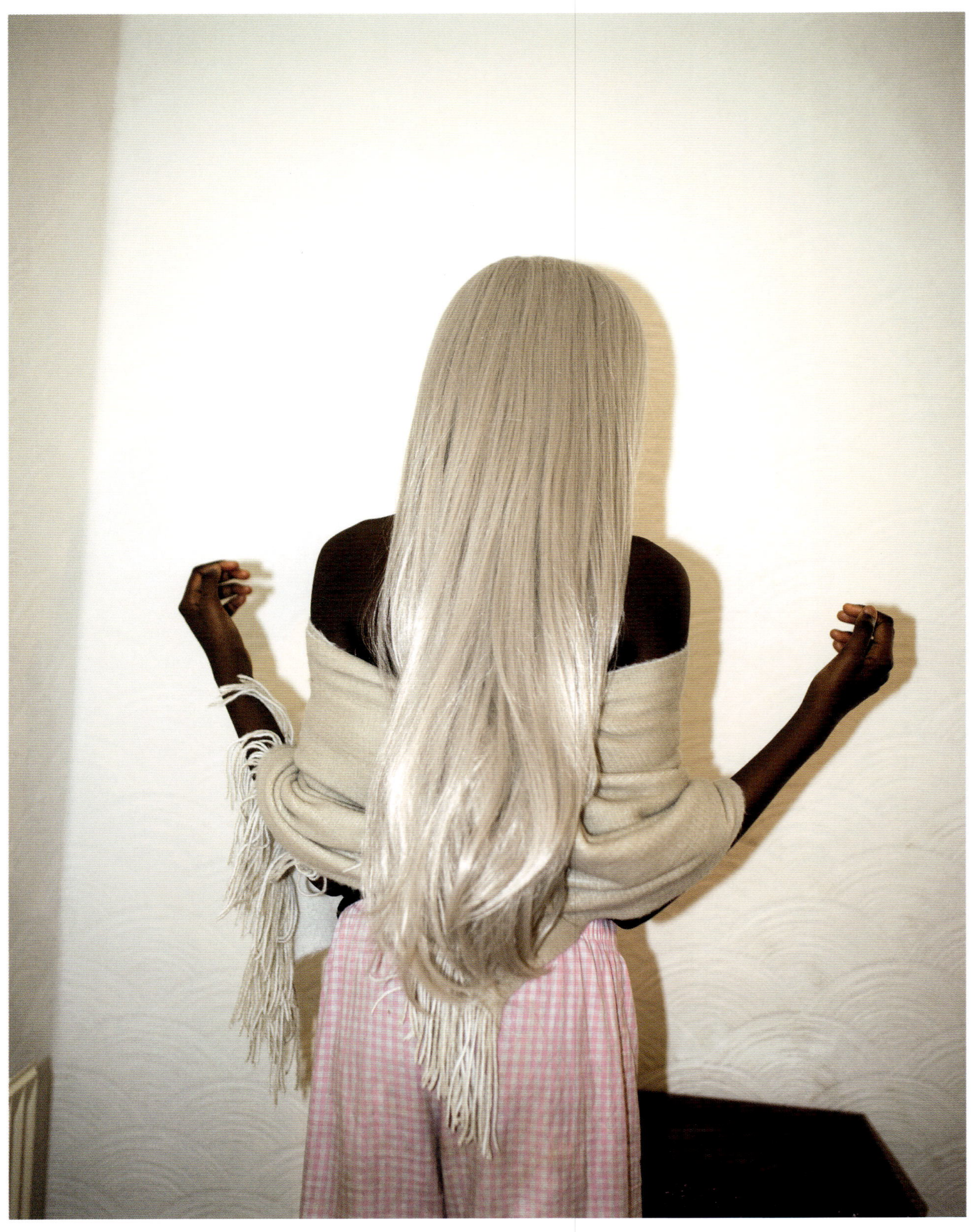

Untitled 3, 2016, Noises in the Blood series

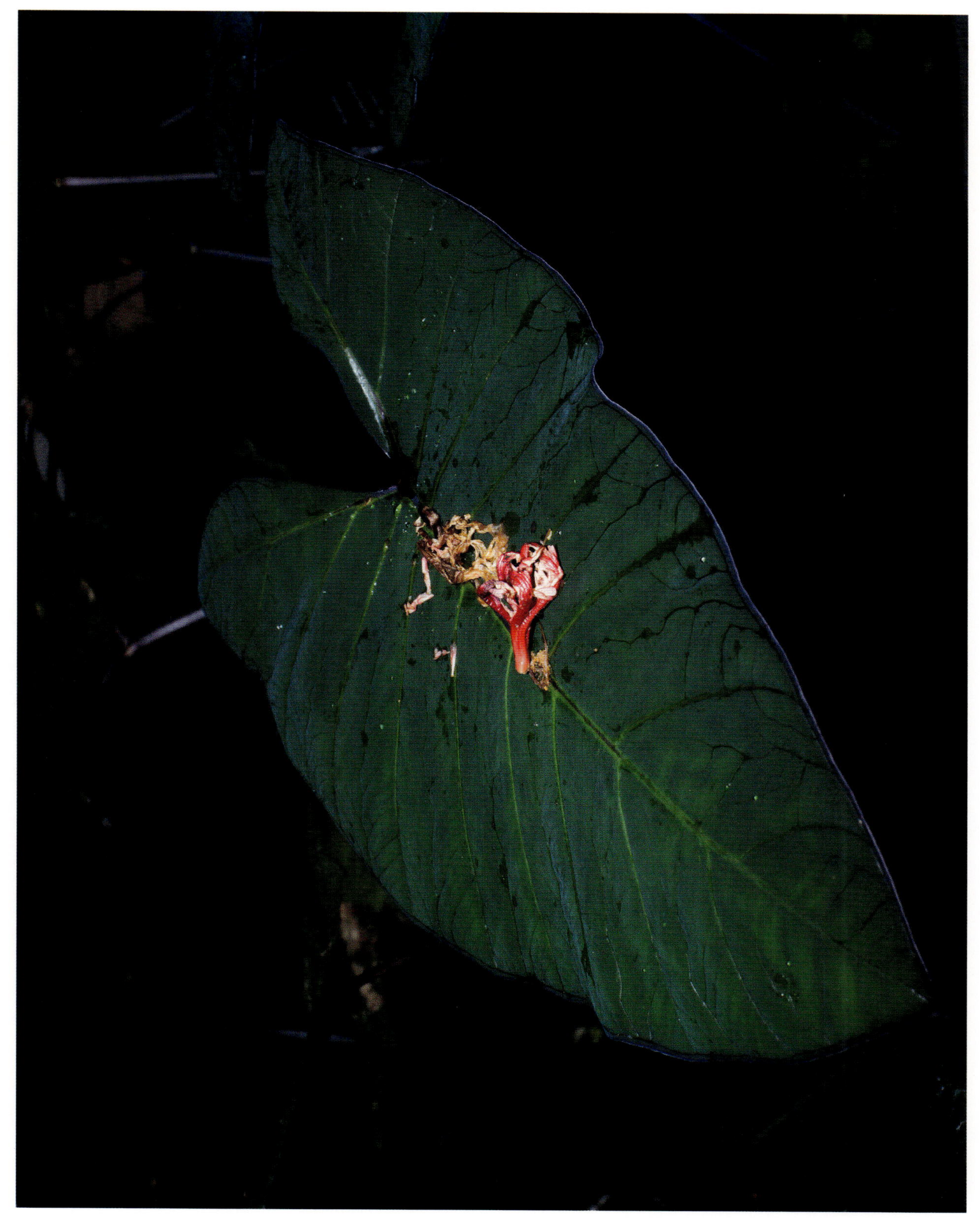

Untitled 4, 2016, Noises in the Blood series

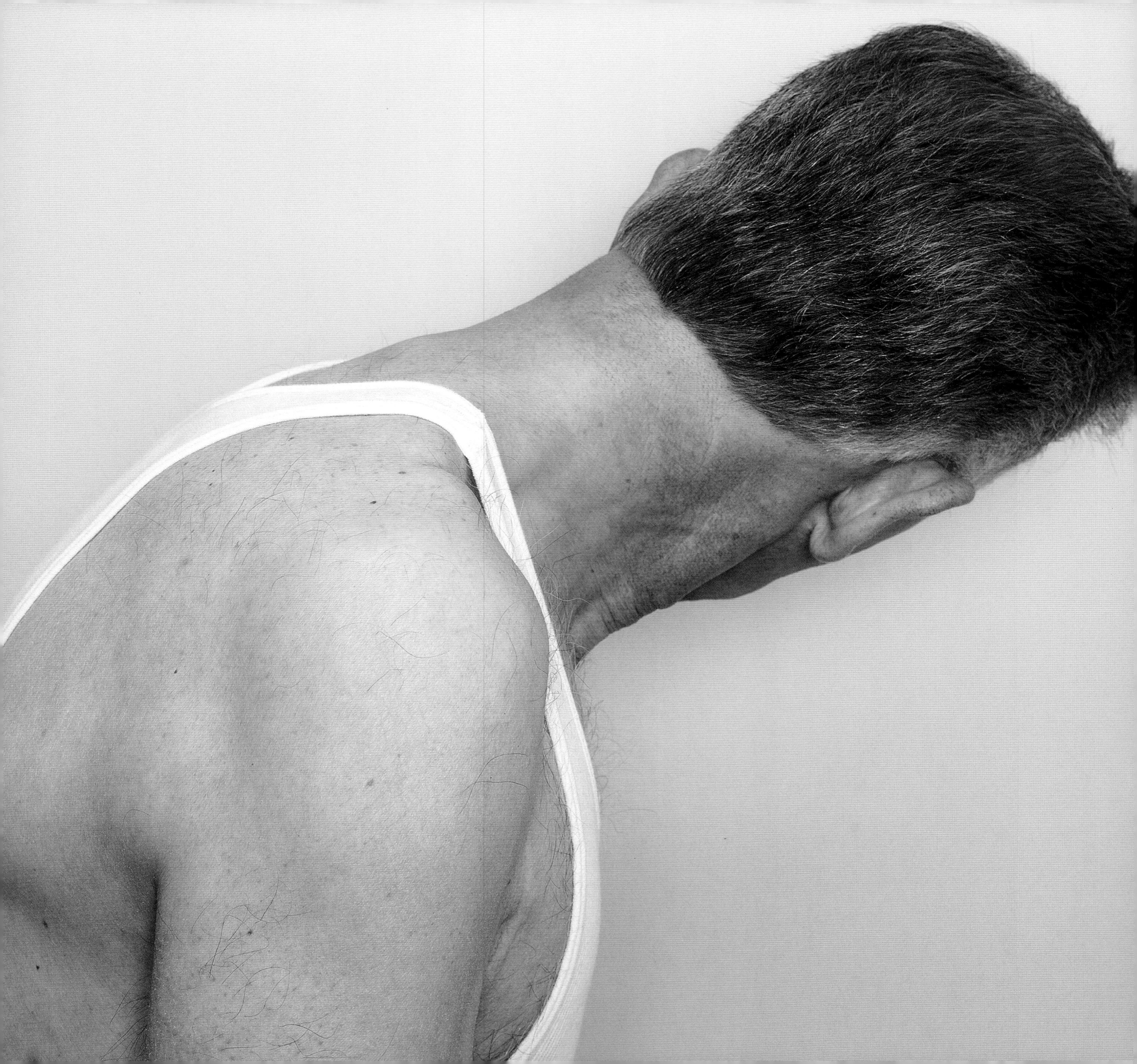

MARIELA SANCARI

...
She had to return
to the end to begin
again
...

With the publication of her extraordinary book *Moisés*, Mariela Sancari demonstrated the possibility of picturing a secret. The book is named after her father, who committed suicide when his daughters – Sancari and her twin – were fourteen years old. They were not allowed to see his body and weren't told why; they speculated that this might have been connected to the cause of his death, or to his Jewish identity. But they did not know.

The not knowing became the wellspring, eventually, for *Moisés* (La Fabrica, 2015). In the intervening years, the sisters half-believed they might find their father sitting in a café, or walking down the street. In Sancari's words, 'Thanatology asserts that not seeing the dead body of our beloved ones prevents us from accepting their death. Contemplating the body of the deceased helps us overcome one of the most complex stages of grief: denial.'

Sancari placed a classified advert in a Buenos Aires newspaper, asking for men aged around seventy, which was the age her father would be, had he lived, to study a photograph of Moisés and, if they saw a resemblance, to come forward. Sancari photographed the men who had responded to her request in her father's clothes, which the family had kept close during a spontaneous evacuation to Mexico from Argentina in the aftermath of his death, and in the ensuing decades. The palpable desire for the return of a beloved father finds its voice in photographing strangers. Sancari asks one man to comb her hair; we witness this intimacy because she chooses to be visible in a couple of otherwise solitary portraits. There is something inexplicably poignant in the act of turning the lens on, or paying attention to, a group of older men, with their lined faces and their knowing eyes. However, we will never know what exactly they saw in the newspaper image of Moisés that spoke to them so deeply – what it was that reminded them of themselves.

Since 1997, Sancari has lived in Mexico City. She worked as a newspaper photographer for five years before focusing on more personal work, including the series *The Two Headed Horse*, in which she creates portraits of herself and her twin, apart, entwined, clasped in a tenderly sexual embrace. Is this a pure form of self-love, or consolation? She also photographs precious objects such as their father's gold cigarette lighter. Two short sentences describe each item; rarely do the memories collide.

Moisés was named book of the year in 2015 by a host of well-known critics – Susan Bright, Tim Clark and Erik Kessels, to name a few. The latter likened the raw emotional power of the work to Seiichi Furuya's *Mémoires*. Indeed the form of the book is structured to mirror the labyrinth of memory. Its pages are interlocking, and necessitate much touching in order to move towards the end, which is, of course, our beginning, as T. S. Eliot reminds us. Sancari understands this from her own experience. She had to return to the end to begin again, with this captivating attempt to reconstitute her father and to unlock, at least in part, the secret of his death.

Untitled, 2014, Moisés series

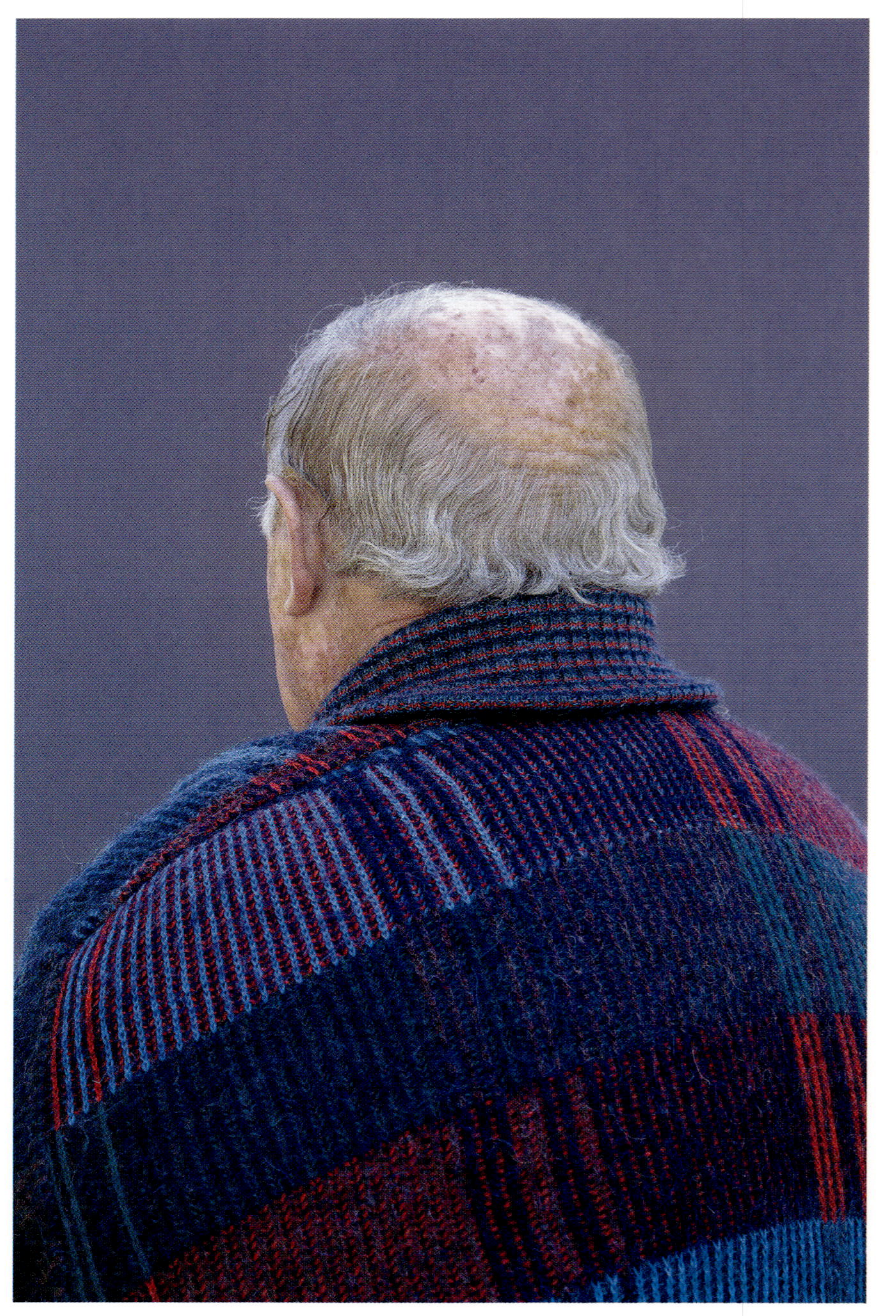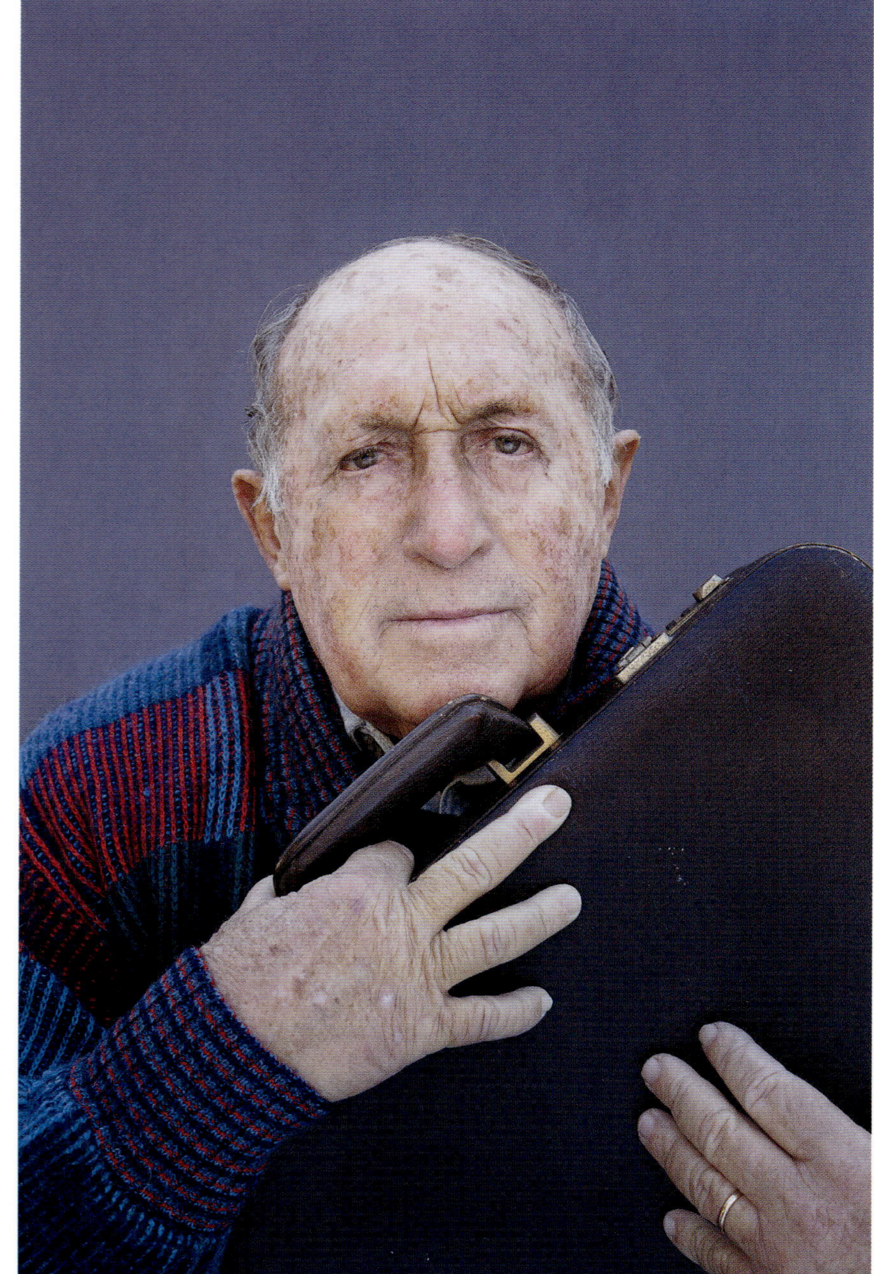

Untitled, 2014, Moisés series

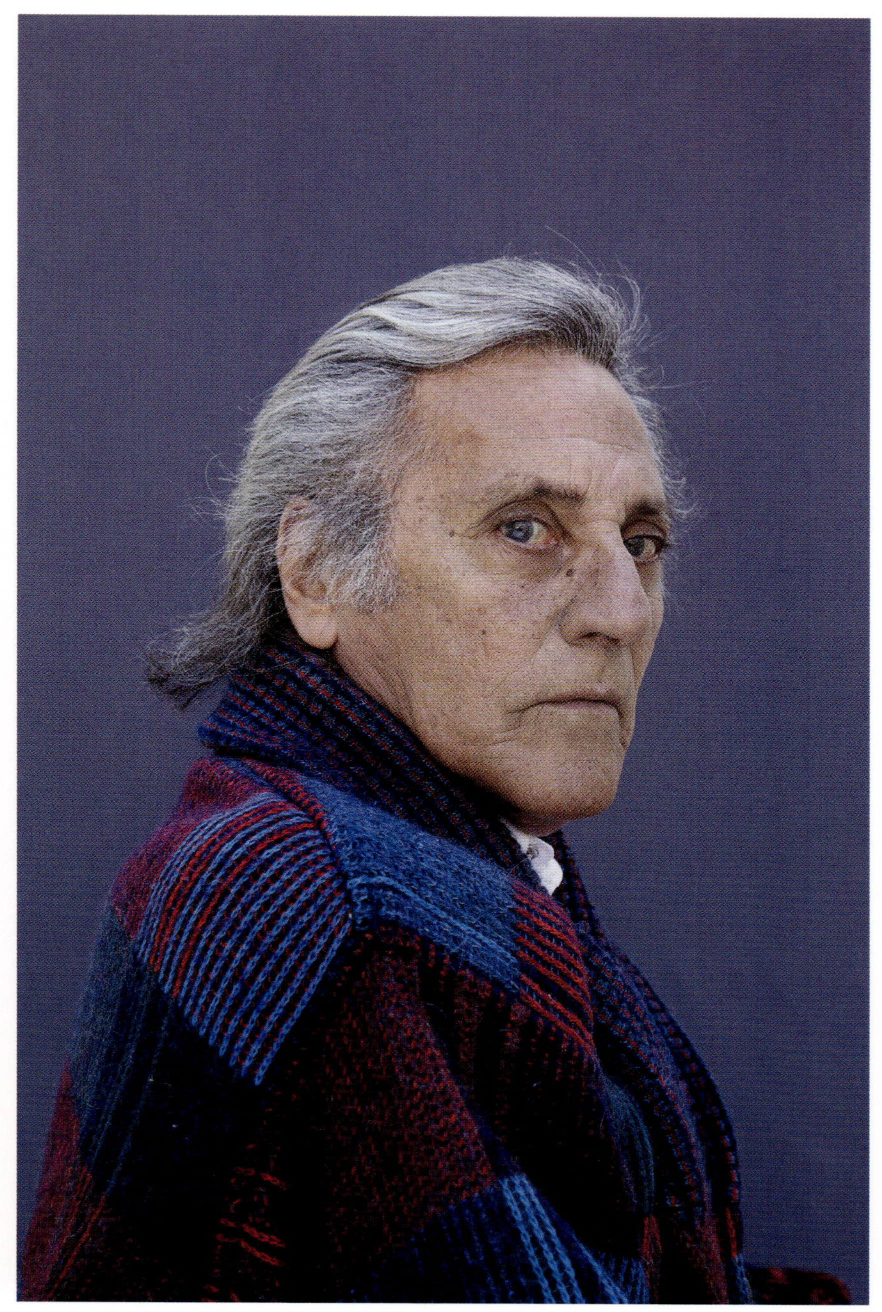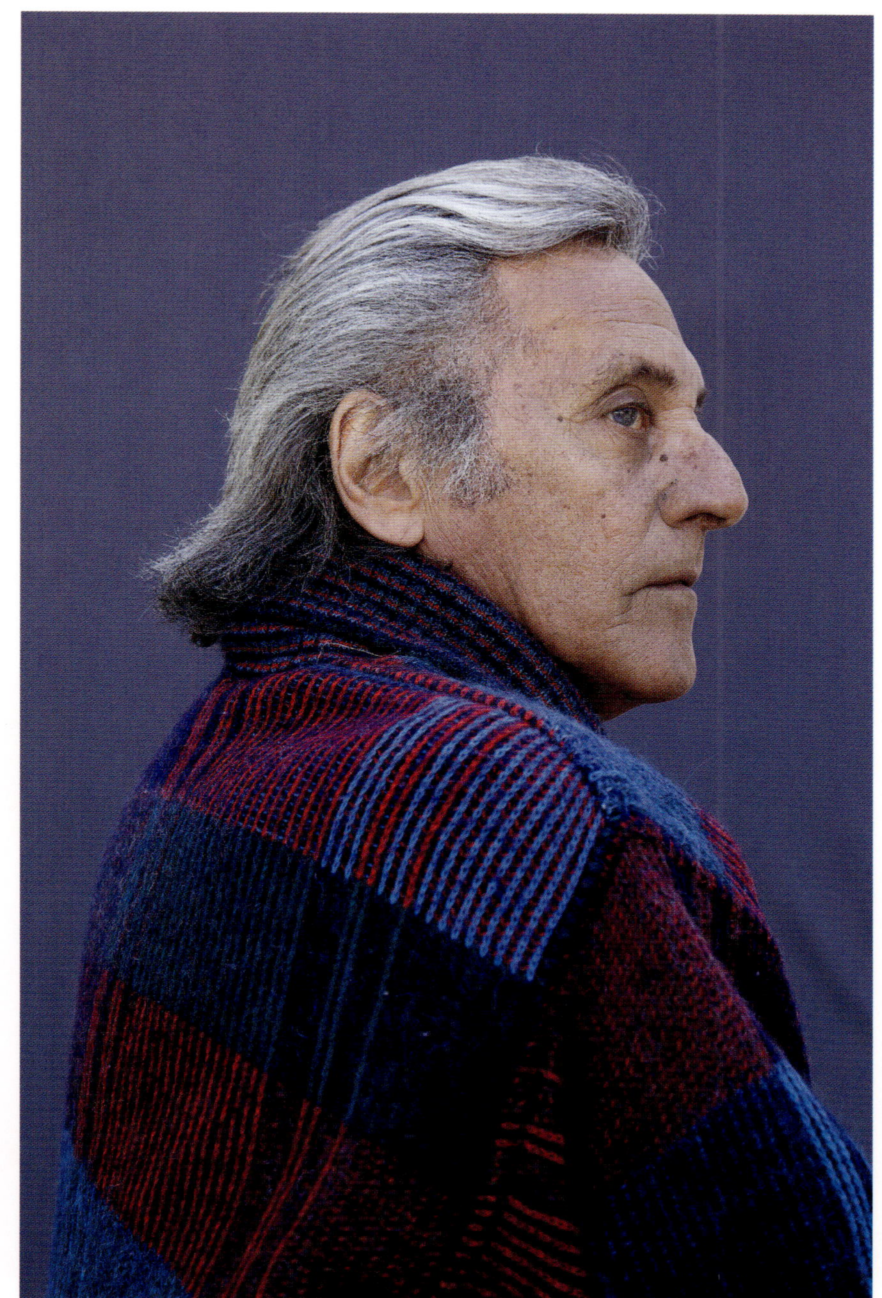

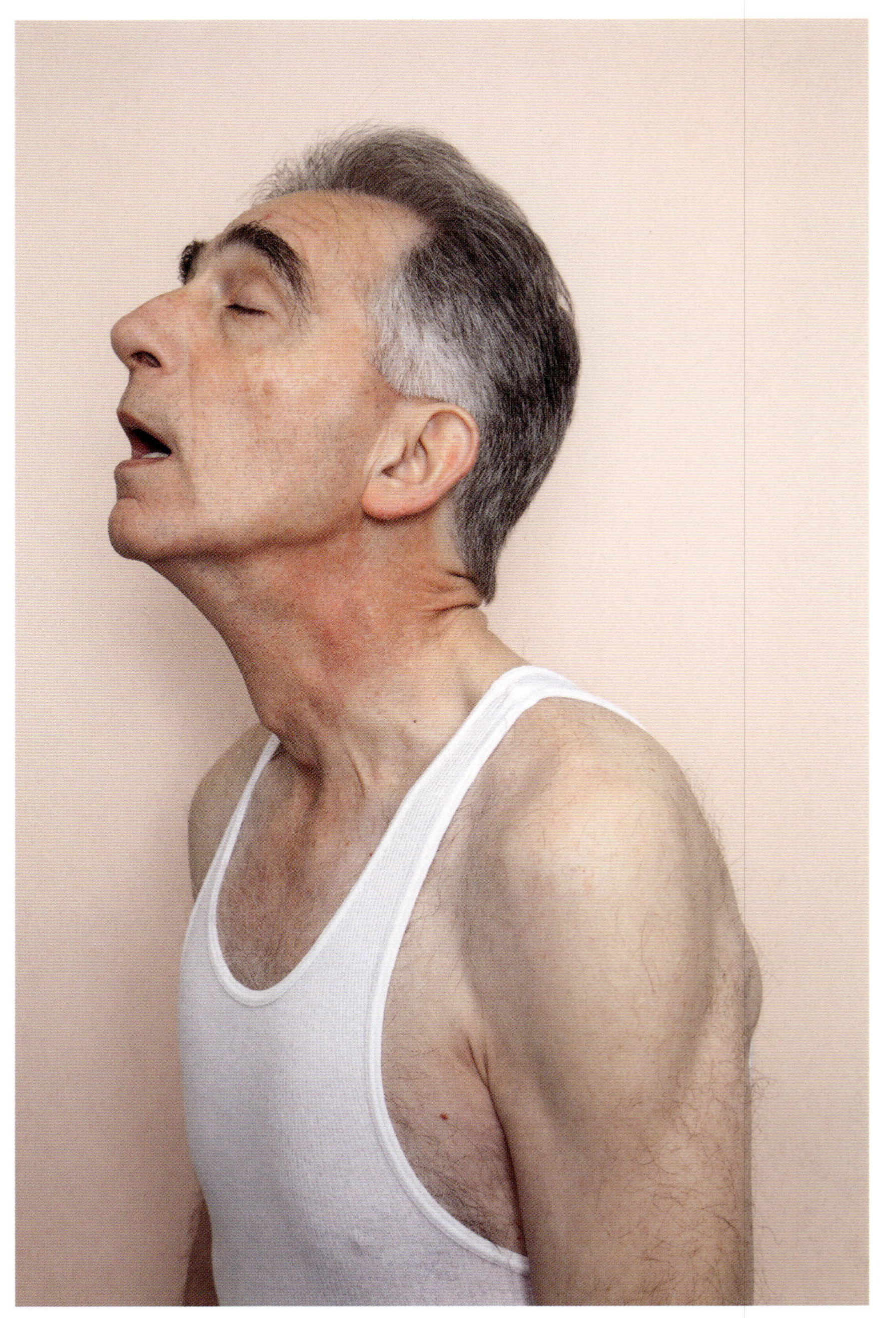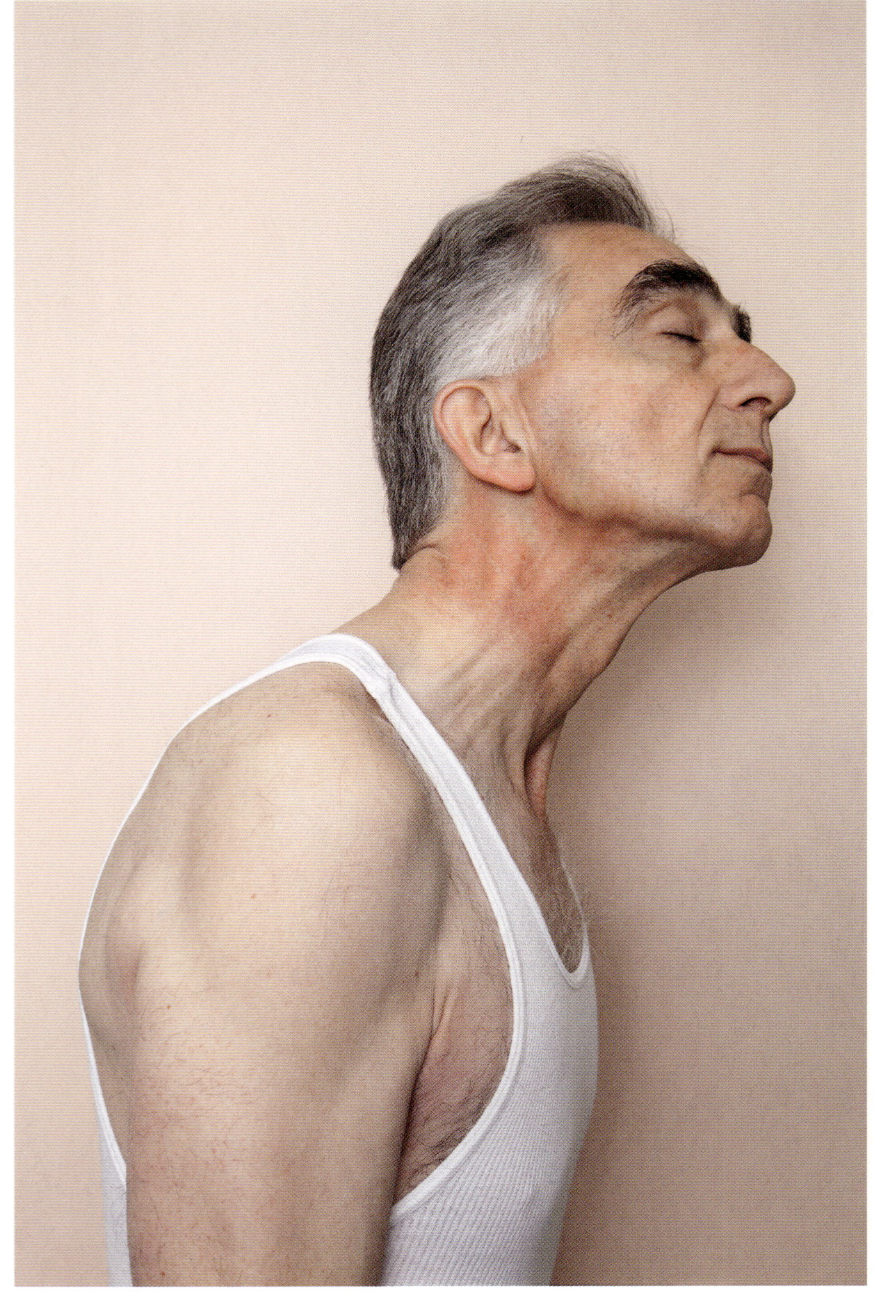

Untitled, 2014, *Moisés* series

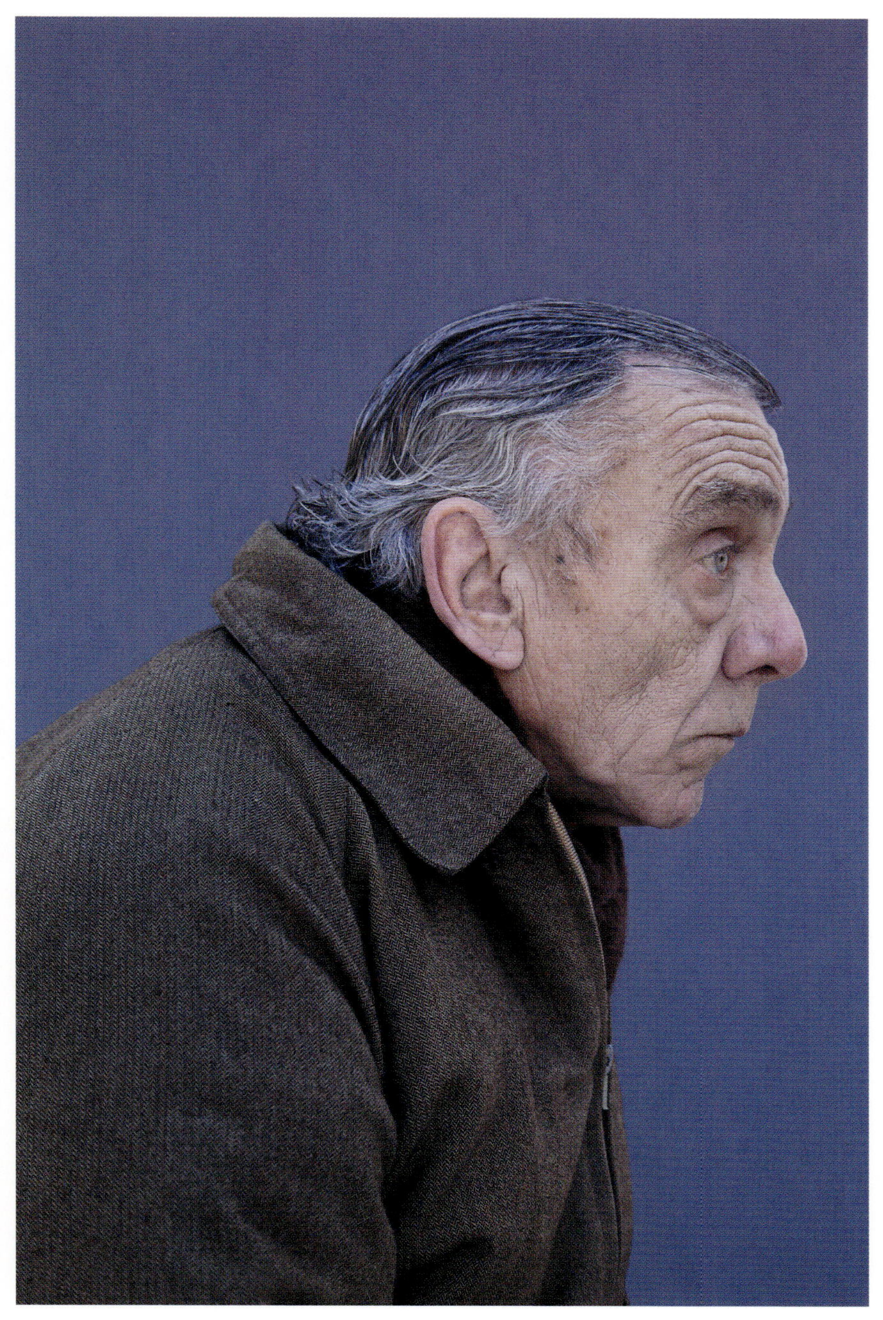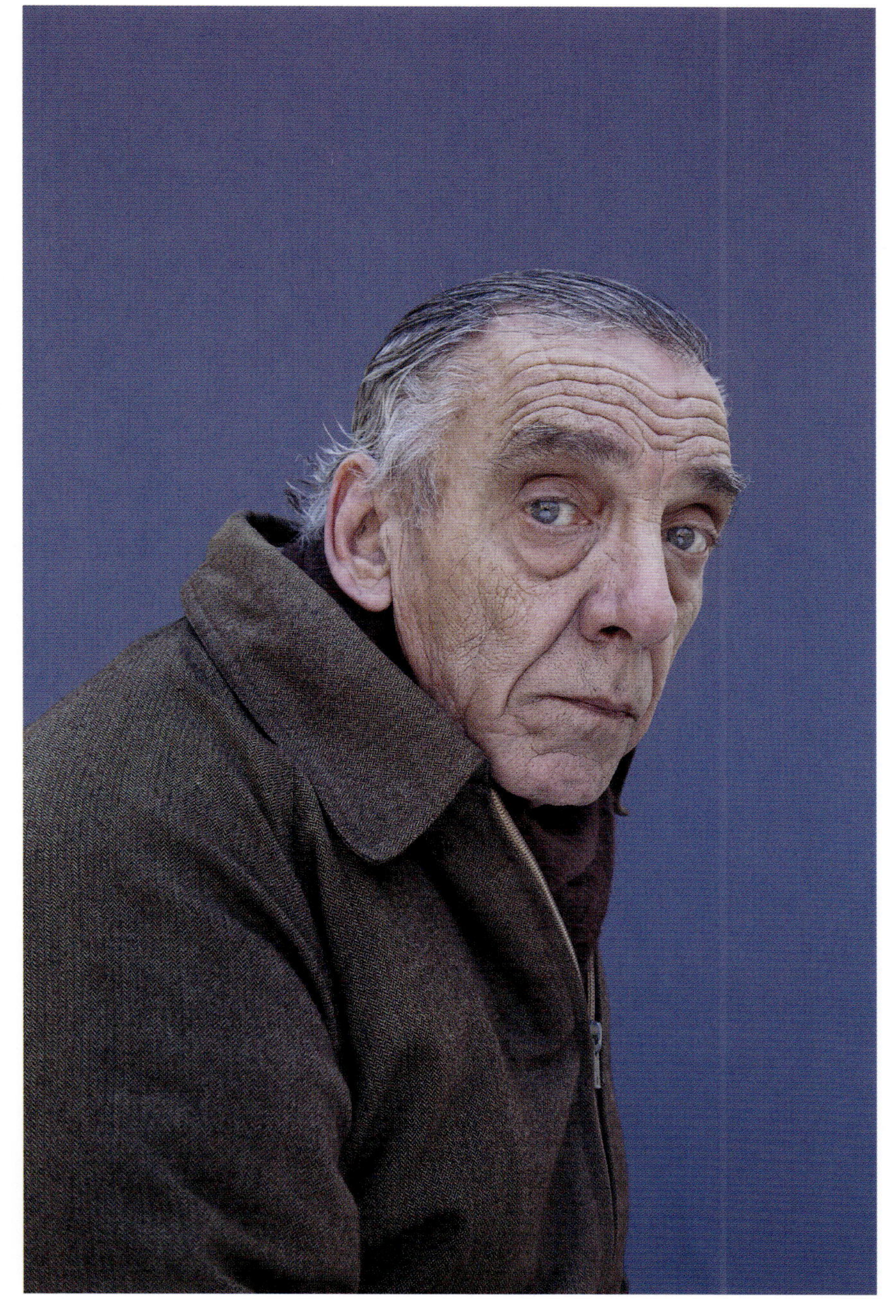

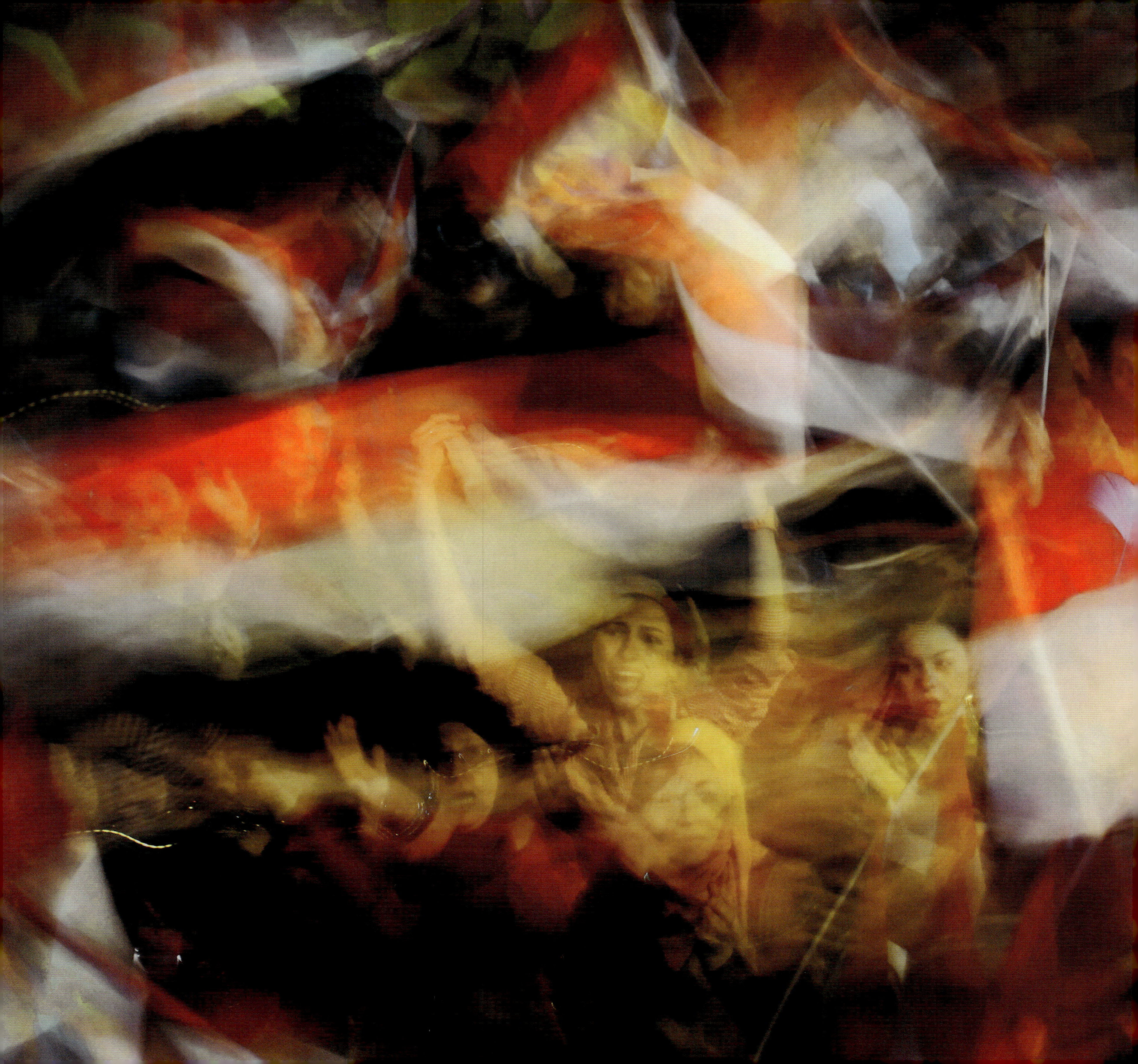

LAURA EL-TANTAWY

...

It is rare to see the personal and political colliding so effectively

...

'I am Egyptian.' These stark words opened Laura El-Tantawy's immersive three-screen installation for the 2016 Deutsche Börse Photography Foundation Prize at the Photographers' Gallery in London. She was nominated for her self-published book *In the Shadow of the Pyramids*, which combines an intensely personal narrative with imagery from the extraordinary sequence of events in January 2011, which saw President Mubarak ousted in a popular revolution.

El-Tantawy was born in Worcester in the UK to Egyptian parents and has lived in Egypt, Saudi Arabia and the US. The death of her maternal grandmother was the catalyst for her starting to create work in the land to which she feels so strongly connected. As a child, her grandparents were as essential to her as her parents; they lived on the floor above in an apartment block in a middle-class suburb of Cairo. Her grandfather, on the death of his wife, was very frail and El-Tantawy, who was studying for an MA in media arts practice at the time, turned her camera towards him. At the same time, she began to photograph from her childhood bedroom window, looking down onto the streets below, through laundry blowing in the wind, which seemed to be ushering in a kind of change.

As the political atmosphere in the country became increasingly febrile in early 2011, El-Tantawy returned to Cairo. 'In Tahrir Square', she says, 'I found myself.' This sense of passionate belonging inspired an unforgettable series of photographs, which are by turns blurred, witnessing a volatile situation, or are so tightly focused on a human face that every pore is visible. With this technique, El-Tantawy has developed a signature style that is often referred to as 'filmic'. Her photographs oscillate between past and future, pausing in the present to register a deep empathy with individual grief.

When El-Tantawy freezes the frame it is as though she stops the world for that moment. This could of course be photography's unique power, but in her hands it is especially potent. Her use of the written word (transformed into spoken word in exhibition installations) bears the traces of the formative words of Egyptian Nobel Laureate Naguib Mahfouz. 'I buried something there,' she says of Tahrir Square. Five years and two presidents since the revolution, and with state terror on the march once more, that 'something' sounds a lot like hope, yet remains indefinable, slightly out of reach.

The imagery from *In the Shadow of the Pyramids*, which was created over a nine-year period, is interwoven with family photographs. The book opens with two single images, facing each other, of each parent, as they looked at the time they first fell in love. Without this encounter, El-Tantawy seems to say, there would be no me. It is rare to see the personal and political colliding so effectively in a single photobook. Nostalgic images of parents, grandparents and siblings punctuate the present, reminding us of the inextricable bonds of family and personal geography and, perhaps, our responsibility in the political fortunes of the country we count on as our home, wherever that may be.

Women of Tahrir, 2013, In the Shadow of the Pyramids series

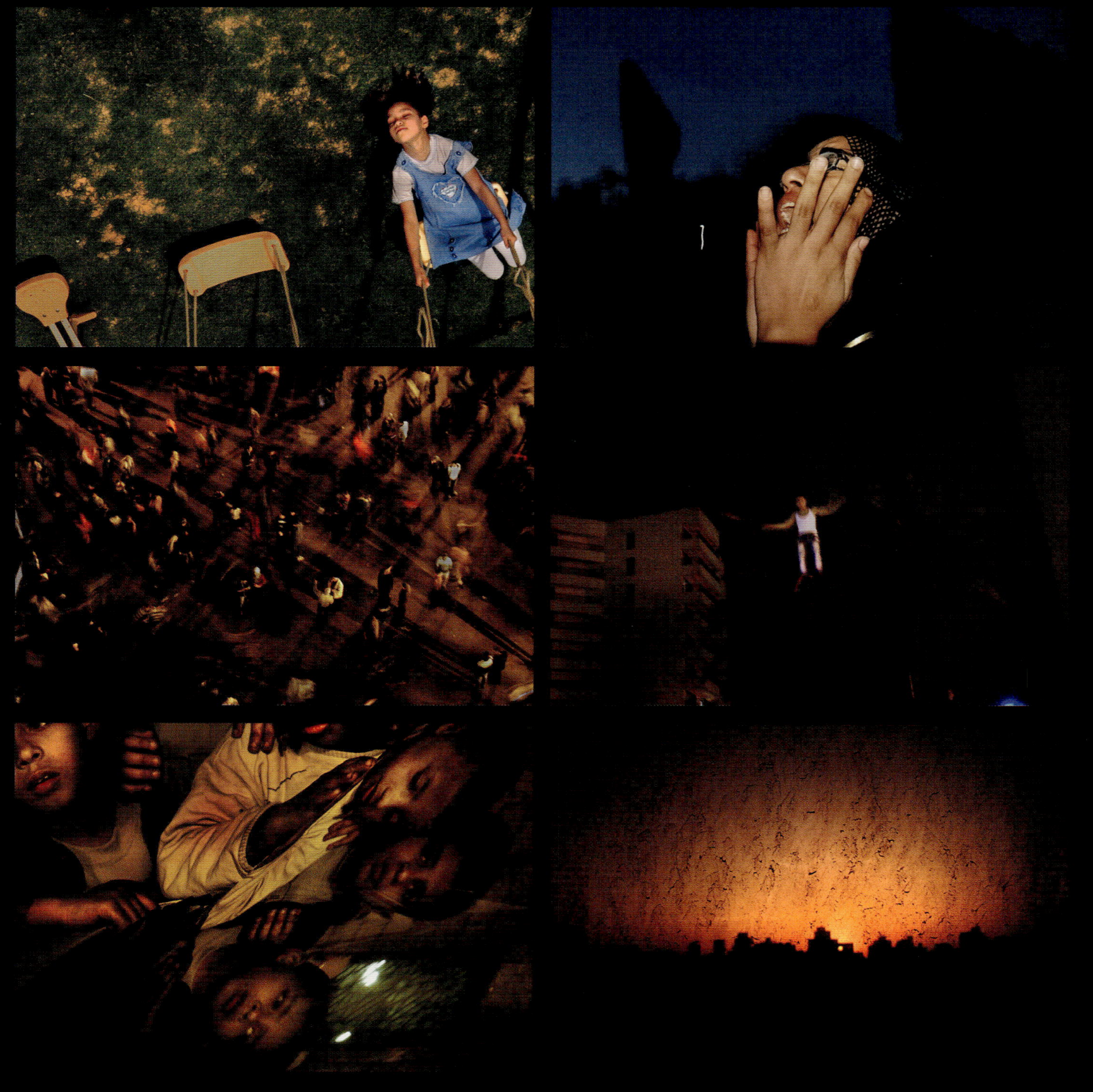

   Firecrackers

Clockwise, from top left:
Girl on Swing, 2007;
Enough!, 2005;
The People Toppled the Regime, 2011;
Sunset Through My Dirty Window, 2013;
Three Boys, 2006;
The Square I Remember, 2011;
all *In the Shadow of the Pyramids* series

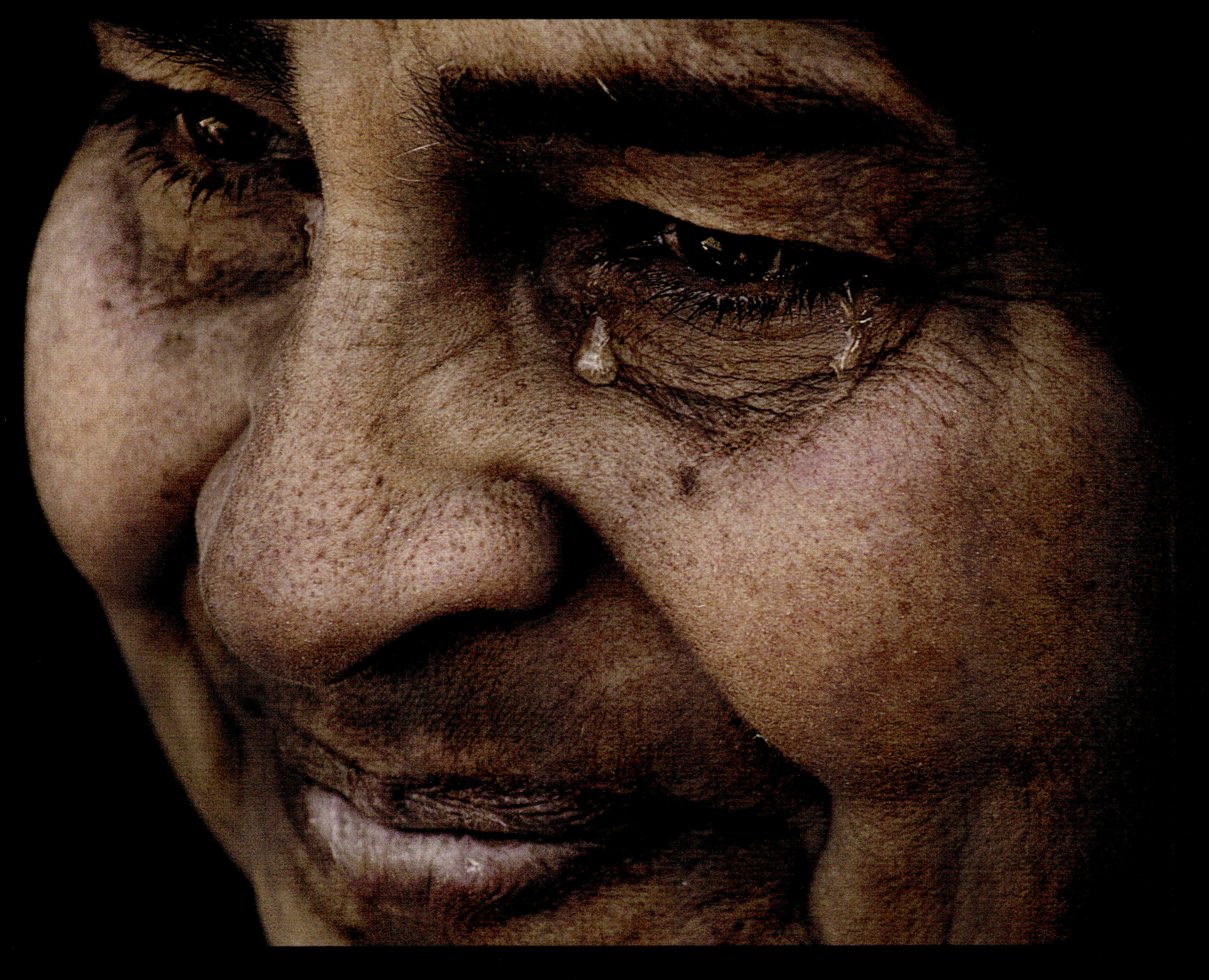

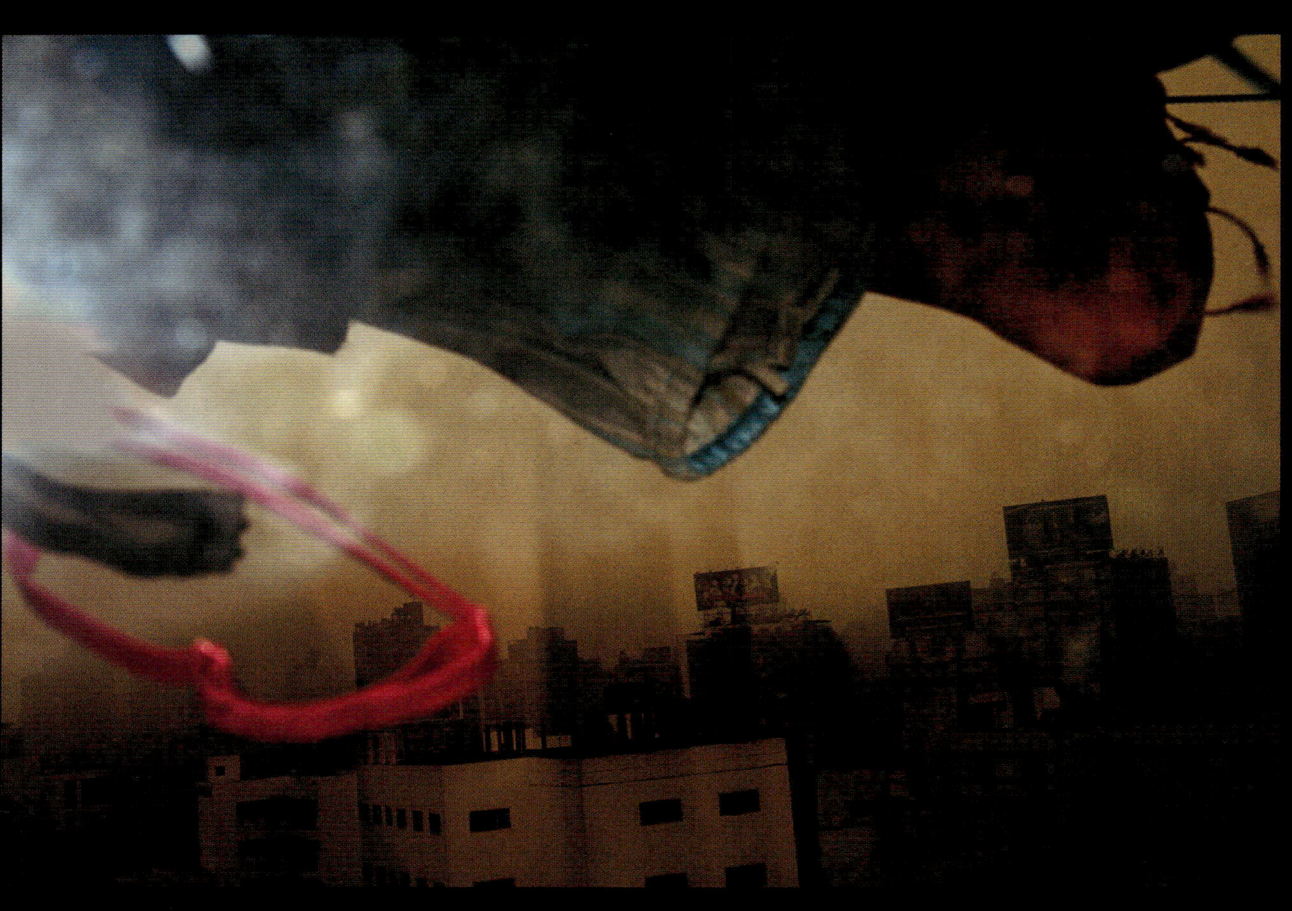

Sand Storm from My Childhood Window, 2007, In the Shadow of the Pyramids

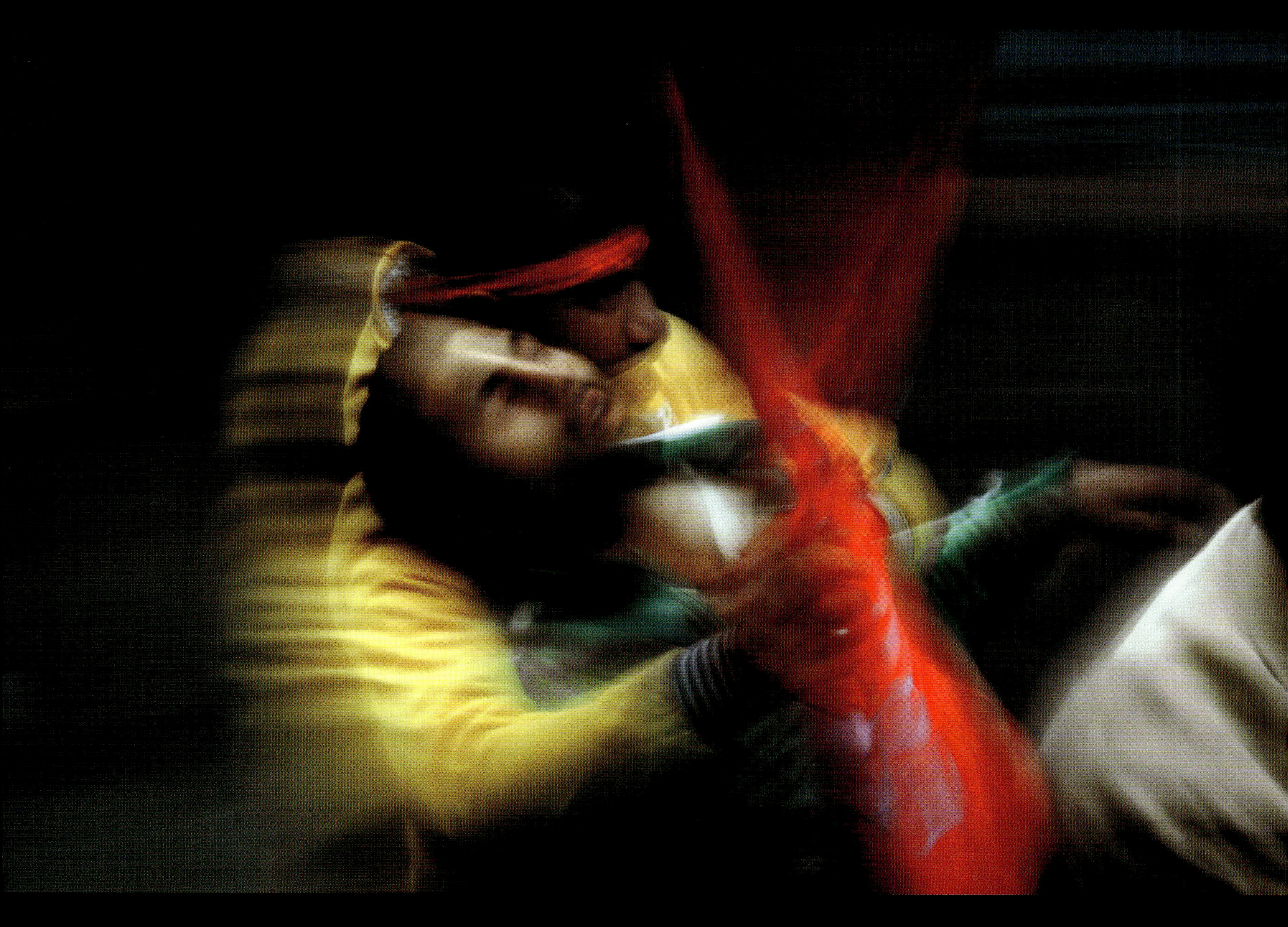

Almost Dead, 2012, In the Shadow of the Pyramids series

Laura El-Tantawy 179

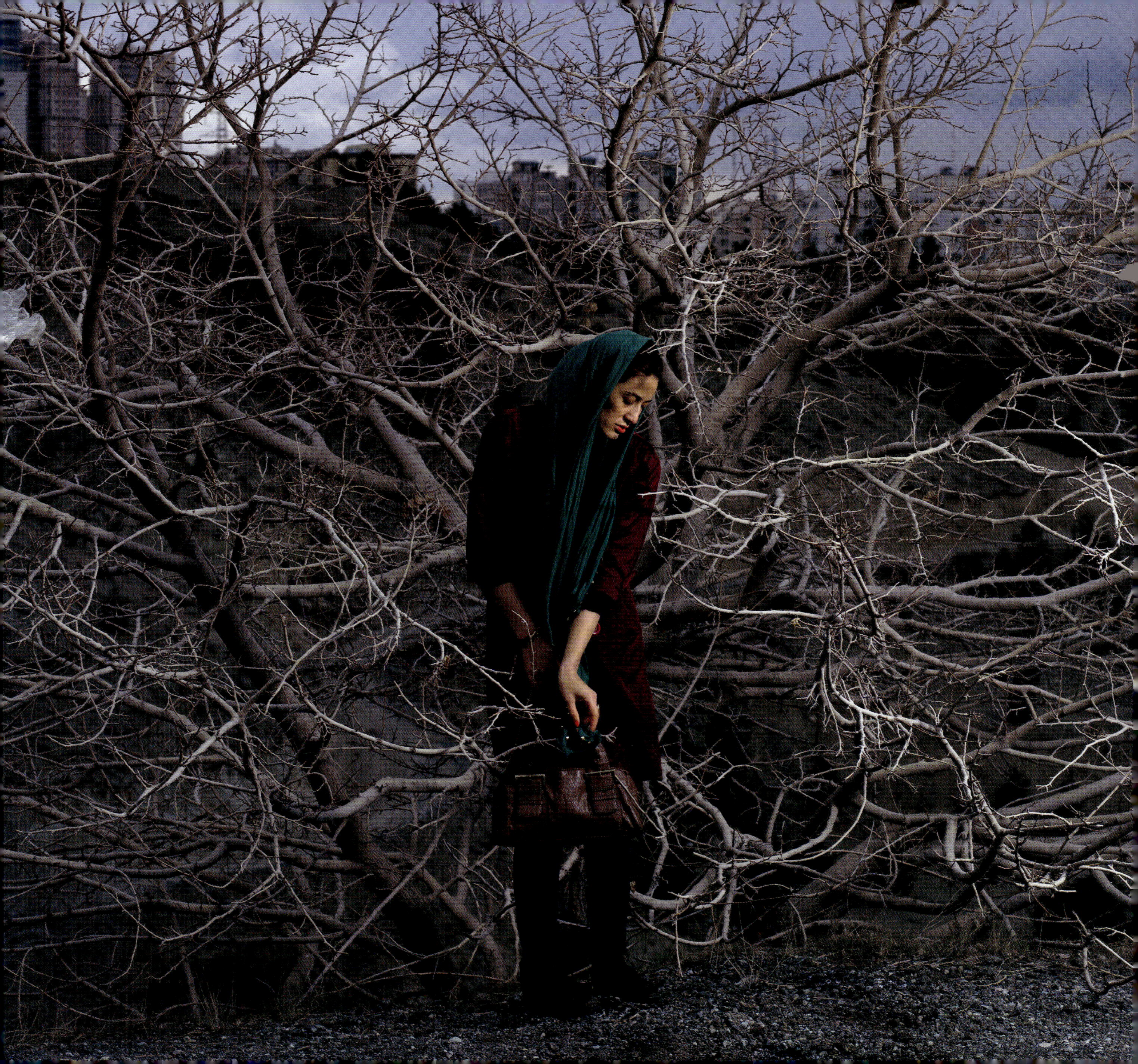

NEWSHA TAVAKOLIAN

...

Blank Pages of an Iranian Photo Album is a politically charged message and a rebuttal to outsiders claiming to know what it is to be Iranian

...

Trained in the language of photojournalism, celebrated Iranian photographer Newsha Tavakolian is much more than a typical newshound. Having photographed her homeland for nearly twenty years, Tavakolian is an experienced mediator of the contrasts, contradictions and intricacies of this complex country.

A magazine photographer from the age of just sixteen, Tavakolian became known for her coverage of the 1999 student uprising in Tehran. Since then she has been amassing a huge collection of photographs that presents an unflinching and honest account of a rapidly modernizing Iran.

The aftermath of the 2009 post-election uprising marked a shift in Iranian photographic approaches, both for Tavakolian and other photojournalists. With authorities using photography to locate and persecute the community, Tavakolian explains that Iranians 'developed a phobia towards having their picture taken, they were simply very scared.' This propelled Tavakolian towards a more conceptual form of documentary practice, manifested in her project *Look*, a series of highly charged portraits taken in her apartment block, metaphorically suspended between the twilight hours.

Much of her work is centred on her contemporaries, those growing up post-revolution and now caught in the classic 'east meets west' dilemma; a desire to maintain tradition and yet move forward and globalize. Tavakolian is mindful to present her work as a challenge to Iranian stereotyping, counteracting misconceptions that her generation is 'lost', but acknowledging they are certainly under-represented and unheard.

Her first photobook, *Blank Pages of an Iranian Photo Album*, is a politically charged message and a rebuttal to outsiders claiming to know what it is to be Iranian. The book borrows from the widely understood significance of the family photo album, which remains sacrosanct in Iran as a record of hopes and dreams for the future. Tavakolian calls it 'the showcase' for her generation. However, many of these memories end abruptly and pages are left blank. Tavakolian populates these blank pages, envisaging the present day and symbolizing the abandonment of hope and unlived dreams felt by many of her generation.

The book is imbued with childhood snapshots alongside the contemporary photographs of ten people; a continuation of the photo album from their childhood. Tavakolian's subjects define a generation, but they are also interchangeable. Her images serve as

visual representations of both Tavakolian herself and every millennial Iranian, particularly the middle classes. We see women undergoing plastic surgery procedures, a man scaling an empty pool, an abandoned outdoor cinema. All this is set against the backdrop of the historic and the traditional, with the spirit of the revolution omnipresent; two men converse in a café while footage of the uprising plays in the background and a family review a propaganda poster in the middle of the street.

Tavakolian was accepted into the Magnum Photos collective as a nominee in 2014. She is at the vanguard of a new generation of female documentarians and is a trailblazer for those who wish to understand and represent the political and social complexities of the Middle East at this time of great change.

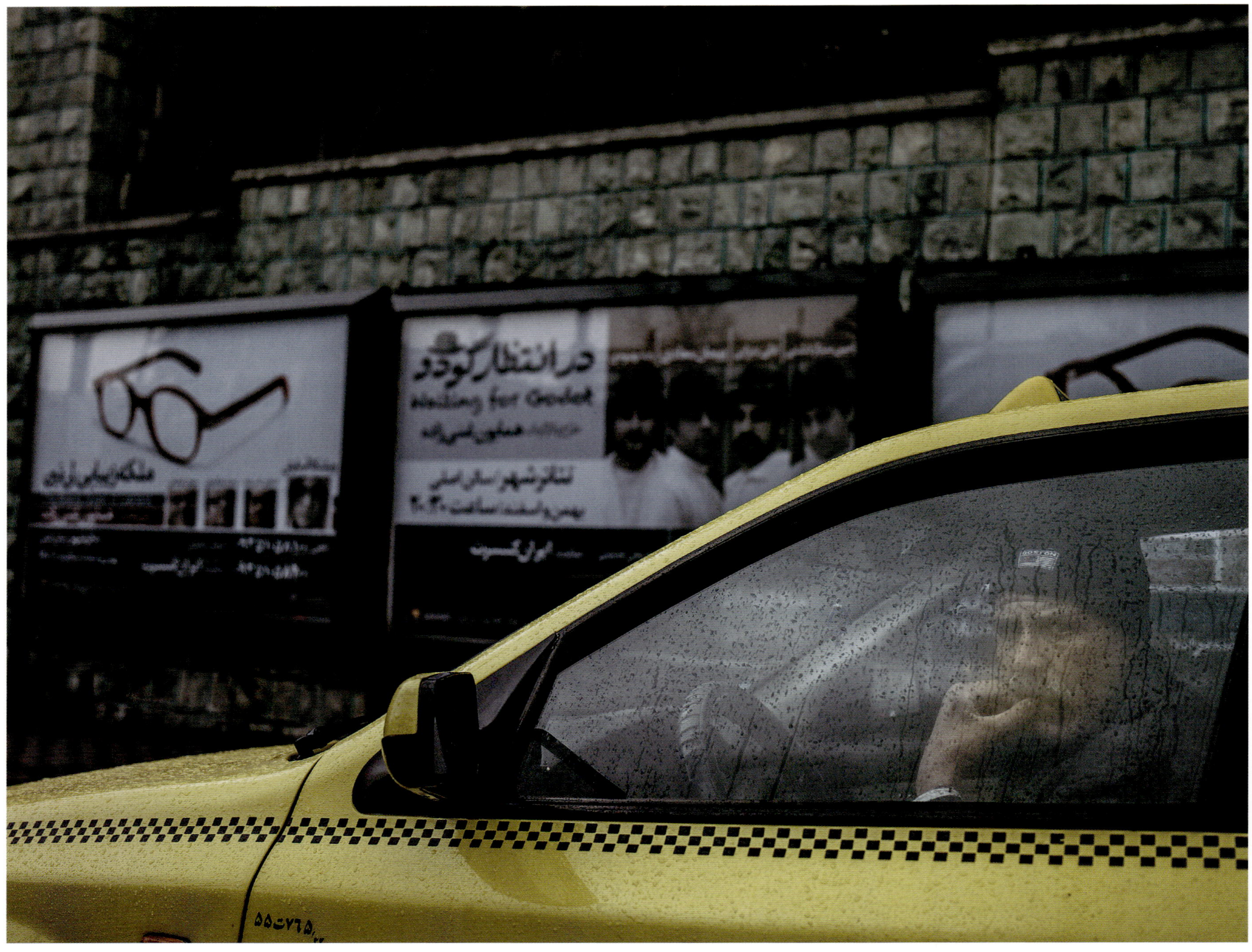

Untitled, 2014–15, Blank Pages of an Iranian Photo Album series

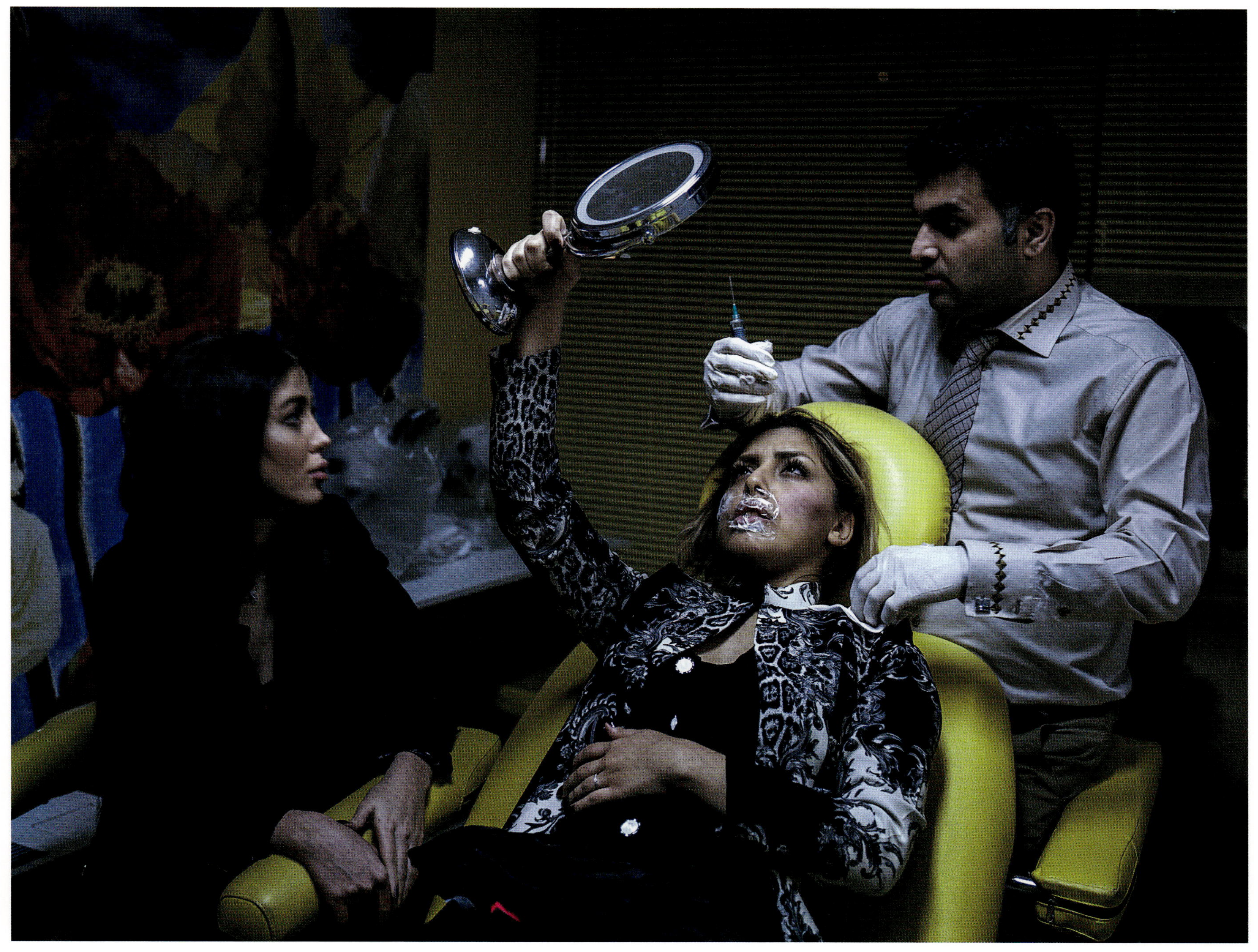

Untitled, 2014–15, Blank Pages of an Iranian Photo Album series

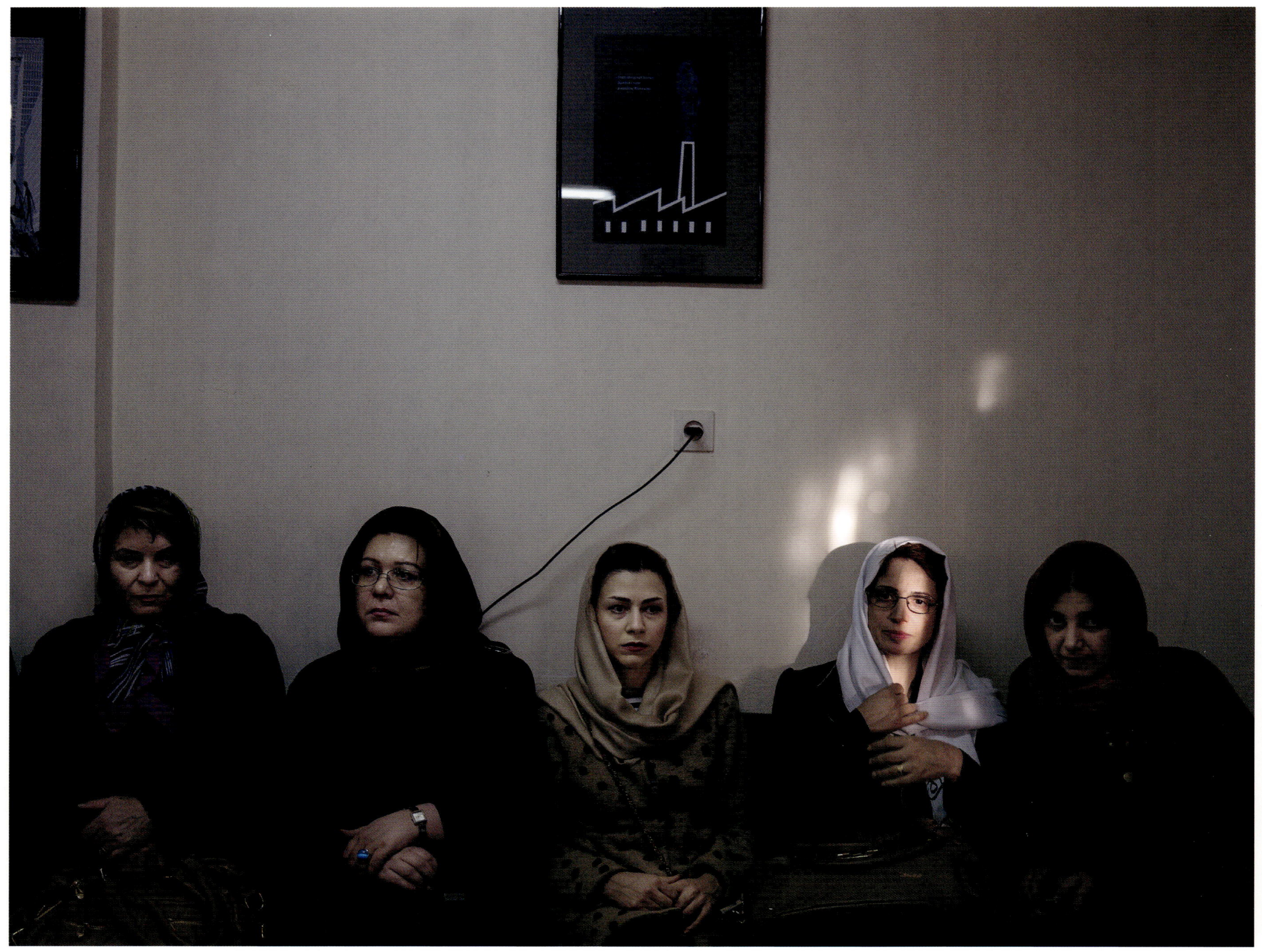

Untitled, 2014–15, Blank Pages of an Iranian Photo Album series

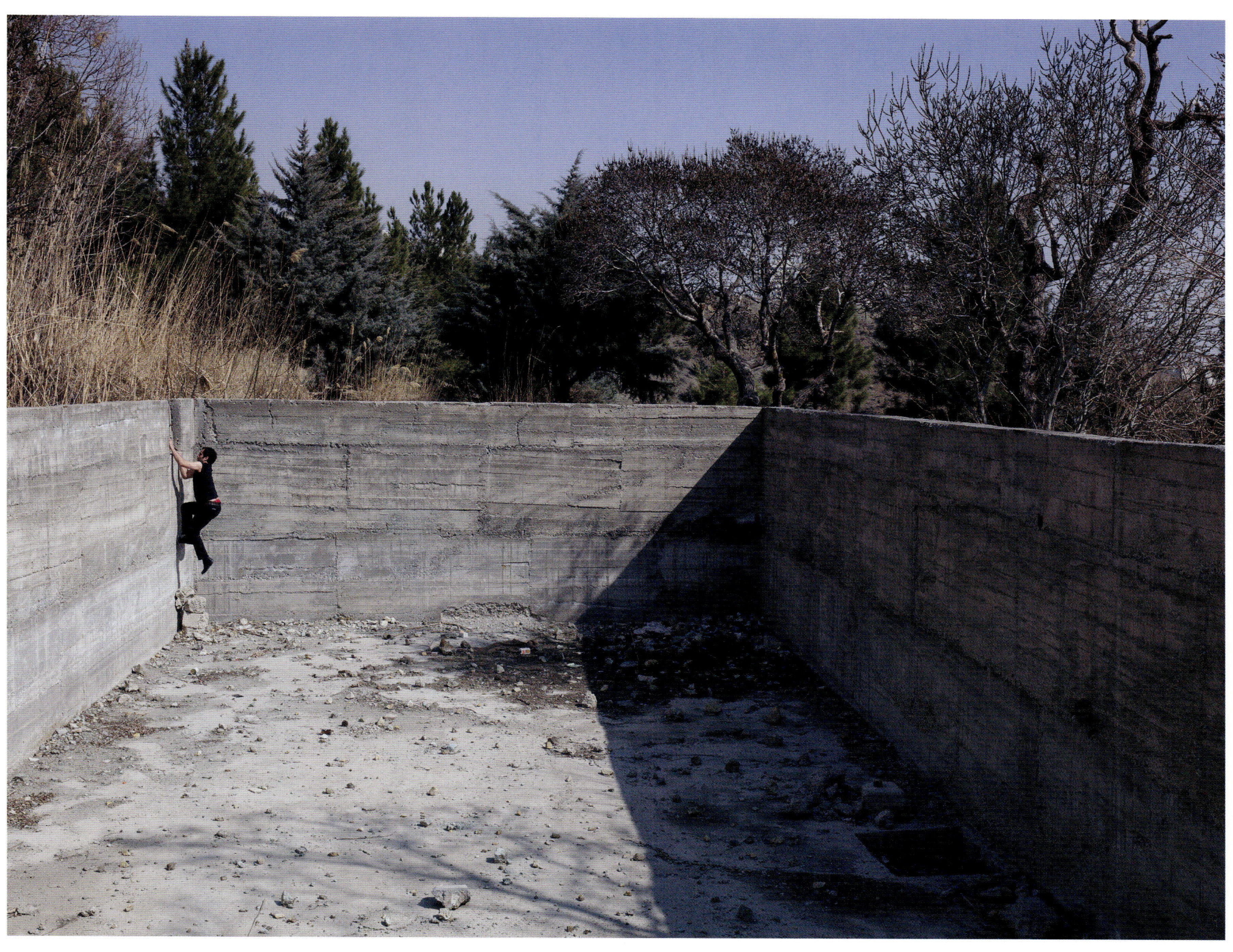

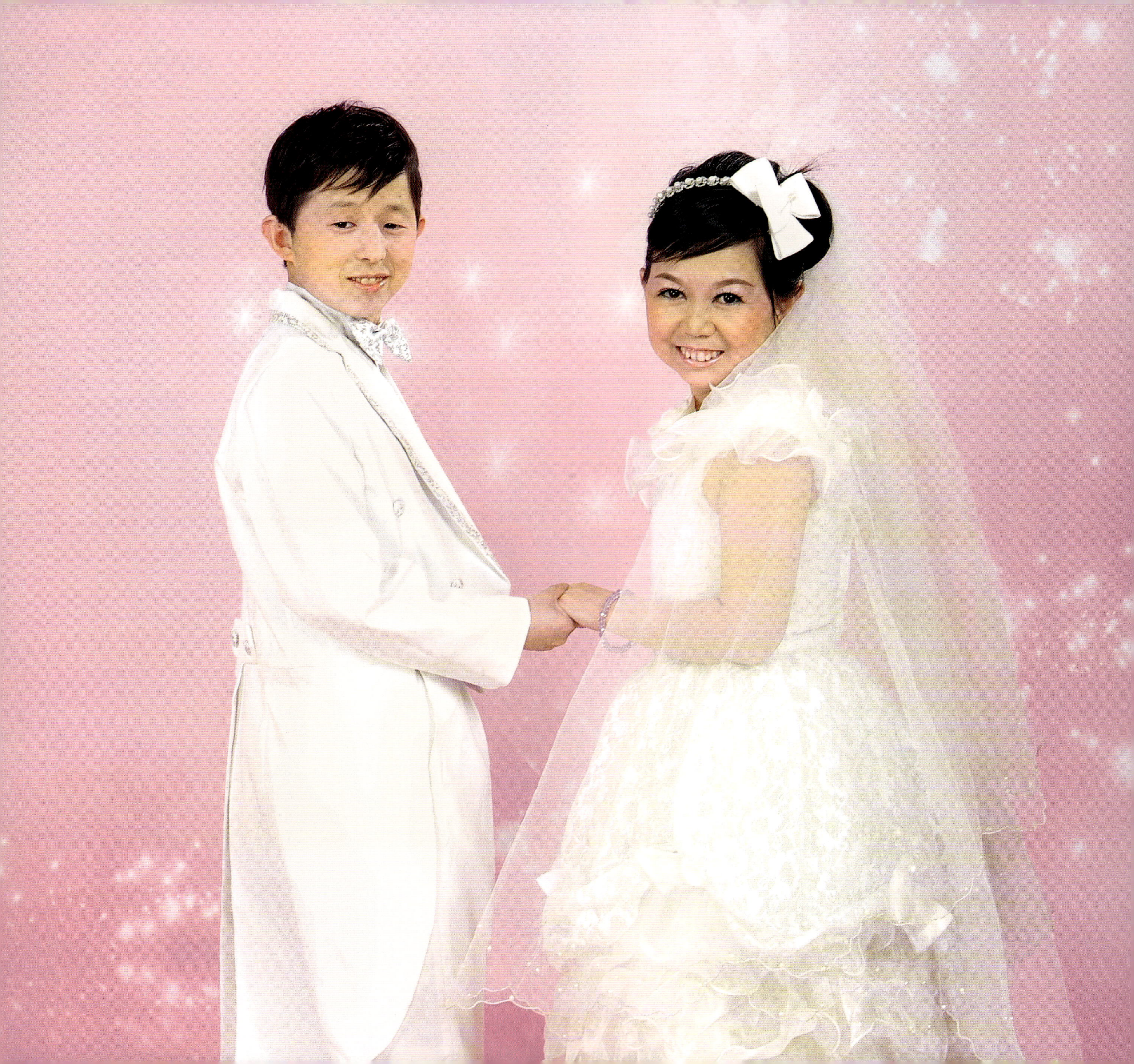

SANNE DE WILDE

...
De Wilde found most of the residents considered The Kingdom of the Little People 'a wonderful place and even a kind of paradise'
...

The work of Belgian photographer Sanne De Wilde explores physical stereotyping, although this is not immediately apparent when looking at her explosive and utterly unique work.

De Wilde's early work included *Snow White*, an otherworldly portrait series of people with albinism, which highlights the fragility and beauty of the condition. It was, however, *The Dwarf Empire*, De Wilde's MA graduation project at the Royal Academy of Fine Arts in Ghent, Belgium that catapulted her to international recognition in 2013. She won the International Photography Award Emergentes DST and became a finalist for the Unseen Photo Fair's Dummy Award.

The project is set in China, at The Kingdom of the Little People, a highly questionable fantasy theme park in Yunnan province and 'home' to over seventy-five people with dwarfism. The park is the perfect embodiment of capitalist culture; founded in 2009 by real estate developer Chen Mingjing, it combines entertainment with a level of 'social care'. Twice a day, the residents literally sing for their supper to an audience of predominantly Chinese tourists.

De Wilde photographs the often mundane lives of the residents between their performances. We see behind the façade:

the specially constructed dormitories, the park's 'Emperor' on his mobile phone, the costumed performers and the mushroom-style landscape where this fantasy plays out. *The Dwarf Empire* could be seen as a moral tale of subjectivity – by Western standards the park seems unscrupulous, but De Wilde found most of the residents considered it 'a wonderful place and even a kind of paradise...not just a community, but a sense of belonging'.

De Wilde deftly negotiates issues of voyeurism and exploitation by getting close to the residents. So close, in fact, that the project takes a surprising turn and De Wilde herself becomes a part of the story. Having attempted to explore their objectification, it's clear that the tall, striking, blue-eyed blonde is herself a novelty in the park. The dwarves, and the tourists, turn the lens on her, and in doing so heighten the concept of 'otherness' which De Wilde's photography often explores – the way we view people and what that ultimately says about us. De Wilde describes her work as not being 'about people who are "different" from the norm [but how] other people become different because of the way they see things.'

The Dwarf Empire's presentation method helps to elaborate the lurid, fantasy element of the project: it is a lavishly thick

book, bound in tactile gold foil. It is more fairytale than photobook, split into two chapters containing De Wilde's exceptional photography amid vernacular imagery, and tourist brochures and fold-out posters with portraits and biographical information for each resident, such as height, which appears so omnipresent in both the project and their lives.

An important component of the book's two chapters is the dwarves' photographs of De Wilde. They are affectionate and playful, and everyone seems to be smiling. It's a final reinforcement of the complexity of both the project, and The Kingdom of the Little People itself.

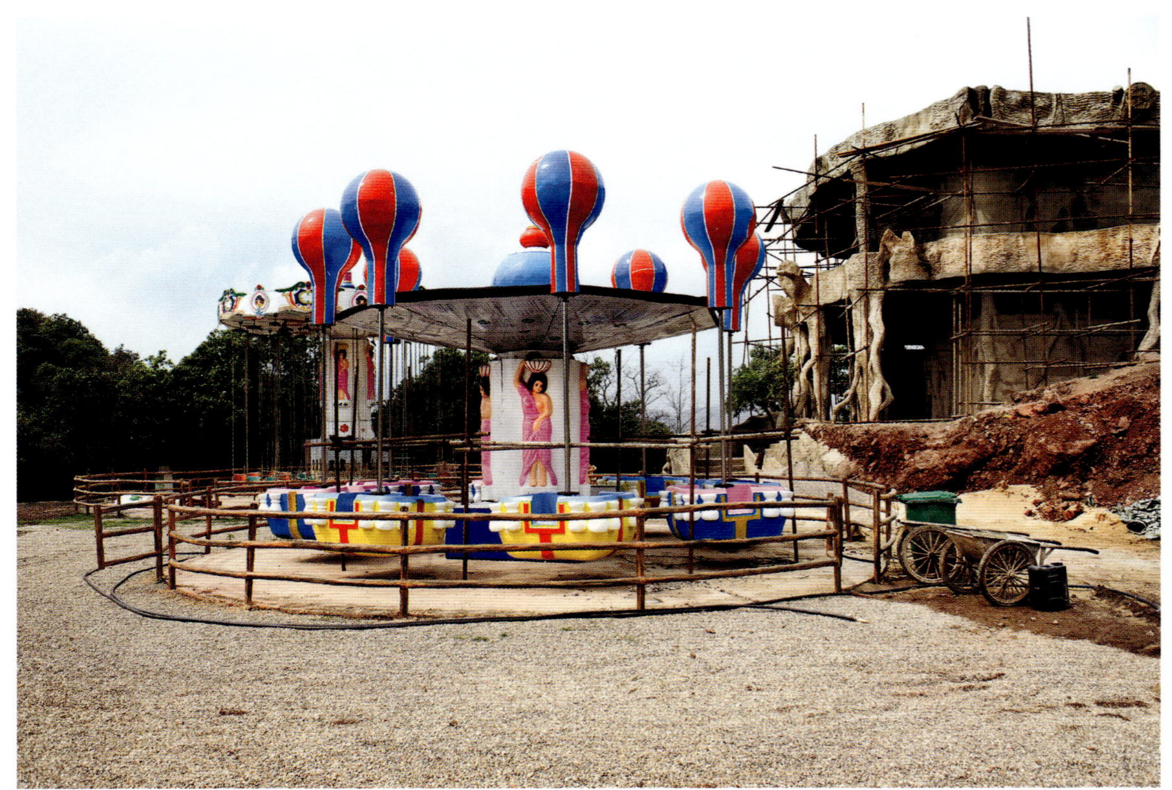

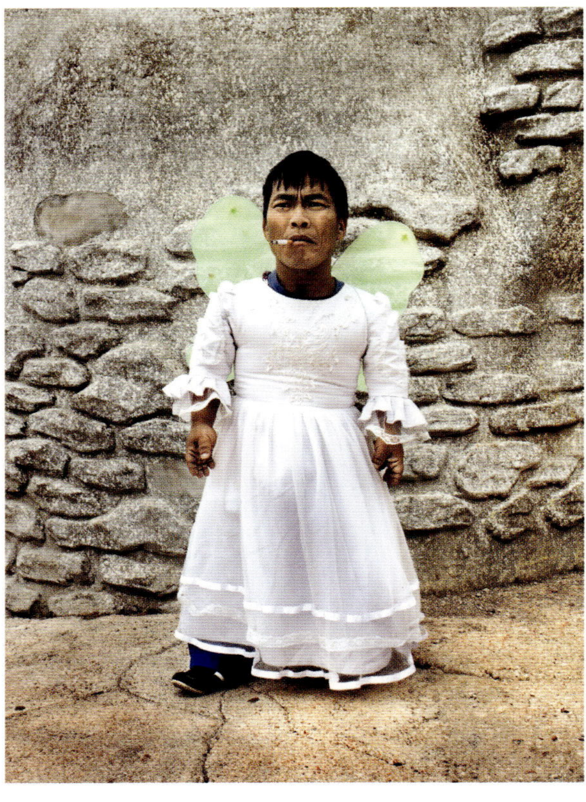

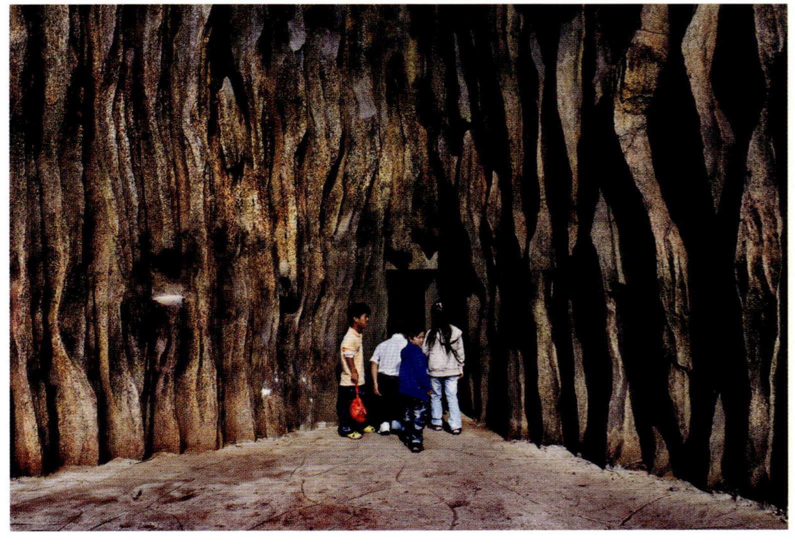

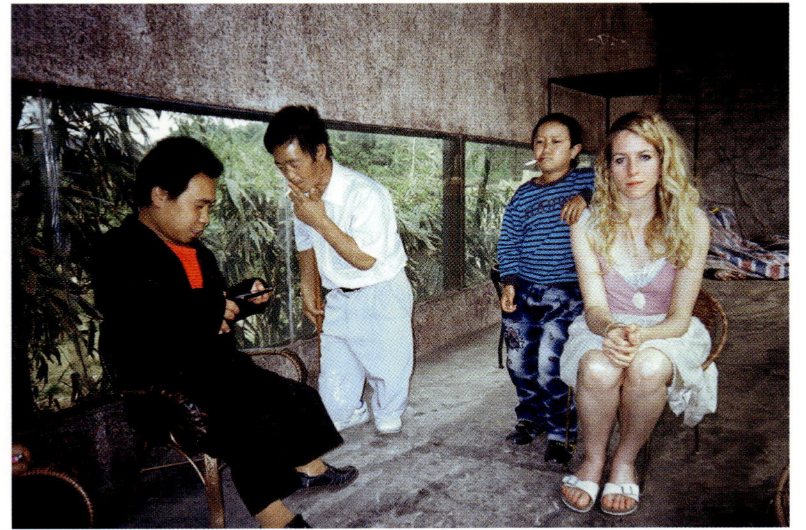

The Dwarf Empire series, 2011

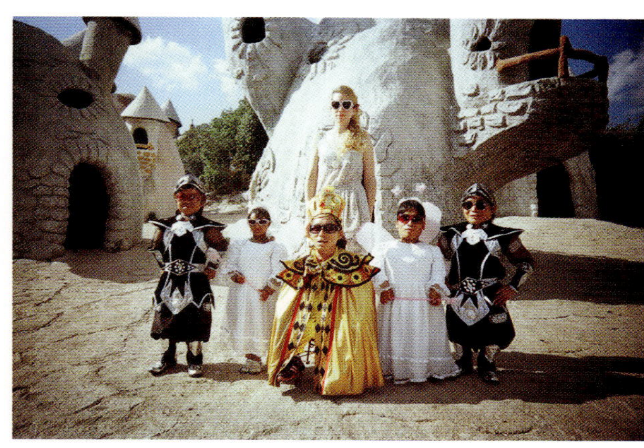

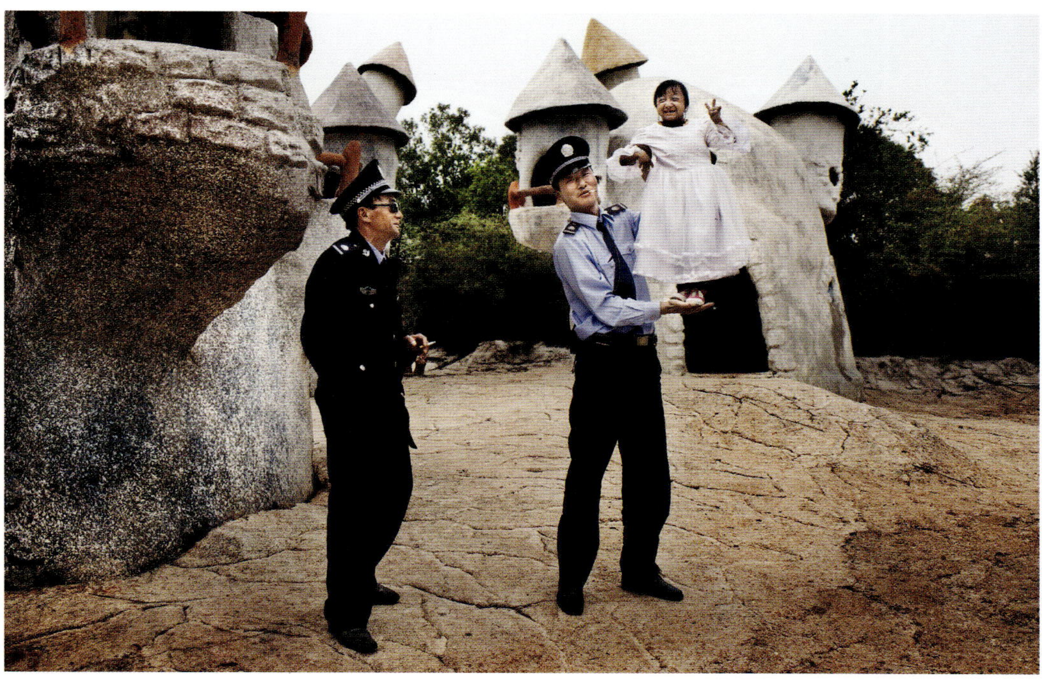

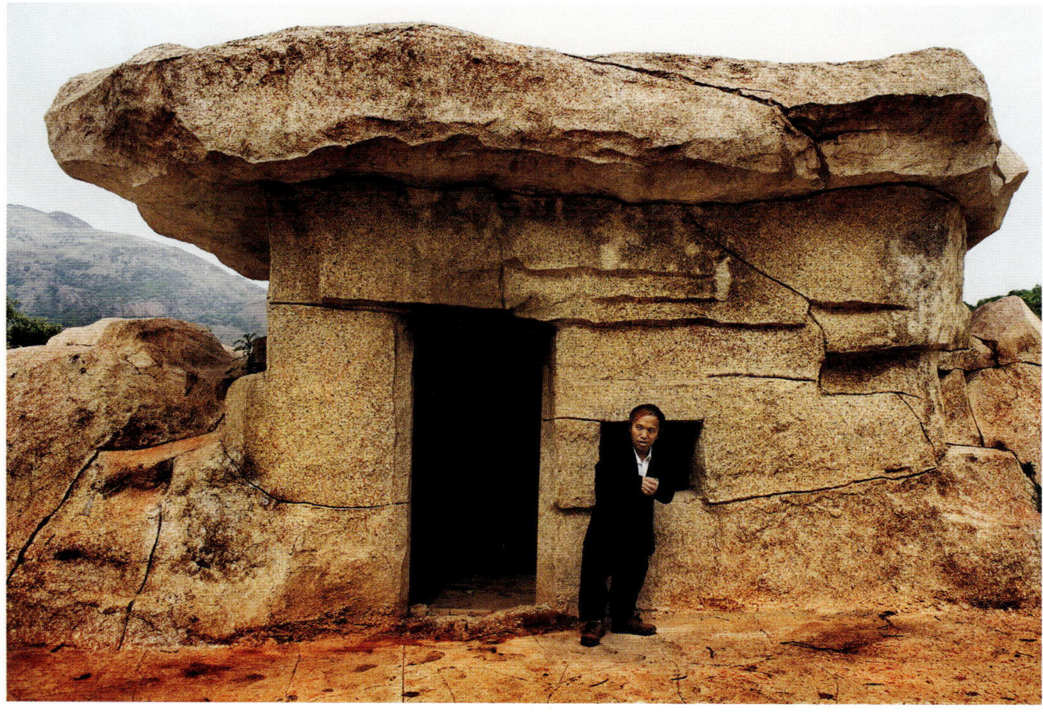

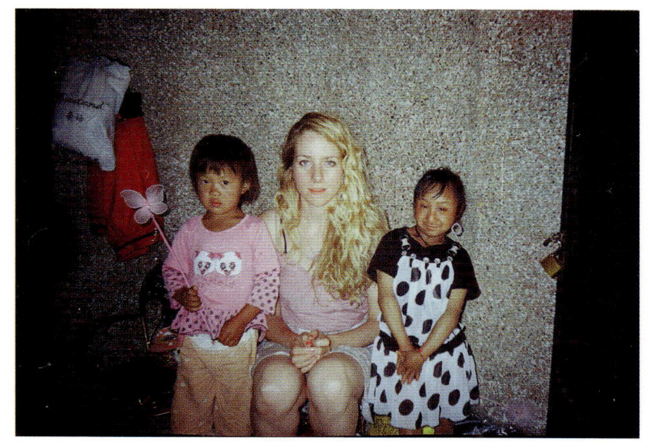

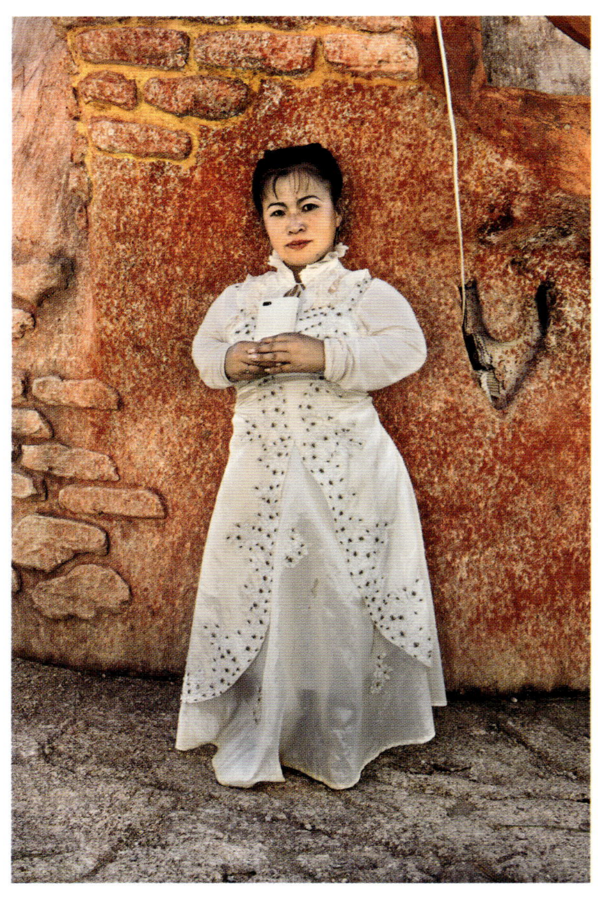
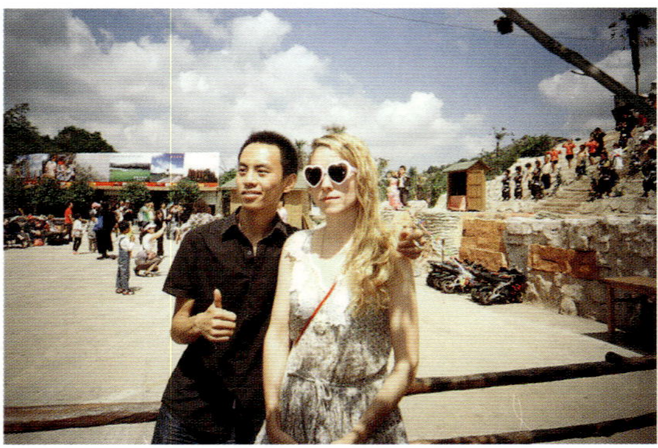
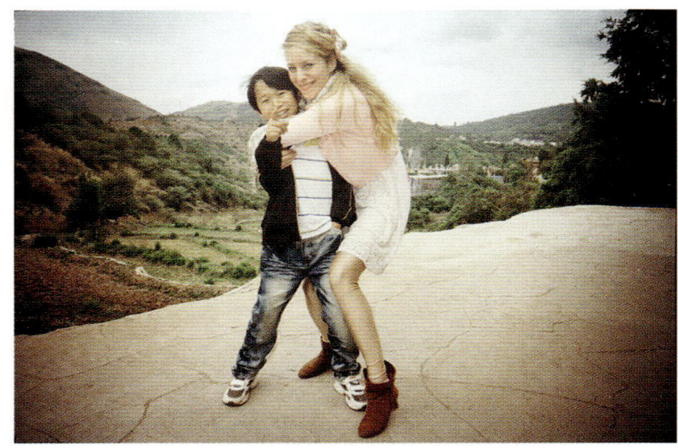
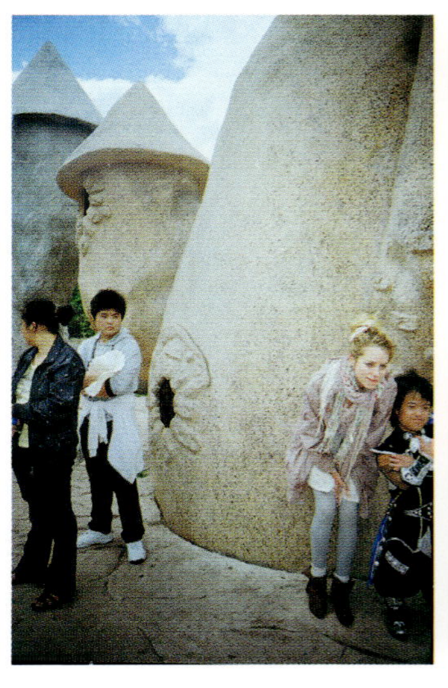
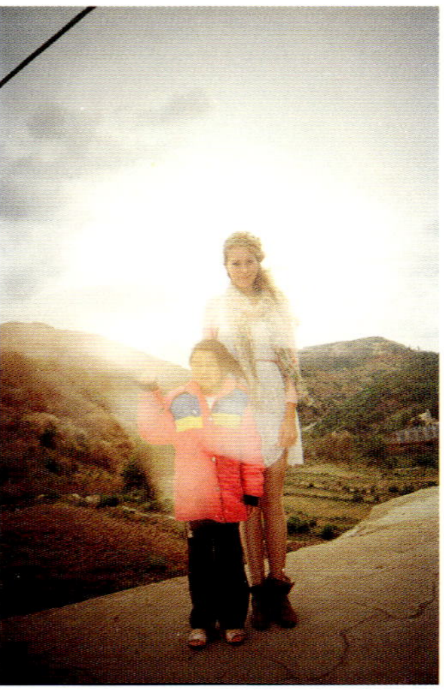
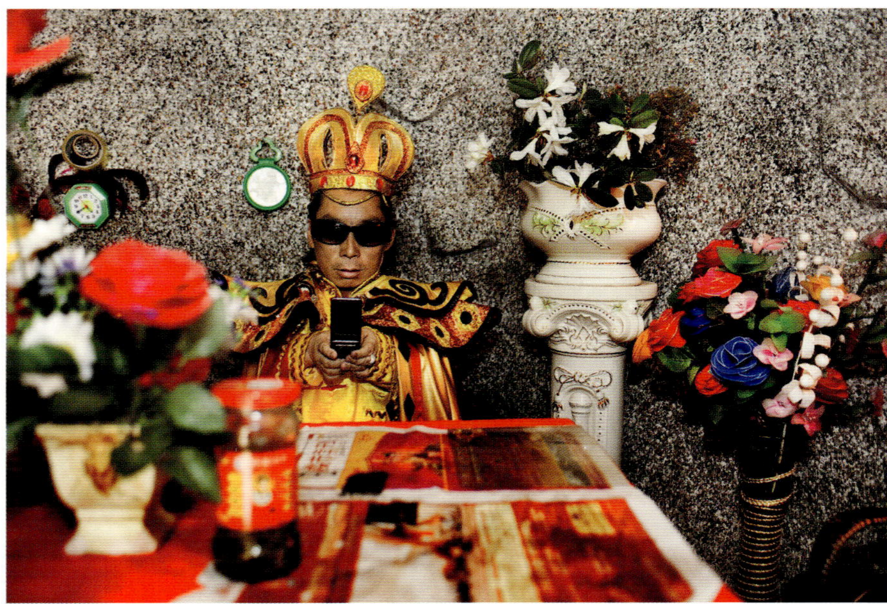

Above left: *The Dwarf Empire* series, 2014;
all other images: *The Dwarf Empire* series, 2011

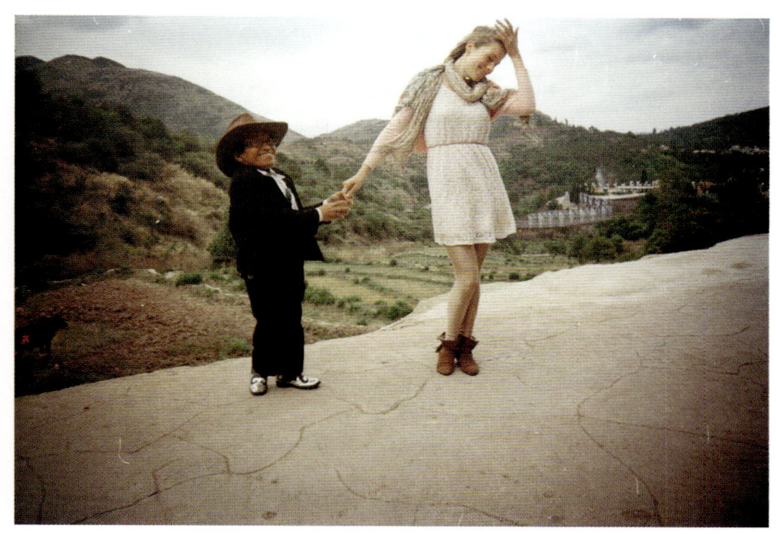

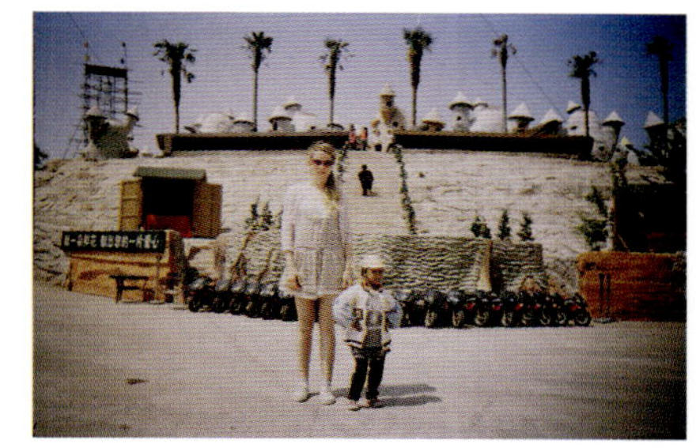

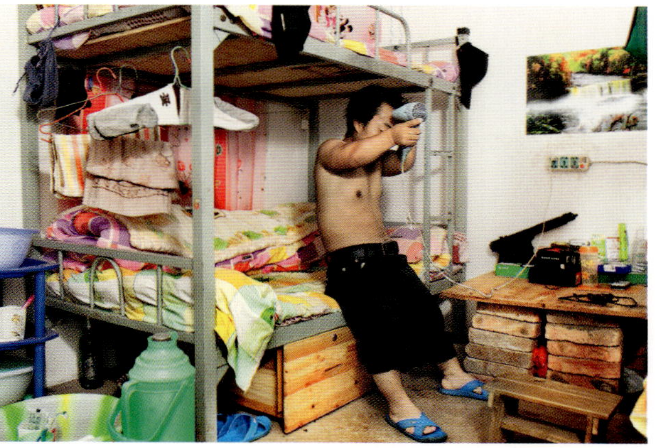

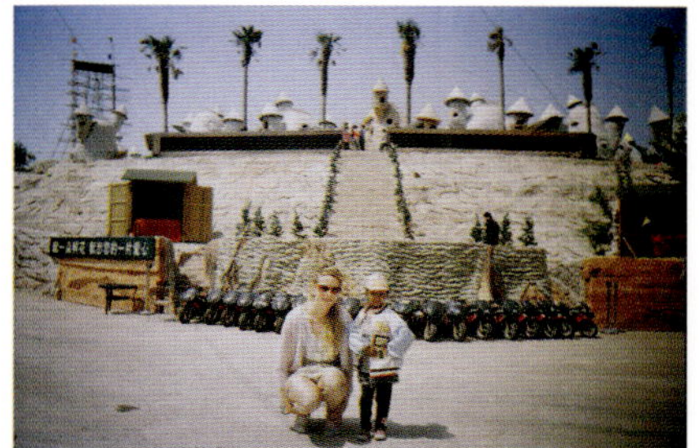

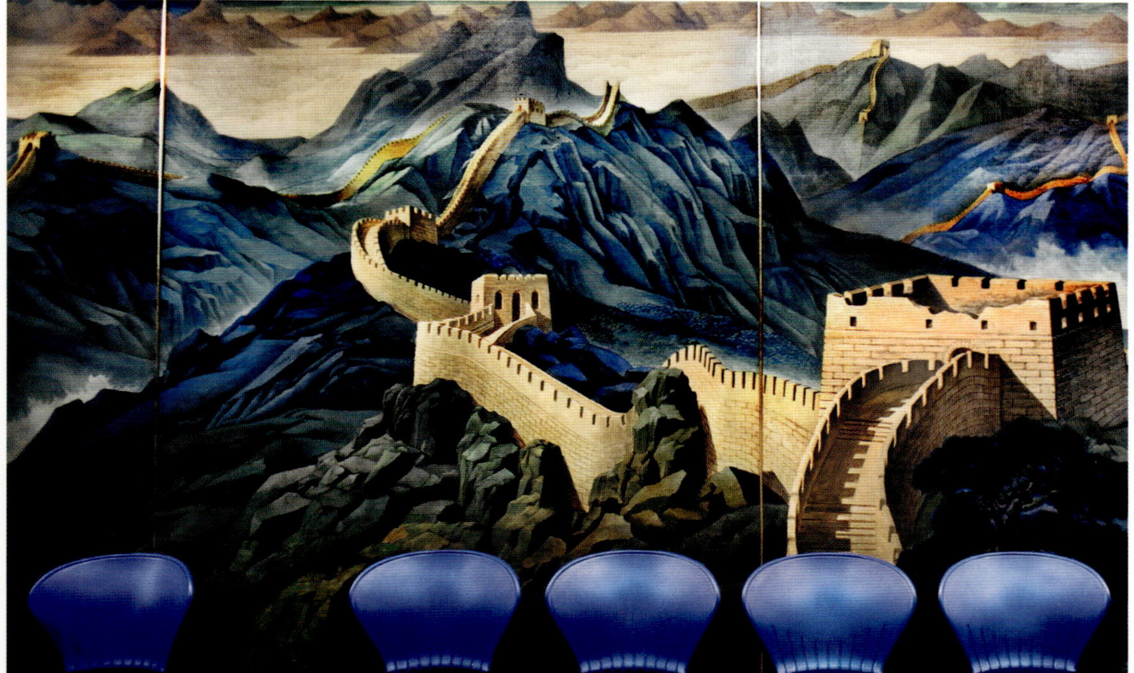

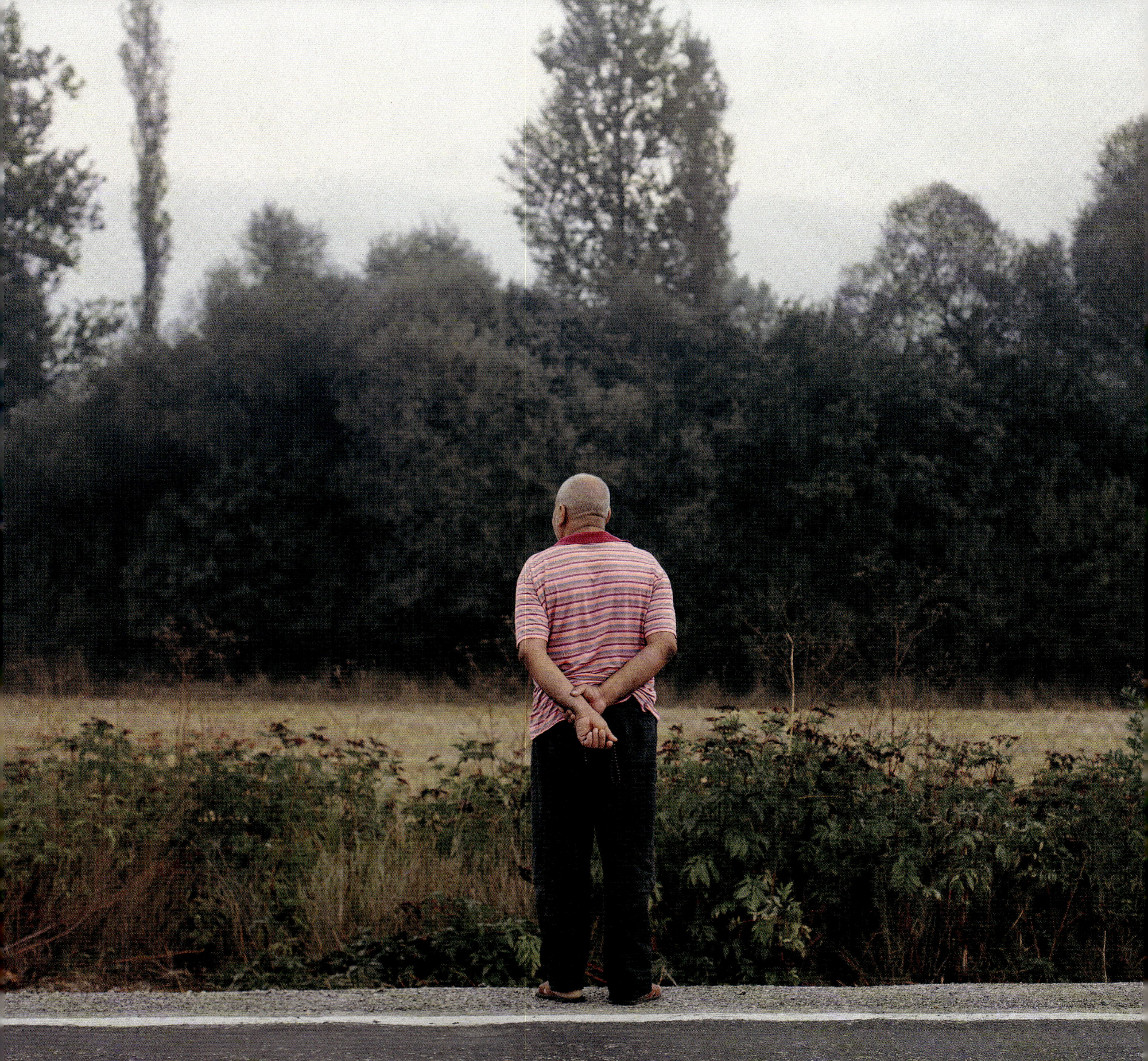

CEMRE YESIL

...

For Birds' Sake is a tale of possession, obsession and deep contradictions
...

Turkish photographer Cemre Yesil is a specialist in intimate visual details. She is studying for a PhD at the London College of Communication and also has an MA in visual arts and a BA in photography. For Yesil, the project culmination is as considered and important as the conception of the work itself. A prolific book publisher (six and counting), her book designs are emblematic of the projects they represent and her detailed, highly contemplated exhibitions often border on installation or performative art.

In her new work *Milk Tooth* Yesil interrogates the notion of relationships and, in particular, the paradigm of mother and child. She photographs grown children languishing in their mother's arms, punctuated by small details of teeth and archival images of children from the turn of the century. Using allegories of double portraits and the embrace, Yesil explores the manifestation of empathy between subject and viewer through the presence of these two motifs. In *Gelatista* she documents the destruction of her photography, presenting the visceral and violent act as a metaphor for a failed relationship.

Her poetic prose *For Birds' Sake* is the work that first attracted attention. Produced in collaboration with friend and artist Maria Sturm, it is fundamentally a love story, an unconventional romance full of mystery, addiction and passion. In Istanbul, a symbolic meeting point of east and west and a region of great storytelling, a group of men dedicate their lives to the illegal raising of birds and the cultivation of the most beautifully sorrowful song.

It is a tale of possession, obsession and deep contradictions. Each bird is caught in the wild and kept in a covered cage to encourage its sweet sorrow as it searches for a mate. The men then gather in cafés to listen to the mournful chorus and compete for the 'best' song. It is something only a highly trained ear can detect. Yesil and Sturm's images reveal the incongruity in both an undeniable dedication to caring for the birds, coupled with the desire to keep them captive. There is something contrary, too, about a tradition cultivated by men, but with a gentleness that is distinctly feminine – something that Yesil captures beautifully.

Because this practice is so secretive the photographs themselves become metaphoric and melodic, presented like visual clues to the identity of the project and stimulating the imagination. There is a palpable sense of quiet, of patience and of waiting. We see hooks, covered boxes and shrouds but never the birds themselves. This notion of covering, shrouding and veiling is deeply rooted in many different cultures. The concept of freedom, too, especially for women, is historically complex. The birdmen become symbolic of the complexity of these ideas and the inconsistency of independence itself.

Yesil has relocated back to Istanbul, and with this experienced the unease and excitement that such changes can bring. She uses her photography as a tool with which to incite communication and promote interaction with her environment. Through projects such as *For Birds' Sake* and *Milk Tooth* she creates conversations and connections for both herself and her audience, drawing upon the similarities in all of us: we were once children, we are all somebody's child; we have all experienced joy, love, loss and jealousy. These are the emotions that make us uniquely human, and which Yesil is so adept at making visible.

Arap Nedim Listening to Bird Songs, 2014, For Birds' Sake series

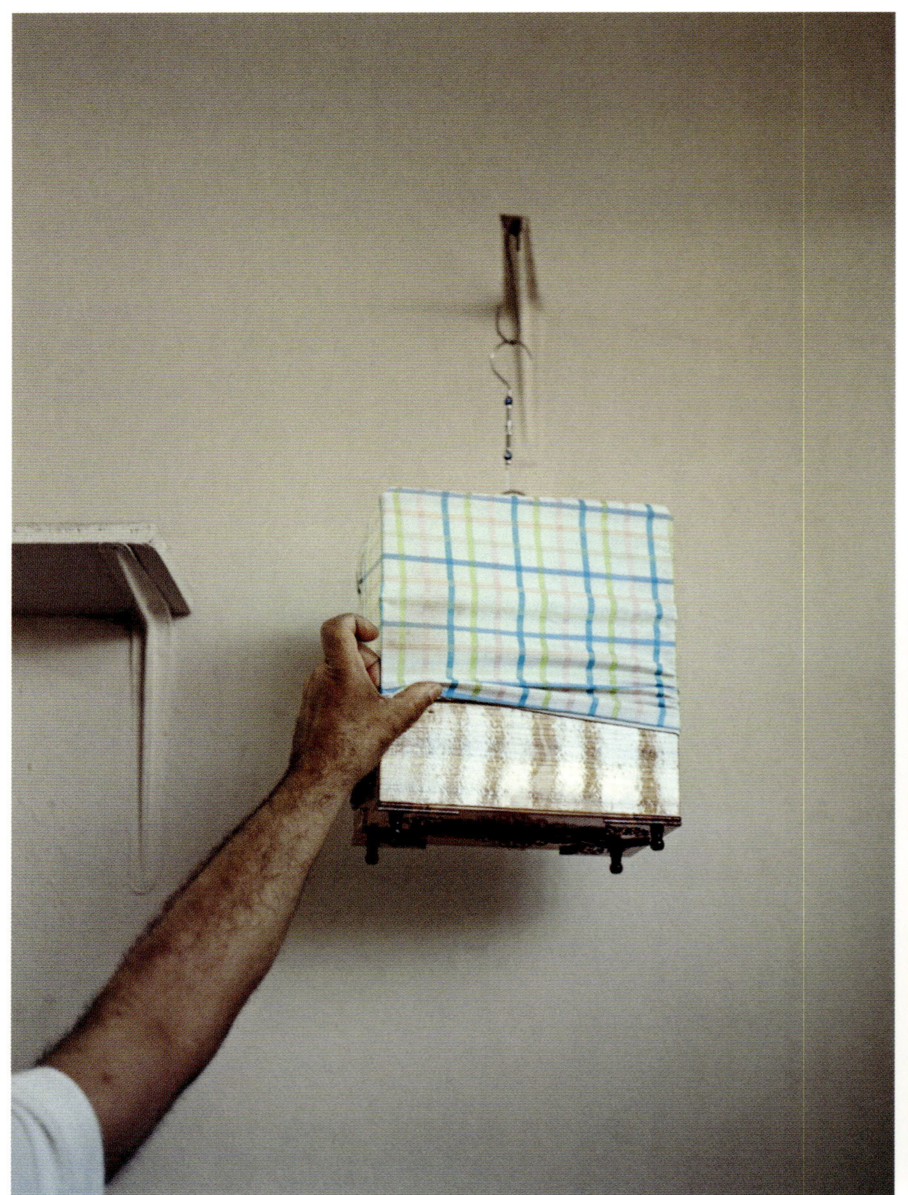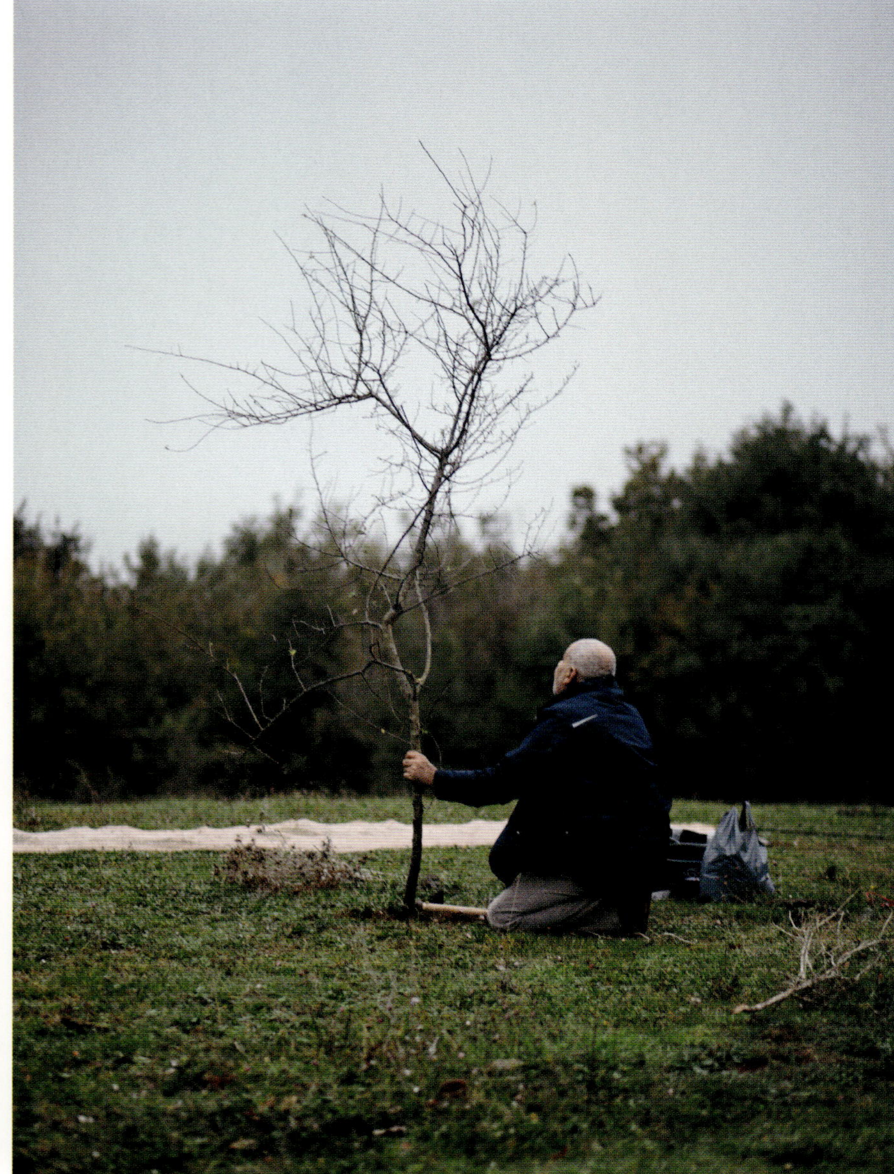

Above left: *Cage and Hand #4*, 2014; above right: *Holding a Tree*, 2014; both *For Birds' Sake* series

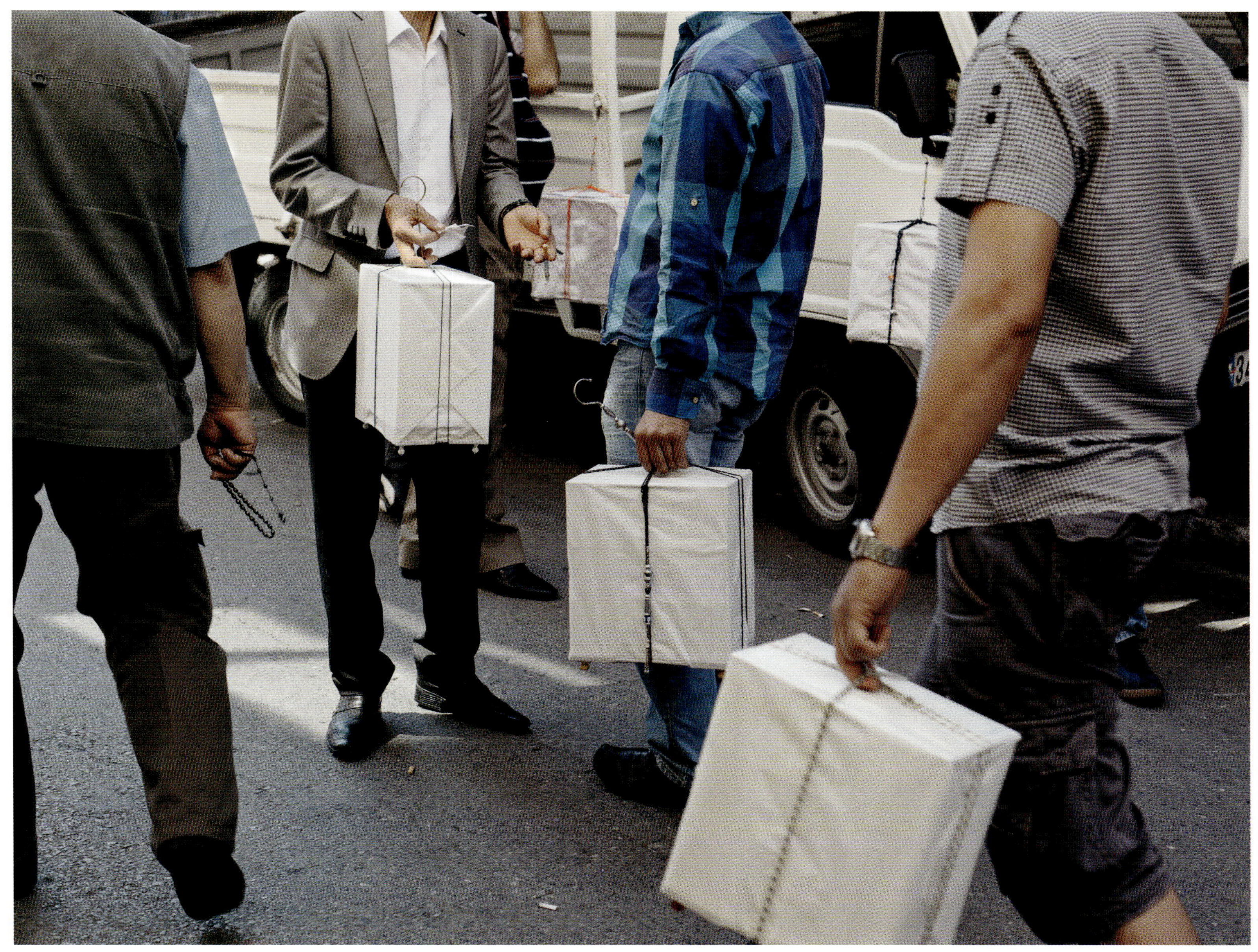

Birdmen Waiting for their Turn to Compete, 2014, For Birds' Sake series

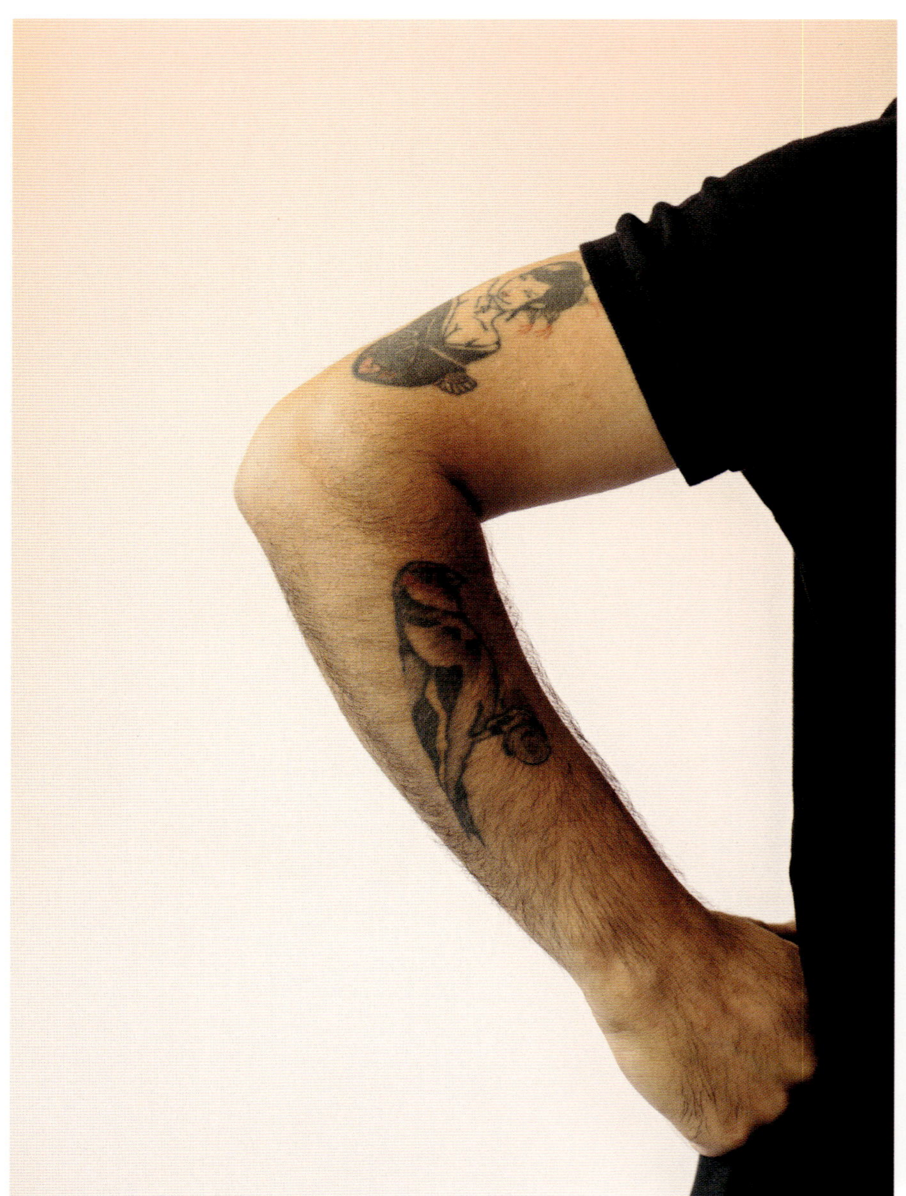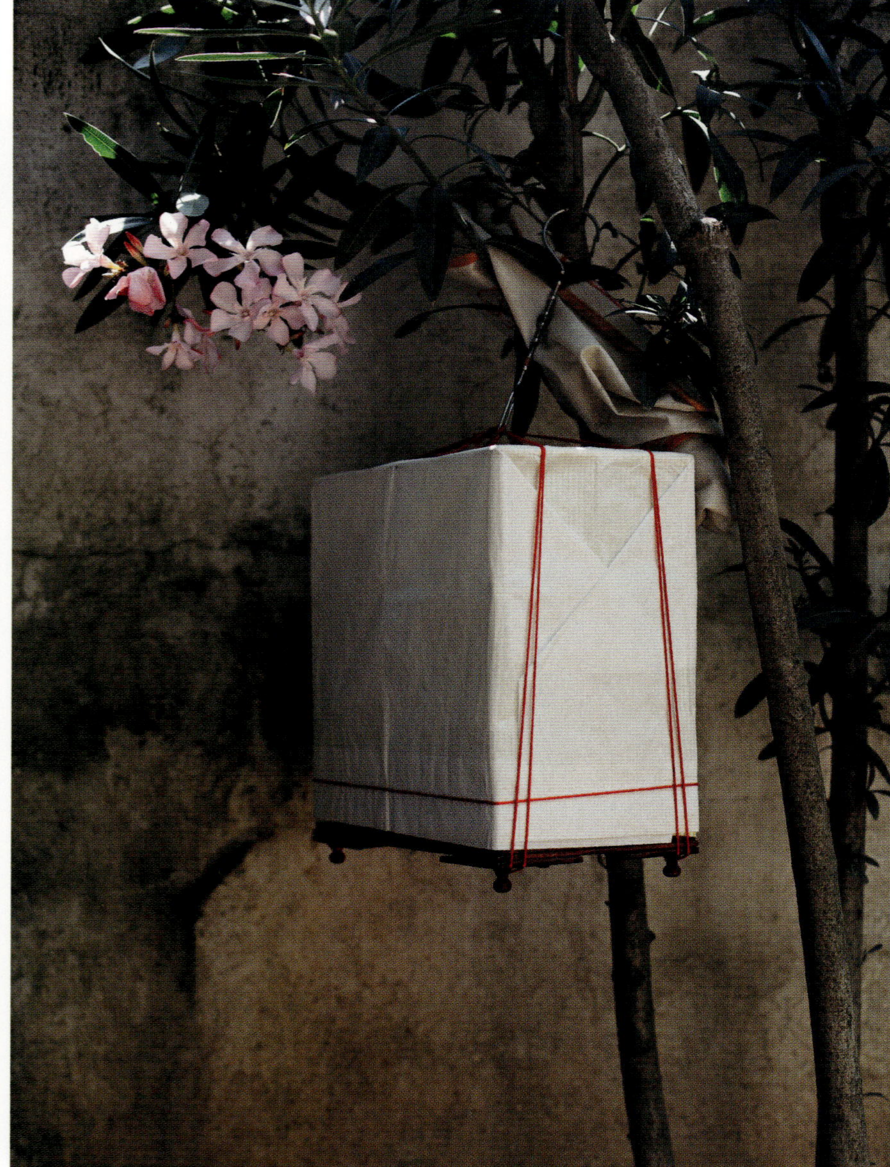

Above left: *Goldfinch Tattoo*, 2014; above right: *Cage #3*, 2014; both *For Birds' Sake* series

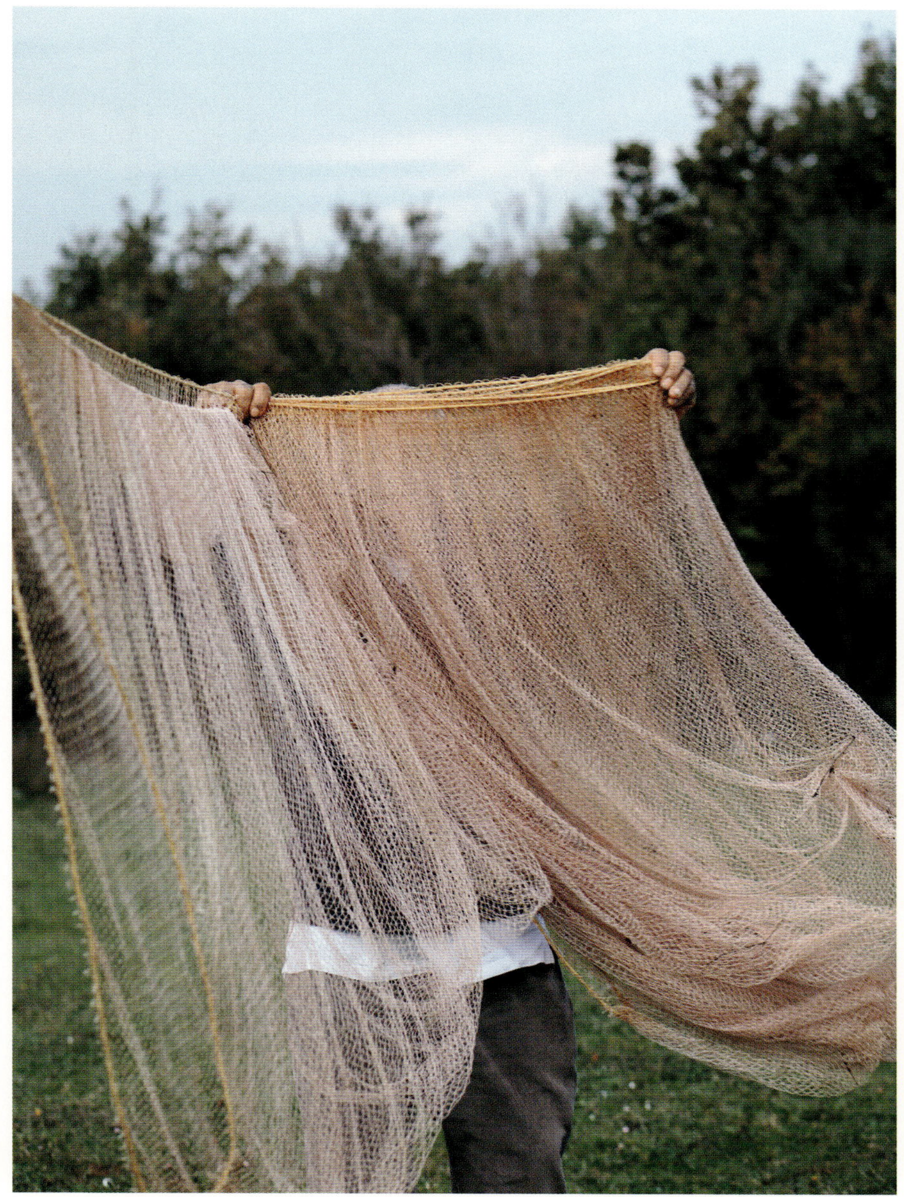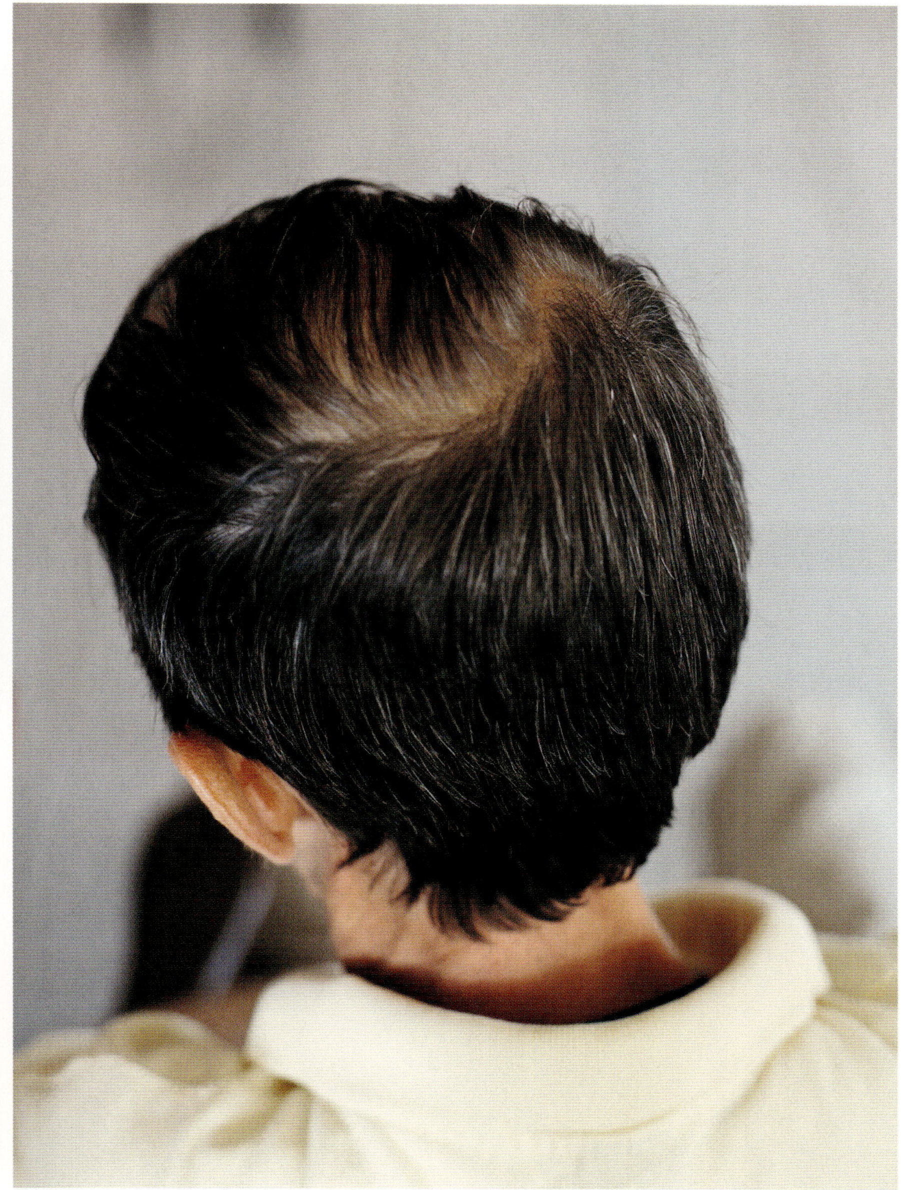

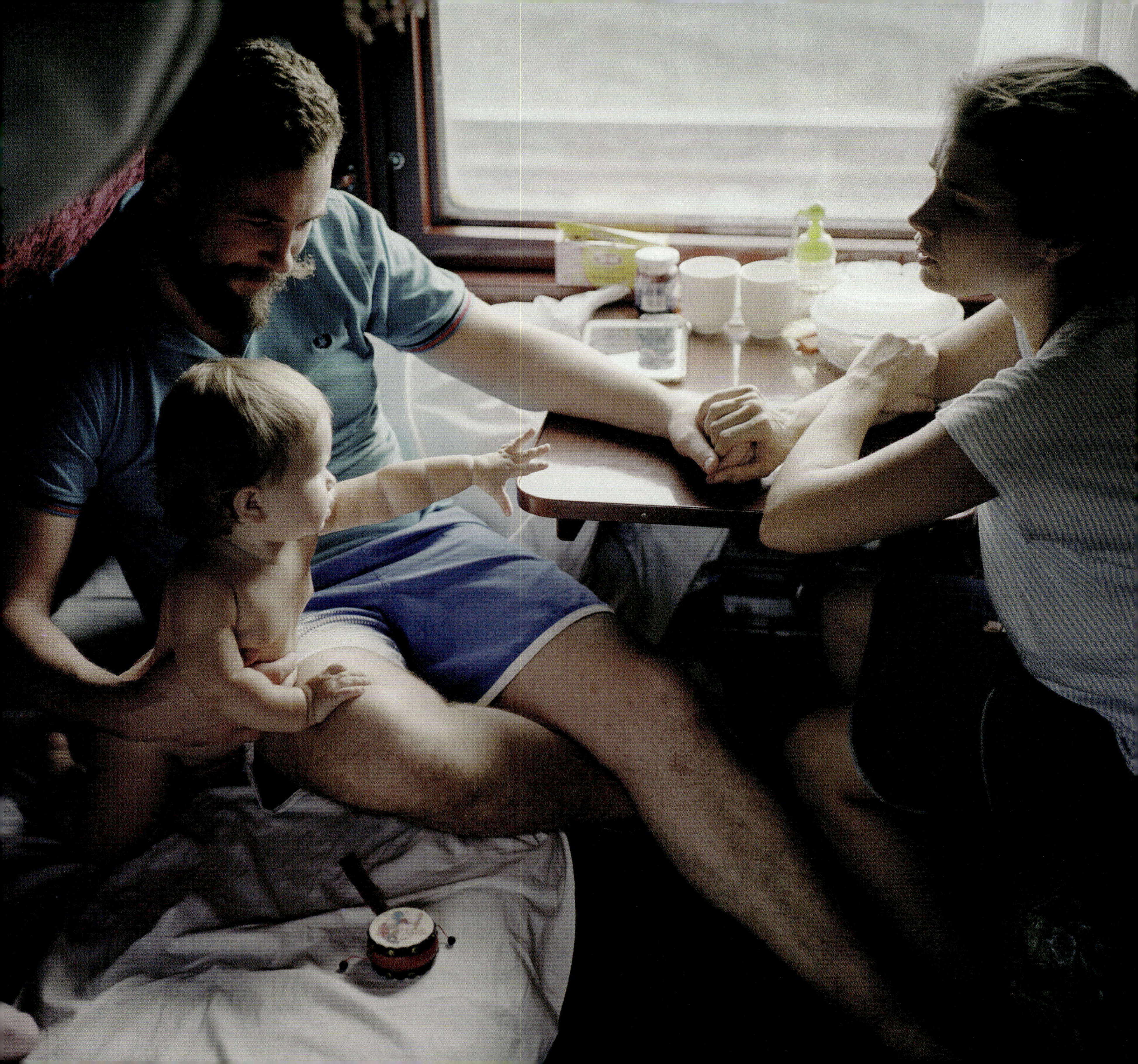

YUNYA YIN

Sometimes, although rarely, a new photographic talent is part of a graduation show and everybody notices. This is how it was for Yunya Yin, a twenty-six-year-old photographer from Sichuan, China.

During the summer of 2015 Yin returned to China to create her major project for her MA at the London College of Communication. She travelled back west much more slowly on the Trans-Siberian express. Over the 126-hour journey Yin observed poignant vignettes of life unfolding. Her unthreatening and gentle presence made her the perfect compassionate voyeur, a welcome guest at the tables of others. The photographs, shot through with clear light, have an oneiric quality that Yin herself associates with a kind of timelessness. She photographed a tiny baby, unaware of its journey on board this historic train, which has linked cultures and people for decades. She photographed friends, families, dreamers, lovers, united briefly in time and space.

For Yin, it was the very essence of this epic voyage that she wanted to capture. She wasn't interested in the demographics of the passengers, or even the reason for their trips. In addition to her delicate interior shots, Yin also photographed the view outside as the train cut its path through the changing landscapes. With the precision of

a miniaturist, she observed scenes playing out: moments of exchange between fellow humans who inhabit this planet that can never be seen again. Inside her viewfinder Yin held each moment in motion as though she were catching a falling star.

It is apposite that she found her inspiration in the work of acclaimed photographer Sun Jun, who learnt the art of traditional Chinese painting when he was just seven years old. Often working in fashion – as well as art – photography, Sun Jun fuses traditional elements with modern, creating a unique and distinctive style, which has quite clearly been an influence in the creation of Yin's own aesthetic.

Yin studied for her undergraduate degree at the Beijing Film Academy from 2009 until 2013. In 2014, she moved to London to study for an MA in photojournalism and documentary photography. After her graduation show in January 2016, Yin was nominated for the Magnum Photos Graduate Photographers Award, won the 'student' category in the prestigious PDN 2016 awards, and was the recipient of a residency at the coveted Planche(s) Contact Festival of Photography, Deauville, 2016. Her new project, made exclusively for Deauville, was displayed in the city in November 2016.

Her second long-term project, *Imaginary Adolescence*, finds a space in which to explore the boundaries between fact and fiction in documentary photography.

Yin understands the unreal quality of life on the cusp of adulthood: the intensity, the nonchalance, the sense of anticipation. To make vivid this condition, Yin has injected colour to the images, via Photoshop. The gap between reality and fantasy allows for free play of her imagination and, in turn, the creation of the exquisite imagery that is fast becoming her signature.

A Russian Family, 2015, The Timeless Trans-Siberian Railways series

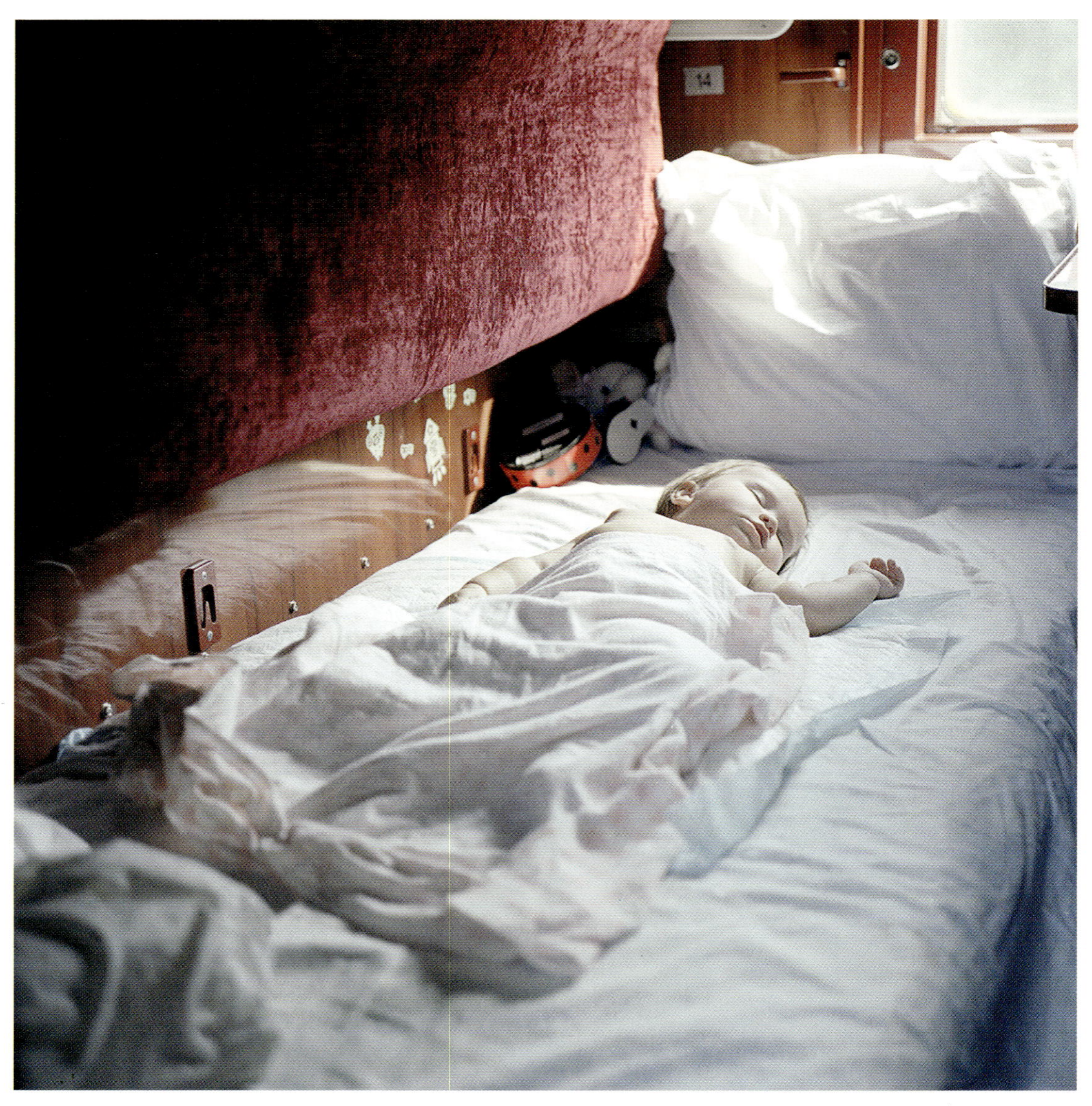

Dolphin, 2015, The Timeless Trans-Siberian Railways series

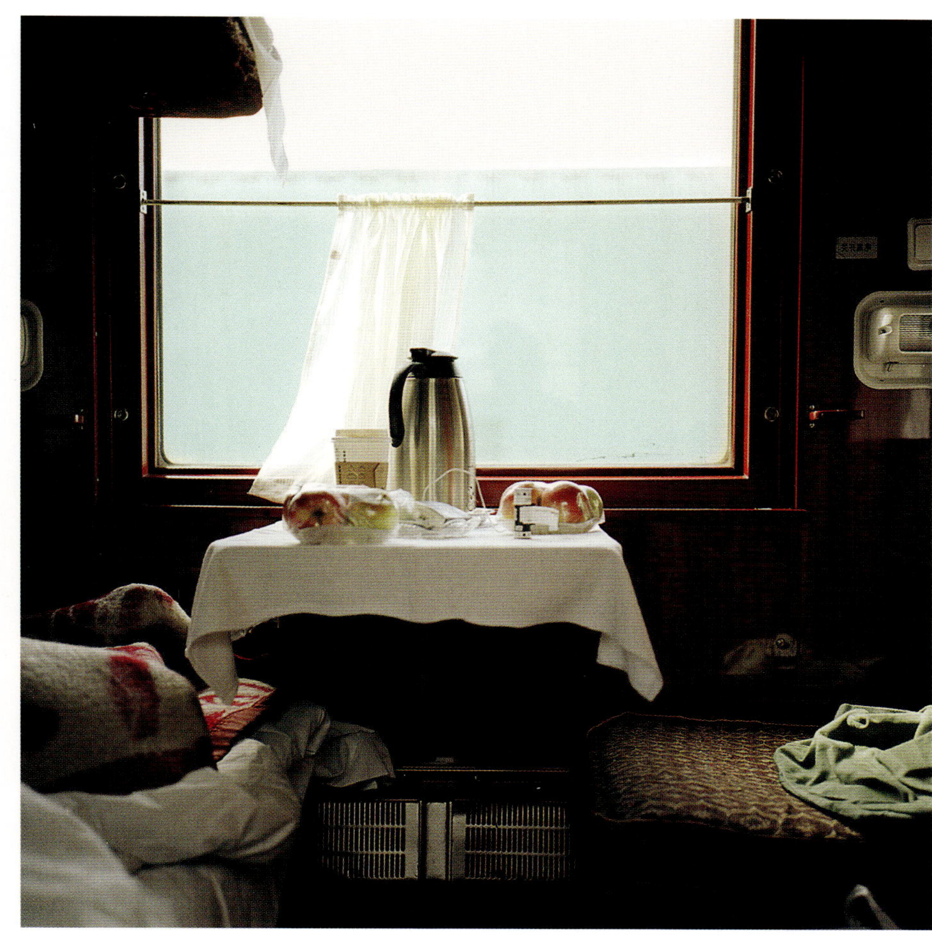

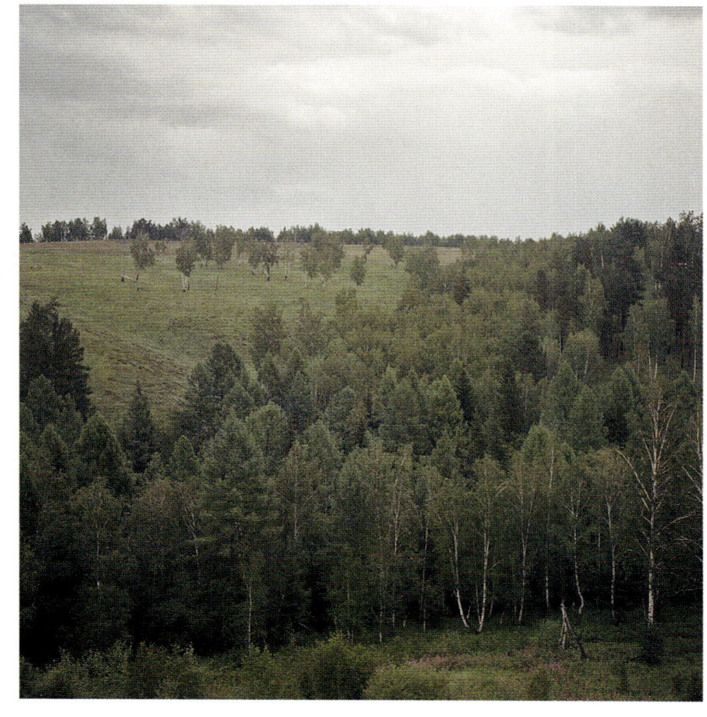

Above: *Carriage no.9*, 2015;
right: *Landscape I: Birch-woods*, 2015;
both *The Timeless Trans-Siberian Railways* series

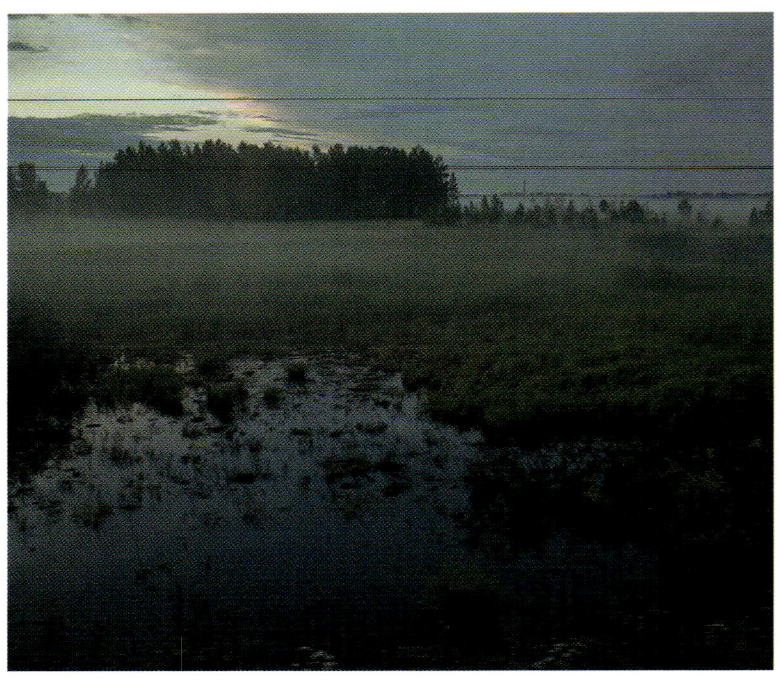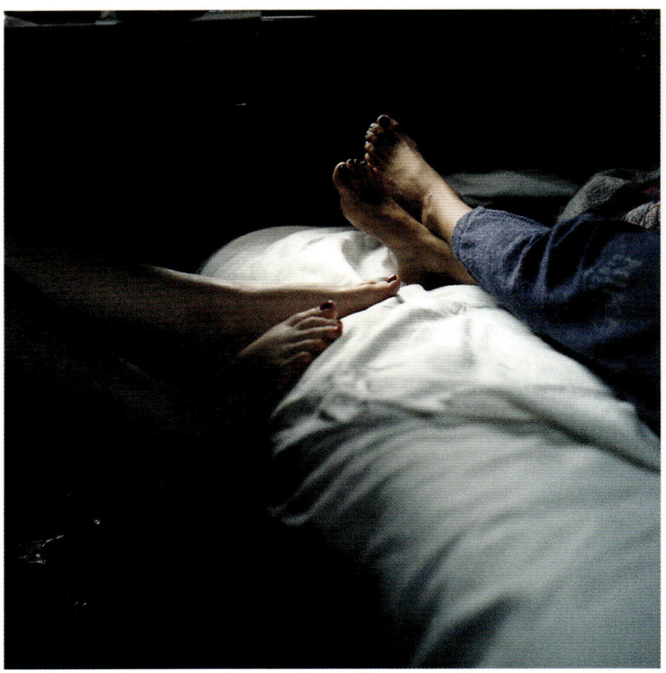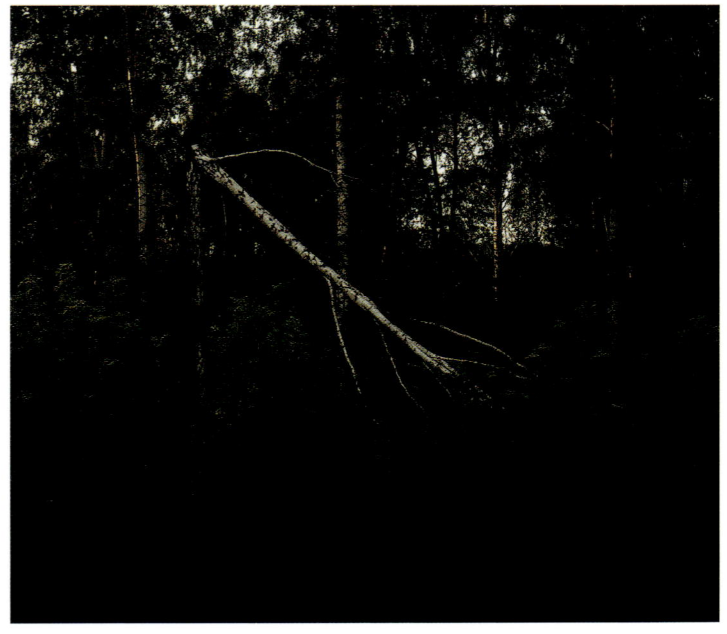

Above left: *Landscape 2: Untitled*, 2015;
above right: *Untitled 2*, 2015;
above: *Landscape 3: Untitled*, 2015;
all *The Timeless Trans-Siberian Railways* series

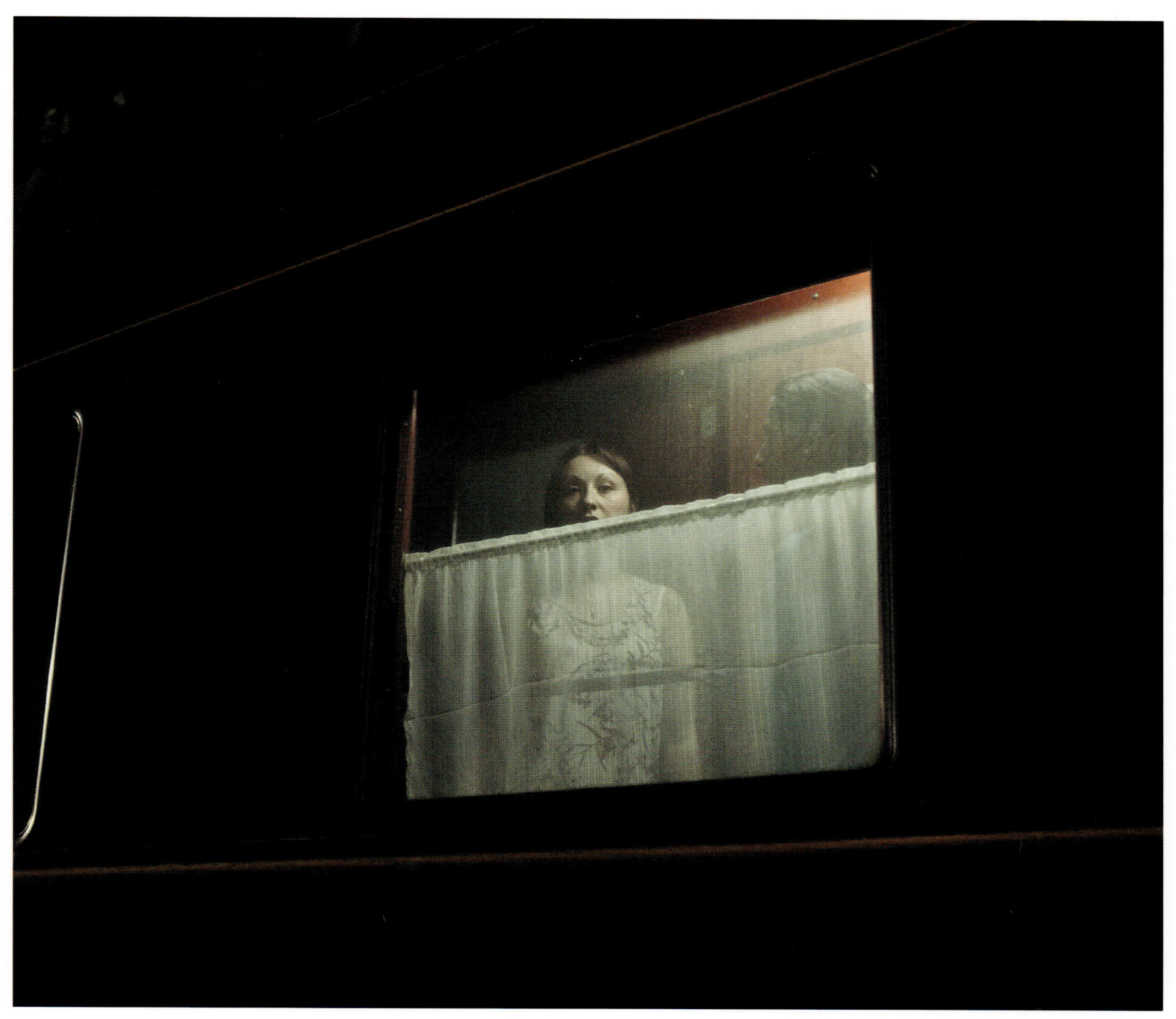

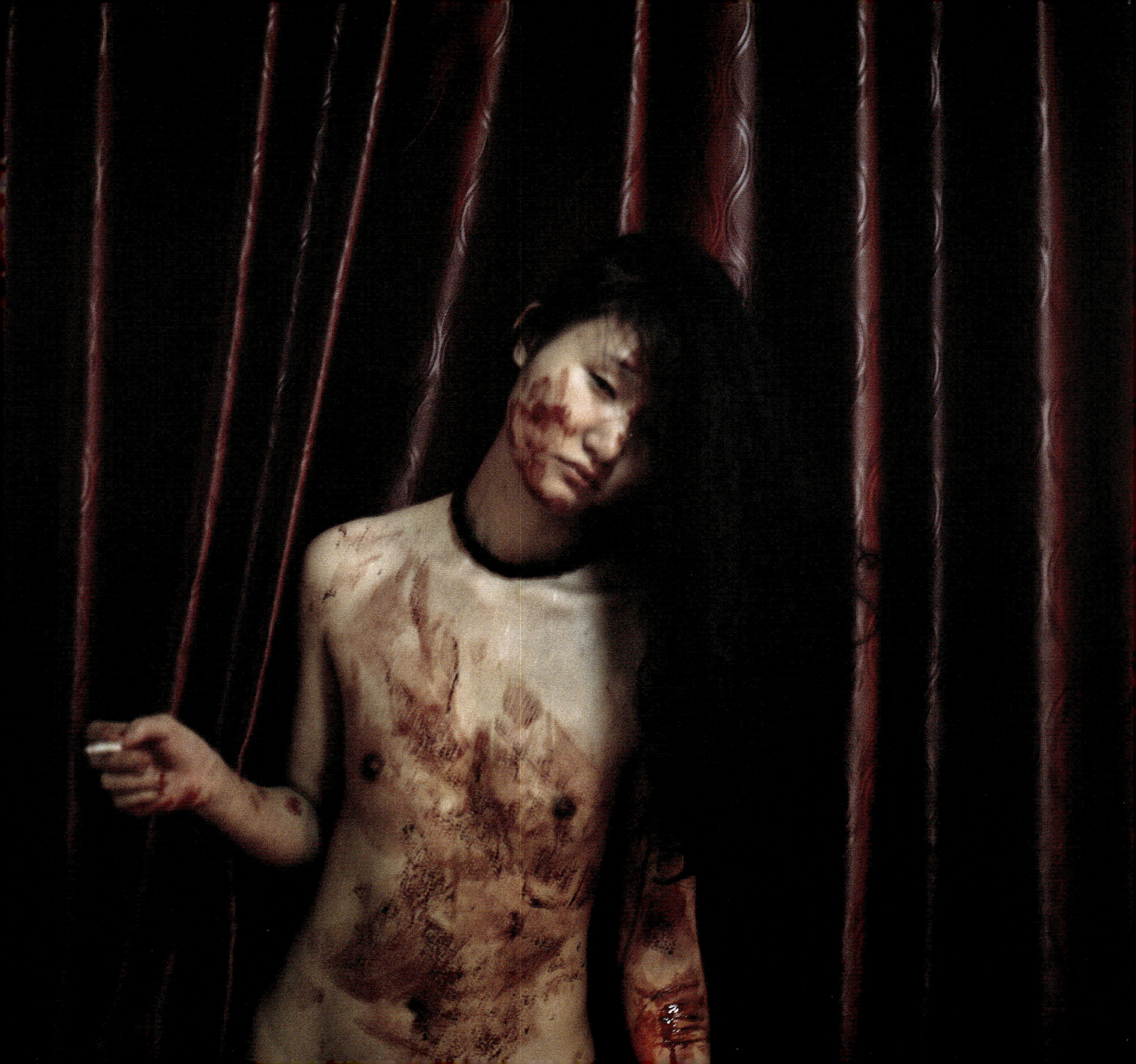

CHEN ZHE

The unsettling work of Chinese artist Chen Zhe seeks to make sense of our inner lives and propensity for self-destruction. Born and raised in Beijing, Chen currently lives and works in her home town, but studied at the School of Visual Arts, New York, and was also a graduate of the Art Centre College of Design in Los Angeles.

Chen is a self-confessed self-harmer and has wrestled with her condition for nearly a decade. Her first body of work, *The Bearable*, began in 2007 as a reflective documentation of her personal history, seeking to both confront and overcome this relationship with her own body. It became the starting point for *The Bees* in 2010, which sought to expand these ideas through encounters with other people, mainly young adults in her native Beijing and other major Chinese cities. The bees are a gentle metaphor for Chen to describe visually the paradoxical nature of self-harm in order to preserve existence itself. She references Virgil's *The Georgics*: '...if hurt, they breathe Venom into their bite, cleave to the veins And let the sting lie buried, and leave their lives Behind them in the wound.'

The two bodies of work are bound together in Chen's book *Bees & The Bearable* (Jiazazhi Press, 2016), which won best photobook at Fotobookfestival Kassel and the Unseen Dummy Awards. It serves as a closing statement for Chen's long and deeply personal exploration. In her collection of observations, letters, diary entries and exchanges with people of shared experience, Chen finds an alternative means of portraying an often misunderstood condition.

Chen's work gets under the skin in more ways than one. Beautiful and tender in places, but disquieting and uneasy in others, she delves deep into the human psyche to show us the nature of self-harm in all its layered complexity: fragile, violent, chaotic and calming. She explores it as both a rational coping strategy and a frenzied emotional release, offering us many viewpoints but no conclusions and no explanation of her own motivations to self-harm.

In describing her work, Chen references the Chinese words 'Tong(痛)' meaning pain and 'Kuai(快)' meaning pleasure. She says, 'If you combine the two characters, there comes a particular phrase "Tong-kuai(痛快)" that means wholeheartedly enjoying something; very delighted... Think of the stimulations you get when swimming in cold water, picking at your scabs or biting on the ulcer on the side of your tongue. You would notice that, in these actions, both the sense of pain and pleasure are awakened, and the resistance and the attraction coexist.'

Her visceral photographs are both cold and detached in places, and highly empathic in others. In one image, a listless woman is covered in blood. In another, a hooded figure contemplates a city skyline, looking as though they may jump. Blood is a recurring feature and the viewer can't help but feel complicit, as though they have witnessed something they shouldn't. Within the work are nods to notions of fading memory, scientific exploration and religious or spiritual enlightenment.

Bees & The Bearable is a brave and devastatingly honest body of work. As both sufferer and documentarian, Chen presents an autobiographical truth that touches on the fallibility and vulnerability of the human condition.

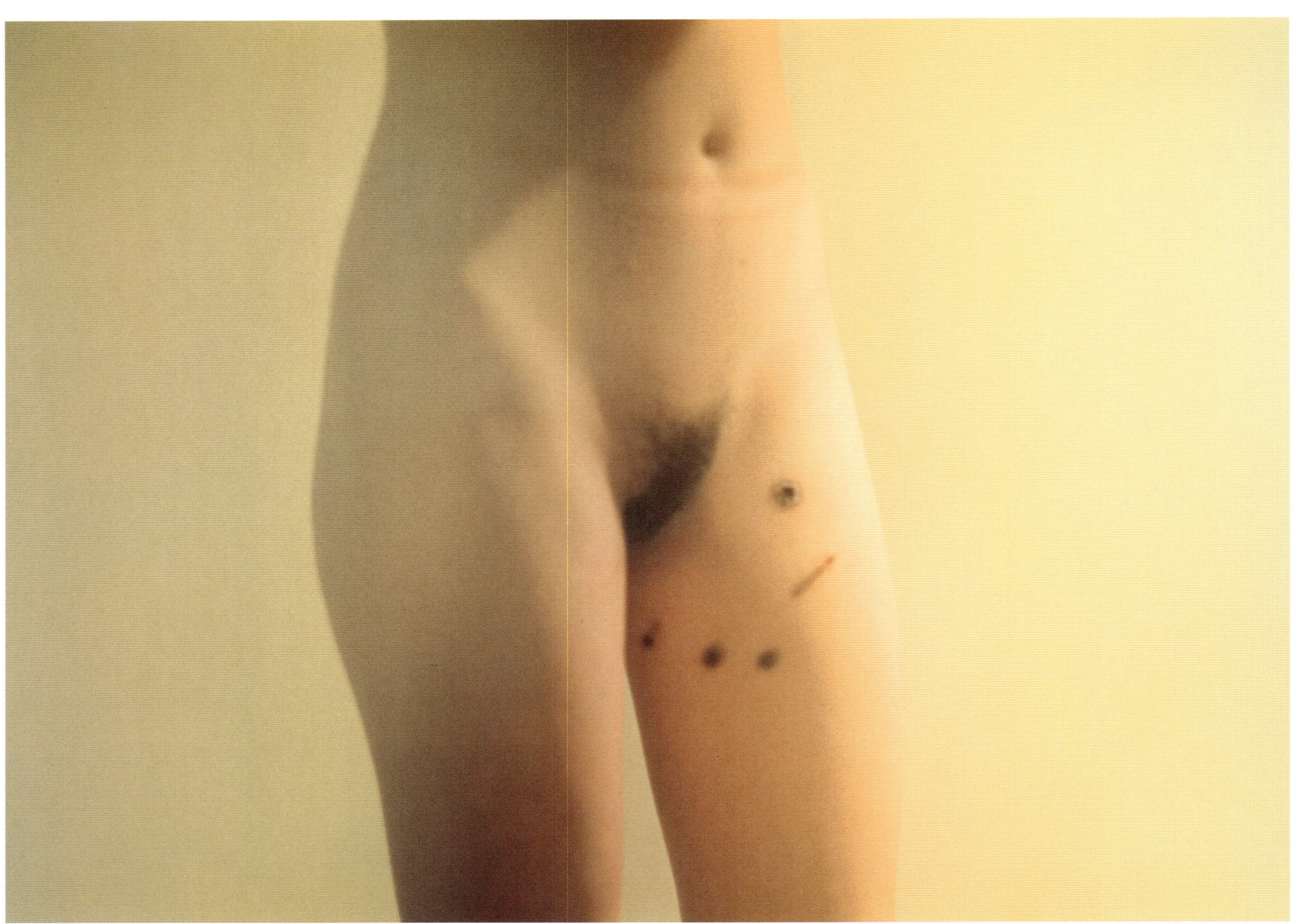

Bees # 054-06, 2010

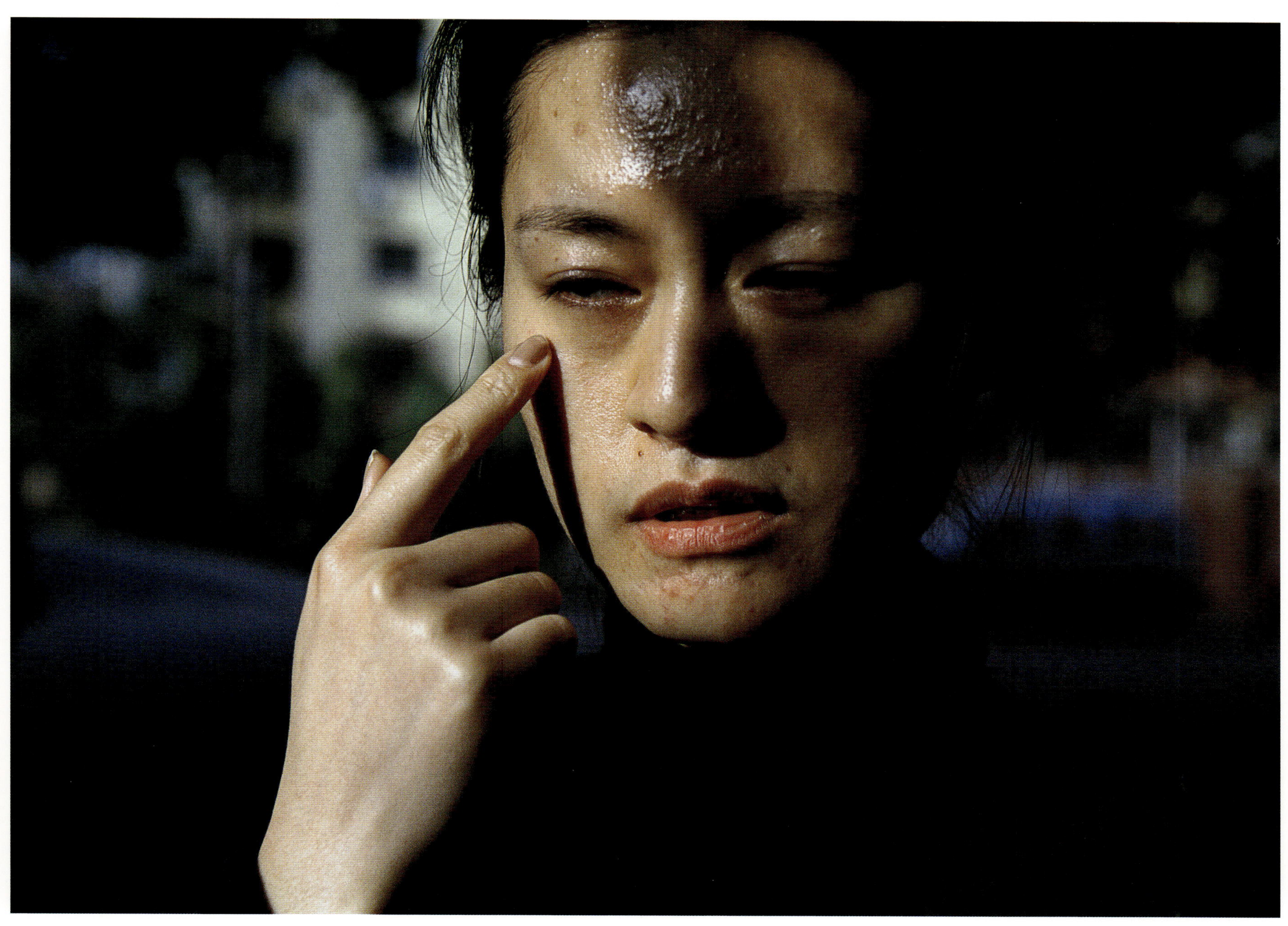

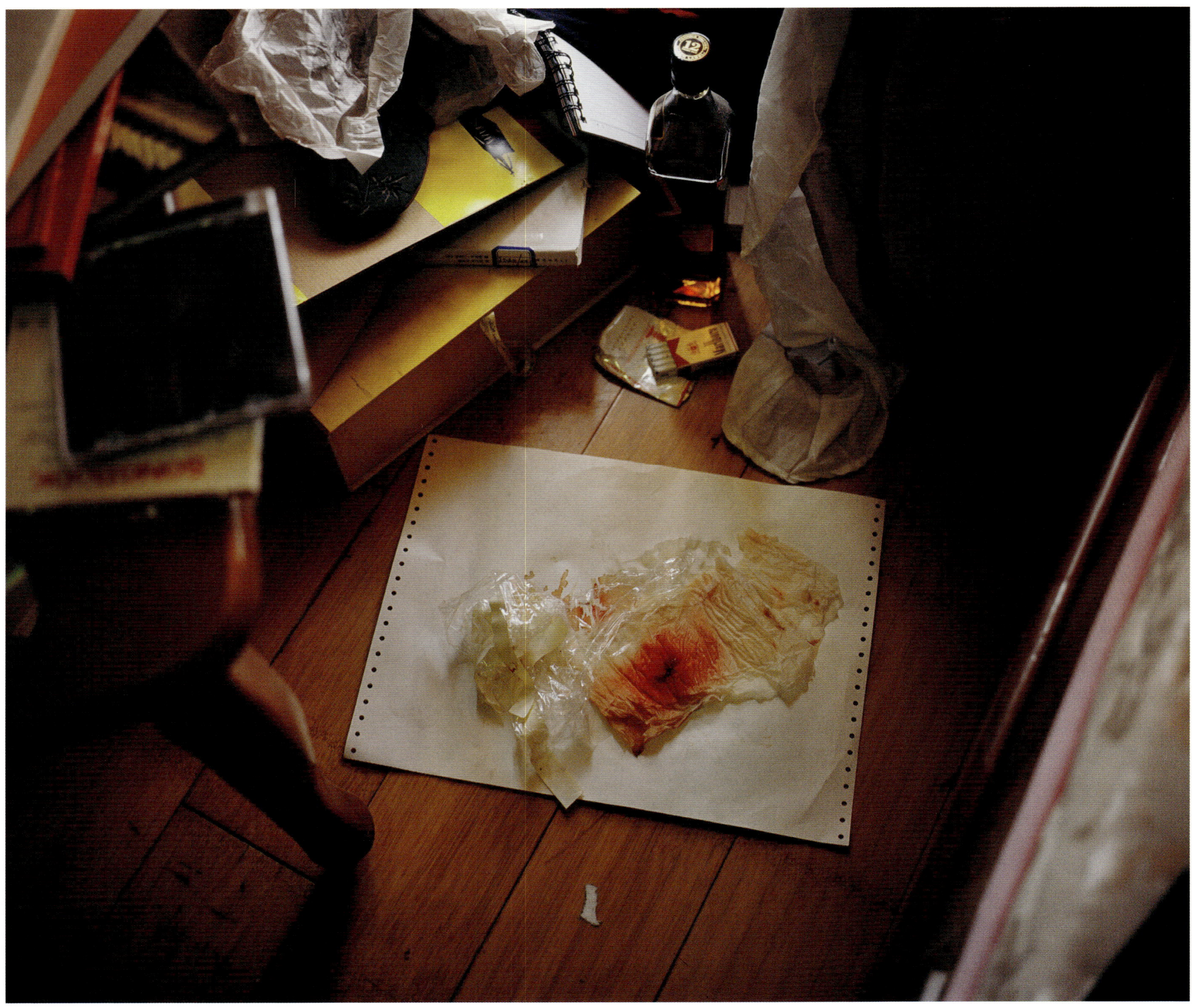

Bees # 009-01, 2010

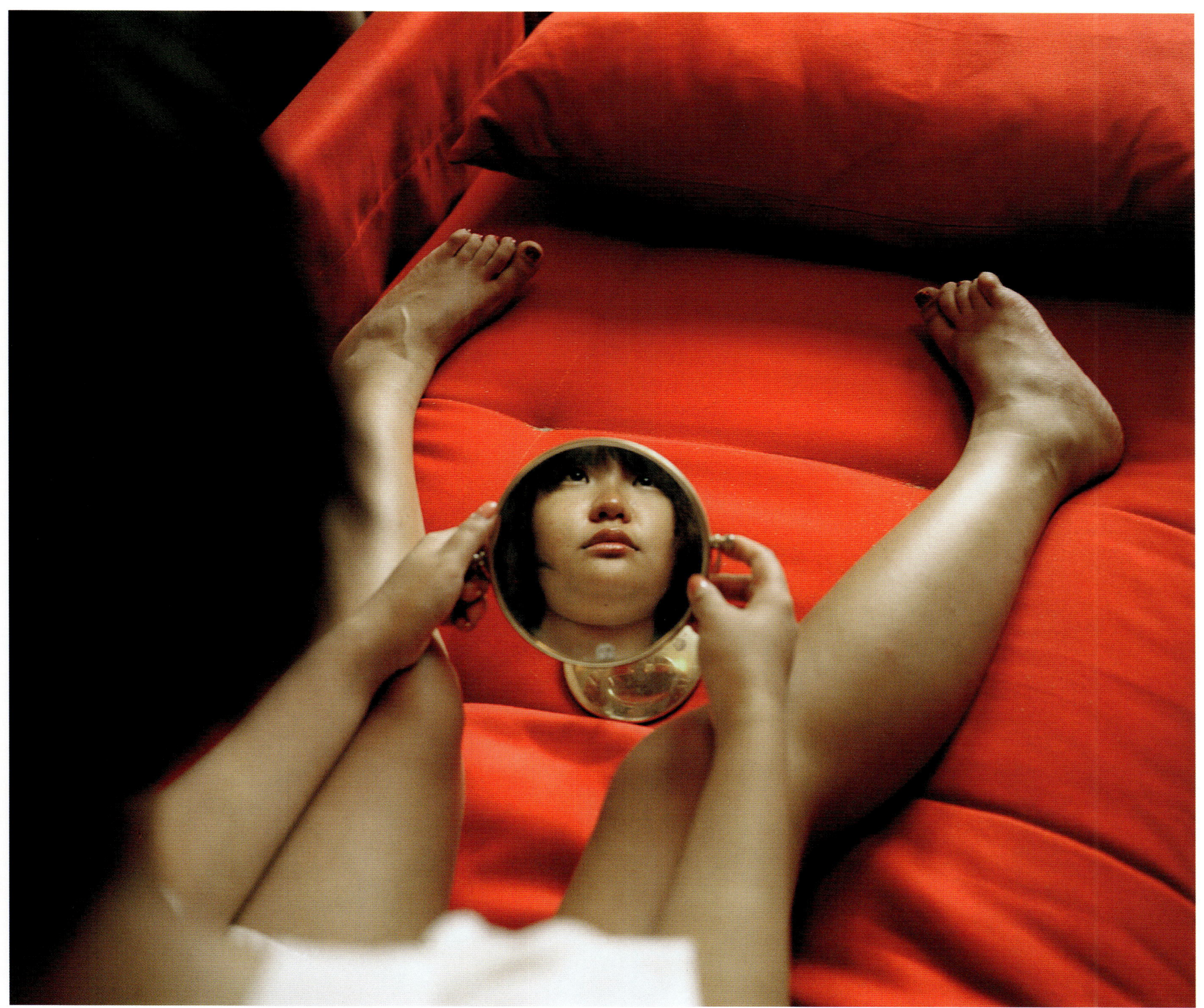

YING ANG

Ying Ang is based in Melbourne, Singapore and New York and has exhibited internationally in group and solo shows in various cities from New York to Arles. She graduated as valedictorian for the 2009–2010 class of documentary photography and photojournalism at the International Center of Photography in New York; her portfolio was acquired for the permanent collection of the Sagamihara City Museum in Japan. Ang is the director of the Reflexions Masterclass in Europe.

Ang self-published her book *Gold Coast*, which won the New York Photo Festival and Encontros Da Imagem book prizes in 2014. The book was also a finalist for Australian Photobook of the Year, the CREATE Award, the Guernsey Photography Festival Prize for 2015 and was acquired for the Rare Books Collection at the State Library of Victoria in Melbourne. *Gold Coast* was also listed by FlakPhoto, LensCulture, Voices of Photography, Mark Power/Magnum Photos, Asia Pacific Photobook Archive and Self Publish Be Happy as a top photobook of 2014 and was recently honoured with a nomination for the prestigious Prix Pictet award for 2015. Ang has been chief curator for the print exhibitions at the OBSCURA Festival of Photography and was the keynote speaker at the inaugural Photobook New Zealand, 2016.

—

EVGENIA ARBUGAEVA

Evgenia Arbugaeva was born in 1985 in the town of Tiksi, which is located in the Russian Arctic. In her personal work she often looks into her homeland – the Arctic, discovering and capturing its remote worlds and the people who inhabit them. Arbugaeva has been a winner of various competitions.

She has received the ICP Infinity Award, the Leica Oskar Barnack Award and the Magnum Foundation Emergency Fund Grant. Her work has been exhibited internationally and has appeared in such publications as the *New Yorker*, *Le Monde* and *National Geographic Magazine* among others.

—

BEHNAZ BABAZADEH

Behnaz Babazadeh is an Afghan-American artist who received her MA in fine arts from Parsons School of Design in New York in 2012. Her work spans photography, sculpture and film, and challenges the Western preconceptions of women in burkas with a series of works made from materials found in a candy shop. Babazadeh is a TEDxMidAtlantic speaker.

—

POULOMI BASU

Poulomi Basu is an Indian storyteller, artist, investigative journalist and activist. She was born and raised by her mother in Calcutta. After her father's sudden death when she was seventeen, her mother told her to leave home and follow her dreams. Her work documents the role of women in isolated communities and conflict situations.

Basu has spoken at many events: in 2015 she shared a platform with the parents of the Nirbhaya New Delhi rape victim and spoke about her social activist initiative, The Rape in India Project; in 2016 she spoke at the UN Young Changemakers Conclave about the social impact of sustainable development with specific reference to her long-term project *A Ritual of Exile* and her collaboration with NGO WaterAid and their 'To Be a Girl' campaign, which raised

£2 million, using her work; and in 2016 she was invited to speak at the National Geographic Annual Seminar in Washington D.C. Basu was featured alongside Hillary Clinton in Refinery29's 'amazing women from around the world give you their best advice' feature. She was also part of the VII Mentor Program.

She is the director of Just Another Photo Festival, a travelling guerrilla visual media festival that democratizes photography by taking it to the people and forging new audiences. Her festival was shortlisted by the *British Journal of Photography* as 2015's most 'cool and noteworthy' photo festival and in 2016 it was described as an alternate voice of the 'audience' in J. M. Colberg's *Conscientious Photography Magazine*. Her ongoing work *A Ritual of Exile* won the FotoEvidence Book Award, 2017. *Centralia* was shortlisted for a MACK First Book Award in 2017, Magnum Emergency Fund in 2016 and was a W. Eugene Smith finalist in 2016. The Magnum Foundation also awarded Basu the What Works Human Rights Fellow Grant in 2016, and she was a nominee for the Foam Paul Huf Award in 2015 and 2017. She won second place in the Firecracker award in 2015 for *Mothers of ISIS Foreign Fighters,* which will be exhibited at *Poetics of War and Secrecy* in Oxford in 2017. She was a Magnum Foundation Human Rights Fellow in 2012.

Her works have been exhibited in a variety of venues, such as the Bronx Documentary Center, New York, House of Commons, Palace of Westminster, and St James' Palace, London, Commonwealth Health Ministers Meeting, Geneva, Human Rights Watch Fundraising Exhibition in the US as well as in villages and fringe communities in the streets of India.

ENDIA BEAL

Endia Beal is a North Carolina-based artist, educator and activist, who is internationally known for her photographic narratives and video testimonies that examine the personal and contemporary stories of women of colour working within the corporate space. Beal currently serves as the director of Diggs Gallery and as assistant professor of art at Winston-Salem State University.

Beal has been featured in several online editorials including the *New York Times*, NBC, BET, the *Huffington Post, Slate Magazine* and *National Geographic Magazine*. Her work has also appeared in *Essence Magazine, Marie Claire Magazine* (South Africa), *Newsweek* (Japan) and *Photo District News*. Her work has been exhibited in several institutions such as the Columbia Museum of Art, South Carolina, the Harvey B. Gantt Center for African-American Arts + Culture based in Charlotte, North Carolina, and the Aperture Foundation in New York.

–

HALEY MORRIS-CAFIERO

Haley Morris-Cafiero is part-performer, part-artist, part-provocateur, part-spectator; she explores the act of reflection in her photography. Her photographs have been widely exhibited in solo and group exhibitions throughout the world, and have been featured in numerous newspapers and magazines, in print and online, including *Le Monde, New York Magazine* and *Salon*. Born in Atlanta, Georgia, she is a graduate of the University of North Florida, where she earned a BA in photography and a BFA in ceramics in 1999. Morris-Cafiero was nominated for the Prix Pictet in 2014 and was a Fulbright finalist in 2016. She has an MFA in art from the University of Arizona.

Her monograph, *The Watchers*, was published in 2015. Morris-Cafiero is a photography professor and lives in Tennessee. She is represented by TJ Boulting Gallery in London. *The Watchers*, a monograph of her work, was published in 2105 by the Magenta Foundation.

–

JUNO CALYPSO

Juno Calypso was born in London in 1989. She completed her BA in photography at the London College of Communication in 2012. Since graduating, she has won several awards, including the 2013 Catlin Art Prize visitors' choice and the Series Award at the 2016 British Journal of Photography International Photography Award. Calypso is currently one of the 2016 Foam Talents and has been selected for several international photo festivals such as reGeneration3, the first Photo Vogue Festival and Lianzhou Foto Festival in China. Her video work has been screened at Photo London, Tate Modern, London, and the Photographers' Gallery, London. Calypso lives and works in London.

–

NATASHA CARUANA

Natasha Caruana is a photographic artist living and working in London. She has an MA in photography from the Royal College of Art, London, and is a senior lecturer of photography at the University for the Creative Arts, Farnham, UK.

Caruana's art practice is grounded in research concerned with narratives of love, betrayal and fantasy. Significant to all her work is the questioning of how today's technology affects relationships. In 2014 Caruana won the prestigious BMW Artist in Residence Award at Musée Nicéphore Niépce, Chalon-sur-Saône, France. The award led to solo shows at the Rencontres d'Arles and Paris Photo, and to the monograph *Coup de Foudre*.

Her work has been shown across Australia, China, France, India, Lithuania, Portugal, Saudi Arabia and the US. Her *Married Man* and *Fairytale for Sale* series has been included in numerous contemporary photographic catalogues, printed as monographs, and have toured widely – most recently in *Public, Private, Secret* at the International Center of Photography Museum, New York, *The Real Thing*, Flowers Gallery, New York, and *Feminine Masculine*, Photo50, London.

–

SCARLETT COTEN

Scarlett Coten is an independent French photographer who dedicates herself essentially to personal, long-term projects. The Arab countries are at the heart of her photographic practice, which explores the themes of identity and intimacy. After studying at L'Ecole Nationale Supérieure de la Photographie in Arles, Coten travelled to Egypt in 2000 and created her first important series, *Still Alive*, spending months in the Sinai desert with the Bedouins. Coten was awarded the Humanity Photo Award in 2004 in Beijing and her book was nominated for an award at the New York Photo Festival in 2009.

Since 2012, Coten has been engaged in the ongoing project *Mectoub*, photographing men in the Arab countries of the Mediterranean basin, travelling from North Africa to the Middle East. Her work has been shown in many solo and group exhibitions around the world from France to the US. She has also won many awards.

BIEKE DEPOORTER

Bieke Depoorter was born in 1986 in Kortrijk, Belgium. She received an MA in photography at the Royal Academy of Fine Arts in Ghent in 2009. Her early colour photography work is the result of a unique approach: she captures the privacy of people whom she meets by chance and she gets to invite her into their homes. She captures indescribable, fragile and intense moments, always with kindness.

For the *Ou Menya* series, Depoorter travelled for three months to remote villages in Russia, guided by the Trans-Siberian Railway. This work won her several awards, including the Magnum Expression Award in 2009. Her first book, *Ou Menya,* was published by Lannoo (Belgium) in 2011.

For a similar long-term project entitled *I Am About to Call it a Day* she went to the US. The book about the project was jointly published in 2014 by Hannibal (Belgium) and Edition Patrick Frey (Switzerland). With *Sète#15* Depoorter explores the thin line between fiction and documentary for the first time. These photographs were taken during an artistic residency for the festival ImageSingulières. She presents a nocturnal vision of the city, with a filmic dream-like atmosphere. Her photographs convey the muted pulsations of a sleeping city.

Depoorter finished *Dvalemodus,* her first short movie, in 2017. She directed it with musician Mattias De Craene. The film talks about everlasting darkness in a small village in northern Norway.

She became a nominee of the Magnum Photo collective in 2012 and a full member in 2016.

MARIA GRUZDEVA

Maria Gruzdeva was born in Russia in 1989 and is now based in London. She mainly works on long-term projects that are underpinned by extensive research. In her work she explores such issues as collective memory, sense of place and belonging, and the relationship between landscape and identity.

Her work has been exhibited in Russia, the UK, France, Greece and Japan and has been featured in a number of photographic festivals, including the Rencontres d'Arles, France and the Festival of Political Photography in Finland.

Gruzdeva has been awarded the IdeasTap Photographic Award with Magnum Photos, the Magenta Flash Forward for Emerging Photographers, the Gabriele Basilico Prize in Architecture and Landscape Photography as well as many other awards. In 2016 she was named one of the 30 Under 30 Europe in the arts category by Forbes.

Her work has been published in three monographs: *Direction-Space!* (Dewi Lewis Publishing, 2011), *Border: A Journey Along the Edges of Russia* (Schilt Publishing, 2016) and *The Song of Tkvarcheli* (Danilo Montanari Editore, 2017).

–

ALMA HASER

Alma Haser was born in Haslach, Germany, in 1989 and completed her BA at Nottingham Trent University in 2010. She has exhibited in solo and group exhibitions at the Photographers' Gallery, London, Print Sales Gallery, London, De Soto Gallery, Los Angeles, Australian Centre for Photography, Darlinghurst, QSS Gallery, Belfast, Fort Worth Contemporary Arts, Texas, Four Corners

Gallery, London, The Art Foundation, Athens, Queensland Centre for Photography, Australia, Neubacher Shor Contemporary, Toronto, M Shed, Bristol, Aspex Gallery, Portsmouth, National Portrait Gallery, London, PhotoIreland Festival, Dublin, Foto8 Gallery, London, and Guernsey Photography Festival. Haser received fourth prize in the National Portrait Gallery's Taylor Wessing Photographic Portrait Prize in 2012 and won the Magenta Foundation Bright Spark Award in 2013. She lives and works in Hastings, East Sussex.

–

MAYUMI HOSOKURA

Mayumi Hosokura was born in Kyoto in 1979 and graduated from Ritsumeikan University and the Institute of Photography at Nihon University of Art. She has participated in numerous group exhibitions in Japan and gained attention both at home and internationally for *Kazan* (2009–11), which depicted her strong yet delicate sensitivity towards the city. Her work has been shown internationally at Paris Photo and the Unseen Photo Fair in Amsterdam. In 2016, a book of her work, *Transparency is the New Mystery*, was published by MACK. The book includes some of Hosokura's best works of nudes and minerals.

–

CORINNA KERN

Corinna Kern is a German photojournalist and documentary photographer based in Israel. Inclined towards the counter-cultural and non-mainstream, her work gives intimate insights into the lives of people on the margins of society. Capturing the humanity behind their non-conformist choices from an insider's perspective, Kern's candid photography aims to challenge preconceived notions.

Kern's background was in video editing at Westdeutscher Rundfunk, one of Germany's major TV stations, but in 2012 she devoted herself to her passion by studying for an MA in photojournalism at the University of Westminster, London. She graduated with a distinction in 2013 and was selected for a mentorship with Getty Images Reportage. She was awarded the Getty Images Reportage Emerging Talent Award in 2014. She decided to base herself in South Africa for two years in order to work extensively on personal long-term projects. In 2016 she relocated to Israel where she continues to focus on people and communities of diverse cultures and backgrounds, while freelancing for international publications and photo agencies.

Her work gained international recognition through prestigious photo awards such as Pictures of the Year International, NPPA Best of Photojournalism, Sony World Photography Awards, International Photography Awards, Lensculture and many others. Her work has been published online and in print by *TIME Lightbox*, the *New York Times*, *Stern*, *Der Spiegel*, CNN, Vice, *Magazine du Monde*, *Die Zeit*, *Marie Claire* and the *Guardian* among others.

–

KATRIN KOENNING

Katrin Koenning is a German photographer with a particular interest in our physical and emotional connection to place and environment. She currently lives in Melbourne, Australia, where she works as a freelance photographer and lecturer in photography. Her photographs have been exhibited in numerous Australian and international solo and group exhibitions, and her work has featured in festivals such as Noorderlicht, FORMAT, Athens Photo Festival, PhotoIreland Festival, the New York Photo Festival, Delhi Photo Festival, Gijon International Photojournalism Festival and Voies Off, Arles.

Koenning's photographs have been published in *Photographers' Sketchbooks*, *Hijacked 3*, Documentum, the *Guardian*, the *New York Times*, *Der Spiegel*, *GUP Magazine*, the *Financial Times Magazine*, *Bloomberg Businessweek*, *Marie Claire Magazine* and *SBS Australia* among many others. She has won a number of awards including the 2015 Daylight Photo Award, Australia's Top Emerging Documentary Photographer, the Troika Editions FORMAT Exposure Prize and the JGS Award (Forward Thinking Museum). Her work is held in numerous public and private collections across Australia and Europe, and she is a former editor of the *Australian PhotoJournalist Magazine*.

Her first book, *Astres Noirs*, in collaboration with Sarker Protick, is due to be published in June this year by Chose Commune.

–

ANASTASIA TAYLOR-LIND

Anastasia Taylor-Lind is an English-Swedish journalist who has been working for leading editorial publications for over a decade on issues relating to women, population and war. She is a 2016 Harvard Nieman Fellow and recently finished a year of research at the university on war and how we tell stories about modern conflict. She is currently a Logan Fellow at the Carey Institute for Global Good, New York, where she is working on a book about the visual representation of contemporary warfare and the photojournalists who cover it. She is also a TED fellow. Taylor-Lind has written about her experiences as a photojournalist for the *New York Times*, *TIME LightBox*, *Nieman Reports* and *National Geographic Magazine*. As a photographer, her focus has been on long-form narrative reportage for monthly magazines. She is a regular *National Geographic Magazine* contributor, and she also contributes to *Vanity Fair*, the *New Yorker*, *TIME*, the *New York Times*, the *Sunday Times*, the *Telegraph* and the *Guardian*.

Her first book, *Maidan: Portraits from the Black Square*, which documents the 2014 Ukrainian uprising in Kiev, was published by GOST books.

—

DIANA MARKOSIAN

Diana Markosian is an Armenian-American artist whose images explore the relationship between memory and place. Born in the former Soviet Union, her family immigrated to the US when she was a child, leaving her father behind. In 2010, she received her MA from Columbia University's Graduate School of Journalism. Her work has since taken her to some of the most remote corners of the world, where she has produced both personal and editorial work. Her images can be found in publications such as *National Geographic Magazine*, the *New Yorker* and the *New York Times*. She became a Magnum nominee in 2016.

—

DIANA MATAR

Diana Matar is an artist who works with photography, testimony and archive. Often spending years on a theme, she attempts to capture the invisible traces of human history. Her works are concerned with power and violence and the question of what role aesthetics might play in their depiction. Matar graduated from the Royal College of Art, London, in 2008. She has been the recipient of the Deutsche Bank Pyramid

Award for Fine Art, the International Fund for Documentary Photography Award and Arts Council England Individual Artist Grant. Her work has been shown at Tate Modern, London, Institut du Monde Arabe, Paris, the National Museum of Singapore and the Museum Folkwang, Essen, among many other international institutions. Her first monograph, *Evidence*, was published in November 2014 by Schilt Publishing, Amsterdam, and chosen by the *New York Times* photography critic Teju Cole as best book of the year. Her work is in the collections of the Museum of Contemporary Photography, Chicago, the Museum of Fine Arts, Houston, the Santa Barbara Museum of Art, the George Eastman Museum, Rochester, New York and the Victoria & Albert Museum, London among others.

—

CHLOE DEWE MATHEWS

Chloe Dewe Mathews is a photographic artist based in St Leonards-on-Sea in the UK. After studying fine art at Camberwell College of Arts and Oxford University, she worked in the feature film industry before dedicating herself to photography.

Her work has been exhibited at museums and galleries such as Tate Modern, London, the Irish Museum of Modern Art, Dublin, Museum Folkwang, Essen, and Fotomuseum Antwerp, as well as being published widely in newspapers and magazines such as the *Guardian*, the *Sunday Times*, the *Financial Times*, *Harper's* and *Le Monde*.

Dewe Mathews' first monograph, *Shot at Dawn*, was published by Ivorypress in 2014 and in the same year she became the Robert Gardner Fellow in Photography at the Peabody Museum of Archaeology and Ethnology, Harvard University.

Public and private collections have acquired her work, including the British Council Art Collection, the Irish State Art Collection and the National Library of Wales. She has also received commissions from institutions such as the Contemporary Art Society, Oxford University and Photoworks.

Her awards include the British Journal of Photography International Photography Award, the Julia Margaret Cameron New Talent Award and most recently the Royal Photographic Society Vic Odden Award.

—

ZANELE MUHOLI

Zanele Muholi is a visual activist. She was born in 1972 in Umlazi, Durban, and now lives in Johannesburg. She co-founded the Forum for the Empowerment of Women (FEW) in 2002, and in 2009 founded Inkanyiso, a forum for visual (activist) media. Muholi's self-proclaimed mission is 'to re-write a black queer and trans visual history of South Africa for the world to know of our resistance and existence at the height of hate crimes in SA and beyond'. She continues to teach and co-facilitate photography workshops for young women in the townships.

Muholi studied advanced photography at the Market Photo Workshop in Newtown, Johannesburg, and in 2009 completed an MFA in documentary media at Ryerson University, Toronto. She is an honorary professor at the University of the Arts, Bremen. Muholi has won numerous awards including the ICP Infinity Award for Documentary and Photojournalism (2016), Africa'sOut! Courage and Creativity Award (2016), the Outstanding International Alumni Award from Ryerson University (2016), the Fine Prize for an emerging artist at the 2013 Carnegie

International, a Prince Claus Award (2013), the Index on Censorship Freedom of Expression art award (2013), the Casa Africa award for best female photographer and a Fondation Blachère award at Les Rencontres de Bamako biennial of African photography (2009).

Her *Faces and Phases* series has been shown in such places as the North Carolina Museum of Art, Documenta 13, the South African Pavilion at the 55th Venice Biennale, and the 29th São Paulo Biennale. She has had solo exhibitions at various institutions, including the Mead Art Museum, Amherst, Gallatin Galleries, New York, Open Eye Gallery, Liverpool, Brooklyn Museum, New York, Akershus Kunstsenter, Lillestrøm, Einsteinhaus, Ulm, Schwules Museum, Berlin, Williams College Museum of Art, Williamstown and Casa Africa, Las Palmas. Her *Somnyama Ngonyama* series was recently exhibited in a solo show at the Standard Bank Gallery during the National Arts Festival in Grahamstown.

Muholi's most recent group shows include *Où poser la tête*, the Institute of Contemporary Art Indian Ocean, Mauritius (2016), *Supporting Alternative Visions*, the Prince Claus Fund Gallery, Amsterdam (2016), the Berlin Biennale (2016), *Mina/Meg*, the Kulturhistorisk Museum, Oslo (2016), *Systematically Open: New Forms of Production of the Contemporary Image*, LUMA, Parc des Ateliers, Arles (2016), *Reality of My Surroundings*, the Nasher Museum of Art, North Carolina (2016), *African Art Against the State*, the Williams College Museum of Art, Williamstown (2016), *After Eden/ Après Eden: The Walther Collection*, La Maison Rouge, Paris (2015), *Making Africa: A Continent of Contemporary Design*, the Vitra Design Museum, Weil am Rhein, and at the Guggenheim Bilbao (2015).

Muholi was shortlisted for the 2015 Deutsche Börse Photography Prize for her publication *Faces and Phases* (2006–14, Steidl/The Walther Collection). Other publications include *Zanele Muholi: African Women Photographers #1* (Casa Africa and La Fábrica, 2011); *Faces and Phases* (Prestel, 2010) and *Only Half the Picture* (Stevenson, 2006).

–

AIDA MULUNEH

Aïda Muluneh was born in Ethiopia in 1974. She left the country at a young age and spent an itinerant childhood between Yemen and England. After several years at a boarding school in Cyprus, she finally settled in Canada in 1985. In 2000, she graduated from the communication department at Howard University in Washington, D.C., having majored in film. After graduation she worked as a photojournalist at the *Washington Post*; her work has also been included in several other publications.

Her images can be found in the permanent collection at the Smithsonian Institution's National Museum of African Art, the Hood Museum of Art, New Hampshire, and the Museum of Biblical Art, New York. In 2007, she received the European Union Prize in the Rencontres africaines de la photographie in Bamako, Mali, and in 2010 she won the CRAF International Award of Photography in Spilimbergo, Italy. She is also the founder and director of the first international photography festival in East Africa, the Addis Foto Fest. Muluneh continues to curate and develop cultural projects with local and international institutions through her company DESTA (Developing and Educating Society Through Art) For Africa Creative Consulting PLC (DFA) in Addis Ababa, Ethiopia.

ANJA NIEMI

Anja Niemi was born in Norway and is considered 'one of the most compelling modern artists working today' according to the *British Journal of Photography*. Niemi always works alone, photographing, staging and acting out the characters in all of her photographs.

Her critically acclaimed series include *Do Not Disturb, Starlets, Darlene & Me, Short Stories* and *The Woman Who Never Existed*. These works have been exhibited worldwide in, among other cities, London, New York, San Francisco, Oslo and Paris. Her work is highly collectable and is included in many art collections.

She has published three books: *Photographing In Costume, Short Stories* and *The Woman Who Never Existed*.

–

REGINE PETERSEN

Regine Petersen was born in 1976 in Hamburg, Germany. She has a diploma in communication design from the Hamburg University of Applied Sciences (2006) and an MA in fine art/photography from the Royal College of Art, London (2009). Her work has been exhibited internationally, with the most recent solo shows at Foam Museum, Amsterdam (2015), Photoforum Pasquart, Biel, Switzerland (2015) and the Museum for Photography, Brunswick, Germany (2016). She was a recipient of the National Media Museum Bursary UK in 2010, the Alfried Krupp von Bohlen and Halbach Foundation Grant in 2012 and the Outset/Unseen Exhibition Fund in 2014. Her publication *Find a Fallen Star* (Kehrer Verlag) received the German PhotoBook Award in 2015.

JILL QUIGLEY

Jill Quigley is from County Donegal in Ireland and is currently based in Belfast. In 2014 she completed an MFA in photography at Ulster University, having previously studied art history at Trinity College Dublin. She works with installations and photography, making interventions in architecture that disrupt the space and highlight the contrasting prosaic and aesthetic understanding of it.

She has participated in group exhibitions at the FORMAT Festival, Derby, Belfast Photo Festival, the Photographers' Gallery, London, the Encontros da Imagem Festival, Portugal, the Library Project, Dublin and the Perlman Teaching Museum, Minnesota. She has held solo exhibitions at Belfast Exposed and Seen Fifteen in London, which was nominated for the Workweek Prize. Quigley's work won the ESPY Student Prize, was highly commended at the Jill Todd Photographic Award and has been nominated for the Magnum Graduate Photographers Award and the Prix Pictet.

–

MAGDA RAKITA

Magda Rakita studied finance in Poland, her home country. In 2013 she was awarded an MA in photography and photojournalism from the London College of Communication. Rakita works on self-initiated projects and with media and NGOs worldwide. She is particularly interested in social and development issues, especially those affecting women and older generations. Her work uses multimedia, participatory projects and writing. She has received several awards including runner up for the IdeasTap Photographic Award with Magnum Photos and second place at the International Photography Awards. Her work has been exhibited worldwide.

–

LUA RIBEIRA

Lúa Ribeira Cendán was born in A Coruña, Galicia, Spain in 1986. She has a BA in audiovisual communication and graphic design from the University of Vigo. She received a grant to continue her studies at Tecnológico de Monterrey, Mexico, and graduated from the University of Barcelona in 2008. In 2016 she received a BA in documentary photography from the University of South Wales, Newport.

Ribeira has been awarded the Jerwood-Photoworks Grant, 2018. In 2015 she was awarded a Firecracker Photographic Grant and a Ditto Press Scholarship, and in 2016 the Reginald Salisbury Fund. She has participated in the Independent AIR's Residency, Denmark (2015) and various group exhibitions in the UK, Spain, Italy and Germany. Her work was selected by PHotoEspaña 2014, the *British Journal of Photography*, Ian Parry Scholarship (2015), Encontros da Imagem Discovery Awards (2015), the Gazebook Photobook Festival and *A Fine Beginning, Contemporary Welsh Photography*. Currently, she is preparing a solo show (along with a publication) at Fishbar Gallery, London, curated by Olivia Arthur and Philipp Ebeling.

–

MARIELA SANCARI

Mariela Sancari was born in Buenos Aires, Argentina, in 1976. She has lived and worked in Mexico City since 1997. Her work revolves around identity and memory and the way they are intertwined and affected by each other. She examines the thin and elusive line dividing memories and fiction.

She has received numerous awards for her work: she won the VI Bienal Nacional de Artes Visuales Yucatán in 2013 and the PHotoEspaña Descubrimientos Prize in 2014. Her work was selected for the XVI Bienal de Fotografía from Centro de la Imagen and received an honourable mention at the XI Bienal Monterrey FEMSA among others.

Her first book, *Moisés*, was selected by several curators and reviewers, such as Sean O'Hagan, Tim Clark, Erik Kessels, Jörg Colberg, Larissa Leclair, Yumi Goto and Colin Pantall, as one of the best photobooks published in 2015.

–

LAURA EL-TANTAWY

Laura El-Tantawy is an Egyptian photographer. She was born in Worcester in the UK to Egyptian parents. She attended high school in Saudi Arabia, started university in Cairo and completed her degree in the US. Living between east and west for much of her life has been a source of both immense enlightenment and considerable anxiety as she contemplates notions of home, identity, culture and, ultimately, 'the self'. It is through the allure of photography as an artistic medium of limitless boundaries that she chooses to explore these themes. With her characteristically painterly and impressionistic eye on reality, El-Tantawy explores social and environmental issues that are relevant to her background. Her self-published monograph, *In the Shadow of the Pyramids*, was shortlisted for the 2016 Deutsche Börse Photography Foundation Prize and is in the private collection of the Tate Modern, London, and the Fotomuseum Den Haag.

NEWSHA TAVAKOLIAN

Newsha Tavakolian is a self-taught
photographer who began working
professionally in the Iranian press at the age
of sixteen. She worked at *Zan*, a women's
daily newspaper, and two years later was
the youngest photographer to cover the 1999
student uprising, which was a turning point
for the country's blossoming reformist
movement, and for Tavakolian personally
as a photojournalist. A year later she joined
the New York-based agency Polaris Images.

In 2002 she started working internationally,
covering the war in Iraq. She has since
covered regional conflicts, natural disasters
and made social documentary stories.
Her work has been published in international
magazines and newspapers such as
*Time Magazine, Newsweek, Stern, Le Figaro,
Colors*, the *New York Times, Der Spiegel,
Le Monde, NRC Handelsblad*, the
New York Times Magazine and *National
Geographic Magazine*.

In 2009 Tavakolian covered the presidential
elections in Iran, which resulted in chaos
and forced her to halt her photojournalistic
work temporarily. She then started working
on projects that are a mix of social
documentary photography and art. Her work
has been displayed in dozens of international
art exhibitions and has been on show in
museums such as the Victoria & Albert
Museum, London, the Los Angeles County
Museum of Art, the British Museum, London,
and the Museum of Fine Arts, Boston.

In 2014 she was chosen as the fifth
laureate of the Carmignac Gestion
Photojournalism Award and in 2015 she was
chosen as the principal laureate of the
Prince Claus Award. She became a Magnum
nominee in 2014.

SANNE DE WILDE

Sanne De Wilde was born in Belgium and
graduated from the Royal Academy
of Fine Arts in Ghent in 2012. Her photo
series *The Dwarf Empire* was given
the Photo Academy Award in 2012, as well
as the International Photography Award
Emergentes DST in 2013. Her series *Samoa
Kekea*, which is about albinism in Samoa,
won her the Nikon Press Award in 2014
for most promising young photographer.
The *British Journal of Photography* selected
De Wilde as one of 'the best emerging
talents from around the world'. Since 2013
De Wilde has worked as a photographer
for the Dutch newspaper and magazine
De Volkskrant in Amsterdam.

—

CEMRE YESIL

Cemre Yesil is a Turkish photographer living
in Istanbul. She has a BA in photography and
an MA in visual arts from Sabanci University
in Istanbul. She is currently a practice-based
PhD student at the London College of
Communication. Her work has been exhibited
and published internationally. She was
nominated for the Foam Paul Huf Award
in 2014, the ING Unseen Talent Award in 2016
and Lead Awards in 2016.

In 2015 the *British Journal of Photography*
listed Yesil as one of the twenty-five most
promising new talents in a global survey
of emerging photographers for her work
For Birds' Sake. A selection from her *An/other*
series is in the Istanbul Modern Art Museum's
photography collection.

Apart from her personal projects, Yesil
lectures on photography at Istanbul Bilgi
University and Koç University. Her recent
publications include *Cut/Kesik* (2010),

We Have Not Lived through such a Thing
(2012), *This Was* (2013), *OCC Retrospective*
(2014, *Orta Format Magazine*), *The House
We Used to Call Home* (2014) and *For Birds'
Sake*, in collaboration with Maria Sturm
(2016, La Fabrica), which was shortlisted
for Prix du Livre d'Auteur at the Rencontres
d'Arles in 2016. She has had three solo
exhibitions and a number of duo exhibitions
with Maria Sturm in 2016 and 2017 with the
work *For Birds' Sake*.

Yesil is the founder of FiLBooks which is
dedicated to photobooks, artist talks and
workshops in Karaköy, Istanbul. She is
represented by Daire Gallery in Istanbul.

—

YUNYA YIN

Yunya Yin was born in 1990 in Sichuan, China.
She graduated from Beijing Film Academy
in 2013 and then moved to the UK to study
for an MA at the University of the Arts
London. In 2016 she was the winner of PDN
Photo Annual (student work) for *The Timeless
Trans-Siberian Railways*. She was also
nominated for the Magnum Photos Graduate
Photographers Award in the same year.

Her work has been used by BBC News,
and has appeared in *Aesthetica Magazine*
and *The Week* among other publications. She
is currently a freelance photographer.

—

CHEN ZHE

Chen Zhe was born in 1989. She is a photo-
based artist born and based in Beijing. She
received her BFA in photography and imaging
from the Art Center College of Design in Los
Angeles in 2011. Zhe received the Three
Shadows Award in 2011, the Inge Morath

Award from the Magnum Foundation in 2011, Lianzhou Festival Photographer of the Year Award in 2012 and the Xitek New Talent Award in 2015.

Her work has been included in public and private collections and exhibited internationally at the Unseen Photo Fair, Amsterdam, Contact Photography Festival, Toronto, Fotohof Gallery, Salzburg, and Tokyo Photo, as well as at the Ullens Center for Contemporary Art, Beijing, Minsheng Art Museum, Shanghai and the Power Station of Art, Shanghai. Chen was subject of the TV documentary films *Chinese Viewfinder* in 2013, produced by ARTE, France, and *China Through the Lens of Youth* in 2014, produced by NHK, Japan. Her debut publication, *Bees,* was selected as one of the best books of 2012 by Photo-Eye and Feature Shoot, and her latest book, *Bees & The Bearable,* was named the best photobook of the year by Kassel Fotobookfestival in 2016.

POULOMI BASU

Page 30: Martine, from Brussels, whose son died in Syria in February 2015. Martine's son was an eighteen-year-old high-school drop-out who told his mother that his Arab surname did not appeal to employers. He was lured by recruiters from radical groups who said they did not care about his lacklustre CV.

Page 32, above left: Saliha Ben Ali, forty-nine, left Vilvoorde when the pressure of staying there became too much after her nineteen-year-old son Sabri died in Syria in December 2013. This is the view from her window in Brussels, where she now lives.

Page 32, above right: According to Saliha, this is the most important photograph she has of her son Sabri. In this picture, he is saying goodbye: this is how she wants to remember him.

Page 32, below left: Sabri knew that his mother would never let him enter the bloody chaos of Syria, so he said he was going to a wedding. One morning in August 2013 Saliha, Sabri's mother, discovered his room was empty. She knew he was on his way to join the ranks of some 6,500 Europeans designated as foreign fighters in Syria. She found a djellaba, a traditional robe, which he said he was going to wear to the wedding, hidden under his bed. These clothes are some of the few items Saliha has to remember her son by.

Page 32, below right: Martine received a text message saying her son had been killed in an attack on the Deir Ez-Zor airport. He reportedly joined ISIS the year before.

Page 33: A selfie of Sabri wearing his favourite Adidas sweater, one of the few items of his that his mother, Saliha, has kept.

Page 34: Photograph of Sabri, Saliha's son. The letter reads:

My son,

One day you decided to leave. Without a word, you left to go over there and time froze.
We are not angry at you because for us, it was not your choice.

With all our love always,
Mother
Papa
Ismael
Mehdi
Likeb

We all miss you!

Page 35: 'When you are pregnant you have pain and afterwards you have a baby that's there but when your baby dies you have pain but are left with nothing.'

Saliha is the lead coordinator of Aux Parents Concernés, a Brussels-based non-profit organization seeking family support and a role in prevention programmes against extremism.

Basu would like to thank Lisa Bode for her text.

—

ENDIA BEAL

Page 36: 'It is a benefit for corporate America to have diverse perspectives that align with the company's strategy in order to gain a broader market share and truly embrace diversity and inclusion.' Jessica, 28

Page 38, left: 'I feel nervous about entering the corporate environment, but I will not let that change my attitude towards success as a black woman.' Mel, 21

Page 38, right: 'Honestly, it can be intimidating. The major industries that come together to make corporate "America", a country that claims to be all inclusive, is mainly comprised of one type of person. That person is the white male…and there isn't a book you can read or a certification you can get to make you more of a white male – you are or you aren't. With that being said, if I were to approach this question as if I were giving advice to my younger self on the corporate experience I have gained I would say, as an African-American woman in the corporate world you must approach every situation with confidence. You must know who you are and what you are capable of intellectually. You must remember to be on guard because there will be stereotypes already assumed that you do not want to fit into. You must remember that you may sometimes be surpassed for opportunity simply because you are a woman and simply because you are black. However, with determination and the power rooted in you from the tears of your ancestors, you will eventually bloom into a beautiful flower filling up the board room with your intelligence and creativity and then, only then is when you let curly hair down. Not a moment before.' Shakiya, 24

'I feel as though the corporate world is not representational of me as a black woman and also as an individual. There are too many restrictions on appearance in corporate America. I am more of a free spirit, I fully believe in expressing myself. I don't feel as though I should have to compromise the majority of things about me to fit the corporate mold. I can definitely see myself in a more creative field where I can have the option to express myself.' Kyandra, 21

Page 39: 'Corporate America is already geared towards the success of men in the business. So as a woman – a woman of color at that – I always have to be better than the best to even be considered for the same opportunities. The way I wear my hair, my posture and my outfit do not define who I am or what I know, they externalize my confidence.' Taylor, 21

Page 40: 'In corporate America it is twice as hard to not only be a woman, but also a black woman. As black women we get more responsibility, but hardly enough power.' Tianna, 20

Page 41, above left: 'Corporate America is intimidating, but my hope to succeed allows it to also be promising. I feel like I will have to fight twice as hard to exceed my competition for respect and wage.' Sabrina, 23

'I join the band of minority women in corporate America as a faceless heroine. I believe corporate has lost its servitude for humanity and I feel obligated to supply it. I noticed that big-name corporations are making an effort to equal the playing field by hiring minority and female leaders…but it's an indication that there are highly skilled players on the bench ready to be called into play.' Katrina, seated, 23

Page 41, above right: 'I believe I can dominate corporate America. Although I will need to network a lot more than my white counterparts to get my foot in the door, I believe once in, I will excel.' Dontia, 21

Page 41, below left: 'I tend to view the corporate space as an exciting challenge. Because I was fortunate to grow up in a household with two master's degree-bearing parents, I was always a few feet away from inspiration. Upon growing up and realizing

that this fortune is relatively idiosyncratic of the black community, I'm inspired to serve as a role model for others.' Annie, 22

Page 41, below right: 'I don't see myself in the corporate space. I see myself in a more open environment where you are free to express your creativity and ideas with others.' Aja, 19

—

MARIA GRUZDEVA

Page 73: This is also symbolic of the local facility Zvezdochka.

Page 74: The Alpha group is an elite Russian counter-terrorism unit.

—

CORINNA KERN

Pages 90–95: George smokes a cigarette while taking a bath on 12 December 2013 in London. As one of the only accessible spaces in his home, George's bathtub has become the place where he washes the dishes, does his laundry, stores items, repairs bikes, has his coffee, smokes, reads a book or, last but not least, takes a bath.

—

DIANA MARKOSIAN

Page 108: Yepraksia watched the Ottomans kill the Armenians. She saw them throw the bodies into the river, which she described as 'red, full of blood'.

Page 110, above right: The Akhurian River is a tributary of the Araks, which Armenians crossed over to escape the massacres of 1915.

Page 110, below left: This is the first time Yepraksia has seen this place for 100 years.
Page 110, below right: Hundreds of thousands of Armenians were forced to march to Der Zor, Syria, in 1915 and 1916. For Armenians, this location in the Syrian desert, now controlled by ISIS, is synonymous with Auschwitz.

Page 111: After the genocide, Turkey erased Armenia from its history, not mentioning who built or inhabited it. Today, the city of Ani remains abandoned, apart from the occasional presence of Turkish border guards.

Page 113: This was the first time Movses had seen his home for ninety-eight years.

—

ZANELE MUHOLI

© Zanele Muholi. Courtesy of Stevenson, Cape Town/Johannesburg and Yancey Richardson, New York.

—

JILL QUIGLEY
The photographs are pigment prints.

—

MAGDA RAKITA

Page 156: Evon sits in a room where she lives with her sister, grandmother and other members of her extended family. Evon's grandmother supports the whole family by running a small restaurant in West Point.

Page 158: Girls play with soap bubbles in the tight alleyways of West Point.

Page 159: A girl seated in a classroom plays with a shower cup used during the rainy season to protect her hair. For Rakita, the image symbolizes the suffocation of the schooling system and the challenges the girls face when fighting for access to education.

Page 160: Hawa during boxing training. She is the only girl attending boxing lessons at the local club.

Page 161: Girls share their lunch while chatting to a friend. Food provided by the More Than Me Foundation is often an important contribution towards the girls' diet and helps to convince families to allow their daughters to go to school. It also prevents the poorest girls from selling their bodies for food in order to survive.

—

YUNYA YIN

The photographer's reflections:

Page 198: The family reminds me of the fundamental emotion of human love.

Page 200: It is the third day on the train. The baby is sleeping in the Siberian sunshine.

Page 201, above: Class 9, my space.

Page 201, below: Green – the dominant colour of the whole journey.

Page 202, above left: The swamps appeared nearly 10,000 years ago. For a long time Russia has used Siberia as a place of exile for criminals and political prisoners because of its abominable natural conditions.

Page 202, above right: I defined my experience as a 'timeless journey', attributing an unregulated feeling to my images. The work consists of nature, architecture, landscapes and people.

Page 202, below: The project explores the relationship between time and space, humans and their environments.

Page 203: The pictures do not conform to a clear and strict narrative. As though in a dream-like state, I provide the viewer with scattered fragments, giving them the power to try and make sense of my images in their own way.

—

CHEN ZHE

The photographs are archival pigment prints on German etching paper.

ACKNOWLEDGMENTS

With thanks to all our Firecrackers, past and present, and especially the photographers who agreed to be featured in this book.

To Ken Sethi, Howard Lee, Mark Foxwell and Gabrielle Brooks at Genesis Imaging for their continued support of Firecracker and the annual Firecracker Photographic Grant.

And with thanks to everyone who has helped to support Firecracker over the years and who champions wonderful women in photography: Hannah Watson, Emma Bowkett, Simon Bainbridge, Di Smyth, Marc Hartog, Sophie Wright, Francesca Sears, Olivier Laurent, Monica Allende, Shoair Mavlian, Sean O'Hagan, Michael Mack, Aidan Sullivan, Michael Benson, Fariba Farshad, Lee Grant, Karen McQuaid, Janice McLaren, Louise Clements, Marie Teresa Salvati, Harry Hardie, Rebecca McClelland, Zelda Cheatle, Nuno Ricou Salgado, Yasmin Keel, Val Williams, Brigitte Lardinois, Anna Fox, Matthew Flowers, Ghislain Pascal, Sinazo Chiya, Rodrigo Orrantia, Lauren Heinz, Ame Snyman, David Krut, Meghan Allyn Johnson, David Kogan, and to Andrew Sanigar, for believing this could be something!

Special thanks to Russell Parker, Madeleine Houghton, Charlie Cloke, Denise and David Rogers, Susan Meiselas, Martin Parr and David Hurn.